Solicitors and Money Laundering

THIRD EDITION

D1344043

Related titles available from Law Society Publishing:

Companion to the Solicitors' Code of Conduct
Peter Camp

Solicitors' Accounts Manual (10th edition)
Solicitors Regulation Authority & The Law Society

Solicitors and the Accounts Rules
Peter Camp

Solicitors' Code of Conduct 2007
Solicitors Regulation Authority & The Law Society

The Solicitor's Handbook 2008
Andrew Hopper QC and Gregory Treverton-Jones QC

SOLICITORS AND MONEY LAUNDERING

A Compliance Handbook

THIRD EDITION

Peter Camp

The Law Society

Peter Camp, the author of *Solicitors and Money Laundering*, quotes extensively from the Law Society's official Practice Note in the text of this book. For the avoidance of doubt, the views expressed in this publication should be taken as those of the author.

Readers should note that the Law Society's official Anti-money Laundering Practice Note can be found at www.lawsociety.org.uk and represents the Law Society's views on this subject.

ISBN 978-1-85328-753-4

First edition published in 2004
Second edition published in 2007
This third edition published in 2009 by the Law Society
113 Chancery Lane, London WC2A 1PL

Typeset by J&L Composition Ltd, Filey, North Yorkshire
Printed by TJ International Ltd, Padstow, Cornwall

FSC
Mixed Sources
Product group from well-managed
forests and other controlled sources
Cert no. SGS-COC-2482
www.fsc.org
© 1996 Forest Stewardship Council

The paper used for the text pages of this book is FSC certified. FSC (The Forest Stewardship Council) is an international network to promote responsible management of the world's forests.

Contents

vii

B – GUIDANCE MATERIAL

C – FORMS AND PRECEDENTS

Foreword

The Proceeds of Crime Act 2002 and associated Money Laundering Regulations have been with us for some years now and much progress has been made among practitioners in understanding and implementing their provisions. Solicitors and other regulated professionals have made significant efforts to familiarise themselves with the regime and regulators have developed comprehensive guidance to assist with some of the more complex issues which can arise. At the same time, improved partnership working between law enforcement authorities and the regulated sector has resulted in significant benefits to the overall operation of the regime.

The law and practice concerning anti-money laundering, however, continues to develop and evolve. It is more important than ever that solicitors are up to date with the current law and understand how it impacts on their practice. Solicitors remain at risk from criminals seeking to exploit professional advisers and, as this book reminds us, 'It is no longer possible for solicitors to "turn a blind eye" to a client's potential criminal transaction'.

This third edition of Peter Camp's *Solicitors and Money Laundering* includes guidance on the Money Laundering Regulations 2007 which came into force in December 2007. These Regulations incorporate a risk based approach to customer identification and due diligence and will have a direct impact on solicitors and their dealings with their clients. Once again, Peter Camp has illustrated some of the complexities of the regime with practical scenarios and has included key texts and legislation in the appendices. I am pleased to commend this book to the profession.

Sir Stephen Lander
Chair, Serious Organised Crime Agency
October 2008

Preface

The Third EU Directive on money laundering required EU governments to adopt new obligations on anti-money laundering procedures by 15 December 2007. The UK government brought into force the Money Laundering Regulations 2007 implementing the requirements of the Directive on 15 December 2007. Further amendments to the definition of the 'regulated sector' and to the offence of 'tipping off' came into force on 26 December 2007.

The third edition of this book contains a detailed commentary on these changes, together with material covering the basic obligations on solicitors arising out of the Proceeds of Crime Act 2002 and the Terrorism Act 2000.

Both the Proceeds of Crime Act and the Money Laundering Regulations require a court to consider relevant guidance in determining whether an offence has been committed under the statute or the Regulations. Relevant guidance for these purposes is defined as guidance issued by a supervisory body and approved by the Treasury. The Law Society's most recent Anti-money Laundering Practice Note dated 22 February 2008 has been submitted to the Treasury for approval. The full text of this Practice Note is contained in the Appendix to this book. At the time of writing the Treasury has not formally approved the Practice Note. However, it is likely that that the main changes that are likely to occur before approval will be as a result of developments in the section on FATF countermeasures. Details of these developments appear in the main text of the book.

As with the two previous editions, I have quoted extensively from the Law Society's Practice Note. I am also very grateful to the Society's anti-money laundering policy adviser, Emma Oettinger, for her many helpful comments on the text. However the responsibility for the views expressed in the book remains mine and only where the context allows should these views be taken as being endorsed by the Law Society.

Peter Camp
November 2008

Table of cases

Table of statutes

Table of statutory instruments and European legislation

STATUTORY INSTRUMENTS

EUROPEAN LEGISLATION

PART I

Substantive Law

CHAPTER 1

Money laundering and the solicitors' profession: an overview

1.1 INTRODUCTION

In recent years, successive governments have taken steps to increase intelligence information regarding serious criminal activities. To this end they have introduced legislation which requires the disclosure of knowledge or suspicion of criminal activities. This legislation is aimed at those whose services may be used by the perpetrators of crimes, typically banks and other financial institutions and professional businesses such as solicitors and accountants. Failure to disclose can be a serious crime in itself. Initially the requirements to disclose were limited to crimes involving terrorism and drug trafficking (see the Prevention of Terrorism (Temporary Provisions) Act 1989 and the Drug Trafficking Offences Act 1986). However, in 1994, requirements to disclose a wider range of criminal activities (i.e. activities relating to indictable offences) were introduced by an amendment to the Criminal Justice Act 1988 contained in the Criminal Justice Act 1993. More recently, more draconian measures requiring disclosure were introduced in the Proceeds of Crime Act 2002 (PoCA 2002). Amendments have been made to PoCA 2002 as a result of the Serious Organised Crime and Police Act 2005 (SOCPA 2005), and the Terrorism Act 2000 and Proceeds of Crime Act 2002 (Amendment) Regulations 2007, SI 2007/3398.

In addition to the criminal law, regulation of businesses which potentially could be used by criminals was introduced with the Money Laundering Regulations 1993 (replaced by the Money Laundering Regulations 2003, which, in turn were replaced by the Money Laundering Regulations 2007, SI 2007/2157). All three sets of Regulations were introduced into UK law as a result of European Directives, the 2007 Regulations as a result of the Third Directive on Money Laundering.

Where disclosure is necessary, the procedure is normally for disclosure to be made to the Serious Organised Crime Agency (SOCA). SOCA became operational on 1 April 2006, bringing together the National Criminal Intelligence Service (NCIS), the National Crime Squad and the investigative branches of HM Revenue & Customs and the Home Office Immigration Service. SOCA has as its core objective the reduction in the harm caused to

3

the UK and its citizens by organised crime, including the trafficking of drugs and people. It works very closely with the revenue departments which continue to be responsible for tackling revenue and tax fraud. The agency has a UK-wide remit.

The solicitors' profession is an ideal target for criminals. Criminal property must be converted into apparently legitimate assets if it is not to be at risk of seizure by the authorities. Use of a solicitor's services to buy or sell property (real estate or business property) using the proceeds of crime or merely 'laundering' criminal proceeds through a solicitor's client account will potentially involve the solicitor in criminal activities. It is not possible for solicitors to argue that they did not know that their client was using their services in this way. The legislation imposes severe penalties on those who do not report when they know or suspect that they are involved with criminal property.

1.2 WHAT IS MONEY LAUNDERING?

The traditional view that money laundering simply involved 'cleaning dirty cash' (i.e. converting criminally obtained cash into clean money) is no longer appropriate. (One view is that the term 'money laundering' derived from the activities of Chinese laundries in Chicago in the hey-day of American organised crime.) 'Money laundering' encompasses a far wider range of criminal activities and today can be undertaken by the perpetrator of the original crime as well as by third parties on behalf of the perpetrator or others. It is an attempt to hide the proceeds of crime (by integrating such proceeds into other legitimate property or by confusing the audit trail) in such a way that the authorities cannot trace the proceeds back to the original crime.

There are three generally accepted stages to the money laundering activities of the criminal community:

1. **Placement**: where cash is converted into non-cash assets.
2. **Layering**: where several transactions are undertaken for no other reason than to confuse the audit trail between the original crime and subsequent proceeds.
3. **Integration**: the final destination of the criminal proceeds.

Solicitors could find themselves inadvertently involved in any of these stages.

1.2.1 Placement

A large proportion of criminal property starts life as cash (this is particularly the case where drug trafficking is involved). The first thing the holder of such cash will wish to do is to convert the cash into a non-cash asset. It is increasingly difficult to pay large sums of cash into a bank account or through any other financial institution. The money launderer will therefore need to approach this in a more subtle way. Frequently this will involve a number of local cash businesses, for example, taxi firms or retail shops. These businesses will regularly bank large amounts of cash and such deposits, being in the usual way of business, will not attract their banks' suspicion. If the money launderer can persuade owners of these businesses to bank some of the criminal cash at the same time as their own takings, substantial amounts of criminal money can be deposited in the banking system without suspicion being aroused. A cheque can then be drawn in favour of the criminal (or more likely some third party on behalf of the criminal) for the appropriate amount less, of course, the commission for providing this service.

Solicitors' involvement in placement is rare to the extent that it is unlikely that many solicitors will agree to receive large amounts of cash deposits. Clearly, if a client attempts to put the firm into funds for a transaction or for substantial costs using cash, suspicion should be aroused and steps should be taken to ascertain the legitimacy of funds. Where this proves to be impossible solicitors should act on their suspicion. However, it is possible that solicitors may be involved on the periphery. If, when acting for a cash business, a solicitor becomes aware of suspicious circumstances which point to the possibility of placement, the solicitor must take appropriate steps to avoid the risk of criminal liability. Further, solicitors asked to act on, say, a company formation, must be satisfied as to the commercial reason for the formation. Companies are frequently formed with a view to setting up bogus businesses in order that criminal proceeds can be laundered through those businesses.

1.2.2 Layering

Once any cash has been converted into a non-cash asset (e.g. a deposit account at a bank) the next stage in the money laundering activity is to ensure that the criminal property cannot be traced back to the crime. This stage is equally important for the criminal whose criminal property did not start as cash (e.g. where the crime involved fraud or the acquisition of non-cash assets illegally). As a result of PoCA 2002 provisions relating to confiscation and civil recovery of criminal proceeds (see **Chapter 8**) it is of particular importance to the criminal to ensure that any property cannot be traced back to the original crime. Civil recovery provisions mean that it is now necessary for the authorities only to discharge a civil onus of proof (i.e. on the balance of probabilities) in order to seek and obtain a recovery order. Criminal property is defined in PoCA 2002 as constituting a person's benefit from criminal conduct or representing such a benefit in whole or part, directly or indirectly (PoCA 2002, s.340). Consequently it does not matter how remote property is from the original crime; if the audit trail allows the authorities to trace the property back to the original proceeds of the crime (on the balance of probabilities) a recovery order may be granted. Layering is the attempt to ensure that this cannot happen.

Solicitors may frequently be involved inadvertently in the layering transaction. A firm's client account is ideal for layering purposes. If money can be passed through a client account and out the other side by a 'clean' client account cheque or bank transfer, this can amount to one step in the layering process. Obviously solicitors must be suspicious where potential clients ask that money be accepted into client account for onward transmission where the solicitor is not involved in any legal or commercial transaction on behalf of that client. The Solicitors' Accounts Rules 1998 provide additional guidance on the use of client account for non-legal purposes. Note (ix) to Rule 15 of the Rules states:

> In the case of *Wood and Burdett* (case number 8669/2002 filed on 13 January 2004), the Solicitors' Disciplinary Tribunal said that it is not a proper part of a solicitor's everyday business or practice to operate a banking facility for third parties, whether they are clients of the firm or not. Solicitors should not, therefore, provide banking facilities through client account. Further solicitors are likely to lose the exemption under the Financial Services and Markets Act 2000 if a deposit is taken in circumstances which do not form part of a solicitor's practice. It should be borne in mind that there are criminal sanctions against assisting money launderers.

Again, the criminal is more likely to use subtle means of passing money through client account, rather than an 'up front' request. Frequently solicitors are involved in abortive transactions and most of these will be legitimate. However, consider the following scenario. A solicitor is instructed by a new client. Appropriate money laundering verification procedures are followed (for details of these requirements, see **Chapter 9**). The client instructs the solicitor on a property transaction; the client is buying commercial property for consideration of in excess of £1 million. The client explains that there is an urgency surrounding this transaction; the deal must be completed by a specified date or it is likely to collapse. The solicitor agrees with the firm acting for the vendor that, because of the deadline, the two firms will proceed on the basis of a simultaneous exchange of contracts and completion – not an uncommon procedure. A week before the planned completion date, the purchaser's solicitor is put in funds by way of a cheque or BACS payment. The funds cover the amount required to complete plus costs and disbursements including stamp duty. A day or two before the planned completion date the client telephones his solicitor and explains that there has been a hitch in the arrangements. For whatever reason given, the transaction cannot proceed to completion. Since no contracts have been exchanged there is no legal reason why the client cannot, at this stage, pull out of the deal. The client asks that the solicitor bills for the work done and returns the balance of the money held in client account. Is this a genuine abortive transaction or a successful layering exercise which has allowed the client to pass in excess of £1 million through the client account and out the other side?

Solicitors and their staff must be concerned about any deal which does not complete where substantial sums are placed in their client accounts before being returned to the client or a third party on behalf of the client. Solicitors must also question the commerciality of deals and, after any appropriate investigation, act on any suspicion they may have. (For further examples of layering, see **paragraph 1.3**.)

1.2.3   Integration

The final stage in the money laundering exercise is integration – the final destination for the criminal proceeds. After passing the funds through a number of layering transactions, the criminal should be fairly confident that funds are now unlikely to be traced back to the original crime. The criminal is now ready to invest the funds in a legitimate investment which will give a legitimate return and, for all intents and purposes, allow the appearance of non-criminal wealth.

The authorities have indicated that they believe that much of the criminal funds invested in the UK end up in commercial property. The UK commercial property market is an ideal final destination for criminal funds sourced from both the UK and abroad. There is the potential for capital growth as well as rental income. Inevitably, if funds are invested in commercial property, a solicitor is involved in the conveyancing. This involvement can bring the solicitor within the scope of the criminal law.

However, commercial property is not the only asset used as the final destination for criminal funds. Some funds will be invested in genuine business deals (company acquisitions, corporate finance, partnership finance, or joint ventures). Any asset purchase or funding deal could potentially involve a firm in the money laundering exercise.

1.3   HOW ARE SOLICITORS INVOLVED?

It should be clear from the above that solicitors could be involved in any or all three stages in a typical money laundering exercise. The following paragraphs expand on the details of a solicitor's potential involvement indicating that there really is no common area of practice that is not at risk. A departmental checklist can be found in **Chapter 12**.

1.3.1   Advice

It is clear from the substantive law that a solicitor need not be in possession of cash or other criminal property in order to run the risk of involvement in money laundering. One of the more dangerous offences from a solicitor's point of view is that of 'arrangements' contained in PoCA 2002, s.328 (for full details and commentary on this section, see **Chapter 2**). This section provides that an offence is committed if a person:

> enters into or becomes concerned in an arrangement which he knows or suspects facilitates (by whatever means) the acquisition, retention, use or control of criminal property by or on behalf of another person.

Thus a solicitor who gives advice knowing or suspecting that the advice facilitates the acquisition of criminal property could be guilty of this offence which carries a maximum punishment of 14 years' imprisonment. Tax evasion is a crime. In February 1999, Jack Straw MP (the then Home Secretary) said, 'Tax evasion offences are criminal offences . . . The [money laundering] legislation . . . does not treat them in any special way . . .' If a solicitor gives advice to a client which assists in a client's legitimate tax avoidance this is acceptable (and, indeed, a normal activity for solicitors). If, however, the advice facilitates tax evasion such advice could lead to a charge under PoCA 2002, s.328.

1.3.2 Use of client account

A major reason why money launderers might target a solicitor's practice is the solicitor's client account. For all intents and purposes a client account is like a bank account. Any use of client account for other than a legitimate underlying legal purpose should give rise to suspicion. Solicitors must be careful not to mistake what appears to be a legitimate use of client account with improper use leading to money laundering. As noted above, those intent on money laundering will use subtle means to avoid a solicitor's suspicion. A solicitor delivers a bill of costs to a client following the successful completion of a transaction. The client sends a cheque in payment of the costs. Sometime later, the same sum is received into the solicitor's client account by way of a BACS transfer. The payment comes from a third party who informs the firm that they have agreed to pay the client's costs associated with the transaction. One way or another, the solicitor will have to return the overpaid costs to the client or third party – money has been passed through client account and out again on a genuine client account cheque.

Particular care must be taken when a solicitor is asked to act as a stakeholder (i.e. holding money in client account on behalf of a third party until the happening of a specified event). This is an everyday occurrence in conveyancing transactions and where the property or other transaction appears genuine, no great risk will occur. However, if the instructions are such that the solicitor is only being asked to act as stakeholder without involvement in the underlying transaction, this should give rise to concern and appropriate enquiries should be made to check the legitimacy of the transaction. Solicitors' undertakings or guarantees are particularly useful to criminals. If they can persuade their victims to part with funds against the undertaking of a solicitor 'to hold the funds to the order of' the victim until the happening of a specified event, the victim is more likely to readily part with the funds.

Solicitors and their cashiers must at all times be vigilant to the possible misuse of client account. Unusual transactions and transactions involving the movement of funds through client account where, for whatever reason, there is no underlying legal transaction should be considered carefully and, if necessary, reported internally in accordance with the firm's procedures (for details of such procedures, see **Chapter 11**).

1.3.3   Purchase or sale of property/assets

Either as part of the layering exercise or as the final destination for criminal proceeds, property purchase or sale can form part of a money laundering exercise. If a client is involved in providing false information to a bank or building society as part of a mortgage transaction, the loan becomes criminal property (the proceeds of mortgage fraud). The property purchased with the mortgage funds becomes criminal property. When the property is sold, the proceeds of sale become criminal property. If the proceeds of sale are used to purchase another asset, that other asset becomes criminal property. If the asset is used as security to borrow money, that money becomes criminal property. The definition of criminal property is wide enough to catch all these items (for full details of the definition, see **paragraph 2.2**). A solicitor's involvement in any of these activities could risk involvement in money laundering if the solicitor knows or suspects that criminal property is involved.

Conveyancing and property lawyers are clearly at risk. The Law Society issued specific guidance for solicitors undertaking property work in December 2005. This has been replaced by the section on property work in Chapter 11 of the Law Society's Anti-money Laundering Practice Note (paragraph 11.4): see **paragraph 1.4**. However, the risk is not limited to real property transactions. Transactions involving shares, other securities and investments could equally give rise to risk of money laundering.

1.3.4   Hiding behind corporate or other vehicles or devices

Criminals involved in the laundering of criminal proceeds will frequently wish to avoid the use of their own names (particularly in the light of the identification procedures set out in the Money Laundering Regulations (see **Chapter 9**)). Consequently they are likely to seek to hide behind a corporate identity or seek to distance themselves from the transaction through the use of trusts or powers of attorney. Solicitors instructed to create companies or draft trust deeds or powers of attorney are clearly at risk of involvement in money laundering where such vehicles are being used for criminal purposes. Equally, solicitors instructed to act as directors, trustees or donees under a power of attorney where there is no commercial or other reason for the appointment may find themselves acting as a front for criminals.

1.3.5 Drafting documentation

A major need for any successful money launderer is the ability to move funds from one account to another or across one frontier to another jurisdiction. To do so through the legitimate banking system, an apparently genuine reason for the transfer of the funds will have to be found; a reason which will satisfy the suspicions of the bankers involved. If the launderer is able to produce genuine documentation prepared by a reputable firm of solicitors, this task will be made much easier.

Loan documentation, drafted by solicitors, can be used as a reason for the transfer of funds – funds paid to discharge the loan or funds received to discharge a loan.

1.3.6 Confidentiality and privilege

Money launderers will frequently make use of a solicitor's services in the mistaken belief that any information given in the course of a solicitor's retainer is confidential and sometimes subject to the concept of privilege. They believe that a solicitor is prohibited from disclosing information received in the course of practising as a solicitor. Consequently any suspicion (or knowledge) of a criminal purpose will, they believe, not be passed on to the authorities.

It is undoubtedly true that such an obligation applies in both a solicitor's duty in law and in professional conduct. Lord Denning MR stated in *Parry-Jones* v. *The Law Society* [1969] 1 Ch 1:

> as between solicitor and client there are two privileges. The first relates to legal proceedings – commonly called 'legal professional privilege'. . . The second privilege arises out of the confidence subsisting between solicitor and client. . . . The law implies a term into the contract whereby a professional man is to keep his client's affairs secret.

The money laundering legislation has made serious inroads into the duties of confidentiality and privilege. First, the definition of legal professional privilege for criminal proceedings has been codified by the Police and Criminal Evidence Act 1984 (PACE). Section 10 of that Act provides:

(1)   . . . items subject to legal privilege means –

    (a) communications between a professional legal adviser and his client or any person representing his client in connection with the giving of legal advice to the client;

    (b) communications between a professional legal adviser and his client or any person representing his client or between such an adviser and any other person made in connection with or in contemplation of legal proceedings and for the purposes of such proceedings; and

    (c) items enclosed with or referred to in such communications and made:

        (i) in connection with the giving of legal advice; or

        (ii) in connection with or in contemplation of legal proceedings and for the purposes of such proceedings they are in possession of a person who is entitled to possess them.

(2)   Items held with the intention of furthering a criminal purpose are not items subject to legal privilege.

PACE, s.10(2) provides that items are not to be considered as privileged where they are held 'with the intention of furthering a criminal purpose'. The House of Lords in *R* v. *Central Criminal Court ex p. Francis and Francis* [1989] 1 AC 346, held that the 'intention' in PACE, s.10(2) did not have to be the solicitor's intention. Provided someone had the intention to further a criminal purpose, items held would not be privileged.

Secondly, PoCA 2002 requires solicitors to disclose their knowledge or suspicions of a client's involvement in money laundering in certain circumstances (either by way of a defence or by way of an obligation). PoCA 2002 provides that such disclosures made by a solicitor in accordance with the requirements are 'not to be taken to breach any restriction on the disclosure of information (however imposed)' (see s.338 and **Chapter 2**). However, the Court of Appeal in *Bowman* v. *Fels* [2005] EWCA Civ 226 stated:

> There is nothing in the language of [PoCA 2002] to suggest that Parliament expressly intended to override legal professional privilege ... Much stronger language would have been required if [PoCA 2002] could be interpreted as bearing a necessary implication that legal professional privilege was to be overridden.

Privilege, as it applies to money laundering scenarios, is a complex topic. It is covered in **Chapters 4** and **5** of this book and Chapter 6 of the Law Society's Anti-money Laundering Practice Note (see **paragraph 1.4**).

1.4   LAW SOCIETY'S GOOD PRACTICE ADVICE

A number of criminal offences contained in PoCA 2002 (notably s.330 and 331 – see **Chapters 5** and **6**), the Terrorism Act 2000 (notably s.21A – see

Chapter 5) and the Money Laundering Regulations 2007, SI 2007/2157 (reg.45(2) – see **Chapter 9**) all provide that:

> In deciding whether a person committed an offence . . . the court must consider whether he followed any relevant guidance which was at the time concerned –
>
> (a) issued by a supervisory authority or any other appropriate body;
> (b) approved by the Treasury; and
> (c) published in a manner it approved as appropriate in its opinion to bring the guidance to the attention of persons likely to be affected by it.

A supervisory body, for these purposes, includes the Law Society.

The Law Society issued Guidance on PoCA 2002 and related matters to the solicitors' profession ('Money Laundering Guidance: Professional Ethics', Pilot Edition) in January 2004. The Guidance was significantly amended in the light of *Bowman* v. *Fels* by the replacement of the original Annex 3 to the Guidance. On 3 September 2007, the Law Society replaced this Guidance with a Practice Note (the Anti-money Laundering Practice Note), and the latest version of this Practice Note is dated 22 February 2008. The Law Society is seeking Treasury approval of the Practice Note. Extracts from the Practice Note appear throughout the text of this book, and the full text of the Practice Note is available at **Appendix B1** and on the Law Society's website (**www.lawsociety.org.uk**).

1.5 CONCLUSION

It should be clear from the above that solicitors are at risk from inadvertent involvement in money laundering. The risk arises from the types of transactions which solicitors are frequently involved with, and from the fact that a criminal charge can follow from a solicitor's suspicion – it is not necessary for the solicitor to *know* that a client is involved in criminal activities. PoCA 2002 contains a number of obligations relating to a solicitor's possible involvement in money laundering activities. It is no longer possible for solicitors to 'turn a blind eye' to a client's potential criminal transaction. Any suspicion must be acted upon and the firm must ensure that adequate safeguards and systems are in place requiring all partners and members of staff to be aware of the dangers of inadvertent involvement and to understand the detailed requirements of the legislation.

CHAPTER 2

Criminal offences: arrangements (PoCA 2002, s.328)

2.1 INTRODUCTION

The Proceeds of Crime Act 2002 (PoCA 2002) received Royal Assent in June 2002. PoCA 2002 is a substantial Act and contains many provisions outside the scope of this book. Part 7 of PoCA 2002 deals with money laundering offences. Part 8 contains the offence of prejudicing an investigation. These provisions replace previous money laundering offences contained in the Criminal Justice Act 1988 (as amended by the Criminal Justice Act 1993), and the Drug Trafficking Act 1994. Part 7 came into force on 24 February 2003. Various parts of PoCA 2002 have been amended by the Serious Organised Crime and Police Act 2005 (SOCPA 2005). In particular, SOCPA 2005 has made amendments to Part 7 of PoCA 2002, some of which came into force on 1 July 2005 and others on 21 February 2006 and 15 May 2006. In addition, the Terrorism Act 2000 contains further money laundering offences relating to terrorist property (these offences are dealt with in **Chapters 3** and **5**). Further amendments were made to both PoCA and the Terrorism Act as a result of the Terrorism Act 2000 and Proceeds of Crime Act 2002 (Amendment) Regulations 2007, SI 2007/3398 which came into force on 26 December 2007.

There are five criminal offences dealt with in PoCA 2002, Part 7. These are:

- s.327 – concealing.
- s.328 – arrangements.
- s.329 – acquisition, use and possession.
- ss.330, 331 and 332 – failure to disclose.
- ss.333A–E – tipping off: regulated sector.

Of these five offences, the offences contained in ss.327–9 (the 'money laundering offences') are, perhaps, of greatest risk for solicitors. The offence of 'arrangements' (s.328) has the greatest potential scope for solicitors' involvement. This offence is dealt with in this chapter – subsequent chapters deal with the other offences.

The offence in s.328 is not new. Similar offences were to be found in the amended Criminal Justice Act 1988 (applying to the laundering of the proceeds of indictable offences), and the Drug Trafficking Act 1994 (applying to the proceeds of drug trafficking). However, PoCA 2002 brings these offences into one statute and makes some subtle but important changes to the way this offence applies.

2.2 THE OFFENCE

Section 328 provides:

> A person commits an offence if he enters into or becomes concerned in an arrangement which he knows or suspects facilitates (by whatever means) the acquisition, retention, use or control of criminal property by or on behalf of another person.

The offence is a serious one with severe penalties available to the courts for those found guilty. Under PoCA 2002, s.334 the penalty on summary conviction is imprisonment for a term not exceeding six months or a fine not exceeding the statutory maximum or to both, or on conviction on indictment, to imprisonment for a term not exceeding 14 years or a fine or both.

There are a number of points that can be made concerning this section.

A person commits an offence if he enters into or becomes concerned in an arrangement . . .

A solicitor is commonly going to enter into or become concerned in an arrangement as a result of the retainer between the solicitor and client. In many cases, it will be the client who 'enters into' the arrangement and the solicitor will merely be 'concerned in' the client's arrangement. This will, however, be sufficient to bring the solicitor within the wording of the section.

The Court of Appeal in *Bowman* v. *Fels* [2005] EWCA Civ 226 has excluded certain activities from the definition of 'arrangement' for the purposes of s.328. The excluded activities are described as 'litigation from the issue of proceedings and the securing of injunctive relief or a freezing order up to its final disposal by judgment' (para.83 of the judgment). The judgment states that legal proceedings are a state-provided mechanism for the resolution of issues according to law. Parliament, according to the judgment, cannot have intended that proceedings or steps taken by lawyers in order to determine or secure legal rights and remedies for their clients should involve them in 'becoming concerned in an arrangement which facilitates the acquisition, retention, use or control of criminal property', even if they suspect that the outcome of such proceedings might have such an effect (para.84 of the judgment).

The exclusion also covers consensual resolution of issues in a litigious context. The Law Society's view (supported by Counsel's opinion) is that settlements, negotiations, out of court settlements, Alternative Dispute Resolution (ADR) and tribunal representation are not arrangements. However, consensual arrangements entered into independently of litigation (i.e. in a transactional matter) will still be within the scope of s.328, as will sham litigation created for the purposes of money laundering. Acting on behalf of a victim to recover property which has been criminally acquired will not give rise to an offence under s.328. See paragraph 5.4.3 of the Law Society's Anti-money Laundering Practice Note (see **Appendix B1**).

In the case of *P* v. *P* [2003] EWHC Fam 2260, Dame Elizabeth Butler-Sloss suggested that the act of negotiating an arrangement would equally amount to being 'concerned in' the arrangement. The Court of Appeal's judgment in *Bowman* v. *Fels* provides support for the proposition that *P* v. *P* can no longer be regarded as good law in this respect and (at para.67) states:

> To enter into an arrangement involves a single act at a single point in time; so too, on the face of it, does to 'become concerned' in an arrangement, even though the point at which someone may be said to have 'become' concerned may be open to argument.

The Law Society's Practice Note acknowledges the fact that the Court of Appeal did not consider the conduct of transactional work in their judgment in *Bowman* v. *Fels*. However, the Note states that the court's approach to what constitutes an arrangement under s.328 provides some assistance in interpreting how that section applies to transactional work. The Society's view is that the judgment provides support for a restricted understanding of what amounts to an arrangement in transactional work. The Note suggests that:

- entering into or becoming concerned in an arrangement involves an act done at a particular point in time;
- a person does not enter into or become concerned in an arrangement under s.328 and no offence is committed until such an arrangement is made; and
- no preparatory or intermediate step taken in the course of transactional work which does not itself involve the acquisition, retention, use or control of property will constitute the making of an arrangement under s.328.

Solicitors may be involved in preparatory steps which may bring the arrangement into existence but ultimately a criminal offence will only have been committed if the arrangement does exist and, in the present (not the future), the arrangement has the effect of facilitating money laundering. Until an arrangement under s.328 exists, the solicitor can continue with any preparatory steps relating to the transaction without committing an offence. However, if the solicitor considers that the preparatory steps will inevitably lead to an arrangement and the solicitor would become concerned with that arrangement, the solicitor must either cease acting (so as not to become concerned in the arrangement) or seek a defence (usually by way of an authorised disclosure (see **Chapter 4**)).

. . . which he knows or suspects . . .

The section introduces a double test of knowledge or suspicion. First, it is necessary for the prosecution to show that the alleged offender knew or suspected that the arrangement would facilitate the acquisition, retention, use or control of criminal property. Secondly (as noted below), the definition of 'criminal property' for these purposes requires that the alleged offender knows or suspects that the property constitutes or represents the benefit (directly or indirectly) from criminal conduct.

Knowledge should not cause a problem when interpreting this section. If a solicitor knows that the arrangement will facilitate money laundering then the solicitor risks a criminal conviction if no steps are taken to avoid liability. Difficulties can arise when a client admits to the commission of a crime (for example, tax evasion). The solicitor may withdraw from the matter and thus will not be concerned in the arrangement. However, in this situation, a solicitor may still have an obligation to report under PoCA 2002, s.330 (see **Chapter 5**) but the concept of privilege may provide a defence.

Suspicion is a more difficult concept. The test is a subjective test for the purposes of s.328. However, some people are more suspicious than others. What will amount to suspicion for the purposes of this section? The Law Society's Practice Note quotes from the case of *Da Silva* [1996] EWCA Crim 1654 (a case based upon earlier money laundering legislation). Longmore LJ stated:

> It seems to us that the essential element in the word 'suspect' and its affiliates, in this context, is that the defendant must think that there is a possibility, which is more than fanciful, that the relevant facts exist. A vague feeling of unease would not suffice.

Any unusual or unexpected transaction must raise a concern which warrants enquiry. It is not necessary to know the exact nature of the criminal offence nor to have evidence that money laundering is taking place. Transactions that should give rise to concern and therefore should be investigated include:

- **Unusual settlement transactions**
  Consider the circumstances where, on an asset purchase, less funds are required on completion than expected by reference to the contractual

16

provisions. Clients may excuse this by indicating that they have paid a direct deposit to the vendor. This typically indicates a possible mortgage or loan fraud. The property (i.e. the asset being purchased) is being over-valued for security purposes. The genuine price paid is the lesser amount.

- **Unusual instructions**

  The key to avoiding criminal liability is to know the client and know the typical transactions expected to be undertaken in the firm. Accepting instructions in a matter which is outside the normal type of work under-taken by the firm should give rise to a risk assessment – enquiries should be made to ensure that this is a legitimate transaction and one that the firm has competence to undertake.

  For example, a small traditional firm specialising in private client work should be suspicious if a new client requires the firm to act on a complex commercial transaction involving significant values. If the remuneration offered seems too good to be true, it probably is! Criminals wishing to launder money might take the (often erroneous) view that a small firm has less sophisticated money laundering procedures in place. Equally, larger commercial firms should be suspicious where commercial clients instruct them on private client matters beyond the scope of their normal work. Even if they have staff who are competent (or who could gain competence) the question should always be asked: 'Why are we being instructed?'

- **Secretive client**

  The Money Laundering Regulations 2007, SI 2007/2157 (see **Chapter 9**) require solicitors to carry out customer due diligence (CDD) on most new clients (i.e. obtain evidence which verifies the client's identity). A client who is unwilling or unable to produce such evidence should give rise to concern. To continue to act without such evidence may put the firm in breach of the Regulations and the lack of such evidence without good reason may give rise to suspicion that any arrangement might facilitate the acquisition, retention, use or control of criminal property. It is good prac-tice to apply CDD to all new and existing clients even if this is not strictly required by the Regulations. By doing so, a solicitor is going somewhere towards allaying suspicion. Without such evidence, the authorities' case for showing suspicion is made easier.

  In particular, where the client is a corporation or trust it may be neces-sary to identify and verify the identity of a 'beneficial owner' (i.e. share-holders of a company or the trustees/beneficiaries of the trust fund). It is too easy for launderers to hide behind such vehicles, so the identification procedures must now be applied to those controlling the appropriate vehicle. Details of the requirements relating to client and beneficial owner identification and recommended procedures are contained in **Chapter 9** and **Chapter 11**.

- **Cash transactions**

  In a solicitor's practice, large cash transactions are usually rare and as such should give rise to concern. These might involve sale or purchase transactions involving cash or large sums of cash used to discharge the solicitor's costs. Of course, the use of cash in any transaction is not unlawful. Of itself, a client proposing to use cash does not commit an illegal act. However, it must put the solicitor on notice that the transaction might be one involving 'placement' (see **Chapter 1**) and as such the solicitor should not proceed unless satisfied as to the legitimacy of the transaction.

  In some ethnic communities, cash is still the preferred currency for business transactions. Solicitors acting for members of such communities may be satisfied that a cash transaction is the norm. However, in most circumstances the use of large sums of cash should give rise to a sensible concern.

  Many firms impose a cash limit (i.e. a maximum sum that can be accepted in cash). Frequently this is set at £500 but some firms have set a limit as low as £250.

  Where cash is legitimately used, solicitors should refer to guidance in the Solicitors' Accounts Rules 1998 (SAR). The Solicitors Regulation Authority's 'Guidelines: Accounting Procedures and Systems' are contained in Appendix 3 SAR. These state (Guideline 3) that 'the firm should have procedures for identifying client money and controlled trust money, including cash, when received in the firm, and for prompt recording the receipt of the money . . .'

  In earlier guidance ('Complying with the Solicitors' Accounts Rules: A Practical Guide' published by the Law Society, 1996) the following was stated:

  Receipt of Cash

  When cash is received from a client, particularly a large amount, consideration should always be given to the Money Laundering Regulations.

  Any cash receipts should be counted in the presence of the client by the relevant fee earner and another member of staff. Care should be taken to check for any forged bank notes.

  A receipt should be issued to the client and the client's signature should be obtained. A copy of the receipt should be retained on a central file. A posting slip should then be completed in the same manner as for cheques but should specify that the sum was received in cash. The cash, together with the posting slip, should immediately be passed to the accounts department for banking that day.

  Withdrawal of cash

  The following points should be considered when withdrawing client's money in cash:

  - A posting slip should be completed in duplicate by the fee earner. The original should be passed to the accounts department and the copy retained on the client's file. The posting slip should indicate why cash is required.

- The fee earner should seek the client's written authority to make a withdrawal by cash and a copy of that authority should be passed to the accounts department and retained on a central file.
- The cash should be counted by the fee earner in the presence of the client/recipient and another member of the firm.
- A signed receipt should be obtained and a copy passed to the accounts department for retention on a central file.
- Particular attention should be paid to security when withdrawing cash from the bank.
- It is a breach of the Accounts Rules to have client petty cash, as all client's money should be held in a client account at a bank or building society. Petty cash will usually be required only in respect of office expenditure, though it may be used to pay disbursements on behalf of a client, e.g. oath fees.

- **Suspect territories**

  The definition of criminal property includes, in certain cases, property derived from overseas transactions (see below). Consequently solicitors should be satisfied as to the source of any funding used as part of transactions and in particular should be aware of the dangers of receiving funds from overseas suspect territories.

  Some countries worldwide have lower levels of regulation than others. Particular care must be taken when any party to the transaction is based in or moves money from or to such countries. The Financial Action Taskforce (FATF) was formed in 1989. It is an intergovernmental body with members from 31 countries and the European Commission. It publishes and updates a list of non-co-operative countries and territories (NCCTs). At the time of writing (August 2008) there are no countries listed as NCCTs. However, this can be regularly checked by logging on to the Financial Action Taskforce website (**www.fatf-gafi.org**).

  Although there are currently no NCCTs it should be noted that on 16 October 2008, FATF warned of higher risks of money laundering and terrorist financing by deficiencies in the systems in Iran, Uzbekistan, Turkmenistan, Pakistan, São Tomé and Northern Cyprus. Transactions with these countries can present a higher risk of money laundering which should be taken into account as part of a firm's risk assessment as required by the Money Laundering Regulations 2007 (see **Chapter 9**).

- **Source of funds**

  Generally, enquiries do not need to be made into every source of funds received by the firm. However, note that if the client is a PEP (Politically Exposed Person) within the meaning of the Money Laundering Regulations 2007, measures must be undertaken to establish the source of wealth and source of funds (reg.14(4) – see **Chapter 9**). Where funds are received from a source other than a client, further enquiries may have to be made. For example, it is reasonable to expect that funds required from a sole trader in respect of a personal matter may drawn on a business bank account (i.e. by way of drawings) but if a client produces a cheque drawn on their employer's bank account for use in a personal matter further enquiries may be necessary.

Accounts staff should be vigilant and should monitor whether funds received are from a creditable source.

... facilitates (by whatever means) the acquisition, retention, use or control ...

The arrangement (where a solicitor 'enters into or becomes concerned in an arrangement') must be such that the solicitor knows or suspects that it facilitates the acquisition, retention, use or control of criminal property. This is a very wide concept. Previous legislation (e.g. the Criminal Justice Act 1988 as amended) simply referred to the act of facilitating the retention or control of criminal property. PoCA 2002 extends this to now include 'acquisition and use'.

All of the examples given in **Chapter 1** could be said to be facilitating the acquisition, retention, use or control of criminal property. The use of the words 'by whatever means' ensures that the act of facilitation could be undertaken by a solicitor by placing money in client account; by transferring funds; by acting on the purchase/sale of property; or, as noted previously, simply by giving advice.

... criminal property ...

Section 340(3) defines criminal property. Property is criminal if:

(a) it constitutes a person's benefit from criminal conduct or it represents such a benefit (in whole or part and whether directly or indirectly), and
(b) the alleged offender knows or suspects that it constitutes or represents such a benefit.

Section 340(2) defines criminal conduct as that which:

(a) constitutes an offence in any part of the United Kingdom, or
(b) would constitute an offence in any part of the United Kingdom if it occurred there.

The first point to note from this definition is that criminal property can be the benefit (however small) of a crime or it can (directly or indirectly) represent the benefit of a crime. The property does not have to be the original criminal proceeds. As a result of this definition, if cash is stolen, it is criminal property. If the stolen cash is used to buy an asset, the asset will be criminal property. If the asset is used as security to obtain a loan, the loan will become criminal property.

Section 340(5) provides that a person benefits from conduct if he obtains property as a result of or in connection with the conduct. Property includes (s.340(9)) money; all forms of property real, personal, heritable or moveable; or things in action and other intangible or incorporeal property. Further, property is obtained by a person if he obtains an interest in it, which is defined in relation to land as any legal estate or equitable interest or power and in relation to other property as including references to a right (including a right to possession) (s.340(10)).

Where a person receives a pecuniary advantage as a result of conduct he is taken to have received a sum of money equal to the value of the pecuniary advantage for the purposes of these provisions (s.340(6)).

The definition does not impose strict liability to the extent that in addition to the requirement that the property constitutes or represents a person's benefit from criminal conduct, the alleged offender must know or suspect that it constitutes such benefit. Suspicion, for these purposes, will be tested on a subjective basis and the comments on the interpretation of 'suspicion' noted above are equally relevant here. It should therefore be appreciated that in considering the offence under PoCA 2002, s.328 (arrangements) there is a double test of knowledge or suspicion:

- there must be knowledge or suspicion that the arrangement facilitates the acquisition, retention, use or control of criminal property; and
- there must be knowledge or suspicion that the property constitutes or represents a person's benefit from criminal conduct.

The benefit must have derived from criminal conduct. The previous legislation limited this to benefit from indictable offences (i.e. serious criminal offences), drug trafficking and terrorism offences. PoCA 2002 does not replicate this restriction. Any criminal act which gives rise to a benefit can form the basis of a money laundering offence.

Further, the criminal conduct need not have occurred in the UK. As can be noted from the definition in s.340(1), the conduct will be criminal if it would have constituted a crime if it had occurred in the UK. Originally, there was no requirement in the statute that the conduct must constitute a crime in the jurisdiction in which it occurred.

This led to the so-called 'Spanish bullfighter' problem. The argument was made that any legitimate income earned by a bullfighter in Spain would amount to criminal property in the UK. Bullfighting in Spain is legal, but it is a criminal activity in the UK. Anyone who, with knowledge or suspicion, facilitated the retention, use etc. of this income could be guilty of an offence.

However, SOCPA 2005 provides for a defence where the accused knows or believes on reasonable grounds that the criminal conduct was not unlawful in the place where it occurred. This amendment came into effect on 15 May 2006 (see **paragraph 2.3** for details).

Overseas criminal property (i.e. the benefit of overseas crime) cannot form the basis of a money laundering offence if the conduct undertaken overseas is not a crime in the UK. An obvious example would be a sum of money sourced from an overseas jurisdiction where money was removed from the jurisdiction in breach of that jurisdiction's exchange control regulations. Since the UK does not currently have exchange control regulations, the activity of removing the funds from the overseas jurisdiction would not constitute a crime if it had occurred in the UK. It may be, however, that a client who is willing to breach overseas exchange control regulations might be prepared to breach other obligations. Solicitors should carefully consider all the surrounding facts before determining that a client in breach of overseas exchange control regulations does not give rise to concern.

One problem associated with this definition relates to the proceeds of tax evasion. As noted above, UK tax evasion is a criminal offence and as such can give rise to money laundering. What about the proceeds of overseas tax evasion? Can such proceeds form the basis of a money laundering charge if such proceeds are brought into the UK?

There appears to be a divergence of views on this. Some commentators take the view that the proceeds of overseas tax evasion should be treated in exactly the same way as the proceeds of UK tax evasion. However, others take the view that the offence concerned should be defined by reference to the overseas tax authority. In this case the activity will not be a UK crime if it had occurred in the UK. For example, it is undoubtedly a crime in the US to evade US taxation. If the definition of the crime includes the specific victim (i.e. the US tax authorities) the evasion of US tax would not be a crime in the UK if it had occurred in the UK.

Solicitors should, however, err on the side of caution. Until such time as the courts give a definitive interpretation of overseas criminal conduct for these purposes it would seem sensible to act upon any knowledge or suspicion of such overseas activities and follow the appropriate procedures to avoid personal liability.

Finally, in relation to the definition of criminal property, it should be noted that PoCA 2002 makes it clear (in s.340(4)) that it is immaterial for the purposes of the definition:

(a) who carried out the conduct;
(b) who benefited from it;
(c) whether the conduct occurred before or after the passing of this Act.

The money laundering offences contained in PoCA came into force on 24 February 2003. However, provided the money laundering offence occurred on or after 24 February 2003, it does not matter that the criminal conduct giving rise to the money laundering offence occurred before that date. Further, it is not necessary for the criminal conduct to have resulted in a conviction before a person is prosecuted for a money laundering offence.

. . . by or on behalf of another person

To be guilty under PoCA 2002, s.328, the accused must facilitate the acquisition, retention, use or control of criminal property 'by or on behalf of another person'. This offence is not aimed at the original perpetrator of the crime but at some other person who assists in the laundering of the criminal property of the perpetrator or other person.

However, in the context of a solicitor's practice, this does not mean that a solicitor can only be guilty of an offence where the act of facilitation is done for or on behalf of the solicitor's client. In most cases, the risk of committing this offence will arise from a client retainer in circumstances where the client is acting suspiciously. Since knowledge or suspicion is a necessary element of the crime, it follows that such knowledge or suspicion is most likely to arise in relation to the client's conduct from information received in the course of acting for a client.

In some cases, a solicitor may be acting for an innocent client but, nonetheless, the solicitor's actions could facilitate the acquisition, retention, use or control of criminal property by the person on the other side of the transaction. Completing the transaction in these circumstances could give rise to liability under PoCA 2002, s.328. Take, for example, a solicitor acting for a lender of money (a bank or building society) but not acting for the borrower. The lender's solicitor acquires certain information in the course of acting that gives rise to a suspicion that the borrower has given false information as part of the borrower's loan application. To continue to completion without taking appropriate steps could be facilitating the acquisition of criminal property by the borrower. The false information relied upon by the lender could bring about a loan or mortgage fraud; the loan itself could therefore be criminal property.

This particular point is worth making to clients and members of staff who might find a solicitor's money laundering procedures to be burdensome and unhelpful. Clients should be notified that the procedures are not simply designed to ensure that a solicitor is not involved with money laundering. A good system is designed to ensure that innocent clients are not inadvertently dragged into a money laundering investigation as a result of other parties to the transaction who might have criminal intent.

2.3 DEFENCES

Section 328(2) provides for a defence where the accused makes an authorised disclosure in accordance with the provisions of PoCA 2002, s.338. Since the defence under s.338 applies equally to the offence of concealing (s.237 – see **Chapter 3**) and to the offence of acquisition, use and possession (s.329 – see **Chapter 3**), details of the defence are to be found in **Chapter 4**.

Disclosure in accordance with s.338 is by far the most important and relevant defence for solicitors. However, there are four further defences specified in the section.

First, it is a defence that the accused intended to make a disclosure under s.338 but had a reasonable excuse for not doing so (s.328(2)(b)). Although there is currently no judicial definition of what would amount to a 'reasonable excuse', solicitors should note that the duty of confidentiality would not provide a reasonable excuse for these purposes. PoCA 2002 provides that disclosures made by a solicitor under s.338 are 'not to be taken to breach any restriction on the disclosure of information (however imposed)' (see s.338(4)).

However, *Bowman* v. *Fels* has confirmed that common law legal professional privilege (LPP) is not overridden by PoCA. The Law Society's original guidance on *Bowman* v. *Fels* suggested that where LPP applied a solicitor would be prevented from making a disclosure unless the client provided a waiver of privilege. If the client refused, the solicitor had to withdraw from the transaction to avoid becoming concerned in an arrangement. The Society's Anti-money Laundering Practice Note (February 2008) changes this guidance. It states (paragraph 5.5.1):

> This defence applies where a person intended to make an authorised disclosure before doing a prohibited act, but had a reasonable excuse for not disclosing. Reasonable excuse has not been defined by the courts, but the scope of the reasonable excuse defence is important for legal professional privilege.
>
> . . . . you are prevented from disclosing if your knowledge or suspicion is based on privileged information, and legal professional privilege is not excluded by the crime/fraud exception. You will have a reasonable excuse for not making an authorised disclosure and will not commit a money laundering offence.
>
> There may be other circumstances which would provide a reasonable excuse, however these are likely to be narrow. You should clearly document the reason for not making a disclosure on this ground.

Secondly, it is a defence that the act (i.e. the prohibited act of facilitation) 'is done in carrying out a function [the accused] has relating to the enforcement of any provision of [PoCA 2002] or of any other enactment relating to criminal conduct or benefit from criminal conduct'.

Thirdly, a new defence has been added by SOCPA 2005 following an amendment that was brought into force on 15 May 2006. The new s.328(3) provides that an offence is not committed under s.328 if the accused:

- knows or believes on reasonable grounds that the relevant criminal conduct occurred outside the UK; and
- the relevant criminal conduct is not unlawful under the criminal law of the place where it occurred and is not of a description prescribed by order made by the Secretary of State.

The Proceeds of Crime Act 2002 (Money Laundering: Exceptions to Overseas Conduct Defence) Order 2006, SI 2006/1070 is the Order referred to in the amendment and lists the criminal offences for which the definition of 'criminal conduct' remains unchanged. The offences listed are those which are punishable by imprisonment for a maximum term in excess of 12 months if committed in the UK unless the benefit arises from an offence under:

- the Gaming Act 1968;
- the Lotteries and Amusements Act 1976; or
- ss.23 or 25 of the Financial Services and Markets Act 2000.

As a result of this Order, the position regarding criminal property sourced from abroad has not changed greatly. Solicitors faced with overseas money or assets must first apply the basic definition of 'criminal property'.

- Is this money or are the assets derived from an overseas activity which would have been a criminal offence if it had occurred in the UK? If the answer to this question is 'no', the property will not be 'criminal property'. If the answer is 'yes', a further question must be asked.
- Are there reasonable grounds for knowing or believing that the activity was not unlawful under the criminal law of the country where the activity occurred? If the answer is 'no', the property will be 'criminal property' as defined by PoCA 2002. If, however, the answer is 'yes', the solicitor must further consider the offence in the UK.
- Is the offence punishable in the UK for a maximum term of in excess of 12 months? If the answer is 'yes' and the offence is so punishable, then despite the fact that the activity abroad is not an offence in that country, the property will be 'criminal property' (unless the offence is one of those specified and contained in the Gaming Act 1968, the Lotteries and Amusements Act 1976 or the Financial Services and Markets Act 2000). If the answer is 'no', the property will not be criminal property.

Fourthly, a defence has been added by SOCPA 2005 for deposit-taking bodies where the body operates and maintains an account and the criminal property is of a value less than the threshold amount. The threshold amount is determined in s.339A and is currently £250 (although the section provides for circumstances where this sum can be increased). This particular amendment came into force on 1 July 2005 but as solicitors are not deposit-taking bodies, this amendment is unlikely to affect them.

CHAPTER 3

Criminal offences: other money laundering offences

3.1 INTRODUCTION

Although the offence involving 'arrangements' is likely to have a significant impact on solicitors, there are two other money laundering offences contained in the Proceeds of Crime Act 2002 (PoCA 2002), both of which involve criminal property (as defined). Section 327 of PoCA 2002 creates the offence of 'concealing etc.' and PoCA 2002, s.329 creates the offence of 'acquisition, use and possession'. Both these offences could give rise to difficulties unless solicitors take appropriate action to avoid risks. Both offences carry the same penalty on conviction as that applicable to 'arrangements', i.e. on summary conviction, imprisonment for a term not exceeding six months or a fine not exceeding the statutory maximum or both, or on conviction on indictment, imprisonment for a term not exceeding 14 years or a fine or both.

In addition to these two offences, further money laundering offences are contained in the Terrorism Act 2000, ss.16–18. Details of these offences are included at the end of this chapter.

3.2 CONCEALING ETC.: THE OFFENCE

Section 327 of PoCA 2002 makes it an offence to:

- conceal criminal property;
- disguise criminal property;
- convert criminal property;
- transfer criminal property;
- remove criminal property from England and Wales or from Scotland or from Northern Ireland.

PoCA 2002 also makes it clear (s.327(3)) that for these purposes concealing or disguising criminal property includes concealing or disguising its nature, source, location, disposition, movement or ownership or any rights with respect to it.

Solicitors are likely to be at risk from this offence where money is held in client account and is subsequently transferred to a client or third party. Potentially, there is an overlap between this offence and the offence of 'arrangements' – transferring funds could amount to an arrangement facilitating the use of criminal property. The offence does not specifically refer to the need for the acts to be carried out with knowledge or suspicion. However, since the requirement of the offence is to conceal etc. criminal property and the term 'criminal property' is defined, knowledge or suspicion is a required element of this offence. As has been noted (see **Chapter 2**) the definition of criminal property requires that the alleged offender knows or suspects that property constitutes or represents a benefit from criminal conduct.

A solicitor who holds money in a client account and who transfers such funds or arranges for the removal of such funds from the UK could be guilty of an offence where the solicitor simply suspects that the money constitutes or represents a benefit from criminal conduct. It is therefore important that firms adopt systems to ensure all members of staff act in an appropriate manner when money is paid into client account. Frequently money is paid into a solicitor's client account by BACS or other electronic means. If the solicitor is not expecting this sum, or is initially unaware of the identity of the client or client matter to which the funds are to be applied, it is not appropriate simply to instruct the bank to return the funds to the source without considering the possibility of money laundering offences. If the solicitor has any suspicion concerning the funds, returning the funds to the source could amount to the offence of concealing.

In *Bowman* v. *Fels* the Court of Appeal confirmed that certain activities were excluded from the scope of the s.328 arrangements offence (for details, see **paragraph 2.2**). The excluded activities were described as 'litigation from the issue of proceedings and the securing of injunctive relief or a freezing order up to its final disposal by judgment' (para.83 of the judgment). The exclusion also covered consensual resolution of issues in a litigious context. The Law Society's view (supported by Counsel's opinion) is that settlements, negotiations, out of court settlements, Alternative Dispute Resolution (ADR) and tribunal representation are excluded activities – see paragraph 5.4.3 of the Law Society's Anti-money Laundering Practice Note (see **Appendix B1**).

Paragraph 95 of the Court of Appeal's judgment states:

> For the reasons we have already given, the issue or pursuit of ordinary legal proceedings with a view to obtaining the court's adjudication upon the parties' rights and duties is not to be regarded as an arrangement or a prohibited act within ss. 327–9.

As a result of this paragraph, it would appear that the excluded activities listed by the Court of Appeal (and logically the additional activities listed by the Law Society) also have no relevance in the operation of PoCA 2002, s.327.

An important point to note is that the s.327 offence (unlike the offence in s.338) is not limited to committing the prohibited act for or on behalf of another. Obviously a solicitor could be charged with concealing etc. criminal property on behalf of a client. However, the perpetrator of the original criminal act can also be guilty if the perpetrator conceals etc. his own criminal property. This has an important result. The offence of concealing etc., therefore, amounts to money laundering and in certain specified circumstances (notably under PoCA 2002, s.330) a solicitor is required to disclose knowledge or suspicion of any person engaged in money laundering (for details of this requirement, see **Chapter 5**). This might require a solicitor to report a client where the solicitor knows or suspects that a client is removing his own criminal property from the jurisdiction (e.g. where the solicitor is aware that the client has evaded UK taxation and is buying a property abroad). This could be so, even if the solicitor is not involved in any arrangement relating to that criminal property.

3.3 CONCEALING ETC.: DEFENCES

Like the offence of arrangements the most important defence in s.327 is one of disclosure. Provided a solicitor makes an authorised disclosure under s.338 (and, if necessary, has appropriate consent to continue acting) no offence will be committed under s.327. Details of this important defence are contained in **Chapter 4**.

Also, in common with the offence of arrangements, four further defences are available.

First, it is a defence that the accused intended to make a disclosure under s.338 but had a reasonable excuse for not doing so (s.327(2)(b)). As noted above, it is unlikely the duty of confidentiality would provide a reasonable excuse for these purposes. PoCA 2002 provides that disclosures made by a solicitor under s.338 are 'not to be taken to breach any restriction on the disclosure of information (however imposed)' (see s.338(4)).

However, *Bowman* v. *Fels* has confirmed that common law legal professional privilege (LPP) is not overridden by PoCA 2002. The Law Society's original guidance on *Bowman* v. *Fels* suggested that where LPP applied a solicitor would be prevented from making a disclosure unless the client provided a waiver of privilege. If the client refused, the solicitor had to withdraw from the transaction to avoid committing a prohibited act (i.e. concealing). The Society's Anti-money Laundering Practice Note (February 2008) changes this guidance. (Paragraph 5.5.1 is quoted at **paragraph 2.2**, and can be found in **Appendix B1**.)

Secondly, it is a defence that the act (i.e. the prohibited act of concealment etc.) 'is done in carrying out a function [the accused] has relating to the enforcement of any provision of [PoCA 2002] or of any other enactment relating to criminal conduct or benefit from criminal conduct'.

Thirdly, a new defence has been added by SOCPA 2005. This amendment came into force on 15 May 2006. The new s.327(2A) provides that an offence is not committed under s.327 if the accused:

- knows or believes on reasonable grounds that the relevant criminal conduct occurred outside the UK; and
- the relevant criminal conduct is not unlawful under the criminal law of the place where it occurred and is not of a description prescribed by order made by the Secretary of State.

Commentary on this defence and on the order made by the Secretary of State can be found in **Chapter 2**.

Fourthly, a defence has been added by SOCPA 2005 for deposit-taking bodies where the body operates and maintains an account and the criminal property is of a value less than the threshold amount. The threshold amount is determined in s.339A and is currently £250 (although the section provides for circumstances where this sum can be increased). This particular amendment came into force on 1 July 2005, but as solicitors are not deposit-taking bodies, this amendment is unlikely to affect them.

3.4 ACQUISITION, USE AND POSSESSION: THE OFFENCE

Section 329(1) makes it an offence to:

- acquire criminal property;
- use criminal property;
- have possession of criminal property.

Clearly this offence could apply to solicitors – particularly in relation to the holding of client money where such money is criminal property. The offence is not, however, limited to money.

As with the offence of concealing (s.327) criminal property for the purposes of s.329 is defined in the same way as for the offence of arrangements (s.328 – see **Chapter 2**). An element of knowledge or suspicion is necessary.

The interpretation of this offence (like the offence of concealing (s.327) and arranging (s.328)) has been changed as a result of *Bowman* v. *Fels*. As noted above, the activities excluded from the scope of the s.328 arrangements offence ('litigation from the issue of proceedings and the securing of injunctive relief or a freezing order up to its final disposal by judgment') would also appear to be excluded from s.329 as a result of para.95 of the Court of Appeal's judgment where it is stated:

For the reasons we have already given, the issue or pursuit of ordinary legal proceedings with a view to obtaining the court's adjudication upon the parties' rights and duties is not to be regarded as an arrangement or a prohibited act within ss. 327–9.

Also, like the offence of concealing (s.327), the offence under s.329 can apply to the perpetrator of a crime. A thief who steals property is guilty under the Theft Act 1968. Having acquired the stolen property and having possession of the stolen property means that the thief can also be charged and convicted under PoCA 2002. For the same reasons as noted above (PoCA 2002, s.330 and see **Chapter 5**) a solicitor may be required to report knowledge or suspicion that a client is engaged in money laundering (the definition of money laundering includes the offence under s.329) simply because the solicitor knows or suspects that the client has committed a crime and is therefore in possession of criminal property.

One problem with this offence arises from the wide definition of criminal property for these purposes (see **Chapter 2**). Since criminal property includes property which represents a benefit from criminal conduct, it is quite possible that property which is legitimately obtained by a person could be treated as criminal property simply because an audit trail is capable of tracing the property back to a crime. Further, a solicitor may be concerned about the payment of costs from a client whom he knows has no legitimate source of income. Potentially the solicitor in these circumstances could be guilty of an offence on the basis of his possession and suspicion that the money is criminal property.

Fortunately, the legislators have foreseen this problem and a defence of 'adequate consideration' is available (see **paragraph 3.5**).

3.5   ACQUISITION, USE AND POSSESSION: DEFENCES

A defence is available where a person makes an authorised disclosure under PoCA 2002, s.338. This is dealt with in **Chapter 4**.

Also, in common with the offence of concealing (s.327), four further defences are available.

First, it is a defence that the accused intended to make a disclosure under s.338 but had a reasonable excuse for not doing so (s.329(2)(b)). As noted above, the duty of confidentiality will not provide a reasonable excuse for these purposes. Section 338(4) states that 'an authorised disclosure is not to be taken to breach any restriction on the disclosure of information (however imposed)'. Note also the comments arising from the Court of Appeal's judgment in *Bowman* v. *Fels* and the Law Society's amended guidance on this aspect of the case.

Secondly, it is a defence that the act (i.e. the prohibited act of acquisition, use or possession) 'is done in carrying out a function [the accused] has relating to the enforcement of any provision of [PoCA 2002] or of any other enactment relating to criminal conduct or benefit from criminal conduct'.

Thirdly, a new defence has been added by SOCPA 2005. This amendment came into force on 15 May 2006. The new s.329(2A) provides that an offence is not committed under s.329 if the accused:

- knows or believes on reasonable grounds that the relevant criminal conduct occurred outside the UK; and
- the relevant criminal conduct is not unlawful under the criminal law of the place where it occurred and is not of a description prescribed by order made by the Secretary of State.

Commentary on this defence and on the order made by the Secretary of State can be found in **Chapter 2**.

Fourthly, a defence has been added by SOCPA 2005 for deposit-taking bodies where the body operates and maintains an account and the criminal property is of a value less than the threshold amount. The threshold amount is determined in s.339A and is currently £250 (although the section provides for circumstances where this sum can be increased). This particular amendment came into force on 1 July 2005, but as solicitors are not deposit-taking bodies this amendment is unlikely to affect them.

There is, however, the further defence of 'adequate consideration'. Section 329(2)(c) provides that a person does not commit an offence under s.329(1) if 'he acquired or used or had possession of the property for adequate consideration'. Subsection (3) gives further guidance on this defence.

First, consideration is to be taken as inadequate for the purposes of acquisition of property if the value of the consideration is significantly less than the value of the property. Secondly, a person uses or has possession of property for inadequate consideration if the value of the consideration is significantly less than the value of the use or possession. Finally, the provision by a person of goods or services which that person knows or suspects may help another to carry out criminal conduct is not consideration.

As a result of these provisions solicitors should treat the defence of adequate consideration with care. Take the following scenario by way of example. A solicitor is acting for a client on a house purchase. The solicitor is aware that the client is on benefits and has no legitimate source of income. When it comes to the payment of the solicitor's fees, the client makes the payment in cash. The solicitor suspects that the cash may be the proceeds of crime but takes the view that the provision by him of the conveyancing services amounts to adequate consideration. This defence is likely to be flawed. First, it is highly probable that the solicitor was suspicious about the house purchase transaction. If that was the case then completing the house purchase is likely to be an offence under s.328 (arrangements). Secondly, the defence of adequate consideration could not apply to the costs if the solicitor suspects that the services have helped the client to carry out criminal conduct.

However, in other circumstances, the defence may be of benefit. The Crown Prosecution Service guidance for prosecutors (referred to in paragraph 5.5.2 of the Law Society's Anti-money Laundering Practice Note) states that the defence will apply where professional advisers receive money for or on account of costs provided that the charges are reasonable and there is no suspicion that the client is using their services to carry out criminal conduct.

3.6 TERRORISM ACT 2000, SS.16–18

3.6.1 Offences

Further money laundering offences appear in the Terrorism Act 2000.

Section 16 of the Act provides:

(1)   A person commits an offence if he uses money or other property for the purposes of terrorism.
(2)   A person commits an offence if he –

   (a)   possesses money or other property, and
   (b)   intends that it should be used, or has reasonable cause to suspect that it may be used, for the purposes of terrorism.

Section 17 of the Act provides:

A person commits an offence if –

   (a)   he enters into or becomes concerned in an arrangement as a result of which money or other property is made available or is to be made available to another, and
   (b)   he knows or has reasonable cause to suspect that it will or may be used for the purposes of terrorism.

These offences are similar to POCA 2002, s.329 (acquisition, use and possession) and s.328 (arrangements). The offences require knowledge or reasonable cause to suspect that the money or property may be used for the purposes of terrorism. This suggests, unlike the equivalent PoCA offences (see **Chapter 2**), the Terrorism Act 2000 imposes an objective test of suspicion; i.e. were there factual circumstances from which an honest and reasonable person should have formed suspicion?

Section 18 of the Terrorism Act 2000 provides:

(1)   A person commits an offence if he enters into or becomes concerned in an arrangement which facilitates the retention or control by or on behalf of another person of terrorist property –

    (a) by concealment,
    (b) by removal from the jurisdiction,
    (c) by transfer to nominees, or
    (d) in any other way.

(2) It is a defence for a person charged with an offence under subsection (1) to prove that he did not know and had no reasonable cause to suspect that the arrangement related to terrorist property.

The offence is similar to that covered under PoCA 2002, s.327 (concealing). It covers arrangements made to facilitate the retention or control of terrorist property and provides that such facilitation can be by concealment, etc. or in any other way. Like the offence under PoCA 2002, s.328 (arrangements) it is not necessary for the accused to have possession of the terrorist property – for example, advising a client in circumstances where the advice assists in the retention of terrorist property will be sufficient.

The crime itself does not specify a requirement for knowledge or suspicion. However, subsection (2) provides for a defence if the person charged can show that he had no knowledge and no reasonable cause to suspect that the arrangement related to terrorist property. Two points are worthy of note regarding this defence. First, the reference to 'no reasonable cause to suspect' suggests that, like the previous offences noted under the Act, an objective test will be used to determine suspicion. If the individual did not suspect (subjectively) no defence will be available if a reasonable person would have suspected. Secondly, the onus of proving no knowledge or reasonable cause for suspicion rests upon the defence – not the prosecution. Once the prosecution prove that an arrangement exists which falls within subsection (1) a conviction will follow unless the defence can discharge their onus of proof.

It is obviously necessary for the legislation to cover activities relating to terrorist property in addition to those offences involving criminal property. If property used by terrorists is the proceeds of crime, then the offences in PoCA 2002 can obviously be relevant. However, it is also possible that quite legitimate funds are made available for terrorist purposes. It is this possibility which gives rise to the money laundering offences under the Terrorism Act 2000.

The Act defines terrorist property for the purposes of s.18. Section 14 of the Act states:

(1) In this Act 'terrorist property' means –

    (a) money or other property which is likely to be used for the purposes of terrorism (including any resources of a proscribed organisation),
    (b) proceeds of the commission of acts of terrorism, and
    (c) proceeds of acts carried out for the purposes of terrorism.

(2) In subsection (1) –

(a) a reference to proceeds of an act includes a reference to any property which wholly or partly, and directly or indirectly, represents the proceeds of the act (including payments or other rewards in connection with its commission), and

(b) the reference to an organisation's resources includes a reference to any money or other property which is applied or made available, or is to be applied or made available, for use by the organisation.

The penalty on conviction under the Terrorism Act 2000, ss.16–18 is, on indictment: imprisonment for a term not exceeding 14 years, a fine or both; or on summary conviction: imprisonment for a term not exceeding six months, a fine not exceeding the statutory maximum or both. Further offences under the Terrorism Act 2000 are considered in **Chapter 5**.

3.6.2 Defences

A defence, by way of disclosure, to ss.16–18 of the Terrorism Act 2000 applies under s.21, which allows for a disclosure to a constable of suspicion or belief that the money or other property is terrorist property, and the disclosure of information on which the suspicion or belief is based. There are provisions in s.21(6) permitting the disclosure to be made to the firm's nominated officer.

New defences have been introduced by the Terrorism Act 2000 and Proceeds of Crime Act 2002 (Amendment) Regulations 2007, SI 2007/3398. These include new defences where there is:

• involvement in an arrangement with prior consent of SOCA (s.21ZA);
• disclosure after entering into an arrangement (s.21ZB); and
• a reasonable excuse for failure to disclose (s.21ZC).

The Law Society has issued a separate Practice Note on the Terrorism Act 2000 named 'Anti-terrorism Practice Note – The conflicting duties of maintaining client confidentiality and reporting terrorism' (see **Appendix B2**).

CHAPTER 4

Authorised disclosures

4.1 INTRODUCTION

The three money laundering offences created by the Proceeds of Crime Act 2002 (PoCA 2002) (s.327 concealing; s.328 arrangements; and s.329 acquisition, use and possession) all have a common defence available. Each section provides for this defence using the same wording:

> a person does not commit such an offence if –
>
> (a) he makes an authorised disclosure under section 338 and (if the disclosure is made before he does the act mentioned in subsection (1) *[the prohibited act]*) he has the appropriate consent.

For solicitors, the authorised disclosure defence is probably the most important and widely used defence. PoCA 2002 has introduced some complex rules, and failure to comply with these rules will often render the defence ineffective.

In most cases, it will be necessary for solicitors to make an authorised disclosure before undertaking the act prohibited by the relevant section. In these cases, it is important that the concept of appropriate consent is considered carefully.

4.2 AUTHORISED DISCLOSURES (POCA 2002, S.338)

4.2.1 Definition

Section 338(1)(a) of PoCA 2002 defines an authorised disclosure as a disclosure made to:

- a constable;
- a customs officer; or
- a nominated officer.

In each case the disclosure, made by the alleged offender, should relate to the knowledge or suspicion that the property is criminal property.

4.2.2 Disclosure to Serious Organised Crime Agency

In practical terms, the reference in s.338(1)(a) to a constable or a customs officer means that the disclosure is made to the Serious Organised Crime Agency (SOCA). For practical details associated with disclosures to SOCA, see **Chapter 10**.

4.2.3 Disclosure to a nominated person

Disclosure to a nominated officer is disclosure to a firm's Money Laundering Reporting Officer (MLRO). In practice, many firms' internal money laundering procedures will identify a person (frequently a partner) who has been appointed as MLRO. The Money Laundering Regulations 2007 and PoCA 2002 refer to this person as a 'nominated officer'.

Section 338(5) states that a disclosure to a nominated officer is a disclosure which is made to a person nominated by the alleged offender's employer to receive authorised disclosures. Further, the disclosure must be made in the course of the alleged offender's employment. As originally drafted, PoCA 2002 required the disclosure to be made to the nominated officer in accordance with procedures established by the employer for this purpose. This requirement was removed as a result of an amendment to PoCA 2002, contained in SOCPA 2005, s.105(2). Consequently, any disclosure to a nominated officer in the course of employment (whether it is in accordance with internal procedures or not) will serve as a defence.

However, it is still important for all firms to adopt appropriate procedures for internal disclosure of knowledge or suspicion of money laundering and for these procedures to include the appointment of a person to the role of nominated officer. Firms subject to the Money Laundering Regulations 2007 (see **Chapter 9** for full details) must appoint a nominated officer. Firms not subject to the Regulations should still consider making such an appointment to enable members of the firm to make internal disclosures and thereby to benefit from the authorised disclosure defence.

It is not strictly necessary for the nominated officer to be a partner or principal in a firm of solicitors. However, in practice, the individual should be a senior member of the firm's management. Severe penalties (including imprisonment for up to five years) can be imposed upon the nominated officer for a failure to comply with his obligations under PoCA 2002. Further, under the Money Laundering Regulations 2007 a nominated officer must consider, in the light of any relevant information available in the firm, whether a disclosure gives rise to knowledge or suspicion of money laundering. The individual should, therefore, be in a sufficiently senior position to gain access to all relevant information held by the firm concerning clients or others suspected of money laundering.

Although, in the context of a nominated officer, PoCA 2002 refers to a person's employer and a person's employment, s.340(12) provides that:

> references to a person's employer include any body, association or organisation (including a voluntary organisation) in connection with whose activities the person exercises a function (whether or not for gain or reward).

The subsection goes on to state that references to employment must be construed accordingly.

Consequently, a sole practitioner or a member of a limited liability partnership (LLP) or partner in a firm of solicitors, will be able to treat the firm or LLP as an employer for these purposes and will be treated as being in employment when making authorised disclosures.

4.2.4 Form of disclosure

Section 339 allows the Secretary of State, by order, to prescribe the form and manner of any disclosure under s.338 and to provide for the form to include a request for further information specified if the information has not been provided in the disclosure. Section 339(1A) (as inserted by SOCPA 2005) makes it an offence to make a disclosure under s.338 otherwise than in the form or manner prescribed unless the accused has a reasonable excuse not to do so.

At the time of writing (August 2008) no order has yet been made regarding the form and content of disclosures under s.338. If a prescribed form is introduced, the Law Society has stated that it will issue further guidance.

In the meantime, a form of disclosure for use by solicitors when making authorised disclosures to SOCA can be found on its website (**www.soca.gov.uk**; see also **Chapter 10** and **Appendix C4**). The Law Society recommends, as good practice, the use of the SOCA preferred form, and, where possible, for this to be submitted online.

For internal disclosure purposes, firms should publish their own precedent for use by members of the firm. A suggested form of an internal disclosure is given in **Appendix C3**.

4.2.5 Time of disclosure

Section 338(2), (2A) and (3) provide for three alternative conditions regarding the timing of the disclosure.

First, under subsection (2), the disclosure, to satisfy the requirements of the section, can be made 'before the alleged offender does the prohibited act'. The prohibited act for these purposes would be the act of concealment, etc. under s.327; the act of entering or becoming concerned in an arrangement

37

which facilitates under s.328; or the act of acquisition, use or possession under s.329.

This is, by far, the most practical way to approach the defence. As soon as knowledge or suspicion arises a disclosure should be made to the nominated officer. Most firms of solicitors will not wish to encourage their staff and partners to disclose knowledge or suspicion of money laundering directly to SOCA. Internal disclosure allows the firm to maintain control over what is happening in the firm. It allows for policy decisions to be taken centrally by one person (the nominated officer) or, in bigger firms, a panel of senior members of the firm. It therefore makes sense to have internal procedures requiring this defence to be applied by making an internal disclosure as soon as knowledge or suspicion arises and before any prohibited act is undertaken.

As a result of an amendment brought about by SOCPA 2005, the second way in which the disclosure can satisfy the requirements of the section is where the disclosure is made whilst the alleged offender is doing the prohibited act. This will clearly cover the situation where the prohibited act (the act of concealment, the entering into or becoming concerned with an arrangement or the act of acquisition, use or possession) is a continuing act. If the prohibited act has already occurred and is continuing, the second form of disclosure can afford a defence. However, for this defence to apply, two further conditions must be present:

- at the time the act was begun, the accused did not then know or suspect that the property constituted or represented a person's benefit from criminal conduct (and thus the act was not prohibited); and
- the disclosure must be made on the discloser's own initiative and as soon as is practicable after the discloser first knows or suspects that the property constitutes criminal property.

An example of where it might be appropriate to consider this second type of disclosure is where money is held in client account. When originally received by the firm of solicitors, no knowledge or suspicion that the funds were criminal property attached to the possession of the money. However, whilst still in possession of the money, information is received which leads to knowledge or suspicion that the funds are criminal property. The act of holding such funds in client account could amount to being concerned in an arrangement which facilitated the retention or control of criminal property. It might also be an offence under s.329 insofar as the solicitor has possession of criminal property.

Disclosure under the second timing condition is likely to provide the solicitor with a defence. Note, however, that any future dealings with the funds (e.g. by payment to a third party) could amount to a separate money laundering offence for which a further defence would be necessary. Given the existence of knowledge or suspicion, a further disclosure under the first timing condition (i.e. made before the prohibited act of dealing with the funds) would have to be made.

Thirdly, PoCA 2002 provides for a defence where the disclosure is made after the prohibited act.

Section 338(3) (as amended by the Terrorism Act 2000 and Proceeds of Crime Act 2002 (Amendment) Regulations 2007, SI 2007/3398) provides that a disclosure made after the alleged offender does the prohibited act may provide a defence if two further conditions apply. These are that:

- he has a reasonable excuse for the failure to make the disclosure before the prohibited act was undertaken; and
- the disclosure was made on the alleged offender's own initiative and as soon as it was practicable for it to be made.

The second and third 'timing options' are clearly not as satisfactory as the first option. If the disclosure is made before the prohibited act, no further condition relating to the disclosure must be met – the defence is available subject to appropriate consent (see **paragraph 4.3**). In order to obtain the benefit of the defence using the second alternative timing requirement, a solicitor will have to show that he was unaware that the property was criminal property when the act commenced; to benefit from the third option, the solicitor will have to show he has a reasonable excuse for failing to make the disclosure earlier. Further, in both the second and third options, it must be shown that disclosure was made on the solicitor's own initiative. It is not yet clear how the courts will interpret the phrase 'a reasonable excuse'. However, the amendment to the section (which came into force on 26 December 2007) substitutes the words 'he has a reasonable excuse' for the previous wording which required that there had to be 'a good reason' for the failure. The new wording is in line with the wording in the three money laundering offences which each provide that no offence is committed if 'he intended to make . . . a disclosure but had a reasonable excuse for not doing so' (see **Chapters 2** and **3**).

Firms, in their internal procedures, should treat the second and third options very much as back-stop procedures, available if necessary but not the norm.

4.2.6 Confidentiality/privilege

Many solicitors are concerned about their duty in confidentiality when making a disclosure. When a solicitor makes a disclosure to a third person (i.e. in this context, SOCA) which concerns the affairs of a client, the question of confidentiality naturally arises. A solicitor's duty in confidentiality extends to all matters communicated to a solicitor by the client or on behalf of the client, except in certain limited exceptional cases. In addition, any information contained in a disclosure may be privileged information. Communications made between a lawyer and a client are privileged if they are confidential and made for the purpose of seeking legal advice from a lawyer or providing legal advice to a client. Further, where litigation has started or is reasonably in prospect, communications made between a lawyer and client; a lawyer and an agent; or a lawyer and a third party are privileged if they are made for the sole or dominant purpose of the litigation.

The duty of confidentiality does not apply to information acquired by a solicitor where the solicitor is being used by a client to facilitate the commission of a crime. The Solicitors' Code of Conduct 2007, Rule 4 covers the topic of confidentiality. The Solicitors Regulation Authority (SRA) has issued guidance on Rule 4. Guidance Note 17 states that: '. . . where you have strong *prima facie* evidence that you have been used by the client to perpetrate a fraud or other crime . . . the duty of confidence does not arise'. Further, s.10(2) of the Police and Criminal Evidence Act 1984 (PACE) states that items are not privileged where they are held 'with the intention of furthering a criminal purpose'. The House of Lords has held that the reference to the word 'intention' in PACE, s.10(2) does not have to be that of the client or the solicitor. It is sufficient that a third party intends the solicitor/client communication to be made with a view to furthering a criminal purpose (see *R* v. *Central Criminal Court ex p. Francis and Francis* [1989] AC 346).

Clearly, if a solicitor is required to disclose information by way of a defence to SOCA, the solicitor must ensure that such disclosure does not give rise to a breach of the duty in confidentiality or an improper disclosure of privileged information.

Section 338(4) of PoCA 2002 provides: 'An authorised disclosure is not to be taken to breach any restriction on the disclosure of information (however imposed).'

In *Bowman* v. *Fels*, the Court of Appeal considered the effect of PoCA 2002, s.338(4) on common law legal professional privilege (LPP). It was argued before the court that Parliament, by s.338(4), must have intended authorised disclosures to override LPP. However, the court stated that this provision is used to protect what would otherwise be a breach of a duty of confidence in circumstances which did not amount to the violation of a fundamental human right. The court stated much stronger language would be required if the legislation was to be interpreted as implying that LPP was to be overridden.

The Law Society's Anti-money Laundering Practice Note (see **Appendix B1**) provides guidance on the effect of LPP on a solicitor's ability to make an authorised disclosure. In particular, paragraph 12.2 contains a flow diagram dealing with the question 'Do I have a defence?' The Note confirms that LLP extends to transactional work and also confirms that the authorised disclosure defence does not override LPP. The flow diagram suggests the following steps should be taken where knowledge or suspicion is based on information subject to common law LPP and continuing to act would put the solicitor at risk of committing one or more of the money laundering offences (ss.327–329):

- is there *prima facie* evidence that the solicitor is being used to further a criminal purpose? If the answer is 'yes', LPP no longer applies and a disclosure can be made to SOCA;
- if the answer is 'no', the information continues to be protected as privileged and the defence of 'reasonable excuse' for not disclosing (see **Chapter 2**) could apply;
- if the 'reasonable excuse' defence applies, the reason for failure to report should be fully documented. Further, consideration should be given to seeking a waiver of LPP from the client. If the client agrees, disclosure can be made to SOCA;
- if the client does not consent, it may still be appropriate to continue to act (using the 'reasonable excuse' defence). However, before making this decision, ethical and civil liability risks must be considered. In some cases it may be more appropriate to withdraw.

Before the solicitor seeks a waiver from the client, the solicitor would need to consider the tipping off offences (see **Chapter 7**).

As noted above, if a solicitor has *prima facie* evidence that any communication is made with the intention of furthering a criminal purpose (e.g. by using the solicitor's services to commit a money laundering offence under PoCA 2002, ss.327–329) then any information acquired or communication made in relation to these services will not be confidential nor will it be privileged. Disclosure to SOCA will not be a problem.

However, if a solicitor suspects a client may be using the solicitor's services to commit a money laundering offence, but does not have *prima facie* evidence, the question of confidentiality or privilege depends upon the outcome of any investigation. If the solicitor's suspicions are confirmed, the information or communication is neither confidential nor privileged, and a report can be made to SOCA. If the suspicions turn out to be unfounded, the information or communication will remain confidential and privileged. The Law Society's Practice Note (paragraph 6.4.5) indicates that the sufficiency of *prima facie* evidence depends on the circumstances; it is easier to infer a *prima facie* where there is substantial material available to support an inference of fraud. The court may be asked to give guidance – see *Finers* v. *Milo* [1991] 1 WLR 35.

The Crown Prosecution Service's guidance for prosecutors also indicates that if a solicitor mistakenly believes that information has come into his possession in privileged circumstances, the failure to make a disclosure should not be fatal – the 'reasonable excuse' defence should be available to the solicitor. (Strictly speaking, the CPS guidance on this point refers to the 'privilege' defence in s.330(10) – see **Chapter 5**. However, the Law Society's

Practice Note suggests that a similar approach would be taken where the mistaken belief related to LPP.)

4.3 APPROPRIATE CONSENT (POCA 2002, S.335)

As noted above, ss.327, 328 and 329 provide for a defence where an autho-rised disclosure is made by the accused and 'if the disclosure is made before he does the [prohibited act] he has the appropriate consent'. Also, as noted above, solicitors are encouraged to make any authorised disclosure before the prohibited act rather than relying upon the disclosure being made after the act and having to show that there was a good reason for a failure to make the disclosure earlier.

For this reason, it is vital to understand the meaning of appropriate consent and the rules attached to the definition in PoCA 2002, s.335.

To illustrate this point, consider the following scenario. A solicitor is acting for the vendor on a property transaction. Contracts have been exchanged and a date for completion has been agreed. The solicitor has no concerns about his client but, in the course of the transaction, becomes suspi-cious about the funds used by the purchaser (for whom the solicitor is not acting). Completing the sale is likely to amount to an arrangement which facilitates the acquisition, use or control of criminal property (if the funds do turn out to be criminal property) – PoCA 2002, s.328. Receiving the funds into client account will potentially be the offence of acquisition, use or possession of criminal property – PoCA 2002, s.329. Receipt of such funds may also amount to the offence of concealing – PoCA 2002, s.327. Note that, in accordance with the Court of Appeal's decision in *Bowman* v. *Fels* (see **Chapter 2**) steps which are no more than steps in preparation for completion or in preparation for the holding of client money will not amount to an arrangement. Consequently, the defence of disclosure only becomes neces-sary where the solicitor is undertaking a transaction which will, of necessity, lead to entering into or becoming concerned in an arrangement or to the acquisition, use or possession of criminal property.

In each of the money laundering offences, the defence of an authorised disclosure is available. However, before looking at the defence, the question of confidentiality and privilege must be considered. If the information giving rise to knowledge or suspicion came from the other side (i.e. not from the solicitor's client) it is highly unlikely that the information will be subject to common law LPP – nor will it be confidential and disclosure can be made. However, if the communication came from the solicitor's client it is possibly subject to common law LPP. The solicitor must now decide whether there is *prima facie* evidence that he is being used to further a criminal offence. Subject to 'tipping off' further enquiries can be made of the client. If, following the outcome of any further enquiries, the solicitor is satisfied that there is *prime facie* evidence that he is being used to further a criminal purpose, the information is not privileged and a disclosure can be made to SOCA.

If, however, the solicitor does not have *prima facie* evidence that he is being used to further a criminal offence (the Law Society's Practice Note suggests (paragraph 6.4) that a disclosure should not be made unless the solicitor *knows* of *prime facie* evidence) the client (or if more than one, all the clients) may be approached for a waiver of privilege. If the client(s) agrees to a waiver, a disclosure can be made to SOCA. If the information remains privileged and the client(s) refuses to waive LPP, the solicitor must consider the ethical and civil risks of continuing to act. If the decision is taken to continue to act, the 'reasonable excuse' defence must be relied upon and the reason for failure to report must be fully documented.

If the solicitor discloses his suspicions after completion (i.e. after the prohibited act) the defence will only be available if there was a good reason for the failure to make the disclosure before completion and the disclosure was made on the solicitor's own initiative as soon as it was practicable for him to make it. It is unlikely that the simple contractual requirement to complete by a particular date will be a good reason for failing to make the disclosure before that date although, at the time of writing, there is no judicial interpretation of this term. Consequently, the limited circumstances where the defence might apply in this situation include where the solicitor only became suspicious after the completion. If the conditions are not met, the disclosure does not fall within the definition of an authorised disclosure.

The defence of disclosure might be available if the disclosure was made whilst undertaking the prohibited act, provided that at the time when the prohibited act was begun, there was no knowledge or suspicion that the property (i.e. the funds used by the purchaser) constituted the benefit of criminal conduct. In a conveyancing transaction, where the prohibited act will be completion and/or receiving money into client account, this particular defence is likely to have limited practical benefit.

Assuming the circumstances of the solicitor's suspicion were not privileged and the suspicion arose before the completion date or before suspect funds were received into the solicitor's client account (i.e. the potentially prohibited acts), it would be sensible for the disclosure to be made before any prohibited act was undertaken. In this case, the disclosure would amount to an authorised disclosure. Having made such disclosure, the solicitor could not then proceed to commit the prohibited act without considering the further requirements of PoCA 2002. The defence of authorised disclosure will only continue to apply if the prohibited act is undertaken with appropriate consent. (Note that in this scenario it may also be necessary to consider the offences of failure to disclose under PoCA 2002, ss.330 *et seq.* – see **Chapter 5**.)

Section 335(1) of PoCA 2002 defines appropriate consent as:

- The consent of the nominated officer to do a prohibited act if the authorised disclosure is made to the nominated officer.
- The consent of a constable to do a prohibited act if an authorised disclosure is made to a constable.
- The consent of a customs officer to do a prohibited act if an authorised disclosure is made to a customs officer.

Appropriate consent can therefore be given by a nominated officer (i.e. the firm's MLRO) or by the appropriate authorities (usually SOCA). Since most firms' policies will require members of the firm to report any knowledge or suspicion internally and before the prohibited act, it is sensible for any internal policy to include a requirement that following a disclosure to a firm's MLRO no further work should be undertaken on the file without the MLRO's consent. Given the definition of an 'arrangement' as per *Bowman* v. *Fels* (see **Chapter 2**) it is possible that some work in preparation for the prohibited act could be undertaken without appropriate consent in accordance with PoCA 2002, s.335. However, most firms prefer the decision regarding what is and what is not an 'arrangement' to be taken by those in the firm who have a detailed knowledge of the appropriate law (generally the firm's MLRO) rather than allowing individual fee earners or other members of staff to interpret the complex law. Consequently, a policy which requires no further work on the file without the MLRO's consent allows the MLRO to be involved in any determination as to what might be an 'arrangement' and what might be permissible preparatory activities. Any consent to undertake preparatory activities can be given by the MLRO without considering the rules for consent set out in PoCA 2002. Since preparatory activities do not amount to prohibited acts, no defence is required. However, once the MLRO is satisfied that if the firm were to continue to act, a prohibited act would be committed, appropriate consent can only be given in accordance with the rules set out below.

4.3.1 Appropriate consent by nominated officer

Where disclosure has been made internally to the firm's nominated officer (the MLRO), the officer can only give appropriate consent in accordance with the strict rules set out in PoCA 2002, s.336. This section provides that the nominated officer must not give consent unless the conditions set out in the section are satisfied. There are three conditions, any of which being satisfied will allow the nominated officer to give consent.

Condition 1 (s.336(2))

For this condition to apply the nominated officer must disclose to SOCA (the Act states 'to a person authorised for the purposes of this Part by the

Director General of the Serious Organised Crime Agency') that the property is criminal property. Thereafter, before the nominated officer can give appropriate consent, SOCA must consent to the firm continuing to act in such a way that leads to the prohibited act being undertaken.

SOCA operates a fast track scheme where the arrangement is time sensitive. If, for example, completion of a transaction is imminent, disclosure by the nominated officer to SOCA and the consent of SOCA will be necessary before completion can take place. SOCA has indicated that the time sensitive nature of the arrangement should be explicitly stated and highlighted in the written report faxed or sent electronically to the SOCA Consent Desk.

Condition 2 (s.336(3))

As an alternative to condition 1 above, appropriate consent can be given by a nominated officer if condition 2 applies. The nominated officer must make a disclosure to SOCA that property is criminal property and if, before the end of seven working days starting with the first working day after disclosure has been made, no notice of refusal of consent to undertaking the prohibited act is received from SOCA, consent can be given. A working day for these purposes is defined (s.336(9)) as a day other than Saturday, Sunday, Christmas Day, Good Friday or a day which is a bank holiday under the Banking and Financial Dealings Act 1971.

Obviously, in all cases (but particularly where a solicitor is relying upon this second condition) it is important that the solicitor's records show exactly what has happened.

Condition 3 (s.336(4))

Where disclosure has been made to SOCA by a nominated officer, SOCA will usually acknowledge receipt and either refuse appropriate consent or provide appropriate consent. If consent is given, then obviously the nominated officer can proceed to give appropriate consent to the fee earner. If consent is refused by SOCA, condition 3 may be relevant in determining whether the nominated officer can give consent to the fee earner.

This condition applies where the nominated officer discloses to SOCA that property is criminal property and before the end of seven working days starting with the first working day after disclosure has been made, notice of refusal of consent to undertaking the prohibited act is received from SOCA. Obviously, where SOCA have refused consent, no further work should be undertaken on the file if such work will amount to a prohibited act. However, s.336(4) allows the nominated officer to give appropriate consent to such work after the moratorium period has expired. For these purposes, s.336(8) defines the moratorium period as 'the period of 31 days starting with the day on which the nominated officer is given notice that consent to the doing of the act is refused'.

Note that, unlike the reference to seven working days in the legislation, the reference to 31 days in the definition of the moratorium period is not a reference to working days.

Take the following example by way of illustration of these points.

A solicitor is acting for a client on the disposal of certain assets. Contracts have been exchanged and the completion is fixed for Friday 10 September. On Wednesday 8 September, the solicitor receives certain information from his client that leads him to suspect that the funds being used by the purchaser (for whom the solicitor is not acting) derive from criminal conduct. Completion of the transaction on 10 September is likely to amount to an arrangement which facilitates the retention, use or control of these criminal funds (PoCA 2002, s.328). It would also mean that the solicitor would acquire and possess criminal property when the completion money was placed into his client account (PoCA 2002, s.329). Possibly there would also be a breach of PoCA 2002, s.327 (concealing). In all the circumstances, it would be advisable for the solicitor to report his suspicions. The timetable for reporting is as follows:

8 September	Solicitor reports his suspicions to the firm's nominated officer. Although the contractual completion date is only two days away, completion cannot go ahead without the appropriate consent of the nominated officer. If completion did proceed without the consent, the defence of disclosure would not be available.
8 September	The nominated officer cannot give consent to completion unless he has satisfied one of the conditions in PoCA 2002, s.336. Because of the time sensitive nature of this matter, it is likely that he will contact SOCA using the fast track procedure and seek consent to continuing to act. He makes a disclosure to SOCA, following any necessary waiver of privilege by the client.
9–17 September	Seven working days must be calculated starting with the first working day after the nominated officer makes the disclosure. Consequently, the first working day is Thursday 9 September. Omitting Saturday 11 and Sunday 12 September, the seventh working day is Friday 17 September. If during this period, SOCA consent to the firm undertaking the prohibited act, the nominated officer can give appropriate consent to completion proceeding.

20 September	If before the end of the seven working days (i.e. by midnight on Friday 17 September) the nominated officer has not received consent nor has he received notice of refusal of consent from SOCA, he has received deemed consent and may now give appropriate consent to the matter completing.
17 September – 17 October	If, during the seven working day period, SOCA notifies its refusal to give consent (worst case scenario, the refusal is given on day seven) the moratorium period will apply. This period starts on the day refusal of consent is given and lasts for 31 days. During this period, the prohibited act (i.e. the act of completion) cannot be undertaken since the defence of disclosure will not apply.
18 October	The moratorium period has now expired. Despite the refusal of SOCA, the nominated officer can now give appropriate consent and completion can now take place (assuming the purchaser is still willing or able to complete!)

For the sake of completeness, the following points, dealt with elsewhere in this book, should also be considered:

- Communications with the client (seeking a possible waiver of privilege) and the other side regarding the fact that completion cannot take place on the contractual completion date could amount to the offence of tipping off under PoCA 2002, s.333A – see **Chapter 7**.
- Civil liability. If the client has suffered loss as a result of the delay in completion, there may be civil liability consequences – see Chapter 10 of the Law Society's Anti-money Laundering Practice Note (**Appendix B1**).
- Disclosure on behalf of the client. In this scenario, if the client is innocent (i.e. the suspicions related to the funds of the purchaser) the client will require a defence against a possible charge under PoCA 2002. The client will be entering into an arrangement (i.e. completion) and in consequence will need the same defence as the solicitor. In this case a joint disclosure by the nominated officer on behalf of the firm and the client should be considered – see **paragraph 4.4**.

4.3.2 Offence committed by nominated officer if improper consent is given

Where a member of the firm has made disclosure of knowledge or suspicion of criminal property to a nominated officer by way of a defence, the prohibited act cannot be undertaken without the appropriate consent of the nominated officer. As noted above, there are three alternative conditions that the nominated officer must satisfy before giving consent. If a nominated officer gives consent without satisfying any of these conditions, an offence is committed. Section 336(5) provides that:

A person who is a nominated officer commits an offence if –

(a)   he gives consent to a prohibited act in circumstances where none of the conditions in subsections (2), (3) and (4) is satisfied, and

(b)   he knows or suspects that the act is a prohibited act.

The penalty for such an offence is imprisonment for up to six months and/ or a fine not exceeding the statutory maximum for summary conviction; imprisonment for up to five years and/or a fine for conviction on indictment (s.336(6)).

The nominated officer only commits an offence if the two requirements noted in s.336(5) apply. Not only must the nominated officer be shown to have given consent without any of the three conditions being satisfied but he must also be shown to have known or suspected that the act was a prohibited act.

Where a fee earner reports knowledge or suspicion that property is criminal property and the Money Laundering Regulations 2007 apply (see **Chapter 9**), a nominated officer should investigate the circumstances of the report. Regulation 20(2)(d)(iii) of the Regulations states:

> where a disclosure is made to the nominated officer, he must consider it in the light of any relevant information which is available to the relevant person and determine whether it gives rise to knowledge or suspicion or reasonable grounds for knowledge or suspicion that a person is engaged in money laundering or terrorist financing.

Whether or not the Regulations apply, it would be good practice for the nominated officer to follow this procedure. If, in the light of this internal consideration, the nominated officer comes to the conclusion that there are no grounds for knowledge or suspicion, the nominated officer may give consent to the fee earner continuing to work on the file. For example, this might apply where the fee earner is a junior member of staff or a recently joined employee. A particular aspect of a transaction may arouse the fee earner's suspicion and consequently a report might be made to the nominated officer. On considering the report along with other information held in the firm (including past dealings with the client) the nominated officer may come to the conclusion that there are no grounds for knowledge or suspicion and consent can be given without the need to satisfy any of the three conditions in PoCA 2002, s.336 and without the risk of committing a criminal offence under PoCA 2002, s.336(5). It goes without saying that particular care must be taken in these circumstances. Nominated officers should err on the side of caution and should only give consent outside the conditions of s.336 if, having considered all of the information, they have reached a view that no offence is being committed. In these circumstances it is vital for the nominated officer to record full and proper file notes.

4.3.3   Appropriate consent from the authorities

Section 335(1) of PoCA 2002 defines appropriate consent as:

(a) the consent of the nominated officer to do a prohibited act if the authorised disclosure is made to the nominated officer;

(b) the consent of a constable to do a prohibited act if an authorised disclosure is made to a constable; or

(c) the consent of a customs officer to do a prohibited act if an authorised disclosure is made to a customs officer.

As noted above, most firms will encourage all partners and other members of staff to make their disclosure of knowledge or suspicion internally to the firm's nominated officer. In such cases appropriate consent must be obtained from the nominated officer.

However, a valid defence is available if the disclosure is made to a constable or customs officer (although, in practice, this will be a disclosure to SOCA). There are two circumstances where consent from the authorities will allow the prohibited act to be undertaken.

- **Consent from SOCA.** If a disclosure is made to SOCA, their consent to do the prohibited act will amount to appropriate consent under s.335(1)(b) or (c).
- **Assumed consent from SOCA.** Section 335(2) provides that a person must be treated as having the appropriate consent if that person makes an authorised disclosure to a constable or customs officer and either the condition in subsection (3) or subsection (4) is satisfied.

Condition 1: s.335(3)

If, before the end of seven working days starting with the first working day after disclosure has been made, no notice of refusal of consent to undertaking the prohibited act is received from SOCA, consent can be assumed. A working day for these purposes is defined (s.336(9)) as a day other than Saturday, Sunday, Christmas Day, Good Friday or a day which is a bank holiday under the Banking and Financial Dealings Act 1971.

Condition 2: s.335(4)

If, before the end of seven working days starting with the first working day after disclosure has been made, notice of refusal of consent to undertaking the prohibited act is received from SOCA, no further work should be undertaken on the file if such work is likely to amount to a prohibited act. However, consent can be assumed after the moratorium period has expired. For these purposes, s.335(6) defines the moratorium period as the period of

31 days starting with the day on which the person receives notice that consent to the doing of the act is refused.

These two conditions are very similar to the conditions applicable to the nominated officer when giving appropriate consent. Consequently, the timetable noted above could equally be relevant where a fee earner discloses not to the nominated officer but to SOCA direct.

4.4 AUTHORISED DISCLOSURES BY OR ON BEHALF OF OTHERS

In certain circumstances it is not just the solicitor who might need a defence to the money laundering offences contained in PoCA 2002, ss.327–329. In many transactions it will be the client who enters and the solicitor who will be concerned in an arrangement. In some matters a barrister may also be involved in the arrangement. Consequently, solicitors should consider carefully who might need a defence and what steps can be taken in order to provide that defence.

If a client is an innocent party (and particularly if it is the information provided by the client which has given rise to any suspicion) the solicitor should first consider the privileged nature of the communication giving rise to the knowledge or suspicion. The solicitor should then consider joining in the client to the disclosure to SOCA. If a client has been joined in a disclosure where the solicitor knows or suspects that another has or is intending to use criminal property, the protection of the defence will only apply from the point of time when disclosure was made. Disclosure made by a client does not operate retrospectively and does not provide a defence against activities undertaken before the disclosure.

Any joint disclosure must be to SOCA in order for the client to benefit from it. Although a solicitor may obtain a defence by disclosing knowledge or suspicion to the firm's nominated officer, such a disclosure will not operate as a defence for the client. The nominated officer is the person nominated by the alleged offender's employer and the disclosure must be made during the course of employment.

CHAPTER 5

Failure to disclose: regulated sector

5.1 INTRODUCTION

The money laundering offences contained in the Proceeds of Crime Act 2002 (PoCA 2002) and the Terrorism Act 2000 (see **Chapters 2** and **3**) all require the alleged offender to take some action in relation to criminal or terrorist property. Section 327 of PoCA 2002 requires an act of concealment, etc.; PoCA 2002, s.328 requires a person to enter into or become concerned in an arrangement which facilitates; s.329 requires the acquisition, use or possession; Terrorism Act 2000, s.16 requires use or possession; s.17 requires an arrangement leading to use; and s.18 requires an act of assistance.

Without undertaking any of these acts (or attempting such acts), a solicitor cannot be convicted under these provisions. A solicitor who, for example, interviews a new potential client and, in the course of the interview becomes suspicious of the funds the client intends to use as part of the transaction, may decline to accept the instructions. Simply having suspicion regarding a client's funds would not be sufficient to justify a charge under PoCA 2002, ss.327–329, or Terrorism Act 2000, ss.16–18. Since no offence under these provisions has been committed (or is about to be committed) no disclosure of the suspicions to SOCA or internally by way of defence is necessary.

However, in certain circumstances, a failure to disclose knowledge or suspicion, or reasonable grounds for knowledge or suspicion, of money laundering is an offence even if no act in relation to the criminal or terrorist property is undertaken.

There are four offences of failure to disclose:

- Failure to disclose: regulated sector (PoCA 2002, s.330).
- Failure to disclose: regulated sector (Terrorism Act 2000, s.21A).
- Failure to disclose: nominated officers in the regulated sector (PoCA 2002, s.331).
- Failure to disclose: other nominated officers (PoCA 2000, s.332).

The first two offences are dealt with in detail in this chapter. The remaining two offences are covered in **Chapter 6**.

5.2 FAILURE TO DISCLOSE: REGULATED SECTOR (POCA 2002, S.330)

5.2.1 The offence

Section 330 of PoCA 2002, as amended by SOCPA 2005, provides:

(1) A person commits an offence if the conditions in subsections (2) to (4) are satisfied.

(2) The first condition is that he –

(a) knows or suspects, or
(b) has reasonable grounds for knowing or suspecting,

that another person is engaged in money laundering.

(3) The second condition is that the information or other matter –

(a) on which his knowledge or suspicion is based, or
(b) which gives reasonable grounds for such knowledge or suspicion,

came to him in the course of a business in the regulated sector.

(3A) The third condition is –

(a) that he can identify the other person mentioned in subsection (2) or the whereabouts of any laundered property; or
(b) that he believes, or it is reasonable to expect him to believe, that the information or other matter mentioned in subsection (3) will or may assist in identifying the other person or the whereabouts of any of the laundered property.

(4) The fourth condition is that he does not make the required disclosure to –

(a) a nominated officer; or
(b) a person authorised for the purposes of this Part by the Director General of the Serious Organised Crime Agency, as soon as is practicable after the information or other matter mentioned in subsection (3) comes to him.

There are a number of points that can be made concerning this section and in particular the four conditions that must be satisfied before the offence is committed.

First condition

> . . . knows or suspects, or has reasonable grounds for knowing or suspecting . . .

Like many of the offences contained in PoCA 2002, this offence can be committed with knowledge or suspicion. However, unlike the other offences, the test of knowledge or suspicion is a subjective and objective test. An alleged offender can be found guilty under s.330 if he knows or suspects that another is engaged in money laundering. However, even if subjectively the offender had no actual knowledge or suspicion of matters upon which the charge is based, if the offender has reasonable grounds for knowledge or suspicion of these matters, that will be sufficient for the purposes of this section; the fact that the offender should have known or suspected is all that is required. Consequently, an oversight by a solicitor or incompetence on the part of a solicitor might be sufficient to give rise to liability.

Solicitors must therefore be more proactive in considering whether a particular transaction gives rise to knowledge or suspicion of money laundering. Instead of simply reacting to information which might be suspicious, solicitors should ask themselves: 'Were there factual circumstances from which an honest and reasonable person, engaged in business in the regulated sector, should have inferred knowledge or formed the suspicion that another was engaged in money laundering?' See the Law Society's Anti-money Laundering Practice Note, paragraph 5.3.3 (see **Appendix B1**).

... that another person ...

The reference to another person means that, as with the offence under PoCA 2002, s.328 (arrangements), this offence can be committed where the solicitor's knowledge or suspicion relates to the conduct of a client or some third party. It may be that concerns have arisen regarding the other side's client and that the solicitor's own client is above any suspicion – consideration must still be given to the requirements to report that other person.

... is engaged in money laundering.

Section 340(11) of PoCA 2002 provides a definition for the term 'money laundering'. It states:

Money laundering is an act which –

(a) constitutes an offence under section 327, 328 or 329,
(b) constitutes an attempt, conspiracy or incitement to commit an offence specified in paragraph (a),
(c) constitutes aiding, abetting, counselling or procuring the commission of an offence specified in paragraph (a), or
(d) would constitute an offence specified in paragraph (a), (b), or (c) if done in the United Kingdom.

Money laundering is, therefore, widely defined. Since it includes the offences of concealing, etc. (PoCA 2002, s.327) and acquisition, use and possession (PoCA 2002, s.329) it follows that the perpetrator of the crime can be 'engaged in money laundering' (see **Chapter 3**).

The offence under PoCA 2002, s.330 obliges a solicitor to report knowledge or suspicion even if the solicitor is not involved in an arrangement which is likely to facilitate the acquisition, retention, use or control of criminal property. Unlike an authorised disclosure by way of a defence, this is a disclosure by way of obligation. It is the failure to disclose which is a criminal offence.

Note that the offence under s.330 can also be committed if a solicitor knows or suspects (or has reasonable grounds for knowing or suspecting) that another is engaged in an attempt, conspiracy or incitement to commit a money laundering offence or where another is engaged in aiding, abetting, counselling or procuring such an offence. However, solicitors must be careful to ensure that they do not report in circumstances where to do so would be inappropriate. A required report (termed a protected disclosure – see below) will not breach a solicitor's duty in confidentiality (although note the 'privilege defence' – see below). However, in the light of the Court of Appeal's decision in *Bowman* v. *Fels* (see **Chapter 4**) common law legal professional privilege (LPP) will still apply.

Second condition

> . . . the information or other matter –
>
> (a) on which his knowledge or suspicion is based, or
> (b) which gives reasonable grounds for such knowledge or suspicion,
>
> came to him in the course of business . . ..

Information received, other than in the course of business, does not give rise to an obligation to report. If a solicitor overhears a conversation in a public house suggesting that the speaker is engaged in criminal activities, this will not give rise to compulsory reporting, providing the solicitor is drinking in his private capacity. The fact that the information must be received in the course of business does not restrict the operation of this offence to information received on the office premises. However, the circumstances in which the information is received must suggest that the solicitor is operating in a business capacity at the time of receipt.

> . . . in the regulated sector.

The regulated sector is defined in PoCA 2002, Part 1, Sched. 9. The definition was amended by the Proceeds of Crime Act 2002 (Business in the Regulated Sector and Supervisory Authorities) Order 2003, SI 2003/3074. This order (and thus the amended definition of the regulated sector) came into force on 1 March 2004. Details of the definition of the regulated sector applicable between 1 March 2004 and 14 December 2007 can be found on the SRA's website (**www.sra.org.uk**) under the section on 'Archived rules and guidance'.

However, on 15 December 2007 the definition in PoCA 2002, Part 1, Sched. 9 was replaced as a result of the Proceeds of Crime Act 2002

(Business in the Regulated Sector and Supervisory Authorities) Order 2007, SI 2007/3287. The new definition brings the definition in line with the requirements of the Money Laundering Regulations 2007, SI 2007/2157, reg.3 (application of the Regulations) (see **Chapter 9**).

The new definition provides that a business will be in the regulated sector to the extent that its business consists of one or more of 18 activities listed. Many of the listed activities will have no relevance to solicitors. However, the following business activities should be considered when determining whether solicitors are acting in the regulated sector (the paragraphs are shown below by reference to the lettered paragraphs in the definition):

(b) the carrying on of one or more of the activities listed in points 2 to 12 and 14 of Annex 1 to the Banking Consolidation Directive.

These activities are listed in the Money Laundering Regulations 2007, Sched. 1 (see **Appendix A3**). Of possible relevance to solicitors are:

• money transmission services;
• advice to undertakings on capital structure, industrial strategy and related questions and advice as well as services relating to mergers and the purchase of undertakings; and
• safe custody services.

(d) the provision of investment services or the performance of investment activities by a person (other than a person falling within Article 2 of the Markets in Financial Instruments Directive) whose regular occupation or business is the provision to other persons of an investment service or the performance of an investment activity on a professional basis;

Whilst many solicitors do carry out investment activities, the vast majority of firms are not authorised by the Financial Services Authority (FSA) under the provisions of the Financial Services and Markets Act 2000 because they are able to rely upon providing investment services as 'exempt regulated activities' by satisfying the requirement that such activities are incidental to their professional business. Article 2 of the Markets in Financial Instruments Directive exempts from that Directive (and therefore the definition of the regulated sector under (d) above) 'persons providing an investment service where that service is provided in an incidental manner in the course of a professional activity and that activity is regulated by legal or regulatory provisions or a code of ethics governing the profession which do not exclude the provision of that service'. Consequently, this heading is only likely to apply to solicitors who are authorised by the FSA.

However, note that some activities which are 'exempt regulated activities' will be within the regulated sector as a result of other heads of the definition.

(f) the activities of an insurance intermediary as defined in Article 2(5) of the Insurance Mediation Directive, other than a tied insurance intermediary as mentioned in Article 2(7) of that Directive, in respect of contracts of long-term insurance within the meaning given by article 3(1) of, and Part II of Schedule 1 to, the Financial Services and Markets Act 2000 (Regulated Activities) Order 2001;

Solicitors may advise upon and make arrangements for clients to obtain certain insurance policies (e.g. in a conveyancing transaction, property insurance or defective title insurance; in a private client matter, missing beneficiary insurance; or in litigation ATE insurance). These policies are not 'long-term' and consequently such advice or arrangements will not be within the regulated sector under this head. However, under the exempt regulated activities regime, solicitors may undertake insurance mediation relating to long-term insurance in a limited manner (for example, they may comment on and endorse the advice of an authorised person given in relation to an endowment policy). This would be within the regulated sector, as would mainstream insurance mediation activities relating to long-term insurance policies undertaken by FSA authorised firms.

(k) the activities of a person appointed to act as an insolvency practitioner within the meaning of section 388 of the Insolvency Act 1986 . . .

Solicitors who are appointed as insolvency practitioners will be within the regulated sector. Solicitors who act for external insolvency practitioners or who act in insolvency matters without an appointment as an insolvency practitioner will not be caught under this head. However, depending upon the type of work, they may be caught under paragraph (n) below.

(m) the provision of advice about the tax affairs of another person by a firm or sole practitioner who by way of business provides advice about the tax affairs of other persons;

Solicitors giving tax advice will be within the regulated sector. It appears that any tax advice is capable of triggering the definition of business in the regulated sector. For example, whilst activities relating to will drafting would not bring a solicitor into the regulated sector, if such activities were combined with inheritance tax planning advice this would be considered as business in the regulated sector.

(n) the participation in financial or real property transactions concerning –

(i)   the buying and selling of real property (or, in Scotland, heritable property) or business entities;
(ii) the managing of client money, securities or other assets;
(iii) the opening or management of bank, savings or securities accounts;

(iv) the organisation of contributions necessary for the creation, operation or management of companies; or

(v) the creation, operation or management of trusts, companies or similar structures,

by a firm or sole practitioner who by way of business provides legal or notarial services to other persons;

This paragraph is clearly aimed at extending the regulated sector to many activities undertaken by solicitors. The reference to financial or real property transactions concerning the buying and selling of real property or business entities has the effect of bringing all conveyancing transactions and business acquisitions or disposals within the scope of the regulated sector.

The Law Society's Anti-money Laundering Practice Note provides further guidance on the effect of this paragraph (the guidance strictly relates to the Money Laundering Regulations which use the same wording as used in the definition of regulated sector – see paragraph 1.4.5 of the Practice Note). It states that solicitors will be participating in a transaction by assisting in the planning or execution of the transaction or otherwise acting for or on behalf of a client in the transaction.

The Practice Note also states that managing client money is narrower than simply handling client money. Simply operating a client account is not intended to be caught within the regulated sector but holding money or receiving money on behalf of clients as part of a transaction, or holding or receiving money as attorney or trustee will be caught. Similarly, opening or managing a bank account is wider than opening a solicitor's client account. This head is likely to cover opening or managing bank accounts when acting as trustees, attorneys or receivers.

The Treasury has also confirmed that the following (by themselves) would not generally be viewed as participation in financial transactions:

- Preparing a home information pack (HIP) or any document or information for inclusion in a HIP. This is specifically excluded in Sched.9, para.2(2)(f) and is therefore outside the regulated sector. Any subsequent conveyancing transaction undertaken by the solicitor would, of course, be in the regulated sector.
- A payment on account of costs to a solicitor or payment of a solicitor's bill (because the solicitor is not participating in a financial transaction on behalf of the client).
- Legal advice (assuming such advice does not fall within one or more of the other categories defined as within the regulated sector).
- Participation in litigation or a form of ADR (on the basis that litigation is not a transaction).
- Will writing (unless linked with, for example, tax advice).
- Publicly funded work.

(p) the carrying on of estate agency work (within the meaning given by section 1 of the Estate Agents Act 1979) by a firm or a sole practitioner who carries on, or whose employees carry on, such work.

Solicitors who provide estate agency services will, in respect of those services, fall within the regulated sector.

Third condition

(a) that he can identify the other person mentioned in subsection (2) or the whereabouts of any of the laundered property; or
(b) that he believes, or it is reasonable to expect him to believe, that the information or other matter mentioned in subsection (3) will or may assist in identifying the other person or the whereabouts of any of the laundered property.

This condition was inserted as a result of an amendment contained in SOCPA 2005, and came into force on 1 July 2005. The intention is to avoid the need for disclosure where there is evidence of money laundering which arose in the course of business in the regulated sector but where there is no possibility that the discloser can identify the person engaged in money laundering, the whereabouts of the property or other information which may assist the authorities. For example, in the course of conveyancing (i.e. business in the regulated sector) a solicitor discovers that a client's credit card has been stolen. As a result, the solicitor has reasonable grounds for knowing or suspecting that the thief is engaged in money laundering (the unlawful possession and use of the credit card). However, the solicitor has no information regarding the identity of the thief or of the laundered property. No requirement to disclose will arise in these circumstances.

Fourth condition

. . . he does not make the required disclosure . . .

The required disclosure is disclosure of the identity of the other person, if he knows it, and the whereabouts of the laundered property, so far as he knows it and the information referred to in paragraph (b) of the third condition. This requirement was added by SOCPA 2005 and came into effect on 1 July 2005. Once a solicitor is satisfied that the first three conditions apply, the disclosure must include the information required by the third condition. The disclosure must be to a nominated officer (i.e. the firm's MLRO) or to a person authorised for the purpose by the Director General of SOCA (PoCA 2002, s.330(5)(a) and (b)). Further, the disclosure must be made to SOCA as soon as it is practicable after the information referred to in the third condition comes to the solicitor. Disclosure to SOCA in the usual way (see **Chapter**

10) will satisfy this requirement. Section 339 allows for the Secretary of State to prescribe the form and manner in which a disclosure under s.330 must be made. At the time of writing no such order has been made.

Any disclosure made will be treated as a protected disclosure under PoCA 2002, s.337. This section provides that such a disclosure is not to be taken to be a breach of any restriction on the disclosure of information (however imposed) if three conditions are satisfied. These three conditions are:

- The information or other matter disclosed came to the person making the disclosure in the course of his trade, profession, business or employment.
- The information caused the discloser to know or suspect or gave him reasonable grounds for knowing or suspecting that another was engaged in money laundering.
- The disclosure was made to a constable, a customs officer or a nominated officer as soon as is practicable after the information or other matter comes to the discloser.

Note that in the light of the Court of Appeal's decision in *Bowman* v. *Fels* this provision would not be sufficient to override common law LPP (for details of the *Bowman* v. *Fels* decision relating to privilege, see **Chapter 3**). Solicitors must carefully consider their position before making a disclosure under s.330 and in particular the question of privilege must be addressed. Section 330(6) (see below) specifically includes a defence to the offence of failure to disclose where the information giving rise to knowledge or suspicion arose in privileged circumstances. Prior to *Bowman* v. *Fels*, a view was taken by some commentators that the disclosure of privileged information could be treated as a 'protected disclosure' even if such disclosure was not strictly required by s.330. Consequently, some solicitors might have been tempted to err on the side of caution and to disclose information even if it might have been privileged. This course of action is no longer open to solicitors. LPP is unaffected by the provisions relating to 'protected disclosures' and if the information is privileged it should not be disclosed to SOCA without an appropriate waiver.

Finally, in relation to disclosures, PoCA 2002, s.330(9A) (added by SOCPA 2005) should be noted. This provides that there will not be a disclosure (as defined) to a nominated officer if the person communicating information to the nominated officer is a professional legal adviser or other relevant professional adviser and such communication (which is not intended to be a formal disclosure) is made for the purpose of obtaining advice about the need to make a formal disclosure. This subsection thus allows a full discussion with the nominated officer in order to obtain advice from the nominated officer without making a formal disclosure. For practical situations where this might prove useful, see **Chapter 6**.

. . . as soon as is practicable after the information or other matter comes to him.

Both the third condition and the benefit of protected disclosures require the disclosure to be made as soon as practicable after the information comes into the possession of the discloser. Consequently, to avoid committing the crime and to benefit from the protection of s.337 (protected disclosures), solicitors must not delay in making their disclosures. The Law Society's Anti-money Laundering Practice Note states:

> Our view is that delays in disclosure arising from taking legal advice or seeking help from the Law Society may be acceptable provided you act promptly to seek advice.

5.2.2 Law Society's good practice advice

Section 330(8) of PoCA 2002 states:

> In deciding whether a person committed an offence under this section the court must consider whether he followed any relevant guidance which was at the time concerned:
>
> (a) issued by a supervisory authority or any other appropriate body;
> (b) approved by the Treasury; and
> (c) published in a manner it approved as appropriate in its opinion to bring the guidance to the attention of persons likely to be affected by it.

A supervisory body is defined in PoCA 2002, Sched.9 and the term includes the Law Society.

The Law Society issued guidance on PoCA 2002 and related matters to the solicitors' profession ('Money Laundering Guidance: Professional Ethics', Pilot Edition) in January 2004. The Guidance was significantly amended in the light of *Bowman* v. *Fels* by the replacement of the original Annex 3 to the Guidance. On 3 September 2007, the Law Society replaced this Guidance with a Practice Note (Anti-money Laundering Practice Note), and the latest version of the Practice Note is dated 22 February 2008. The Law Society is seeking Treasury approval of the Practice Note. Extracts from the Practice Note appear throughout the text of this book, and the full text of the Practice Note is available at **Appendix B1** and on the Law Society's website (**www.lawsociety.org.uk**).

5.2.3 Illustrations I

The following scenarios suggest circumstances where a solicitor may be at risk regarding a duty to disclose.

Scenario 1

A solicitor is acting in a corporate acquisition, buying shares on behalf of an individual client. In the course of acting, the solicitor becomes suspicious that funds in the possession of the client and to be used in the purchase derive from criminal activities. The solicitor decides that because of the suspicion, she cannot continue to act for the client. She terminates the retainer, in such a way as to avoid the risk of tipping off or prejudicing an investigation (see **Chapter 7**). Since the retainer has come to an end, the solicitor will not be involved in an arrangement and will not facilitate the acquisition, retention, use or control of criminal property. In order to decide whether a report must nonetheless be made, the solicitor must consider:

- Does she know or suspect that another is engaged in money laundering? On the facts it appears that the client has in his possession criminal property. This would amount to engaging in money laundering as a result of the offence of acquisition, use or possession (PoCA 2002, s.329).
- Has the information on which her suspicion is based come into her possession as a result of business in the regulated sector? The solicitor is acting on the purchase of shares. The transaction involves participation in a financial transaction concerning the buying of a business entity. The solicitor is acting within the regulated sector.

The conclusion is, subject to any defence which might be available (see below), that a protected disclosure should be made as soon as practicable.

Scenario 2

A solicitor is approached by a client for tax advice. She is asked to give advice relating to a legal tax avoidance scheme to be implemented in the UK. The advice given will not amount to an arrangement which facilitates the acquisition, retention, use or control of criminal property. However, in the course of taking instructions, the client discloses to the solicitor that he holds funds abroad derived from overseas trading which have not been disclosed to the appropriate tax authorities. The solicitor is not asked to give advice or provide any services relating to this fund. Should she, nonetheless, report her knowledge? She must consider:

- Does she know or suspect the client is engaged in money laundering? The client possibly has in his possession funds which should have been disclosed to an overseas tax authority (and possibly to the UK tax authorities). Money laundering includes the offence of acquisition, use or possession or an act which would have constituted such an offence if done in the UK (PoCA 2002, s.340(11)). Further enquiries need to be made but if, following these enquiries, there appears to be knowledge or reasonable grounds for knowledge that the client is engaged in money laundering PoCA 2002, s.330 would appear to be relevant.
- Has the information on which her suspicion is based come into her possession as a result of business in the regulated sector? It appears that it has come into her possession as a result of tax advice and in consequence is within the regulated sector.

The conclusion is again, subject to any defence which might be available (see below), that a protected disclosure should be made as soon as practicable.

5.2.4 Defences

There are four defences listed in PoCA 2002, s.330:

(a)   reasonable excuse for not disclosing;
(b)   privileged circumstances;
(c)   lack of specified training;
(d)   money laundering occurred outside the UK.

Reasonable excuse

Section 330(6)(a) states:

> But [a person] does not commit an offence under this section if:
>
> (a)   he has a reasonable excuse for not making the required disclosure.

Reasonable excuse for these purposes has yet to be defined by the courts. Solicitors should, therefore, treat this defence with care.

Section 330(6)(b) provides a defence if the information came into the possession of the solicitor in privileged circumstances (see below). There may be limited circumstances where the statutory defence in s.330(6)(b) does not apply but common law LPP does apply (as a result of the Court of Appeal's decision in *Bowman* v. *Fels* (see **Chapter 2**)).The Law Society's Anti-money Laundering Practice Note states (at para.5.7.1):

> Where common law legal professional privilege has not been expressly excluded, following the reasoning in *Bowman* v. *Fels*, it is considered that the decision not to make a disclosure because the information came to the person in privileged circumstances would be a reasonable excuse.

Crown Prosecution Service legal guidance for prosecutors indicates that if a solicitor forms a genuine but mistaken belief that LPP applies (for example, the client misleads the solicitor and seeks the advice for a criminal purpose) the solicitor would be able to rely on the reasonable excuse defence (see the Crown Prosecution Service website (**www.cps.gov.uk**)).

Privileged circumstances

Section 330(6)(b) states:

> But [a person does] not commit an offence under this section if . . .
>
> (b)   he is a professional legal adviser or relevant professional adviser; and
>
>   (i)   if he knows either of the things mentioned in subsection (5)(a) and (b) [the identity of the person engaged in money laundering and the whereabouts of the laundered property], he knows the thing because

of information or other matter that came to him in privileged circumstances, or

(ii) the information or other matter mentioned in subsection (3) [the identity of the person engaged in money laundering or the whereabouts of the laundered property or information which may assist in identifying the person or property] came to him in privileged circumstances.

Circumstances will give rise to privilege if communicated or given to the professional legal adviser or professional adviser in three cases (s.330(10)):

(a) The information is communicated or given to the adviser by a client (or by the client's representative) in connection with the giving by the adviser of legal advice to the client.

(b) The information is communicated or given to the adviser by a person (or by the person's representative) seeking legal advice from the adviser.

(c) The information is communicated or given to the adviser by a person in connection with legal proceedings or contemplated legal proceedings.

However, PoCA 2002, s.330(11) makes it clear that subsection (10) does not apply to information or other matter which is communicated or given with the intention of furthering a criminal purpose.

These provisions can provide a valuable defence. In the Law Society's view (see Chapter 6 of the Anti-money Laundering Practice Note (see **Appendix B1**)) it is made clear that there is a distinction to be drawn between common law privilege and the s.330(6) defence. The Practice Note states (at para.6.5):

Quite separately from LPP, POCA recognises another type of communication, one which is given or received in 'privileged circumstances'. This is not the same as LPP, it is merely an exemption from certain provisions of POCA, although in many cases the communication will also be covered by LPP.

The Practice Note goes on to state (at para.6.6.1):

When advice is given or received in circumstances where litigation is neither contemplated nor reasonably in prospect, except in very limited circumstances communications between you and third parties will not be protected under the advice arm of LPP.

Privileged circumstances [i.e. the s.330(6) defence], however, exempt communications regarding advice to be provided to representatives, so this may include communications with:

– a junior employee of a client
– other professionals assisting in a transaction such as surveyors or estate agents.

Since *Bowman* v. *Fels* preserves common law LPP, the defence in s.330(6) overlaps with a solicitor's obligations arising from LPP. In practice, external disclosures must not be made in circumstances where the information is privileged. Section 330(6) does, however, apply in one situation not covered by LPP, i.e. as noted in the Law Society's Practice Note, where the information is communicated or given by a 'representative' of a client. In considering whether a disclosure should be made under s.330, solicitors should first consider whether LPP applies to the information. If LPP does not apply because the information was received from a third party, they should then consider whether the third party is a representative of the client, in which case the additional defence in s.330(10) might apply.

A number of further points can be made which should assist solicitors in determining whether privileged or privileged circumstances apply.

WHAT COMMUNICATIONS ARE PRIVILEGED?

Case law can be helpful in determining what amounts to privilege as a matter of law. Chapter 6 of the Law Society's Practice Note (see **Appendix B1**) provides a useful overview of relevant cases.

RELYING UPON THE PRIVILEGED CIRCUMSTANCES DEFENCE

To rely upon LPP or the defence of privileged circumstances in s.330(6) solicitors would have to be satisfied as to two conditions:

- The information must have come to the solicitor in privileged circumstances. Not all communications made by a client are privileged, but only those communicated in connection with the giving or seeking of legal advice or in connection with or contemplation of legal proceedings.
- The information must not have been communicated or given with the intention of furthering a criminal purpose.

If the client or, in the case of the s.330(6) defence, a third party provides information which is unrelated to legal proceedings or the giving or receiving of legal advice, the first condition will not have been satisfied. However, the Law Society's Practice Note, relying upon the decision of the House of Lords in *Three Rivers District Council and others* v. *Governor and Company of the Bank of England* [2004] UKHL 48 at 111, suggests that advice privilege will cover all communications between a professional legal adviser and his client (or, where the statutory defence is being relied upon, the client's representative) relating to a transaction in which the professional legal adviser has been instructed for the purpose of obtaining legal advice, notwithstanding that they do not contain advice on matters of law and construction, provided that they are directly related to the performance by the professional legal adviser of his professional duty as legal adviser of his client.

If the client provides the information with the intention of furthering a criminal purpose, the second condition will not have been satisfied. This will also be the case where a third party intends the communication to be made with the intention of furthering a criminal purpose, even if the client is innocent and is being used by the third party (*R* v. *Central Criminal Court ex p. Francis and Francis* [1989] 1 AC 346).

If the solicitor knows that this is the case (i.e. there is an intention to further a criminal purpose) neither LPP nor the statutory defence under s.330(6) will apply. However, if the solicitor merely suspects that a client (or third party) may be using the solicitor to further a criminal purpose, the courts require *prima facie* evidence of this fact before LPP can be displaced (or the defence in section 330(6) is disapplied). Solicitors may determine whether such evidence exists or may ask the court for directions (see *Finers* v. *Miro* [1991] 1 WLR 35).

This leaves the possibility that a solicitor mistakenly believes the information received from a client is privileged but later it turns out that the client (or a third party) had, all along, intended to further a criminal purpose through communicating the information to the solicitor. When the Proceeds of Crime Bill was passing through the House of Lords an attempt was made to amend the privilege defence by including a defence where the information was privileged or there were reasonable grounds for believing it to be privileged. This amendment was not adopted but a statement by Lord Rooker (the Government spokesman in the House of Lords) and quoted in the guidance from the Crown Prosecution Service is helpful:

> The criminal law is quite clear: where a criminal offence is silent as to its mental element, the courts must read in the appropriate mental element.
>
> Therefore, in circumstances where a legal adviser did not know that information was not legally privileged, the courts would read in a requirement that he could not be convicted unless he did know.

The effect of this statement is that a solicitor therefore only commits an offence under section 330 for failure to disclose if he receives information in circumstances which he knows are not privileged.

As an alternative, the defence of reasonable excuse may be available in these circumstances (see discussion above, and in particular the guidance from the Crown Prosecution Service). However, solicitors should not close their eyes to the obvious, and the genuineness of their belief will be judged by the care they exercise in those circumstances.

WHO IS A PROFESSIONAL LEGAL ADVISER?

Communications between lawyers and clients will be privileged at common law if the appropriate conditions apply. The circumstances in which the information is received is what is important, not the status of the person receiving the information. Consequently, at common law communications made to non-qualified members of a solicitor's staff are capable of being privileged and, in litigation, often communications made to and by experts can be protected as privileged.

Section 330(6) of PoCA 2002 applies the defence of privileged circumstances to professional legal advisers. As originally drafted, this would appear to rule out the defence where information was passed to a non-solicitor employee or, in litigation, to an expert. This anomaly was identified by the Law Society and brought to the attention of the Government.

A SOCPA 2005 amendment contained in s.330(7B) has improved the position. This subsection (which came into force on 21 February 2006) applies where a person is employed by, or in partnership with, a professional legal adviser or a relevant professional adviser in order to provide the adviser with assistance or support. A defence will exist if the information (giving rise to the requirement to disclose) comes to that person in connection with the provision of such assistance or support and the information came to the adviser in privileged circumstances.

RELEVANT PROFESSIONAL ADVISERS

SOCPA 2005 extended the s.330(6)(b) and (7B) defences to 'relevant professional advisers' and this extended defence took effect on 21 February 2006. A 'relevant professional adviser' is defined in a new s.330(14) as an accountant, auditor or tax adviser who is a member of a professional body which is established for accountants, auditors or tax advisers (as the case may be) and which makes provision for testing the competence of those seeking membership and imposes and maintains professional and ethical standards.

Lack of specified training

The third defence appears in PoCA 2002, s.330(7) which provides a defence if a person:

(a) . . . does not know or suspect that another is engaged in money laundering, and

(b) . . . has not been provided by his employer with such training as is specified by the Secretary of State by order for the purposes of this section.

The offence in PoCA 2002, s.330 imposes a subjective and objective test of knowledge or suspicion (see **paragraph 5.2**). This defence applies if the accused can show on a subjective basis that he did not know or suspect another was engaged in money laundering.

In addition it is necessary to show that specified training had not been provided by the person's employer.

Employer for these purposes means someone who employs others, i.e. the defence will only apply to someone who is an employee, not a partner.

Although the definition of employer and employment is extended by PoCA 2002, s.340(12) (see **Chapter 3**), this extended definition only applies to the terms where used for the purposes of a disclosure to a nominated officer.

The specified training requirements are contained in the Money Laundering Regulations 2007, SI 2007/2157 (see **Chapter 9**). Regulation 21 requires a relevant person to take appropriate measures so that all relevant employees are:

(a) made aware of the law relating to money laundering and terrorist financing; and
(b) regularly given training in how to recognise and deal with transactions and other activities which may be related to money laundering or terrorist financing.

Clearly, it would be embarrassing for a firm (not to say unlawful under the Regulations) not to provide employees with training and for an employee to use the defence in s.330(7). Firms must therefore ensure that employees are unable to use such a defence by providing the necessary level of training. For more details of the training obligations, see **Chapter 9**.

Money laundering occurred outside the UK

A new defence (s.330(7A)) has been added by SOCPA 2005 and applies where the accused knows or believes on reasonable grounds that the money laundering is occurring in a particular country or territory outside the UK and the money laundering:

- is not unlawful under the criminal law applicable in that country or territory; and
- is not of a description prescribed by order made by the Secretary of State.

As noted above, money laundering for these purposes is defined by reference to the money laundering offences in PoCA 2002, ss.327–329. Consequently, the Proceeds of Crime Act 2002 (Money Laundering Exceptions to Overseas Conduct Defence) Order 2006, SI 2006/1070 will be the order referred to in s.330(7A).

Where the apparent money laundering occurred in the UK but involved assets derived from activities committed overseas, it will be necessary to ascertain whether the conduct in the UK was, in fact, money laundering – the defences in ss.327–329 relating to overseas criminal conduct could apply, leading to the conclusion that there was no 'engagement in money laundering' (for details of these defences, see **Chapters 2** and **3**).

However, the definition of money laundering includes the offence of acquisition, use or possession or an act which would have constituted such an offence if done in the UK (PoCA 2002, s.340(11)). Consequently, such activities if undertaken abroad could give rise to an obligation to disclose under s.330. Section 330(7A) provides a defence where the money laundering occurred outside the UK provided the two conditions noted above apply.

5.2.5 Illustrations II

The following illustrations indicate how a defence might apply to a possible charge under PoCA 2002, s.330.

Scenario 1

A solicitor is asked to provide tax advice to a client. The client admits that over the last three years he has not fully disclosed his income and capital gains to HM Revenue & Customs. The purpose of the solicitor's instructions is to advise on how to legitimise the situation. Does the solicitor have an obligation to disclose under PoCA 2002, s.330? He must consider:

- Does he know or suspect or have reasonable grounds for knowing or suspecting that the client is engaged in money laundering? On the basis that the client is likely to be in possession of criminal property, the answer would appear to be 'yes'.
- Did the information arise in the course of business in the regulated sector? Tax advice is within the regulated sector.

The initial conclusion therefore must be that a disclosure must be made. Do any of the defences apply? The obvious possibility is the defence of privilege under PoCA 2002, s.330(6). The following points can be made.

- The solicitor is a professional legal adviser.
- The information appears to have been provided in privileged circumstances, i.e. it was communicated by a client in connection with the giving by the solicitor of legal advice to the client.
- It does not appear that the information was communicated with the intention of furthering criminal conduct.

The conclusion is likely to be that the defence of privilege will apply and therefore there is no requirement to make the disclosure.

Scenario 2

A solicitor is acting for a client on a matrimonial dispute. In the course of giving advice relating to ancillary relief the solicitor discovers that the funds to be used in connection with a settlement may constitute the proceeds of tax evasion. Does the solicitor have a duty to report his knowledge or suspicion? He must consider:

- Does he know or suspect that another is engaged in money laundering? The answer would appear to be 'yes' since the funds are in the possession of an individual (his client or the other party to the proceedings) and his suspicion is that they are the proceeds of tax evasion.
- Did the information arise in the course of business in the regulated sector? This is more difficult. If, in the course of giving such advice, the solicitor has

---

given advice about the tax affairs of his client, this will bring the matter within the regulated sector. Do the services involve participation in a financial or real property transaction? If real property is involved in the settlement, again this is likely to bring the matter into the regulated sector. Other financial settlement provisions (i.e. the management of client money) could also bring it within the regulated sector. Probably the only safe course would be to assume that this is within the regulated sector.

- Would any defence arise? Since the information came into the possession of the solicitor in the course of giving legal advice or in connection with legal proceedings it would appear that it is privileged. Note, however, that neither LPP nor the s.330(6) privilege defence attach to communications received from the other side. Consequently, the defence could only apply if the communication came from the client. Even if it turned out later that the client (or a third person) was intending to further a criminal purpose (by including the criminal proceeds in a financial settlement) without *prima facie* evidence of this fact, the solicitor should either be able to rely upon Lord Rooker's statement in the House of Lords (no mental element – see above) or the reasonable excuse defence as per the Crown Prosecution Service's guidance (see **paragraph 5.2.4**).

If the solicitor chooses to withdraw from the retainer, the solicitor is unlikely to be involved in a money laundering offence. Further, even if the solicitor chooses to continue to act for the client, his future actions are unlikely to amount to a money laundering offence. The Court of Appeal's decision in *Bowman* v. *Fels* excludes from the definition of 'arrangements' the consensual resolution of issues in a litigious context (see **Chapter 2**). The offences under s.327 (concealing) and s.329 (acquisition, use and possession) also benefit from the Court of Appeal's decision. Although the settlement might facilitate the acquisition, use, retention or control of criminal property no criminal liability will arise. The Law Society's view is that the effect of the judgment extends to dealing with the final division of assets in accordance with the settlement including the actual handling of the assets which are criminal property.

It should be noted, however, that according to the Court of Appeal, litigation (or consensual resolution) does not 'clean' the criminal property. If the client asks the solicitor to use the property in some future transaction (e.g. conveyancing) the *Bowman* v. *Fels* decision will not assist. At this stage a further re-examination of whether a defence (by way of an authorised disclosure) is required to act on the future transaction must be considered.

For the sake of completeness, the earlier two illustrations are set out below with comments upon possible defences.

Scenario 1

A solicitor is acting in a corporate acquisition – buying shares on behalf of an individual client. In the course of acting, the solicitor becomes suspicious that funds in the possession of the client and to be used on the purchase derive from criminal activities. The solicitor decides that, because of the suspicion, she cannot continue to act for the client. She terminates the retainer, avoiding the risk of tipping off or prejudicing an investigation (see **Chapter 7**). Since the retainer has come to an end, the solicitor will not be involved in an arrangement and will not facilitate the acquisition, retention, use or control of criminal property. In order to decide whether a report must, nonetheless, be made the solicitor must consider:

- Does she know or suspect that another is engaged in money laundering? On the facts it appears that the client has in his possession criminal property. This would amount to engaging in money laundering as a result of the offence of acquisition, use or possession (PoCA 2002, s.329).
- Has the information on which her suspicion is based come into her possession as a result of business in the regulated sector? The solicitor is acting on the purchase of shares. The transaction involves participation in a financial transaction concerning the buying of a business entity. The solicitor is acting within the regulated sector.
- Does the defence of privileged circumstances apply? Although the communication appears to be given by a client seeking legal advice, it also appears that the information is given with the intention of furthering a criminal purpose. The solicitor has decided not to act for the client and on that basis the assumption must be made that the solicitor believes that to continue to act would involve a criminal purpose.

The conclusion is that a protected disclosure must be made as soon as practicable. Failure to do so would risk prosecution under PoCA 2002, s.330.

Scenario 2

A solicitor is approached by a client for tax advice. She is asked to give advice relating to a legal tax avoidance scheme to be implemented in the UK. The advice given will not amount to an arrangement which facilitates the acquisition, retention, use or control of criminal property. However, in the course of taking instructions, the client discloses to the solicitor that he holds funds abroad derived from overseas trading which have not been disclosed to the appropriate tax authorities. The solicitor is not asked to give advice or provide any services relating to this fund. Should she, nonetheless, report her knowledge? She must consider:

- Does she know or suspect the client is engaged in money laundering? She possibly has in her possession funds which should have been disclosed to an overseas tax authority (and possibly to the UK tax authorities). Money laundering includes the offence of acquisition, use or possession or an act which would have constituted such an offence if done in the UK (PoCA 2002, s.340(11)). On the facts, there appears to be knowledge or reasonable grounds for knowledge that the client is engaged in money laundering and it does not appear that the defence in s.330(7A) relating to the money laundering occurring outside the UK would apply. Further enquiries need to be made but if, following these enquiries, there appears to be knowledge or reasonable grounds for knowledge that the client is engaged in money laundering then PoCA 2002, s.330 would appear to be a concern.
- Does any defence apply? It would appear that although the communication was made by a client to the solicitor, this communication was not made in connection with the giving of legal advice by the solicitor to the client. The solicitor is not required to give advice nor provide any legal services regarding this fund.

The conclusion is that a protected disclosure must be made as soon as practicable. Failure to do so would risk prosecution under PoCA 2002, s.330.

5.2.6 Penalty

Under s.334(2) a person guilty of an offence under PoCA 2002, s.330 is liable, on summary conviction, to imprisonment for a period of six months or to a fine not exceeding the statutory maximum or to both; on conviction on indictment, to imprisonment for a term not exceeding five years or to a fine or to both.

5.3 FAILURE TO DISCLOSE: REGULATED SECTOR (TERRORISM ACT 2000, S.21A)

5.3.1 The offence

Section 21A was inserted into the Terrorism Act 2000 by the Anti-terrorism, Crime and Security Act 2001 and amended by the Terrorism Act 2000 and Proceeds of Crime Act 2002 (Amendment) Regulations 2007, SI 2007/3398. It states:

(1) A person commits an offence if each of the following three conditions is satisfied.

(2) The first condition is that he –

   (a) knows or suspects, or
   (b) has reasonable grounds for knowing or suspecting,
   that another has committed or attempted to commit an offence under any of sections 15 to 18.

(3) The second condition is that the information or other matter –

   (a) on which the knowledge or suspicion is based, or
   (b) which gives reasonable grounds for such knowledge or suspicion, came to him in the course of business in the regulated sector.

(4) The third condition is that he does not disclose the information or other matter to a constable or to a nominated officer as soon as practicable after it comes to him.

There are a number of points that can be made concerning this section and in particular the three conditions that must be satisfied before the offence is committed.

First condition

   . . . knows or suspects, or . . . has reasonable grounds for knowing or suspecting . . .

The offence can be committed where there is an objective or subjective test of knowledge or suspicion.

... that another has committed an offence under any of sections 15 to 18 [Terrorism Act 2000]

Section 15 creates an offence of fundraising for the purpose of terrorism. It is an offence to provide money or property or invite another to provide money or property intending it to be used or having reasonable cause to suspect that it will be used for terrorism. Further, it is an offence to receive money or property intending it to be used or having reasonable cause to suspect that it will be used for terrorism.

Section 16 creates an offence of use or possession for the purpose of terrorism. It is an offence to use or possess money or property for the purpose of terrorism or intending it should be used for terrorism.

Section 17 creates an offence of funding arrangements. It is an offence for a person to enter into or to become concerned in an arrangement as a result of which money or other property is made available or is to be made available to another and there is knowledge or reasonable cause to suspect that it will or may be used for the purpose of terrorism.

Section 18 creates the offence of money laundering.

Full details of these offences appear in **Chapter 3**.

Section 21A(11) provides that a person is to be taken to have committed an offence under ss.15–18 of the Terrorism Act 2000 if he has taken an action or has possession of money or property and he would have committed an offence if he had been in the UK at the time. Consequently, activities undertaken overseas can give rise to an obligation to report if such activities would have been an offence under the Terrorism Act 2000 if they had been undertaken in the UK.

Second condition

... the information or other matter on which his knowledge or suspicion is based or which gives reasonable grounds for such knowledge or suspicion came to him in the course of business in the regulated sector.

The offence is limited to disclosing information which came into the possession of the solicitor in the course of business in the regulated sector. This term has been fully defined in **paragraph 5.2.1**.

Third condition

... he does not disclose the information or other matter to a constable or a nominated officer as soon as is practicable after it comes to him.

The reference to a constable includes a reference to a person authorised for the purposes of this section by the Director General of SOCA (s.21A(14)). For practical purposes this means disclosure to SOCA. A nominated officer is defined in the same way as in PoCA 2002. Consequently, the nominated officer appointed by a firm for PoCA 2002 purposes will be the nominated officer for the purposes of Terrorism Act 2000 disclosures.

5.3.2 Law Society guidance and advice

Section 21A(6) of the Terrorism Act 2000 states:

> In deciding whether a person committed an offence under this section the court must consider whether he followed any relevant guidance which was at the time concerned –
>
> (a) issued by a supervisory authority or any other appropriate body;
> (b) approved by the Treasury; and
> (c) published in a manner it approved as appropriate in its opinion to bring the guidance to the attention of persons likely to be affected by it.

A supervisory body is defined in the Terrorism Act 2000, Sched. 3A and the term includes the Law Society.

The Law Society issued Guidance on the Terrorism Act 2000 to the solicitors' profession ('Money Laundering Guidance: Professional Ethics', Pilot Edition) in January 2004. The Guidance was significantly amended in the light of *Bowman* v. *Fels* by the replacement of the original Annex 3 to the Guidance. On 3 September 2007, the Law Society replaced this Guidance with a Practice Note (Anti-money Laundering Practice Note), and the latest version of the Practice Note is dated 22 February 2008. The Law Society is seeking Treasury approval of the Practice Note. Extracts from the Practice Note appear throughout the text of this book and the full text of the Practice Note is available at **Appendix B1** and on the Law Society website (**www.lawsociety.org.uk**).

5.3.3 Defences

There are two defences listed in s.21A(5):

(a) reasonable excuse for not disclosing;
(b) privileged circumstances.

Reasonable excuse

Section 21A(5)(a) states:

> But a person does not commit an offence under this section if –
>
> (a) he has a reasonable excuse for not disclosing the information or other matter
>   . . ..

Reasonable excuse for these purposes has yet to be defined by the courts. Solicitors should, therefore, treat this defence with care.

The commentary earlier in **paragraph 5.2.4** (reasonable excuse defence in PoCA 2002, s.330) would appear to be relevant.

Privileged circumstances

Section 21A(5)(b) states:

> But a person does not commit an offence under this section if . . .
>
> (b)   he is a professional legal adviser or relevant professional adviser and the information or other matter came to him in privileged circumstances . . .

Circumstances will give rise to privilege if communicated or given to the professional legal adviser in three cases (s.21A(8)).

(a)   The information is communicated or given to the legal adviser by a client (or by the client's representative) in connection with the giving by the legal adviser of legal advice to the client.

(b)   The information is communicated or given to the legal adviser by a person (or by the person's representative) seeking legal advice from the adviser.

(c)   The information is communicated or given to the legal adviser by a person in connection with legal proceedings or contemplated legal proceedings.

However, s.21A(9) makes it clear that subsection (8) does not apply to information or other matter which is communicated or given with the intention of furthering a criminal purpose.

The wording of the privilege defence is the same as the defence to PoCA 2002, s.330. Further, the amended s.21A (as a result of the Terrorism Act 2000 and Proceeds of Crime Act 2002 (Amendment) Regulations 2007, SI 2007/3398 which came into force on 26 December 2007) now contains a provision equivalent to that contained in s.330(7B) (see **paragraph 6.2.3**). Where a person is employed by, or in partnership with, a professional legal adviser (or a relevant professional adviser) in order to provide the adviser with assistance or support a defence will exist if the information (giving rise to the requirement to disclose) comes to that person in connection with the provision of such assistance or support and the information came to the adviser in privileged circumstances.

The detailed commentary on the privilege defence earlier in **paragraph 5.2.4** would appear to apply equally to the defence in the Terrorism Act 2000.

5.3.4 Penalty

Under s.21A(12) a person guilty of an offence under s.21A is liable, on summary conviction, to imprisonment for a period of six months or to a fine not exceeding the statutory maximum or to both; on conviction on indictment, to imprisonment for a term not exceeding five years or to a fine or to both.

CHAPTER 6

Failure to disclose: nominated officers

6.1 INTRODUCTION

As noted in **Chapter 5**, there are two other offences contained in the Proceeds of Crime Act 2002 (PoCA 2002) arising from a failure to disclose knowledge or suspicion of money laundering. Both these offences are aimed at nominated officers. These are:

- Failure to disclose: nominated officers in the regulated sector (PoCA 2002, s.331).
- Failure to disclose: other nominated officers (PoCA 2002, s.332).

Both these offences have been amended by the Serious Organised Crime and Police Act 2005 and are dealt with below.

6.2 FAILURE TO DISCLOSE: NOMINATED OFFICERS IN THE REGULATED SECTOR (POCA 2002, S.331)

6.2.1 The offence

Section 331 of PoCA 2002 states:

(1) A person nominated to receive disclosures under section 330 commits an offence if the conditions in subsections (2) to (4) are satisfied.

(2) The first condition is that he –

(a) knows or suspects, or
(b) has reasonable grounds for knowing or suspecting,
that another person is engaged in money laundering.

(3) The second condition is that the information or other matter –

(a) on which his knowledge or suspicion is based, or
(b) which gives reasonable grounds for such knowledge or suspicion,
came to him in consequence of a disclosure made under section 330.

(3A) The third condition is –

   (a) that he knows the identity of the other person mentioned in subsection (2), or the whereabouts of any of the laundered property, in consequence of a disclosure made under section 330,

   (b) that that other person, or the whereabouts of any of the laundered property, can be identified from the information or other matter mentioned in subsection (3), or

   (c) that he believes, or it is reasonable to expect him to believe, that the information or other matter will or may assist in identifying that other person or the whereabouts of any of the laundered property.

(4) The fourth condition is that he does not make the required disclosure to a person authorised for the purposes of this Part by the Director General of the Serious Organised Crime Agency as soon as is practicable after the information or other matter mentioned in subsection (3) comes to him.

There are a number of points that can be made concerning this section and in particular the four conditions that must be satisfied before the offence is committed.

Subsection (1)

A person nominated to receive disclosures . . .

This offence is aimed at those appointed as a nominated officer of a firm. Section 330(9) states that a disclosure to a nominated officer is a disclosure which is made to a person nominated by the alleged offender's employer to receive authorised disclosures under s.330 and is made in the course of the alleged offender's employment.

Although, in the context of a nominated officer, PoCA 2002 refers to a person's employer and a person's employment, s.340(12) provides that:

references to a person's employer include any body, association or organisation (including a voluntary organisation) in connection with whose activities the person exercises a function (whether or not for gain or reward).

The subsection goes on to state that references to employment must be construed accordingly.

As noted in **Chapter 3** it is not strictly necessary for the nominated officer to be a partner or principal in a firm of solicitors. However, in practice, the individual should be a senior member of the firm's management. Because severe penalties can be imposed upon the nominated officer for a failure to comply with his obligations under PoCA 2002, care should be taken to ensure that the nominated officer is aware of his obligations (this is particularly the case when a non-partner or principal is appointed).

. . . under section 330 . . .

Section 330 requires a disclosure of knowledge or suspicion or reasonable grounds for knowledge or suspicion of money laundering to a nominated officer or to SOCA. Details of this offence can be found in **Chapter 5.**

First condition

    (a)   knows or suspects, or
    (b)   has reasonable grounds for knowing or suspecting . . .

Like the offence contained in PoCA 2002, s.330, this offence can be committed where the nominated officer has knowledge or suspicion or reasonable grounds for knowledge or suspicion. A nominated officer can be found guilty under s.331 even if, subjectively, the nominated officer had no actual knowledge or suspicion of matters upon which the charge is based. If the nominated officer has reasonable grounds for knowledge or suspicion, that will be sufficient for the purposes of this section.

    . . . that another is engaged in money laundering . . .

The reference to 'another' means that as with the offence under PoCA 2002, s.330, this offence can be committed where the nominated officer's knowledge or suspicion relates to the conduct of a client or some third party.

Further, the definition of money laundering in PoCA 2002, s.340(11) will apply to this offence. It states:

Money laundering is an act which –

    (a)   constitutes an offence under section 327, 328 or 329,
    (b)   constitutes an attempt, conspiracy or incitement to commit an offence specified in paragraph (a),
    (c)   constitutes aiding, abetting, counselling or procuring the commission of an offence specified in paragraph (a), or
    (d)   would constitute an offence specified in paragraph (a), (b), or (c) if done in the United Kingdom.

For further commentary on this definition, see **Chapter 5**.

Second condition

    . . . the information or other matter –

    (a)   on which his knowledge or suspicion is based, or
    (b)   which gives reasonable grounds for such knowledge or suspicion,

    came to him in consequence of a disclosure made under section 330.

This condition is the key to the offence. The nominated officer only commits an offence under s.331 if the nominated officer fails to act on an internal disclosure made by another member of the firm under PoCA 2002, s.330.

It is vital that all firms adopt appropriate procedures for internal disclosure of knowledge or suspicion of money laundering and that from these procedures it is clear when a formal disclosure has been made to a nominated officer. Many firms will adopt procedures which allow informal discussions to be held between members of staff and more senior members of the management team where there is concern over an individual's responsibilities under PoCA 2002. Sometimes discussions are held with the nominated officer (perhaps on a no-name basis). Where applicable, these procedures must be clearly identified as discussions and not as disclosures. Only by ensuring that procedures identify when a formal disclosure has been made can the nominated officer be sure when potential liability under s.331 arises.

This position has been strengthened by PoCA 2002, s.330(9A) (added by SOCPA 2005) which provides that there will not be a disclosure (as defined) to a nominated officer if the person communicating information to the nominated officer is a professional legal adviser and such communication (which is not intended to be a formal disclosure) is made for the purpose of obtaining advice about the need to make a formal disclosure. This subsection thus allows a full discussion with the nominated officer in order to obtain advice from the nominated officer without triggering the nominated officer's obligations under s.331.

One possibility is for firms to require all internal authorised or protected disclosures to be made formally, in writing and in an approved firm format. Under PoCA 2002, s.339 the Secretary of State may, by order, prescribe the form and manner in which a disclosure under s.330 (failure to report; regulated sector) or s.338 (authorised disclosures) must be made. Although at the time of writing, no order has been made under s.339, it is clear from the wording that the prescribed form could apply to internal disclosures as well as to external disclosures. Until such time as an order is made, it is open to the senior management in the firm to determine the form of internal disclosures. A suggested format for such internal disclosures is contained in **Appendix C3**.

The disclosure by a member of the firm to a nominated officer in accordance with PoCA 2002, s.330 does not automatically require an external disclosure by the nominated officer. It is still necessary for the nominated officer to have knowledge or suspicion or reasonable grounds for knowledge or suspicion that another person is engaged in money laundering, that the necessary information regarding the identity of the person or laundered money is held and for that information to have been received in consequence of a disclosure under s.330. It is possible that a nominated officer, on receiving the disclosure under s.330, considers its contents and comes to the conclusion that there are insufficient grounds to give rise to knowledge or suspicion (either subjectively or objectively).

Where a fee earner makes a disclosure under s.330 the nominated officer should consider the circumstances of the report. Regulation 20(2)(d)(iii) of the Money Laundering Regulations 2007 (see **Chapter 9**) enforces this requirement when the Regulations apply. It states:

> Where a disclosure is made to a nominated officer, he must consider it in the light of any relevant information which is available to [the firm] and determine whether it gives rise to knowledge or suspicion or reasonable grounds for knowledge or suspicion that a person is engaged in money laundering or terrorist financing.

If, in the light of any internal consideration, the nominated officer comes to the conclusion, on both a subjective and objective basis, that there are no grounds for knowledge or suspicion, the nominated officer will have no obligation to report to the authorities. This might apply where, for example, the fee earner is a junior member of staff or a recently joined employee. A particular aspect of a transaction may arouse the fee earner's suspicions and consequently a disclosure under s.330 might be made to the nominated officer. On considering the report along with other information held in the firm (including past dealings with the client) the nominated officer may come to the conclusion that there are no grounds for knowledge or suspicion (either subjectively or objectively).

Finally, nominated officers should consider carefully the fact that for their obligations to have arisen under s.331 there must have been a disclosure under s.330. In other words, the disclosure under s.330 must have followed information received in the course of business in the regulated sector. The definition of the regulated sector can be found, together with commentary, in **Chapter 5.**

This is an important point. Section 332 of PoCA 2002 (see below) imposes an obligation on nominated officers to disclose to the authorities any knowledge or suspicion of money laundering received by way of an internal disclosure outside the regulated sector. For such an obligation to arise, the test of knowledge or suspicion is a subjective test. The objective test only applies to disclosures made in the regulated sector.

Third condition

(a) that he knows the identity of the other person mentioned in subsection (2), or the whereabouts of any of the laundered property, in consequence of a disclosure made under section 330,

(b) that that other person, or the whereabouts of any of the laundered property, can be identified from the information or other matter mentioned in subsection (3), or

(c) that he believes, or it is reasonable to expect him to believe, that the information or other matter will or may assist in identifying that other person or the whereabouts of any of the laundered property.

This is a similar condition to that imposed by s.330(3A). Since the required disclosure under s.330 must include the identity of the person engaged in money laundering, the whereabouts of the laundered property and any information giving rise to knowledge or suspicion (or reasonable grounds for such knowledge or suspicion) the information required by the third condition in s.331 is likely to be provided to the nominated officer.

It will still be necessary for the nominated officer to be satisfied that as a result of the disclosure or as a result of enquiries made after the disclosure, he (the nominated officer) knows or believes that he has information which will satisfy the requirements of the third condition. If this is not the case, no requirement to disclose to SOCA will arise.

Fourth condition

. . . he does not make the required disclosure . . .

The required disclosure is disclosure of:

- the identity of the person engaged in money laundering (if such identity has been disclosed to the nominated officer as a result of a disclosure under s.330);
- the whereabouts of the laundered property (so far as such whereabouts has been disclosed as a result of the s.330 disclosure); and
- the information or other matter on which the knowledge or suspicion is based on or which gives rise to reasonable grounds received as a consequence of the s.330 disclosure.

The disclosure must be to a person authorised for the purpose by the Director General of SOCA (PoCA 2002, s.331(4)). Disclosure to SOCA in the usual way (see **Chapter 10**) will satisfy this requirement.

Any disclosure made will be treated as a protected disclosure under PoCA 2002, s.337. (For the definition of a protected disclosure see **Chapter 5**.) However, in the light of the Court of Appeal's decision in *Bowman* v. *Fels* the wording of s.337 is unlikely to override common law LPP. Consequently, no disclosure can be made where common law LPP applies.

. . . as soon as is practicable after the information or other matter comes to him.

Both the fourth condition and the benefit of protected disclosures require the disclosure to be made as soon as practicable after the information comes into the possession of the nominated officer. Consequently, to avoid committing the crime and to benefit from the protection of s.337 (protected disclosures), nominated officers must not delay in making their disclosures. However, the Law Society's Anti-money Laundering Practice Note states:

Our view is that delays in disclosure arising from taking legal advice or seeking help from the Law Society may be acceptable provided you act promptly to seek advice.

6.2.2 Law Society guidance and advice

Section 331(7) of PoCA 2002 states:

In deciding whether a person committed an offence under this section the court must consider whether he followed any relevant guidance which was at the time concerned:

(a) issued by a supervisory authority or any other appropriate body;
(b) approved by the Treasury; and
(c) published in a manner it approved as appropriate in its opinion to bring the guidance to the attention of persons likely to be affected by it.

A supervisory body is defined in PoCA 2002, Sched. 9, and the term includes the Law Society.

As noted in **Chapter 5**, the Law Society initially issued Guidance on PoCA 2002 and related matters to the solicitors' profession ('Money Laundering Guidance: Professional Ethics', Pilot Edition) in January 2004. The Guidance was significantly amended in the light of *Bowman* v. *Fels* by the replacement of the original Annex 3 to the Guidance. On 3 September 2007, the Law Society replaced this Guidance with a Practice Note (the Anti-money Laundering Practice Note), and the latest version of the Practice Note is dated 22 February 2008. The Law Society is seeking Treasury approval of the Practice Note. Extracts from the Practice Note appear throughout the text of this book and the full text of the Practice Note is available at **Appendix B1** and on the Law Society website (**www.lawsociety.org.uk**).

Consequently, technically s.331(7) will not apply until the Practice Note is approved. However, a court may still take the Note into consideration in deciding whether an offence has been committed under s.331.

6.2.3 Defences

There are two defences available. The first is contained in s.331(6), which states '. . . a person does not commit an offence under this section if he has a reasonable excuse for not making the required disclosure'.

As noted in **Chapter 5**, reasonable excuse for these purposes has yet to be defined by the courts. Solicitors should, therefore, treat this defence with care. There may be limited circumstances where common law legal professional privilege applies (as a result of the Court of Appeal's decision in *Bowman* v. *Fels* (see **Chapter 2**)). The Law Society's Practice Note states:

Where common law legal professional privilege has not been expressly excluded, following the reasoning in *Bowman* v. *Fels*, it is considered that the decision not to make a disclosure because the information came to the person in privileged circumstances would be a reasonable excuse.

The second defence is contained in s.331(6A) and applies where the accused knows or believes on reasonable grounds that the money laundering is occurring in a particular country or territory outside the UK and the money laundering:

- is not unlawful under the criminal law applicable in that country or territory; and
- is not of a description prescribed by order made by the Secretary of State.

As noted above, money laundering for these purposes is defined by reference to the money laundering offences in PoCA 2002, ss.327–329. Consequently, the Proceeds of Crime Act 2002 (Money Laundering Exceptions to Overseas Conduct Defence) Order 2006, SI 2006/1070 will be the order referred to in s.330(7A).

The wording is the same as the wording used in the defence in s.330(7A) (see **Chapter 5**) and in many cases a fee earner may have chosen not to make a s.330 disclosure because of this defence. However, if a s.330 disclosure has been made but the nominated officer is satisfied that the money laundering is occurring outside the UK, s.331(6A) provides a defence provided the two conditions noted above apply and no report to SOCA should be made.

However, in relation to the defence available to a charge under PoCA 2002, s.331 what is notable is the lack of a specific privileged circumstances defence. The judgment in *Bowman* v. *Fels* preserves common law LPP and where the nominated officer determines that the information on which the s.330 disclosure was made to him remains subject to LPP no disclosure will be required under s.331. In these circumstances, the privileged nature of the information should be capable of amounting to a 'reasonable excuse' for not making the disclosure (s.331(6)).

Take the following illustration from **Chapter 5**.

A solicitor is asked to provide tax advice to a client. The client admits that over the last three years he has not fully disclosed his income and capital gains to HM Revenue & Customs. The purpose of the solicitor's instructions is to advise on how to legitimise the situation. Does the solicitor have an obligation to disclose under PoCA 2002, s.330? He must consider:

- Does he know or suspect or have reasonable grounds for knowing or suspecting that the client is engaged in money laundering? On the basis that the client is likely to be in possession of criminal property, the answer would appear to be 'yes'.

- Did the information arise in the course of business in the regulated sector? Tax advice is within the regulated sector.

The initial conclusion therefore must be that a disclosure must be made. Do any of the defences apply? The obvious possibility is the defence of privilege under PoCA 2002, s.330(6). The following points can be made.

- The solicitor is a professional legal adviser.
- The information appears to have been provided in privileged circumstances, i.e. it was communicated by a client in connection with the giving by the solicitor of legal advice to the client.
- It does not appear that the information was communicated with the intention of furthering criminal conduct.

The likely conclusion is that the defence of privilege will apply and therefore there is no requirement to make the disclosure.

However, the firm may have adopted a policy that members of the firm, if in any doubt, should always report any knowledge or suspicion of money laundering to the nominated officer. It is then for the nominated officer to determine whether or not a report should be made to SOCA. This is a sensible policy since it ensures that members of the firm are covered by making such internal reports and allows the nominated officer (who should be more familiar with the detail of the law) to make the final decision.

If the solicitor, in this scenario, reports his knowledge or suspicion to the nominated officer, the information remains subject to LPP and no report to SOCA can be made.

This problem has been somewhat relieved by PoCA 2002, s.330(9A) (added by SOCPA 2005) which provides that there will not be a disclosure (as defined) to a nominated officer if the person communicating information to the nominated officer is a professional legal adviser and such communication (which is not intended to be a formal disclosure) is made for the purpose of obtaining advice about the need to make a formal disclosure. This subsection thus allows a full discussion with the nominated officer concerning the question of privilege without triggering the nominated officer's obligations under s.331. If, following that discussion, the fee earner and the nominated officer come to the conclusion that the information received by the fee earner is privileged, then no s.330 disclosure will be made by the fee earner and no report will need to be made by the nominated officer. If, on the other hand, the discussions lead to the conclusion that privilege does not apply, a formal report will have to be made to the nominated officer by the fee earner and, in turn, the nominated officer will have to consider his obligations under s.331.

However, as noted in **Chapter 5**, LPP does not extend to information received from third parties. If, in the scenario above, the information concerning the client's failure to disclose his income came not from the client but from, say, the client's accountant, common law LPP would not attach to the information. In deciding whether to make a s.330 disclosure, the fee earner (in conjunction with the nominated officer where s.330(9A) is used) could rely upon the s.330(6) defence since this defence extends privileged circumstances for these purposes to information received from a client's representative (see **Chapter 5**). However, if despite the availability of the s.330(6) defence a formal report is made to the nominated officer, then the question of the nominated officer's obligation to disclose to SOCA under s.331 arises. The information is not subject to common law LPP and there is no specific 'privileged circumstances' defence in s.331 extending privilege to information received from a client's representative. In such circumstances a nominated officer may be able to argue that he has a reasonable excuse under s.331(6) for not disclosing.

Some firms approach this problem in a different way. Many firms will have experienced litigators as partners or employees who will be well versed in the legal concept of privilege. An alternative approach is for a firm to identify an individual or small group of individuals (the privilege committee) who have the necessary expertise and to require, as part of the firm's money laundering policy, members of the firm initially to disclose details of any knowledge or suspicion of money laundering to the privilege committee. A decision can then be made as to whether the information is or is not privileged (by reference to both common law LPP and the s.330(6) defence). If it is not privileged a formal disclosure can be made to the nominated officer, who in turn will then disclose to SOCA in accordance with PoCA 2002, s.331. If it is decided that the information is privileged, no formal internal disclosure is made and the issue of whether or not the nominated officer can rely upon the privileged circumstances in relation to his duty to disclose under s.331 becomes redundant.

An argument might be made that by disclosing information to the privilege committee, that committee is now in possession of information suggesting someone is engaged in money laundering. However, it is likely that the committee can benefit from the new s.330(7B). This applies where a person is employed by, or in partnership with, a professional legal adviser in order to provide the adviser with assistance or support. A defence will exist if the information (giving rise to the requirement to disclose) comes to that person in connection with the provision of such assistance or support and the information came to the adviser in privileged circumstances. Consequently, the members of the privilege committee should be able to rely upon the 'privilege' defence and as such they will not be required to report to the nominated officer.

Finally, if a firm chooses to rely upon s.330(9A) and/or to use a privilege committee, it should ensure that regardless of what decision is reached in discussions with the nominated officer or by the privilege committee appointed to consider the question of privilege, the fee earner who first brought his knowledge or suspicion to the attention of the nominated officer or committee must have the right to make a formal disclosure to the nominated officer. Only in this way will the fee earner be covered in respect of any defence (if an authorised disclosure is required) or obligation (if a duty to disclose under PoCA 2002, s.330 arises).

6.2.4 Penalty

Under s.334(2) a person guilty of an offence under PoCA 2002, s.331 is liable, on summary conviction, to imprisonment for a period of six months or to a fine not exceeding the statutory maximum or to both; on conviction on indictment, to imprisonment for a term not exceeding five years or to a fine or to both.

6.3 FAILURE TO DISCLOSE: OTHER NOMINATED OFFICERS (POCA 2002, S.332)

6.3.1 The offence

Section 332 of PoCA 2002 states:

(1) A person nominated to receive disclosures under section 337 or section 338 commits an offence if the conditions in subsections (2) to (4) are satisfied.

(2) The first condition is that he knows or suspects that another person is engaged in money laundering.

(3) The second condition is that the information or other matter on which his knowledge or suspicion is based came to him in consequence of a disclosure made under the applicable section.

(3A) The third condition is –

    (a) that he knows the identity of the other person mentioned in subsection (2), or the whereabouts of any of the laundered property, in consequence of a disclosure made under the applicable section,

    (b) that that other person, or the whereabouts of any of the laundered property, can be identified from the information or other matter mentioned in subsection (3), or

    (c) that he believes, or it is reasonable to expect him to believe, that the information or other matter will or may assist in identifying that other person or the whereabouts of any of the laundered property.

(4) The fourth condition is that he does not make the required disclosure to a person authorised for the purposes of this Part by the Director General of the Serious Organised Crime Agency as soon as is practicable after the information or other matter mentioned in subsection (3) comes to him.

The wording of this section is very similar to the wording in PoCA 2002, s.331. It again is a criminal offence aimed at those appointed as nominated officers and the section obliges a nominated officer to make a required disclosure if the circumstances set out in the section apply. Since the wording of this section is similar to s.331, the commentary above on the application of s.331 can be applied along with the two points of contrast discussed immediately below.

(1) Section 332 applies where the nominated officer receives disclosure under the applicable section. Section 332(5B) defines the applicable section as PoCA 2002, s.337 or s.338; s.331 applies where there is receipt of a disclosure under PoCA 2002, s.330.

This is an important contrast. Obviously, a disclosure under PoCA 2002, s.330 will only apply if the information on which the disclosure is based has been received in the course of business in the regulated sector. Section 332 will require a nominated officer to make a required disclosure where the original information was received in the regulated or non-regulated sector.

Section 332 refers to the nominated officer receiving a disclosure under the applicable section, i.e. PoCA 2002, s.337 or s.338. Section 337 covers protected disclosures and s.338 covers authorised disclosures. Protected disclosures cover a wide range of disclosures. Section 337 provides that such a disclosure is not to be taken to be a breach of any restriction on the disclosure of information (however imposed) if three conditions are satisfied. These three conditions are:

- The information or other matter disclosed came to the person making the disclosure in the course of his trade, profession, business or employment.
- The information caused the discloser to know or suspect or gave him reasonable grounds for knowing or suspecting that another was engaged in money laundering.
- The disclosure was made to a constable, a customs officer or a nominated officer as soon as is practicable after the information or other matter comes to the discloser.

However, in the light of the Court of Appeal's decision in *Bowman* v. *Fels* the wording of s.337 is unlikely to override LPP.

Two circumstances will give rise to protected disclosures. Only the first in the list below would be relevant for the purposes of s.332. The other would be a disclosure in accordance with s.330 and thus the nominated officer's obligations would arise under s.331. In the circumstances below, the assumption is that the solicitor concerned is not involved in concealing (s.327), arrangements (s.328) or acquisition, use or possession (s.329).

- In the course of business in the non-regulated sector a solicitor knows or suspects that a person is engaged in money laundering and makes a disclosure to a nominated officer (even though there is no legal requirement for him to do so).
- In the course of business in the regulated sector a solicitor knows or suspects or has reasonable grounds for knowing or suspecting that a person is engaged in money laundering and makes a disclosure to a nominated officer.

Section 332 also applies where a disclosure is made to a nominated officer by way of a defence to a possible charge under PoCA 2002, ss.327–329 (the money laundering offences) – otherwise known as an authorised disclosure (see **Chapter 3**). Authorised disclosures will be made by way of defence regardless of whether the knowledge or suspicion of money laundering arose in the course of business in the regulated sector.

(2) Section 332 applies where the nominated officer knows or suspects that another person is engaged in money laundering; section 331 applies where the nominated officer knows or suspects or has reasonable grounds for knowing or suspecting that another is engaged in money laundering.

The objective test, when assessing whether the nominated officer knew or suspected another was engaged in money laundering, only applies to s.331. For s.332, the nominated officer must know or suspect using a subjective test only.

6.3.2 Defences

Again, there are two defences. The first appears in s.332(6). This states '. . . a person does not commit an offence under this section if he has a reasonable excuse for not making the required disclosure'.

The second defence is contained in s.332(7) and applies where the accused knows or believes on reasonable grounds that the money laundering is occurring in a particular country or territory outside the UK and the money laundering:

- is not unlawful under the criminal law applicable in that country or territory; and
- is not of a description prescribed by order made by the Secretary of State.

The commentary on both of these defences as apply to s.331 would appear to be relevant.

As with s.331, there is no specific defence of privileged circumstances. However, the judgment in *Bowman* v. *Fels* preserves common law LPP and where the nominated officer determines that the information on which the protected or authorised disclosure was made to him remains subject to LPP no disclosure will be required under s.332. In these circumstances, the privileged nature of the information should be capable of amounting to a 'reasonable excuse' for not making the disclosure (s.332(6)). However, if a protected or authorised disclosure is made to the nominated officer and the information upon which the disclosure was made came not from the client but from the client's representative, no common law LPP would exist. If the disclosure to the nominated officer was made under s.330, the privilege defence in s.330(6) could apply and no obligation under s.331 to disclose to SOCA would arise (see **paragraph 6.2.3**). Section 332 only applies to protected disclosures which are not made under s.330 and to authorised disclosures. As such, the extended defence of privilege does not apply and unless the information is subject to LPP, where the s.332 conditions apply, the nominated officer must disclose to SOCA.

6.3.3 Penalty

Under s.334(2) a person guilty of an offence under PoCA 2002, s.332 is liable, on summary conviction, to imprisonment for a period of six months or to a fine not exceeding the statutory maximum or to both; on conviction on indictment, to imprisonment for a term not exceeding five years or to a fine or to both.

6.4 CONCLUSION

Given a combination of PoCA 2002, ss.331 and 332, it appears that a nominated officer potentially will be required to disclose to SOCA any disclosure received from other members of the firm where such a disclosure gives rise to knowledge or suspicion on the part of the nominated officer of another engaging in money laundering (reasonable grounds for knowledge or suspicion will be sufficient if the obligation arises under s.331). This will be the case regardless of whether or not the member of the firm making the initial disclosure to the nominated officer is obliged to make the disclosure (as a result of PoCA 2002, s.330) or wishes to make the disclosure by way of a defence (PoCA 2002, s.338). However, in both cases consideration should be given to whether or not the information giving rise to the knowledge or suspicion was privileged.

Consequently, it is vital that firms are able to clearly identify when a member of the firm has made a formal report to the nominated officer. It is, perhaps, safer for firms to encourage fee earners and others with concerns to discuss these concerns informally with more senior members of the firm rather than with the nominated officer (relying on s.330(9A) where appropriate to ensure that such a discussion does not amount to a formal disclosure). This should avoid inadvertently imposing an obligation upon the nominated officer to report to SOCA where there is a defence (e.g. privilege) or where no obligation to report arises (e.g. information arising in the non-regulated sector).

CHAPTER 7

Disclosures which prejudice an investigation

7.1 INTRODUCTION

As originally drafted, there were two offences involving disclosures likely to prejudice an investigation contained in PoCA 2002: s.333 (designated 'tipping off') and s.342 (entitled 'offences of prejudicing investigation'). On 26 December 2007, the offence under s.333 was repealed and replaced by new offences under s.333A(1) and 333A(3). Section 342 was amended with effect from that date. The amendments were introduced as a result of the Terrorism Act 2000 and the Proceeds of Crime Act 2002 (Amendment) Regulations 2007, SI 2007/3398. For details of the offences applicable to disclosures before 26 December 2007, see the SRA's website (**www.sra.org.uk**) under the section on 'Archived rules and guidance'.

For solicitors, the main effect of the amendments is that s.333A will only apply where they are acting in the course of business in the regulated sector; s.342 potentially will apply where they are acting in the course of business outside the regulated sector.

7.2 TIPPING OFF: REGULATED SECTOR (POCA 2002, S.333A)

7.2.1 The offences

There are two offences in POCA 2002, s.333A.

The first is contained in subsection (1) and states:

A person commits an offence if –

(a) the person discloses any matter within subsection (2);
(b) the disclosure is likely to prejudice any investigation that might be conducted following the disclosure referred to in that subsection; and
(c) the information on which the disclosure is based came to the person in the course of a business in the regulated sector.

Subsection (2) states:

The matters are that the person or another person has made a disclosure under this Part –

(a) to a constable,
(b) to an officer of Revenue and Customs,
(c) to a nominated officer, or
(d) to a member of staff of the Serious Organised Crime Agency authorised for the purposes of this Part by the Director General of that Agency,

of information that came to that person in the course of a business in the regulated sector.

For this offence to be committed, the solicitor must know that a disclosure has been made which is an authorised disclosure under PoCA 2002, s.338 or a protected disclosure under PoCA 2002, s.337. (For details of authorised disclosure, see **Chapter 3**; for details of protected disclosures, see **Chapters 5 and 6**.) It is sufficient that the disclosure has been made to a firm's nominated officer. It is not necessary for the initial disclosure to have been made externally to SOCA. (The original offence under PoCA 2002, s.333 spoke of 'knowing or suspecting' that a disclosure had been made. The amended offence under s.333A(1) can only be committed where a solicitor knows that a disclosure has been made.)

The disclosure referred to in s.333A(1)(a) can be to the person referred to in the report (i.e. the person suspected of involvement in money laundering) or to any other person. Consequently, if a disclosure has been made, e.g. to SOCA, concerning a solicitor's client, the offence of tipping off can potentially be committed if the prohibited disclosure (likely to prejudice an investigation) is made to:

(a) the client;
(b) any other adviser to the client (e.g. accountant, estate agent, etc.);
(c) the person on the other side of the transaction;
(d) the other side's solicitor;
(e) the other side's other representative or agent.

If the disclosure to, e.g. SOCA, was made concerning the other side's client, then the prohibited disclosure (likely to prejudice an investigation) could also give rise to a criminal offence if it is made to any of those listed above including the solicitor's own innocent client.

Unlike the earlier offence of tipping off (contained in PoCA 2002, s.333), the new offence under s.333A(1) only applies to the regulated sector. The definition of the regulated sector for these purposes is the same as for the offences of 'failure to disclose' – see **Chapter 5**. However, as noted in **Chapter 5**, a number of common activities undertaken by solicitors will be outside the regulated sector. These include:

• Preparing a home information pack (HIP) or any document or information for inclusion in a HIP. This is specifically excluded from the definition of the regulated sector. Any subsequent conveyancing transaction undertaken by the solicitor would, of course, be in the regulated sector.

- A payment on account of costs to a solicitor or payment of a solicitor's bill (because the solicitor is not participating in a financial transaction on behalf of the client).
- Legal advice (assuming such advice does not fall within one or more of the other categories defined as within the regulated sector).
- Participation in litigation or a form of ADR (on the basis that litigation is not a transaction).
- Will writing (unless linked with, for example, tax advice).
- Publicly funded work.

The most common activity undertaken by solicitors which will be outside the regulated sector is litigation. However, the fact that tipping off only applies to the regulated sector is unlikely to make a huge difference in practice for litigators. As a result of *Bowman* v. *Fels* (see **Chapter 2**) most litigation will be outside the scope of the money laundering offences and as such no reports are likely to be made to SOCA. Similarly, since litigation is not within the regulated sector, no reports are likely to be made by way of an obligation under PoCA 2002, s.330 (see **Chapter 5**). If, in the past, despite *Bowman* v. *Fels* and the definition of the regulated sector, internal reports were made to the firm's nominated officer arising from knowledge or suspicion of money laundering in a litigation context, such reports could have led to a tipping off offence under s.333. Now, the communication of internal reports arising in a litigious context (i.e. outside the regulated sector) cannot give rise to an offence under s.333A(1). (However, note the offence of prejudicing an investigation under PoCA 2002, s.342 – see **paragraph 7.3**.)

The requirement in s.333A(1) and (2) is such that there is a double test regarding the regulated sector. Not only does the disclosure to the nominated officer or to SOCA have to be as a result of information obtained in the course of business in the regulated sector, the information regarding the disclosure must have come to the accused in the course of business in the regulated sector.

It cannot be tipping off to include a paragraph about the obligations under the money laundering legislation in the firm's standard client care letter even if the retainer does bring the firm within the regulated sector. For an indication of possible terms of business, see **Chapter 11**.

In the light of s.333A(1), it is important that the firm's internal procedures (particularly when acting in the regulated sector) include a requirement that once an authorised or protected disclosure has been made to the firm's nominated officer, no communication should be made by any fee earner concerning that transaction matter without the consent of the nominated officer. In this way, firms can protect fee earners from inadvertently committing an offence under s.333A(1).

Before making a protected or authorised disclosure to the firm's nominated officer, fee earners should be permitted to make enquiries concerning a client or other party to the transaction in order to allay any possible causes for concern. Following these enquiries, the firm can then decide whether to act for a client or continue to act for an existing client. Since these enquiries will be made before any protected or authorised disclosure, any communication made to a client or other person cannot give rise to an offence under s.333A(1). However, care must be taken regarding these enquiries since it is still possible that such communications could give rise to an offence under PoCA 2002, s.333A(3) (see below) and/or s.342 (see **paragraph 7.3.1**).

Section 333A(3) states:

A person commits an offence if –

(a) the person discloses that an investigation into allegations that an offence under this Part has been committed is being contemplated or is being carried out;
(b) the disclosure is likely to prejudice that investigation; and
(c) the information on which the disclosure is based came to the person in the course of a business in the regulated sector.

Section 333A(1) requires a disclosure to have been made to the nominated officer or to SOCA; s.333A(3) does not require such a disclosure to have been made. Consequently, solicitors are potentially at risk prior to making an authorised or protected disclosure. If they disclose that an internal investigation is being carried out (or even contemplated) such disclosure could be an offence under s.333A(3). This might apply where a solicitor discusses matters with the nominated officer (or any other senior member of staff) with a view to deciding whether a formal disclosure is required and then discloses those discussions to, e.g. a client.

For both offences to be committed, it is necessary under s.333A(1)(b) and (3)(b) for the accused to have made a disclosure which 'is likely to prejudice' any investigation conducted following the authorised or protected disclosure or the investigation being carried out or contemplated.

Two points need to be made regarding the wording of s.333A(1)(b) and (3)(b).

First, the subparagraphs do not require the accused to know or suspect that the disclosure is likely to prejudice any investigation. This, it would appear, is simply a question of the prosecution showing that, as a matter of fact, the disclosure was likely to prejudice any investigation. Certain disclosures are permitted under the Act (see **paragraph 7.2.2**). Section 333D(3) and (4) provide that a person does not commit an offence under s.333A(1) and (3) if he did not know or suspect that the disclosure was likely to be prejudicial.

However, since this appears in the statute as a defence, the onus of proof will rest with the accused. If the prosecution are able to show that, as a matter of fact, the disclosure was prejudicial, it might be difficult for the accused to adduce evidence that, on a subjective basis, the accused did not know or suspect this fact.

Secondly, what amounts to a likelihood of prejudicing an investigation will, ultimately, be for the courts to decide. However, it is clear from the wording of s.333A(1)(b) that the investigation prejudiced by the disclosure must have been conducted following the protected or authorised disclosure. If the disclosure is prejudicial to some other investigation, s.333A(1) will not apply (but perhaps, in these circumstances, there could be a prosecution under PoCA 2002, s.333A(3)).

7.2.2 Permitted disclosures

There are three sections dealing with permitted disclosures. These are:

- s.333B – disclosures within an undertaking or group.
- s.333C – other permitted disclosures between institutions, etc.
- s.333D – other permitted disclosures, etc.

Section 333B – disclosures within an undertaking or group

There are two relevant provisions for solicitors in s.333B. First, an employee, officer or partner of an undertaking does not commit an offence under s.333A (i.e. both the offences in that section are covered by this provision) where the disclosure is to an employee, officer or partner of the same undertaking. Bearing in mind that to commit the offence, there must be a disclosure prejudicial to an investigation, this provision is unlikely to be of great practical assistance but will provide a defence if a prejudicial disclosure is made internally.

Second, the section provides that a professional legal adviser or a relevant professional adviser does not commit an offence under s.333A if the disclosure is to a professional legal adviser or a relevant professional adviser (these terms are defined in **Chapter 5**). However, it is important to note that this provision does not permit disclosures prejudicing an investigation to be made between firms of solicitors and, e.g. firms of accountants because there are two further conditions that must be met before the disclosure is permitted:

- the advisers must perform their professional activities within different undertakings which share common ownership, management or control; and
- both advisers must carry on business in an EEA State or a country imposing equivalent money laundering requirements.

Consequently, whilst this provision might apply to firms with certain overseas offices (different undertakings sharing common ownership) it is unlikely to have widespread application.

Section 333C – other permitted disclosures between institutions, etc.

This section applies to disclosures between credit institutions, financial institutions, professional legal advisers or relevant professional advisers. However, its application is limited to disclosure between persons or businesses of the same type, i.e. a professional legal adviser to another professional legal adviser; it does not apply to disclosures between different types, e.g. a credit institution and a professional legal adviser. The purpose of the section is to permit disclosures which might otherwise be prohibited under s.333A (i.e. those prejudicing an investigation) where the disclosures relate to a client or former client of both advisers or where both advisers are involved in the provision of a service. The purpose of such disclosure must be to prevent an offence being committed under PoCA 2002, Part 7.

In other words, it allows a solicitor acting in a transaction for client A, to disclose to a solicitor acting for client B in the same transaction, information which might prejudice an investigation, providing the purpose of the disclosure was to prevent either client A or client B (or another person) committing a money laundering offence. It would also cover the situation where a solicitor who had previously acted for client A wished to disclose to client A's new solicitor information which might prejudice an investigation, providing the disclosure was for the purpose of preventing a money laundering offence.

Two further conditions must be satisfied under s.333C:

- the adviser to whom the disclosure is made must be situated in an EEA State or another country imposing equivalent money laundering requirements; and
- the adviser making the disclosure and the adviser to whom it is made must be subject to equivalent duties of professional confidentiality and the protection of personal data within the meaning of the Data Protection Act 1998, s.1.

Solicitors should note that this section does not impose a duty on them to disclose information to another solicitor in order to prevent money laundering. Further, the section does not relieve a solicitor from the duty of confidentiality owed to a client nor does the section override the concept of LPP. However, where a solicitor is aware that a client is using the solicitor's services for the purposes of furthering a criminal purpose (meaning any information acquired from the client relating to this purpose is neither confidential nor privileged) the solicitor may choose to disclose information to the solicitor on the other side of the transaction or to the client's new solicitor without being at risk of committing the offence of tipping off under s.333A.

Section 333D – other permitted disclosures, etc.

This section allows a number of disclosures to be made without breaching s.333A.

First, a disclosure (which would otherwise breach s.333A) can be made by a person to that person's supervisory authority. The supervisory authority for this purpose is the authority specified in the Money Laundering Regulations 2007. Under Sched.3 of the Regulations, the Law Society is the supervisory authority for solicitors. Consequently, any disclosure by a solicitor to the Law Society in its role as a supervisory authority would not give rise to a s.333A offence.

Secondly, if the disclosure is for the purpose of:

- the detection, investigation or prosecution of a criminal offence; or
- an investigation under PoCA; or
- the enforcement of a court order made under PoCA,

no criminal offence will be committed under s.333A.

Thirdly, and of most relevance to solicitors, a professional legal adviser (or a relevant professional adviser) does not commit an offence under s.333A if a disclosure is made to the adviser's client and it is made for the purpose of dissuading the client from engaging in conduct amounting to an offence. This allows solicitors to provide advice to a client concerning the client's future intentions without running the risk of tipping off. However, it should be noted that this defence will not apply if the solicitor is aware that a client (or third party) has already committed a criminal offence.

This provision solves the problem of how a solicitor can decline to act further for a client where the solicitor has grounds for believing that the client intends to use the solicitor's services to further a criminal purpose. In these circumstances it would be appropriate to advise the client that a particular course of action would be criminal and try to dissuade the client from undertaking that action. Such disclosure would not amount to a s.333A offence. If the client declined to take the advice, the solicitor could cease acting without risking tipping off. In these circumstances it might still be necessary for the solicitor to consider the impact of PoCA 2002, s.330 (see **Chapter 5**). Remember, this section applies where there is knowledge or suspicion that another is 'engaged in money laundering' and 'money laundering' for these purposes is defined as an act which (*inter alia*) constitutes 'an attempt, conspiracy or incitement' to commit a money laundering offence.

7.2.3 Penalty

Under s.333A(4), a person guilty of an offence under PoCA 2002, s.333A is liable, on summary conviction, to imprisonment for a period of three months or to a fine not exceeding level 5 on the standard scale or to both; on conviction on indictment, to imprisonment for a term not exceeding two years or to a fine or to both.

7.3 OFFENCES OF PREJUDICING INVESTIGATION (POCA 2002, S.342)

7.3.1 The offence

Section 342 states:

(1) This section applies if a person knows or suspects that an appropriate officer (or in Scotland) a proper person is acting (or proposing to act) in connection with a confiscation investigation, a civil recovery investigation or a money laundering investigation which is being or is about to be conducted.

(2) The person commits an offence if –

(a) he makes a disclosure which is likely to prejudice the investigation, or

(b) he falsifies, conceals, destroys or otherwise disposes of, or causes or permits the falsification, concealment, destruction or disposal of, documents which are relevant to the investigation.

For the purposes of money laundering, this offence therefore applies where a solicitor (or member of staff) knows or suspects that an appropriate officer is acting or proposing to act in connection with a money laundering investigation and a disclosure is made which is likely to prejudice the investigation.

The offence can be committed at any stage of a transaction, whether or not an authorised or protected disclosure has been made.

The reference in the section to an appropriate person is a reference to (PoCA 2002, s.378):

(a) an accredited financial investigator;

(b) a constable;

(c) a customs officer.

Further, for the purposes of s.342, in relation to a money laundering investigation, a person authorised for the purposes of money laundering investigations by the Director General of SOCA is also an appropriate officer.

A money laundering investigation is an investigation into whether a person has committed a money laundering offence (PoCA 2002, s.341(4)). A money laundering offence is defined in s.340(11) and is described fully in **Chapter 5**.

97

Like the offence of tipping off, the prohibited disclosure can be made to:

(a) the client;
(b) any other adviser to the client (e.g. accountant, estate agent, etc.);
(c) the person on the other side of the transaction;
(d) the other side's solicitor;
(e) the other side's other representative or agent; or
(f) any other person.

The offence (again like the tipping off offence) does not require knowledge or suspicion that the disclosure is likely to prejudice the investigation. It is sufficient that, as a matter of fact, the disclosure is likely to prejudice the investigation (however, note the defence that the accused did not know or suspect that the disclosure was likely to prejudice an investigation – for a commentary upon this defence, see **paragraph 7.3.2**).

7.3.2 Defences

Introduction

The defences to s.342 can be found in the amended subsection (3). The amendments were made as a result of the Terrorism Act 2000 and Proceeds of Crime Act 2002 (Amendment) Regulations 2007, SI 2007/3398. The section states:

> a person does not commit an offence under subsection 2(a) if –
>
> (a) he does not know or suspect that the disclosure was likely to prejudice the investigation;
> (b) the disclosure is made in the exercise of a function under this Act or of any other enactment relating to criminal conduct or benefit from criminal conduct or in compliance with a requirement imposed under or by virtue of this Act;
> (ba) the disclosure is of a matter within section 333A(2) or (3)(a) (money laundering: tipping off) and the information on which the disclosure is based came to the person in the course of business in the regulated sector,
> (c) he is a professional legal adviser and the disclosure falls within subsection 4.

Each defence will be dealt with in turn.

Section 342(3)(a)

> ... he does not know or suspect that the disclosure was likely to prejudice the investigation ...

As with the offence under s.333A (see **paragraph 7.2.1**) there is no requirement in s.342 for the accused to know or suspect that his disclosure is likely to prejudice an investigation. The prosecution are likely to have to show that, as a matter of fact, the disclosure was likely to be prejudicial. However, by way of a defence, it is open for the accused to show, on a subjective basis, that he did not know or suspect that the disclosure would prejudice an investigation. The onus clearly shifts to the accused to prove the existence of evidence to support the defence. Given that the prosecution will already have adduced evidence that the accused knew or suspected that a money laundering investigation was being or about to be conducted, it might be a difficult onus to discharge.

Undue reliance should not be placed upon this defence.

Section 342(3)(b)

... the disclosure is made in (carrying out a function he has relating to the enforcement of any provision of this Act) [the exercise of a function under this Act] or of any other enactment relating to criminal conduct or benefit from criminal conduct [or in compliance with a requirement imposed under or by virtue of this Act] ...

This defence is clearly aimed at law enforcement officers who, in carrying out their law enforcement activities, may make disclosures which technically could be prohibited by these sections. It is unlikely to be of any benefit to solicitors.

Section 342(3)(ba)

... the disclosure is of a matter within section 333A(2) or (3)(a) (money laundering: tipping off) and the information on which the disclosure is based came to the person in the course of business in the regulated sector,

This new defence was added by the Terrorism Act 2000 and Proceeds of Crime Act 2002 (Amendment) Regulations 2007, SI 2007/3398 and came into effect on 26 December 2007. It has been added as a consequence of the amendments made to the tipping off offence contained in s.333A. The result of this provision is that any disclosure of information caught by s.333A will not be an offence under s.342. Where a solicitor is able to make a permitted disclosure under s.333A, no offence will be committed under s.342. In practice, this means that any disclosure likely to prejudice an investigation based on information received in the course of business in the regulated sector will be dealt with in accordance with s.333A and the permitted disclosures under that section. Section 342 is only likely to apply to prejudicial disclosures based upon information received outside the regulated sector. For a definition of the regulated sector, see **Chapter 5**.

Section 342(3)(c)

> ... he is a professional legal adviser and the disclosure falls within subsection 4.

This is clearly the most relevant of the defences applicable to solicitors working outside the regulated sector and therefore at risk from s.342. Section 342(4) states:

> A disclosure falls within this subsection if it is a disclosure –
>
> (a) to a client of the professional legal adviser in connection with the giving by the adviser of legal advice to the client, or
> (b) to any person in connection with legal proceedings or contemplated legal proceedings.

However, the disclosure will not fall within the terms of this defence if it is made 'with the intention of furthering a criminal purpose' (PoCA 2002, s.342(5)).

The wording of this defence is similar to the defence of privilege contained in PoCA 2002, s.330 (see **Chapter 5**). However, it should be appreciated that the defence of privilege applies to information given *to* a professional legal adviser by a client or other person. This defence applies to information given *by* a professional legal adviser to a client or other person.

Keep in mind that the defence is only necessary if a disclosure has been made in the circumstances envisaged by s.342; in other words, a disclosure has been made which is likely to prejudice an investigation. Despite this fact, it might be possible for a solicitor to make such a disclosure to his client or to a third person if the defence applies.

Since s.342 only applies to information received outside the regulated sector, this defence is of particular importance to litigators (who operate outside the regulated sector) and to those solicitors whose retainer with the client is limited to the giving of legal advice (other than tax advice) which will also be outside the regulated sector.

This defence was first considered in detail by Dame Elizabeth Butler-Sloss in her judgment in the case of *P* v. *P* [2003] EWHC Fam 2260. NCIS (the appropriate authority at the time of her judgment) interpreted s.342(5) very widely, taking the view that if a person intended to use the solicitor for a criminal purpose, even if this was unknown to the solicitor, the benefit of the defence in s.342(4) would be lost.

Dame Elizabeth Butler-Sloss, in her judgment, stated:

> Section ... 342 specifically recognise[s] a legal adviser's duty in ordinary circumstances to make relevant disclosures, even where the result would be to tip off their client, where to do so would fall within the ambit of being in connection with the giving of legal advice or with legal proceedings actual or contemplated. ... Section ... 342(5) must have some purpose and the interpretation suggested by the NCIS

cannot in my view be correct. The exemption is lost if a disclosure to a client is made 'with the intention of furthering a criminal purpose'. . .

But unless the requisite improper intention is there, the solicitor should be free to communicate such information to his/her client or opponent as is necessary and appropriate in connection with the giving of legal advice or acting in connection with actual or contemplated legal proceedings.

The judgment in *Bowman* v. *Fels* (see **Chapter 2**) further supports the statutory exemption: professional legal advisers have a discretion to give advice to their clients about money laundering reports, although there remains no absolute duty to do so. Depending upon the circumstances, solicitors may prefer to withdraw.

In conclusion, solicitors should be able to rely upon this defence where they are properly advising their client or are acting in litigation and are undertaking business outside the regulated sector unless the solicitor's intention is to make the disclosure in furtherance of criminal conduct.

7.3.3 Penalty

Under s.342(7) a person guilty of an offence under PoCA 2002, s.342 is liable, on summary conviction, to imprisonment for a period not exceeding six months or to a fine not exceeding the statutory maximum or to both; on conviction on indictment, to imprisonment for a term not exceeding five years or to a fine or to both.

7.4 TERRORISM ACT 2000

The Terrorism Act 2000 (ss.21D–H, inserted by the Terrorism Act 2000 and Proceeds of Crime Act 2002 (Amendment) Regulations 2007, SI 2007/3398) contain tipping off offences applicable to business in the regulated sector. The wording of these sections is the same as the wording contained in PoCA 2002, ss.333A–E and therefore the commentary above on these sections will be relevant.

CHAPTER 8

Confiscation and civil recovery orders

8.1 INTRODUCTION

This book has not been written to provide a comprehensive commentary on confiscation and recovery orders that can be made by the courts under their powers contained in the Proceeds of Crime Act 2002 (PoCA 2002), but to give guidance on a solicitor's obligations arising out of PoCA 2002, Part 7 (that part of PoCA 2002 dealing with money laundering). However, as noted in **Chapter 1**, a major stage in the money laundering process is layering – the attempt to hide the proceeds of crime in such a way that it cannot be traced back to the original crime.

Those involved in money laundering may frequently attempt to use the services of solicitors to achieve the layering stage. This aim is increasingly important in the light of the confiscation and civil recovery procedures set out in PoCA 2002. If a criminal is able to launder the criminal proceeds successfully, it is unlikely that any recovery of those proceeds will be possible. If the laundering process is unsuccessful, those proceeds may be subject to confiscation or civil recovery.

8.2 CONFISCATION ORDERS (POCA 2002, PART 2)

Under PoCA 2002, s.6 a Crown Court is required to proceed under the section if two conditions are satisfied:

(a) a defendant is convicted of an offence before the Crown Court or is committed to the Crown Court for sentencing or with a view to a confiscation order being considered; and
(b) the prosecutor asks the court to proceed under s.6 or the court believes it is appropriate to do so.

If these two conditions are satisfied, the court must decide whether the defendant has a criminal lifestyle and, if so, whether he has benefited from general criminal conduct. Alternatively, if the court decides that the defendant does not have a criminal lifestyle, it must still consider whether he has benefited from his particular criminal conduct.

A criminal lifestyle for these purposes is defined as arising from a conviction of an offence which constitutes conduct forming part of a course of criminal activity, committed over a period of at least six months and which is listed in PoCA 2002, Sched.2 (serious crimes including specified offences relating to drug trafficking, money laundering, terrorism, people trafficking, arms trafficking, counterfeiting and blackmail). Conduct will form part of a course of criminal activity, if in the proceedings in which he was convicted, he was convicted of three or more other offences from which he has benefited, or if in the period of six years ending with the day when the proceedings started, he was convicted on at least two separate occasions of offences from which he has benefited. The defendant must have obtained a benefit of not less than £5,000.

There is a distinction drawn between general criminal conduct arising from a criminal lifestyle and particular criminal conduct arising from the conduct upon which the specific conviction was based. This distinction is relevant to the assumptions the court can make and the amount recoverable under a confiscation order.

Once a court has decided that a defendant has benefited from either general or particular criminal conduct (the decision is taken by the court on a balance of probabilities – PoCA 2002, s.6(7)), it must decide upon the recoverable amount and make a confiscation order requiring the defendant to pay that amount. (There is a discretion where the court believes that any victim of the criminal conduct has started or intends to start proceedings against the defendant to recover in respect of any loss, injury or damage sustained.)

The amount of the recoverable sum is generally the amount equal to the defendant's benefit from the conduct concerned. If the defendant has a criminal lifestyle, the conduct concerned will be his general criminal conduct and the recoverable sum will be calculated by reference to all of the defendant's criminal conduct, whether the conduct occurred before or after the passing of PoCA 2002 or whether the property was obtained before or after the passing of PoCA 2002. If the defendant does not have a criminal lifestyle, the conduct concerned will be his particular criminal conduct which consists of the conduct constituting the offences for which he was convicted (at the same proceedings) and any other offences which the court will be taking into account in sentencing.

If the court decides that a defendant has a criminal lifestyle, it must make four assumptions in deciding whether the defendant has benefited from his general criminal conduct and in deciding the benefit from this conduct. The four assumptions are:

- Any property transferred to the defendant at any time after the relevant day (generally the first day of the period of six years ending with the date when proceedings were started against him) was as a result of his general criminal conduct.
- Any property held by the defendant at any time after the date of conviction was obtained as a result of his general criminal conduct.
- Any expenditure incurred by the defendant after the relevant day was from property obtained by the defendant as a result of his general criminal conduct.
- In any valuation of property obtained (or assumed to be obtained) by the defendant, he obtained it free of any other interests.

The court should only ignore these assumptions if either one or more of the assumptions is shown to be incorrect or there would be a serious risk of injustice if the assumption were made.

Section 97 of SOCPA 2005 gives the Secretary of State power by order to make provision to allow magistrates' courts to make confiscation orders under PoCA 2002, Part 2. The power for magistrates' courts to make a confiscation order must be restricted to the cases where the amount does not exceed £10,000. Orders above this amount will only be able to be made in the Crown Court.

8.3 CIVIL RECOVERY ORDERS (POCA 2002, PART 5)

In order to make a confiscation order, the criminal must have been convicted of a criminal offence (either in proceedings before the Crown Court or where there has been a committal to the Crown Court for sentencing or a committal with a view to a confiscation order being considered). In all cases, therefore, the court must have been satisfied that, beyond reasonable doubt, the individual had been involved in criminal conduct.

Civil recovery orders were introduced as a result of PoCA 2002. They can be distinguished from confiscation orders on the basis that there is no need for a criminal conviction. These orders allow the recovery of property obtained through unlawful conduct and since the application is made in civil proceedings, the test of whether or not conduct is unlawful is on the balance of probabilities.

Section 240 of PoCA 2002 provides that the general purpose of these provisions is to allow the enforcement authority (SOCA) to recover in civil proceedings before the High Court property which is, or represents, property obtained through unlawful conduct. Further, PoCA 2002, Part 5 allows cash which is, or represents, property obtained through unlawful conduct, to be forfeited in civil proceedings before a magistrates' court.

In both cases it is necessary for there to be unlawful conduct and this is defined in PoCA 2002, s.241 as conduct which is 'unlawful under the criminal law' or conduct which occurs outside the UK and is unlawful under the criminal law of that country and would be unlawful under the criminal law of the UK if it occurred in the UK.

It is for the court to decide on a balance of probabilities whether it is proved that unlawful conduct has occurred (s.241(3)).

8.3.1 Civil recovery in the High Court

Proceedings may be taken by SOCA in the High Court against any person who holds recoverable property (PoCA 2002, s.243(1)). A claim form must be served on the respondent and any other person who holds associated property which SOCA wishes to be subject to a recovery order (PoCA 2002, s.243(2)).

Associated property means (PoCA 2002, s.245) property which is not itself recoverable property but includes:

- Any interest in recoverable property.
- Any other interest in the property in which recoverable property subsists.
- If the recoverable property is a tenancy in common, the tenancy of the other tenant.
- If the recoverable property is part of a larger property, but not a separate part, the remainder of that property.

An interim receiving order can be applied for (either before or after starting the proceedings for a recovery order). This will be an order for the detention, custody or preservation of property and the appointment of an interim receiver (PoCA 2002, s.246). The interim receiver is required to take such steps as the court considers necessary to secure the detention, custody or preservation of the property and to establish whether or not the property to which the order applies is recoverable or associated property (PoCA 2002, s.247). Section 98 of SOCPA 2005 amended PoCA 2002, s.245 allowing SOCA to apply for a property seizing order as an alternative to an order appointing a receiver.

The interim receiving order must prohibit the person to whose property the order applies from dealing with the property, subject to the court making an exclusion to enable the person to meet reasonable living expenses or to carry on any trade, business, profession or occupation (PoCA 2002, s.252). Further, under PoCA 2002, s.253, whilst the order has effect the court may stay any action of legal process in respect of the property. As a result of SOCPA 2005, s.98 defendants who are subject to civil proceedings are able to have access to their frozen assets in order to fund the cost of their legal proceedings.

Where a court is satisfied that property is recoverable, under PoCA 2002, s.266, it must make a recovery order vesting the title to the property in the trustee for civil recovery (a person appointed by the court). The functions of the trustee under PoCA 2002, s.267 are to secure the detention, custody or preservation of the property and, in the case of property which is not money, to realise the value of the property for the benefit of SOCA.

8.3.2 Recovery of cash in summary proceedings

For the purposes of these provisions, cash means:

- notes and coins in any money;
- postal orders;
- cheques of any kind, including travellers' cheques;
- bankers' drafts;
- bearer bonds and bearer shares.

On the application of HMRC or a constable, a magistrates' court may make an order for forfeiture of cash or any part of it if it is satisfied that the cash or part is recoverable property or is intended by any person for use in unlawful conduct (PoCA 2002, s.298) and the cash has been detained under PoCA 2002, s.295 (detention of seized cash – see below). Subject to any appeal, the cash forfeited is paid to the Consolidated Fund (PoCA 2002, s.300).

An officer of HMRC or constable who is lawfully on any premises and who has reasonable grounds for suspecting that there is cash on the premises which is recoverable property or is intended by any person for use in unlawful conduct may search for cash there (PoCA 2002, s.289(1)). Equally, an officer of HMRC or constable who has reasonable grounds for suspecting that a person is carrying cash which is recoverable property or is intended by any person for use in unlawful conduct may require the person to permit a search of any article in his possession or permit a search of his person and may detain the person for as long as necessary (s.289(2) and (3)). Such searches may only be exercised with the prior approval of a judicial officer (or if that is not practicable) a senior officer (a police officer of at least the rank of inspector or an HMRC officer of equivalent seniority).

Following the search the officer of HMRC or constable may seize the cash (PoCA 2002, s.294) and whilst there are still reasonable grounds for suspicion that the cash is recoverable property or is intended by any person for use in unlawful conduct, may detain the cash for a period of 48 hours (PoCA 2002, s.295). This period may be extended by order made by a magistrates' court, initially for a period of three months and on a second application for extension for a further period of two years. The magistrates must be satisfied that the continued detention of the cash is justified while its derivation is being investigated or consideration is given to bringing proceedings against a person for an offence with which the cash is related or where proceedings have started but have not yet been concluded (PoCA 2002, s.295).

Thereafter, on the application of HMRC or a constable, a magistrates' court may make an order for forfeiture of cash or any part of it if it is satisfied that the cash or part is recoverable property or is intended by any person for use in unlawful conduct (PoCA 2002, s.298).

These provisions are subject to a condition that the cash is not less than the minimum amount. This amount is determined by order of the Secretary of State (PoCA 2002, s.303). The current minimum amount is £5,000 (Proceeds of Crime Act 2002 (Recovery of Cash in Summary Proceedings: Minimum Amount) Order 2004, SI 2004/420).

8.4 PRODUCTION ORDERS (POCA 2002, PART 8)

In order to carry out a confiscation, civil recovery or money laundering investigation the authorities may seek a production order requiring the production of material to an appropriate officer or requiring that the appropriate officer be given access to the material. Solicitors' clients might be the subject of an application for such an order and/or solicitors might find themselves the subject of an application.

Confiscation investigations, civil recovery investigations and money laundering investigations are defined in PoCA 2002, s.341. Confiscation investigations are investigations into whether a person has benefited from his criminal conduct, or investigations into the extent or whereabouts of his benefit from his criminal conduct. Civil recovery investigations are investigations into whether property is recoverable property or associated property; who holds the property; or its extent or whereabouts. A money laundering investigation is an investigation into whether a person has committed a money laundering offence.

An appropriate person must make the application. An appropriate person is defined as a constable or an officer of HMRC, if the warrant is sought for the purposes of a confiscation investigation or a money laundering investigation or a named member of SOCA, if the warrant is sought for the purposes of a civil recovery investigation. The application is made to a judge entitled to exercise the jurisdiction of the Crown Court (where it is a confiscation or money laundering officer) or a judge of the High Court (if it is a civil recovery investigation).

The production order, if made, will specify the period within which the order must be complied with and this period will be a period of seven days from the date of the order unless the judge is satisfied that a shorter or longer period is appropriate.

Section 346 of PoCA 2002 sets out the requirements for making a production order. The judge must be satisfied:

- That there are reasonable grounds for suspecting a person has benefited from criminal conduct (confiscation investigation) or property is recoverable or associated property (civil recovery investigation) or that a money laundering offence has been committed (money laundering investigation).
- That there are reasonable grounds for believing that the person specified is in possession or control of the specified material.
- That there are reasonable grounds for believing that the specified material is likely to be of substantial value to the investigation.
- That there are reasonable grounds for believing that it is in the public interest for the material to be produced or for access to the material to be granted.

If an order is made requiring an appropriate officer to be given access to material on any premises, an order can also be made granting entry in relation to the premises (PoCA 2002, s.347).

One important restriction on the granting of a production order and of particular relevance to solicitors and their clients is contained in s.348(1). This states: 'A production order does not require a person to produce, or give access, to privileged material.'

Subsection (2) defines privileged material as 'any material which the person would be entitled to refuse to produce on the grounds of legal professional privilege in proceedings in the High Court'.

However, solicitors must bear in mind the decision of the House of Lords in *R* v. *Central Criminal Court ex p. Francis and Francis* [1989] 1 AC 346. Items are not to be considered as privileged where they are held with the intention of furthering a criminal purpose. The House of Lords held that the intention did not have to be the solicitor's intention. Provided someone had the intention to further a criminal purpose, items held would not be privileged.

CHAPTER 9

Money Laundering Regulations 2007

9.1 INTRODUCTION

The Money Laundering Regulations 2007, SI 2007/2157 came into force on 15 December 2007 and implement the Third European Money Laundering Directive. The full text of the Regulations can be found in **Appendix A3**. The Regulations replace the 2003 Money Laundering Regulations.

The 2007 Regulations impose a requirement that solicitors establish procedures relating to:

(a)   customer due diligence;
(b)   record-keeping, procedures and training.

The Regulations are part of the criminal law. Failure to comply is a criminal offence.

Whilst the Proceeds of Crime Act 2002 (PoCA 2002) and the Terrorism Act 2000 apply to most firms of solicitors (there are few firms, if any, which escape the risk of involvement in money laundering), the Money Laundering Regulations 2007 only apply to relevant persons acting in the course of business carried on by them in the United Kingdom. In theory, parts of a solicitor's practice may well fall outside the requirements of the Regulations. However, most firms take a cautious view and apply the requirements of the Regulations across the whole scope of their activities in order to protect against committing an offence under the statutory criminal law.

Firms of solicitors which are authorised to conduct mainstream regulated activities by the Financial Services Authority (FSA) are subject to the FSA Handbook. Only a small minority of firms are so authorised and this book does not cover details of the FSA Handbook. Guidance for the UK financial sector has been issued by the Joint Money Laundering Steering Group (November 2007).

9.2 RELEVANT PERSONS

The Money Laundering Regulations 2007 only apply to that part of a solicitor's practice which falls within the terms of reg.3 which provides:

> Subject to regulation 4, these Regulations apply to the following persons acting in the course of business carried on by them in the United Kingdom ('relevant persons') –
>
> (a) credit institutions;
> (b) financial institutions;
> (c) auditors, insolvency practitioners, external accountants and tax advisers;
> (d) independent legal professionals;
> (e) trust or company service providers;
> (f) estate agents;
> (g) high value dealers;
> (h) casinos.

The obvious activities affecting solicitors will be where they are providing tax advice (c) or acting as independent legal professionals (d) (although see below for the list of activities caught by the Regulations when acting as an independent legal adviser). However, solicitors will also be caught by the Regulations if they act as insolvency practitioners, trust or company services providers, estate agents, or undertake activities falling within the definition of financial institution.

The wording of reg.3 is nearly identical to the amended wording in PoCA 2002, Sched.9 (the definition of the regulated sector) and solicitors should accept that if they are acting within the regulated sector, they will be subject to the Money Laundering Regulations 2007.

The definition of the regulated sector is covered in **Chapter 5.** Set out below are the activities undertaken within a solicitor's practice which will potentially fall within the definition of the course of business carried on by relevant persons.

9.2.1 Financial institutions

Regulation 3(3)(a) defines 'financial institution' as an undertaking carrying out one or more of the activities listed in points 2 to 12 and 14 of Annex 1 to the Banking Consolidation Directive.

These activities are listed in the Money Laundering Regulations 2007, Sched.1 (see **Appendix A3**). Of possible relevance to solicitors are:

- money transmission services;
- advice to undertakings on capital structure, industrial strategy and related questions; and advice as well as services relating to mergers and the purchase of undertakings;
- safe custody services.

Further, the definition extends (reg.3(3)(c)) to a person whose regular occupation or business is the provision to other persons of an investment service or the performance of an investment activity on a professional basis (other than a person falling within Art.2 of the Markets in Financial Instruments Directive).

Whilst many solicitors do carry out investment activities, the vast majority of firms are not authorised by the FSA under the provisions of the Financial Services and Markets Act 2000 because they are able to rely upon providing investment services as 'exempt regulated activities', satisfying the requirement that such activities are incidental to their professional business. Article 2 of the Markets in Financial Instruments Directive exempts from that Directive (and therefore the definition of an investment service under reg.3(3)(c) above) 'persons providing an investment service where that service is provided in an incidental manner in the course of a professional activity and that activity is regulated by legal or regulatory provisions or a code of ethics governing the profession which do not exclude the provision of that service'. Consequently, this heading is only likely to apply to solicitors who are authorised by the FSA.

However, note that some activities which are 'exempt regulated activities' will be caught by the Regulations as a result of other heads of the definition.

Regulation 3(3)(e) extends the definition of a financial institution to the activities of an insurance intermediary as defined in Art.2(5) of the Insurance Mediation Directive, with the exception of a tied insurance intermediary as mentioned in Art.2(7) of that Directive, when it acts in respect of contracts of long-term insurance within the meaning given by art.3(1) of, and Part II of Sched.1 to, the Financial Services and Markets Act 2000 (Regulated Activities) Order 2001, SI 2001/544.

Solicitors may advise upon and make arrangements for clients to obtain certain insurance policies (e.g. in a conveyancing transaction, property insurance or defective title insurance; in a private client matter, missing beneficiary insurance; or in litigation ATE insurance). These policies are not 'long-term' and, consequently, such advice or arrangements will not be within the scope of the Regulations under this head. However, under the exempt regulated activities regime, solicitors may undertake insurance mediation relating to long-term insurance in a limited manner (e.g. they may comment on and endorse the advice of an authorised person given in relation to an endowment policy). This would bring solicitors within the scope of the Money Laundering Regulations 2007, as would mainstream insurance mediation activities relating to long-term insurance policies undertaken by FSA authorised firms.

9.2.2 Insolvency practitioners

Regulation 3(6) defines an insolvency practitioner as a person appointed to act as an insolvency practitioner within the meaning of s.388 of the Insolvency Act 1986.

Solicitors who are appointed as insolvency practitioners will be within the regulated sector and subject to the Regulations. Solicitors who act for external insolvency practitioners or who act in insolvency matters without being appointed an insolvency practitioner will not be caught under this head. However, depending upon the type of work, they may be caught under **paragraph 9.2.4**.

9.2.3 Tax advisers

Tax advisers will be relevant persons and thus subject to the Money Laundering Regulations 2007. Regulation 3(8) defines a tax adviser as a firm or sole practitioner who by way of business provides advice about the tax affairs of other persons.

Solicitors giving tax advice will be within the scope of the Regulations, and it appears that any tax advice is capable of triggering the Regulations. For example, whilst activities relating to will drafting would not be within the scope of the Regulations, if such activities were combined with inheritance tax planning advice this would be considered subject to the Regulations.

9.2.4 Independent legal advisers

This heading will be of most relevance to solicitors when considering whether the Money Laundering Regulations 2007 apply. Regulation 3(9) defines an 'independent legal professional' as:

> a firm or sole practitioner who by way of business provides legal or notarial services to other persons, when participating in financial or real property transactions concerning:
>
> (a) the buying and selling of real property or business entities;
> (b) the managing of client money, securities or other assets;
> (c) the opening or management of bank, savings or securities accounts;
> (d) the organisation of contributions necessary for the creation, operation or management of companies; or
> (e) the creation, operation or management of trusts, companies or similar structures.

The regulation provides that 'participation in a transaction' means assisting in the planning or execution of the transaction or otherwise acting for or on behalf of a client in a transaction.

As a result of this definition, the Regulations will only apply to solicitors working in a firm or as a sole practitioner – the Regulations therefore do not apply to in-house practice, or to solicitors employed in, e.g. local government or the courts service.

However, reg.3(9) is clearly aimed at extending the scope of the Regulations to many activities undertaken by solicitors. The reference to financial or real property transactions concerning the buying and selling of real property or business entities has the effect of bringing all conveyancing transactions and business acquisitions or disposals within the scope of the regulated sector.

The Law Society's Anti-money Laundering Practice Note (see **Appendix B1**) provides further guidance on the effect of this regulation. It states that managing client money is narrower than simply handling client money. Simply operating a client account is not intended to be caught within the scope of the regulations but holding money or receiving money on behalf of clients as part of a transaction, or holding or receiving money as attorney or trustee will be caught. Similarly, opening or managing a bank account is wider than opening a solicitor's client account. This head is likely to cover opening or managing bank accounts when acting as trustees, attorneys or receivers.

The Treasury has also confirmed that the following (by themselves) would not generally be viewed as participation in financial transactions:

- Preparing a home information pack (HIP) or any document or information for inclusion in a HIP. This is specifically excluded in reg.4(f) and is therefore outside the scope of the Regulations. Any subsequent conveyancing transaction undertaken by the solicitor would, of course, be within the scope of the Regulations.
- A payment on account of costs to a solicitor or payment of a solicitor's bill (because the solicitor is not participating in a financial transaction on behalf of the client).
- Legal advice (assuming such advice does not fall within one or more of the other categories defined as within reg.3).
- Participation in litigation or a form of ADR (on the basis that litigation is not a transaction).
- Will writing (unless linked with, e.g. tax advice).
- Publicly funded work.

9.2.5 Trust or company service providers

These are defined (reg.6(10)) as firms or sole practitioners who, by way of business, provide any of the following services to others:

- forming companies;

- acting, or arranging for another person to act as a director or secretary of a company or as a partner of a partnership;
- providing a registered office, business address, correspondence or administrative address or other related services for a company or partnership or any other legal person or arrangement;
- acting, or arranging for another person to act, as a trustee or as a nominee shareholder for a person (other than a company whose securities are listed on a regulated market).

Solicitors will be undertaking many of these activities under reg.3(9) (independent legal professional participating in transactions concerning the creation, operation or management of trusts, companies or similar structures). However, for the avoidance of doubt, solicitors who are appointed (by way of business) as company officers or partners in client businesses, or trustees will be subject to the Regulations. The Law Society's Practice Note however, confirms that being nominated as a trustee under a will does not amount to being a trust and company service provider, because the trust is not formed until the testator's death.

9.2.6 Estate agency

Estate agency is defined in reg.6(11) as meaning a firm or sole practitioner who, or whose employees, carry out estate agency work (within the meaning given by s.1 of the Estate Agents Act 1979).

Solicitors who provide estate agency services will, in respect of those services, fall within the scope of the Regulations.

9.3 CUSTOMER DUE DILIGENCE

Part 2 of the Money Laundering Regulations 2007 deals with the requirements relating to 'customer due diligence' (CDD) and replaces the identification procedures required by the 2003 Regulations. Significant changes have been made to a solicitor's obligations and changes to internal systems will be required as a result of these obligations.

Regulation 5 states that:

'Customer due diligence measures' means –

(a) identifying the customer and verifying the customer's identity on the basis of documents, data or information obtained from a reliable and independent source;

(b) identifying, where there is a beneficial owner who is not the customer, the beneficial owner and taking adequate measures, on a risk-sensitive basis, to verify his identity so that the relevant person is satisfied that he knows who the beneficial owner is, including, in the case of a legal person, trust or similar legal arrangement, measures to understand the ownership and control structure of the person, trust or arrangement; and

(c) obtaining information on the purpose and intended nature of the business relationship.

This is probably the most onerous of the obligations applicable to solicitors who are subject to the Regulations. It requires firms to have in place procedures which ensure that satisfactory evidence of clients' and beneficial owners' identification is obtained.

9.3.1 Identifying the client

Regulation 5(a) requires a solicitor to identify the customer and verify the customer's identity on the basis of documents, data or information obtained from a reliable and independent source.

The 'customer' for these purposes will obviously be the solicitor's client. 'Identifying' the client is being told or coming to know a client's identification details (i.e. name, address and, where appropriate, date of birth). 'Verifying' is obtaining evidence which supports the identification details.

Verification must be undertaken using documents, data or information obtained from a reliable and independent source. Typically, most firms of solicitors will have been undertaking client identification under the 2003 Regulations using reliable and independent sources. Consequently, the 2007 Regulations should not impose huge changes to procedures relating to client identification.

Risk-based assessment

However, there is one important provision in the Money Laundering Regulations 2007 which did not appear expressly in the 2003 Regulations. Regulation 7(3) states:

A relevant person must –

(a) determine the extent of customer due diligence measures on a risk-sensitive basis depending on the type of customer, business relationship, product or transaction; and

(b) be able to demonstrate to his supervisory authority that the extent of the measures is appropriate in view of the risks of money laundering and terrorist financing.

Consequently, a solicitor's procedures should include a requirement that those undertaking due diligence on a client should adapt their approach by reference to risk factors (i.e. the risk of involvement in money laundering). Firms are encouraged to create identification forms for use by fee earners when undertaking due diligence (for a suggested precedent, see **Appendix C1**).

Such forms should include a risk assessment question to be completed by the fee earner which will demonstrate that risks of possible money laundering have been considered at the outset. This, in turn, will assist firms in satisfying the requirements of reg.7(3)(b) (demonstrating to the Solicitors Regulation Authority (SRA) that the extent of the measures is appropriate in view of the risk).

Chapter 2 of the Law Society's Anti-money Laundering Practice Note (see **Appendix B1**) suggests that a risk assessment can be made by taking into account a number of factors including:

- the firm's risk profile; and
- the client's individual risk profile.

Many firms are able to look at their general risk profile (taking into account such matters as high turnover of clients or a stable existing client base; practice locations; overseas clients; the areas of law practised) and perhaps decide that the majority of their clients (in some firms, well over 90%) fall into a single risk category. Depending upon the firm, this may be low risk, medium risk or high risk. The firm's CDD can then be determined by reference to this risk assessment, with the majority of clients being verified using the firm's standard procedure.

Enhanced CDD

A small number of clients might not fall into the firm's standard risk category. Whilst it would not be a problem to undertake CDD using the firm's standard procedures if a client falls within a lower risk assessment than normal, if a client falls into a higher risk assessment than normal, additional CCD procedures must be applied.

In assessing individual client risk profiles factors to be taken into account might include the ease of satisfying CDD requirements or the type of retainer (i.e. the retainer might suggest a higher risk of money laundering). However, reg.14 specifically identifies a requirement for enhanced CDD in the following situations:

- where the client has not been physically present for identification purposes (i.e. clients are not 'face-to-face');
- where the client is a 'politically exposed person' (PEP); and
- any other circumstances which can present a higher risk of money laundering or terrorist financing.

NON FACE-TO-FACE CLIENTS

Where solicitors act for clients and there is no face-to-face contact with the client, reg.14(2) states that specific and adequate measures must be taken to compensate for the higher risk by applying, for example, one or more of the following:

(a) ensuring that the client's identity is established by additional documents, data or information;

(b) supplementary measures to verify or certify the documents supplied, or requiring confirmatory certification by a credit or financial institution which is subject to the Money Laundering Directive;

(c) ensuring that the first payment is carried out through an account opened in the client's name with a credit institution.

This list is not exhaustive, and alternative forms of enhanced verification could be undertaken by electronic verification (see below) or certification of a client's documentation by a professional person who can be independently contacted to confirm their certification. The Law Society's Practice Note suggests bank managers, accountants, local GPs and the Post Office Identity Checking Service might be appropriate persons.

Regulation 14(2)(c) refers to the first payment being carried out through an account with a credit institution. The Law Society's Practice Note points out that since 1 January 2007, credit institutions in all EU member states must provide the payer's name, address and account number with all electronic fund transfers (see EU Regulation 1781/2006). This can be used as additional verification of a person's identity.

POLITICALLY EXPOSED PERSONS (PEPS)

Regulation 14 also requires enhanced CDD where the client is a PEP. A PEP is defined in reg.14(5) as an individual who is or who has been during the preceding year, entrusted with a prominent public function in a state other than the UK, a community institution or an international body. The definition also covers such an individual's immediate family and known close associates. Schedule 2 to the Regulations gives more detail and lists the following as falling within the definition:

(i) heads of state, heads of government, ministers and deputy or assistant ministers;

(ii) members of parliaments;

(iii) members of supreme courts, of constitutional courts or of other high-level judicial bodies whose decisions are not generally subject to further appeal, other than in exceptional circumstances;

(iv) members of courts of auditors or of the boards of central banks;

(v) ambassadors, chargés d'affaires and high-ranking officers in the armed forces; and

(vi) members of the administrative, management or supervisory bodies of state-owned enterprises.

Before accepting a retainer with a PEP which will be subject to the Money Laundering Regulations 2007, the approval of senior management must be obtained (reg.14(4)(a)). The Law Society's Practice Note suggests that senior management for these purposes might include:

- the head of a practice group;
- another partner who is not involved with the particular matter;
- the partner supervising the file;
- the firm's nominated officer (MLRO); or
- the managing partner.

It obviously makes sense for this approval to be recorded in writing.

In addition to this approval, reg.14(4)(b) requires firms to take adequate measures to establish the source of wealth and source of funds which are involved in the proposed retainer. This can be satisfied by asking the client about their source of funds and wealth. It does not necessarily require the information to be obtained from an independent source, although a higher than normal risk assessment of the PEP might suggest that this would be appropriate.

Finally, reg.14(4)(c) requires enhanced ongoing monitoring where the client is a PEP. The topic of ongoing monitoring is dealt with below. For further details of how to recognise a PEP, see the Law Society's Anti-money Laundering Practice Note (see **Appendix B1**).

OTHER CIRCUMSTANCES WHERE THERE IS A HIGHER RISK

Enhanced CDD is not specifically defined by the Money Laundering Regulations 2007 for this category of higher risk client. However, it might include obtaining additional documents or taking additional measures for the purpose of verifying the client's (and/or beneficial owner's) identity; seeking further information on the purpose of the retainer; or conducting enhanced ongoing monitoring.

Simplified CDD

Most firms will find it easier to work with a choice of two risk factors when assessing risk at the outset of a client retainer: normal risk (i.e. what is normal for the bulk of the firm's clientele) and higher risk. Although there may be clients who pose a lower than normal risk of money laundering or terrorist funding, it is simpler, in most cases, to apply normal CDD to those clients. However, the Regulations specify circumstances where 'simplified CDD' can apply. Regulation 13 states that CDD measures are not required (unless there is a suspicion of money laundering or terrorist financing) if the client, transaction or product falls within those listed in reg.13. The relevant clients, etc. are as follows:

EXCLUDED CLIENTS

- A credit or financial institution which is subject to the requirements of the money laundering directive (i.e. the Third European Money Laundering Directive). This will cover most EEA-based banks, building societies and other financial institutions (e.g. insurance companies and insurance intermediaries). For the full definition of credit or financial institutions, see reg.3(2) and (3).
- A credit or financial institution situated in a non-EEA state which imposes equivalent requirements to those contained in the money laundering directive and is subject to supervision for compliance with those equivalent requirements.
- A company whose securities are listed on a regulated market subject to specified disclosure requirements (i.e. a company listed on an EEA state market or a non-EEA state market with equivalent disclosure requirements).
- UK public authorities and certain EU public authorities.

EXCLUDED PRODUCTS

- Life insurance contracts where the annual premium is no more than 1000 euro or a single premium is no more than 2500 euro.
- An insurance contract for the purpose of a pension scheme where the contract has no surrender clause and cannot be used as collateral.
- Certain pension or superannuation schemes providing retirement benefits to employees.
- Child trust funds.
- Other products with a written contractual base and which fulfil the requirements of para.3 of Sched.2 to the Regulations.

Where simplified CDD applies, it will be necessary to obtain evidence that the client or products provided are eligible for simplified CDD. Such evidence should be recorded in accordance with the requirements of the Regulations (see below). However, although there will not be the need for verification of the client's identity, ongoing monitoring of the client will still be necessary. It will also be necessary to carry out full CDD on such clients where there is a suspicion of money laundering.

Normal CDD

Verification of most clients' identities should follow the basic requirements in reg.5 and thus it should be undertaken on the basis of documents, data or information obtained from a reliable independent source. (Where enhanced CDD is required, it will still be necessary for the firm's normal procedures to be followed in addition to the enhanced procedures. Where simplified CDD is available, the firm's normal procedures verifying the client's identity will only be necessary if money laundering is suspected.)

Detailed guidance on what amounts to satisfactory evidence of identity should appear in the firm's internal procedures. Partners and principals should not leave it to individual fee earners to decide what is and what is not satisfactory. A firm-wide policy should be adopted and the firm's nominated officer should be consulted where, in an individual case, a client is unable to satisfy the requirements of the policy.

The Law Society has provided detailed and comprehensive guidance in its Practice Note on what might amount to satisfactory evidence. This guidance helpfully distinguishes between different categories of clients as set out below.

1. **Natural persons:**

   - UK residents;
   - persons not resident in the UK;
   - individuals: no face-to-face meeting;
   - clients unable to produce standard documentation;
   - professionals.

2. **Partnerships, Limited Partnerships and UK LLPs.**

3. **Companies**:

   - public companies listed in the UK;
   - private and unlisted companies in the UK;
   - public overseas companies;
   - private and unlisted overseas companies.

4. **Other arrangements or bodies:**

   - trusts;
   - foundations;
   - charities;
   - churches and places of worship;
   - schools and colleges;
   - clubs and associations;
   - pension funds.

5. **Government agencies and councils**

The full Law Society guidance on evidence of identity appears in **Appendix B1**.

Firms should tailor this guidance to their own requirements, identifying the common categories of clients relevant to the firm's practice and setting out in the firm's money laundering manual details of the firm's policy regarding identification. Most firms will want to adopt a standard form for use by fee earners in the identification process. Examples of a simple money laundering manual and identification forms can be found in **Appendices C1 and C2**.

Documentary evidence of identity is recommended for most situations, although in some circumstances firms may be prepared to accept evidence from third parties (e.g. credit reference agencies) or to make electronic searches of appropriate databases (e.g. the electoral roll). In each case it will be necessary for the firm to retain a record of the evidence of identity obtained (see below for details of this record). Consequently, the firm's system must ensure that original documentation is photocopied, third party evidence is retained and prints are taken of any electronic evidence relied upon.

Electronic verification and outsourcing

Increasingly, firms are being approached by third party businesses offering to provide money laundering verification services for new clients through electronic means. Commercial agencies have access to a wide range of data sources and such information may satisfy the verification requirements. However, solicitors must still satisfy themselves that the identity given by the client (i.e. name and address) does match the client – any name and address could be provided by a client and an electronic verification, using external databases, will only confirm that the named person lives at the stated address, holds a passport, driving licence, credit cards and has accounts with utility companies, etc. It will not confirm that the person giving the details is the same person whose identity was confirmed by the electronic verification.

The Law Society's Practice Note includes advice on the factors to be taken into account when choosing an electronic verification service provider. It states that solicitors should look for a provider which:

- has proof of registration with the Information Commissioner's Office to store personal data;
- can link an applicant to both current and previous circumstances using a range of positive information sources;
- accesses negative information sources, such as databases on identity fraud and deceased persons;
- accesses a wide range of 'alert' data sources;
- has transparent processes enabling you to know what checks are carried out, the results of the checks, and how much certainty they give on the identity of the subject;
- allows the solicitor to capture and store the information used to verify an identity.

The use of an electronic verification service is an example of 'outsourcing'. Regulation 17(4) states that 'nothing . . . prevents a relevant person applying customer due diligence measures by means of an outsourcing service provider or agent provided that the relevant person remains liable for any failure to apply such measures'. Consequently, regardless of any failure on the part of the outside provider, solicitors will remain responsible for fulfilling their obligations to undertake CDD.

Reliance

Reliance upon another person to undertake CDD must be distinguished from outsourcing. Reliance is a formal procedure under reg.17 which allows a relevant person to rely on another person to apply any necessary CDD. Two conditions must be satisfied before reg.14 applies:

First, the person relied upon must be listed in reg.17(2). This lists:

- credit or financial institutions which are authorised persons (i.e. authorised by the FSA under the Financial Services and Markets Act 2000);
- a relevant person who is an auditor, insolvency practitioner, external accountant, tax adviser or independent legal professional provided that the person is supervised by a professional body.

There are also provisions in reg.17(2) listing equivalent institutions and professional persons who carry on business in another EEA state or non-EEA state provided they are subject to mandatory professional registration required by law, are subject to the money laundering directive or requirements equivalent to the directive and are supervised for compliance purposes.

The second condition is that the person must consent to being relied upon. Whilst the Regulations do not specify that the consent must be in writing, it is clearly sensible to have written confirmation.

One final and important point should be made regarding reliance. Under reg.17(1)(b), notwithstanding the solicitor's reliance upon another person, the solicitor will remain liable for any failure of the other person to apply appropriate CDD measures. Reliance under reg.17 does not relieve the solicitor of responsibility for CDD.

For this reason, it is unlikely that many firms of solicitors will rely upon reg.17. Firms with overseas offices who are introduced to clients by an overseas office may rely upon reg.17 provided the overseas office satisfies the requirements of reg.17(2) – alternatively, such firms may wish to receive information on the client from the overseas office without formally relying upon this information. In this situation the receipt of such information will amount to outsourcing. For further details of 'passporting clients between jurisdictions', see the Law Society's Anti-money Laundering Practice Note, para.4.3.4 (**Appendix B1**).

However, solicitors themselves are capable of being relied upon by another person (since they are independent legal professionals supervised for the purpose of the Regulations by the Law Society (effectively the Solicitors Regulation Authority)). Firms should therefore adopt a policy regarding third party reliance. Fee-earners should be warned not to accept responsibility for a third party's CDD obligations except in accordance with the firm's policy.

9.3.2 Identifying a beneficial owner

Regulation 5(b) requires a solicitor to identify, where there is a beneficial owner who is not the customer, the beneficial owner and take adequate measures, on a risk-sensitive basis, to verify his identity so that the solicitor is satisfied that he knows who the beneficial owner is, including, in the case of a legal person, trust or similar legal arrangement, measures to understand the ownership and control structure of the person, trust or arrangement.

The Law Society's Anti-money Laundering Practice Note suggests that identification of a beneficial owner requires details of the beneficial owner's name and any other identification details which are available (address, registered number, etc.). Unlike the requirements relating to the verification of a client's identity (i.e. document, data or information obtained from a reliable and independent source) the verification of a beneficial owner need only be undertaken by taking 'adequate measures on a risk sensitive basis'. This means that, in many cases, verification of a beneficial owner's identity can be satisfied by checking easily accessible public data or by information provided by the client confirmed by documentary evidence.

However, in high risk situations, the Regulations would require access to a reliable and independent source. The Law Society's Practice Note gives examples of what might be taken into account in considering whether there is a higher risk assessment:

- why your client is acting on behalf of someone else
- how well you know your client
- whether your client is a regulated person
- the type of business structure involved in the transaction
- where the business structure is based
- the AML/CTF (anti-money laundering/counter-terrorist financing) requirements in the jurisdiction where it is based
- why this business structure is being used in this transaction
- how soon property or funds will be provided to the beneficial owner

Where a beneficial owner arises when acting for a corporation, trust or other similar legal arrangement, it is necessary to take measures to understand the ownership and control structure of the client. In most cases, this will be done by identifying the beneficial owner(s) and reviewing the trust deed or partnership document or, in the case of a company, reviewing the company structure. Unless the risk assessment suggests otherwise, there is no reason why this information should not be produced by the client.

Regulation 6 identifies and defines six different classes of beneficial owner. These are:

- body corporate (including an LLP) – reg.6(1);
- partnership (other than an LLP) – reg.6(2);
- trusts – reg.6(3);
- legal entities or arrangements not falling within reg.6(1)–(3) – reg.6(6);
- estates of deceased persons – reg.6(8);
- agency – reg.6(9).

Each of these will be dealt with in turn.

Body corporate (including an LLP)

When acting for a company, solicitors must identify any beneficial owner by reference to two categories.

Regulation 6(1)(a) provides that, except in the case of a company whose securities are listed on a regulated market, a beneficial owner will be any individual who ultimately owns or controls more than 25 per cent of the shares or voting rights in the body. Note that the requirement is a 25 per cent interest plus one share – someone with a simple 25 per cent interest will not be a beneficial owner for these purposes.

Consequently, acting for a company with four or more equal shareholders will not give rise to beneficial owner CDD under this first category; acting for a company with three or fewer equal shareholders will.

The ownership or control giving rise to a beneficial owner may be direct or indirect and may be through a holding of bearer shares. However, voting rights are only those which are currently exercisable and attributed to the company's issued share capital.

Reasonable and proportionate enquiries must be made when acting for a company to determine the existence of any beneficial owners who are shareholders. When such beneficial owners exist, appropriate, risk-based steps must be taken to verify their identity. The Law Society's Practice Note suggests these steps may include the following:

- getting assurances from the client on the existence and identity of relevant beneficial owners;
- getting assurances from other regulated persons more closely involved with the client, particularly in other jurisdictions, on the existence and identity of relevant beneficial owners;
- conducting searches on the relevant online registry;
- obtaining information from a reputable electronic verification service.

Where the holder of the requisite level of shareholding of a company is another company, the Practice Note suggests applying the risk-based approach when deciding whether further enquiries should be undertaken.

Where the holding is through bearer shares, a higher risk of money laundering exists. Difficulties may arise in identifying the current holders of such shares. Nevertheless, the holders of such shares giving rise to a beneficial interest must be identified and verified and assurances should be sought that the holder will notify the solicitor of any change of ownership in the shares.

The second definition of beneficial owner that might arise in a corporate retainer is contained in reg.6(1)(b). This definition applies to any company (listed or unlisted) and defines a beneficial owner as any individual who, otherwise than by shares or voting rights, exercises control over the management of the body. The requirement is for an individual to exercise control over, rather than to be the management of the body. Consequently, the directors of a company will not be beneficial owners under this head (they may be beneficial owners under the 'shares/voting rights' head). This definition is likely to catch, e.g. 'shadow directors' (defined in s.251 of the Companies Act 2006 as meaning a person in accordance with whose directions or instructions the directors of the company are accustomed to act).

Partnership (excluding an LLP)

When acting for a partnership, solicitors must identify any beneficial owner by reference to two categories set out in reg.6(2)(a) and (b).

Regulation 6(2)(a) provides that a beneficial owner will be an individual who ultimately is entitled to or controls more than a 25 per cent share of the:

- capital;
- profits; or
- voting rights.

Again, as with a company, the entitlement or control can be direct or indirect. Four equal partners (in terms of capital, profits and voting rights) would give rise to no beneficial owners under this head. However, it is not necessary for all three elements to be present at the 25 per cent plus level. In a four-partner business with the following capital/profit split (with voting rights linked to capital contributions), all four partners must be treated as beneficial owners when acting for the partnership:

Partner A:	Capital 30%	Profit 20%
Partner B	Capital 30%	Profit 25%
Partner C	Capital 20%	Profit 28%
Partner D	Capital 20%	Profit 27%

However, since a partnership is not a legal entity, when verifying the identity of the client, solicitors may consider carrying out checks on all partners. In this situation, the question of the identity of beneficial ownership becomes redundant. The Law Society's Practice Note suggests that where partnerships are small, all partners will be the clients and should be identified and verified as individuals. Where there is a larger partnership, the client should be treated as if it were a private company. As such the name and business address should be verified along with the names of at least two partners. In this situation other partners may have to be identified and verified as beneficial owners. Where the partnership is made up of regulated professionals, the partnership can either be identified from a reputable professional directory or from the partnership's professional body, or the partner instructing plus one other partner should be identified and verified as individuals. In either case, the identification of beneficial owners might also be necessary.

The Practice Note also includes some examples of verification of beneficial owners in the context of acting for a partnership. Verification can be undertaken by:

- receiving assurances from the client on the existence and identity of relevant beneficial owners;
- receiving assurance from other regulated persons more closely involved with the client, particularly in other jurisdictions, on the existence and identity of relevant beneficial owners;
- reviewing the documentation setting up the partnership such as the partnership agreement or any other profit-sharing agreements.

The second definition of beneficial owner that might arise in a partnership retainer is contained in reg.6(2)(b). This definition catches as a beneficial owner any individual who, otherwise than through sharing capital or profits or exercising voting rights, exercises control over the management of the partnership.

Trusts

Normally, solicitors will be instructed to act for the trustees of a trust fund. In these circumstances the beneficial owners will be, potentially, the beneficiaries of the trust. However, note reg.6(10) which restricts the definition of beneficial owner in the Regulations to a trust which 'administers and distributes funds'.

There are three categories of beneficial owners listed in reg.6(3). Unlike the situation involving companies and partnerships, whenever a solicitor is acting for trustees of an appropriate trust fund, there will always be a beneficial owner to be identified, albeit in many cases simply by reference to the class of persons benefiting from the trust.

Regulation 6(3)(a) defines a beneficial owner as any individual who is entitled to a specified interest in at least 25 per cent of the capital of the trust property. Note that, unlike a company or partnership (where the percentage requirement for a beneficial owner is 'more than 25% . . .') with trusts, the percentage giving rise to a beneficial owner is 'at least 25%'. Thus a trust with four equal beneficiaries each with a specified interest will have four beneficial owners.

To give rise to a beneficial owner under this head of the definition, the individual must have a specified interest in the capital of the trust property.

'Specified interest' is defined in reg.6(4) as a vested interest which is in possession, in remainder or in reversion and which is defeasible or indefeasible. These terms are defined in the Law Society's Practice Note (see **Appendix B1**). Further, the interest must be in the capital of the trust property. A beneficiary who has a life interest in the income of the trust property will not be a beneficial owner.

Regulation 6(5) states that if a company has a specified interest in the capital of the trust property, then an individual who is a beneficial owner of the company must be regarded as having entitlement to the specified interest in the trust property.

Regulation 6(3)(b) provides that where the trust is not one which is set up for or operates entirely for the benefit of individuals referred to in paragraph (a) (i.e. individuals with a specified interest in at least 25 per cent of the trust property) the definition of beneficial interest includes the class of persons in whose main interest the trust is set up or operates.

Consequently, if a solicitor decides that either there are no beneficial owners under paragraph (a) or that there are some beneficial owners under (a) but some other beneficiaries who do not fall within paragraph (a), the definition in paragraph (b) must be considered.

As noted above, if there are four equal beneficiaries with a specified interest in the trust fund, all four will be beneficial owners under paragraph (a) and their identity must be verified individually. If, however, there are five equal beneficiaries with a specified interest, no individual will have at least a 25 per cent interest but the beneficial interest will have to be identified by reference to the class of persons in whose interest the trust was set up.

In most cases (subject to appropriate risk assessments) the solicitor can rely upon the trustees to provide details of the identity of individual beneficiaries and access to the trust deed will provide verification of the class of persons as a beneficial owner.

The Law Society has provided guidance in its Practice Note as follows:

When considering in whose main interest a trust is set up or operates, and there are several classes of beneficiary, consider which class is most likely to receive most of the trust property. For example:

- Where a trust is for the issue of X, then the class is the issue of X as there is only one class.
- Where a trust is for the children of X, if they all die, for the grandchildren of X and if they all die, for charity Y, then the class is likely to be the children of X as it is unlikely that they will all die before the funds are disbursed.
- Where a discretionary trust allows for payments to the widow, the children, their spouses and civil partners, the grandchildren, and their spouses and civil partners, then all interests are equal and all classes will need to be identified.

Where in doubt about which class has the main interest, you should identify all classes.

Note: Interests in parts of the trust property can change significantly between retainers, particularly with discretionary trusts. So it is good practice to obtain an update on any changes from the trustees with each set of new retainers your firm receives in relation to a discretionary trust.

The Practice Note also provides some comprehensive examples involving trust and probate matters – see Chapter 4 of the Practice Note (see **Appendix B1**).

Regulation 6(3)(c) provides the third definition of a beneficial owner in the context of trusts. This is 'any individual who has control over the trust'. Control for these purposes is defined in reg.6(4) and means:

a power (whether exercisable alone, jointly with another person or with the consent of another person) under the trust instrument or by law to –

(a) dispose of, advance, lend, invest, pay or apply trust property;
(b) vary the trust;
(c) add or remove a person as a beneficiary or to or from a class of beneficiaries;
(d) appoint or remove trustees;
(e) direct, withhold consent to or veto the exercise of a power such as is mentioned in sub-paragraph (a), (b), (c) or (d).

In most cases 'control over the trust' will be exercised by the trustees. Where the solicitor is acting for the trustees, they will, of necessity, be excluded from the definition of beneficial owner for the purpose of CDD. However, if a solicitor acts for a beneficiary of a trust fund, the trustees' identity must be verified as part of CDD. However, the definition of control could mean that beneficiaries, acting collectively where they have the power to take or direct action, would be beneficial owners under reg.6(3)(c).

Regulation 6(5)(b) excludes a number of activities from the meaning of 'control' for these purposes. An individual will not have control solely as a result of:

(i)   his consent being required in accordance with section 32(1)(c) of the Trustee Act 1925 (power of advancement);
(ii)   any discretion delegated to him under section 34 of the Pensions Act 1995 (power of investment and delegation);
(iii) the power to give a direction conferred on him by section 19(2) of the Trusts of Land and Appointment of Trustees Act 1996 (appointment and retirement of trustee at instance of beneficiaries); or
(iv) the power exercisable collectively at common law to vary or extinguish a trust where the beneficiaries under the trust are of full age and capacity and (taken together) absolutely entitled to the property subject to the trust . . .

Where, in a trust situation, a beneficial owner must be identified, the Law Society's Practice Note provides some guidance as to the means whereby the identity can be verified. As always, it will be necessary to consider, on a risk-sensitive basis, what appropriate steps need to be taken to verify identity. A family trust fund might be considered less risky than an offshore trust fund. However, subject to risk analysis, the Society suggests that enquiries and verification may be undertaken by:

- getting assurances from trustees on the existence and identity of beneficial owners;
- getting assurances from other regulated persons more closely involved with the client, particularly in other jurisdictions, on existence and identity of beneficial owners;
- reviewing the trust deed;
- obtaining information from a reputable electronic verification service on details of identified beneficiaries.

Executors

Regulation 6(8) deals with the definition of a beneficial owner in the context of an estate of a deceased person in the course of administration. A beneficial owner is defined as 'the executor, original or by representation, or administrator for the time being of a deceased person'. Since in most estate administration retainers a solicitor will be acting for the executor, the concept of a 'beneficial owner' during the administration of the estate will be irrelevant (the requirement to identify a beneficial owner under reg.5(b) (see above) only applies where there is a beneficial owner 'who is not the customer').

The beneficial owner may be relevant if a solicitor is simply acting for a beneficiary during the administration of the estate. In this situation, the executor would have to be identified and verified.

However, the main issue involving estate practitioners will arise if there is continuing trust administration after the completion of the estate administration. Where this is the case, solicitors must identify and verify the trust's beneficial owners in accordance with reg.6(3) – see above.

Legal entities and arrangements not falling within reg.6(1)–(3)

Where a solicitor acts for a client who is not a person, company, partnership or trust (unincorporated associations and foundations are examples of such entities) it will be necessary to identify and verify the identity of a beneficial owner. Regulation 6(11) makes it clear that 'arrangement' and 'entity' means one which administers and distributes funds. Regulation 6(6) defines a beneficial owner in these circumstances as:

(a) where the individuals who benefit from the entity or arrangement have been determined, any individual who benefits from at least 25% of the property of the entity or arrangement;

(b) where the individuals who benefit from the entity or arrangement have yet to be determined, the class of persons in whose main interest the entity or arrangement is set up or operates;

(c) any individual who exercises control over at least 25% of the property of the entity or arrangement.

Category (a) catches individuals who have been identified and who benefit from at least 25 per cent of the property of the entity. Unlike the definition of beneficial owners in the context of trusts, 'property' in reg.6(6)(a) covers both capital and profits of the entity. Regulation 6(7) states that if a company is the beneficial owner in accordance with reg.6(6), then an individual who is a beneficial owner of the company must be regarded as benefiting from or exercising control over the property of the entity.

Acting for an entity with four individuals who benefit equally from the entity's property would require a solicitor to identify and verify the identity of all four individuals as beneficial owners.

An entity with five individuals who benefit equally from the entity's property would not give rise to a requirement to identify beneficial owners. In this case the individuals who benefit from the entity have been determined (i.e. each has a 20 per cent interest), and consequently reg.6(6)(b) will not apply. Unless one or more of the individuals exercises control in accordance with reg.6(6)(c) there will be no beneficial owner as defined.

Regulation 6(6)(b) only applies where the individuals who benefit have yet to be identified. 'Benefit' in this context means 'currently entitled' to the property. Regulation 6(6)(b) will therefore only apply where an individual has a contingent interest or where no determination as to benefit has been made. Where it does apply, it will be necessary to identify the class of persons in whose main interest the entity has been set up or operates. Only the class by definition needs to be identified and recorded. If there is doubt, solicitors should record the class of persons likely to get most of the property.

Regulation 6(6)(c) applies the definition of a beneficial owner to an individual who exercises control over at least 25 per cent of the property of the entity. Control, for these purposes, means control outside the normal management structure and control mechanisms. Consequently, members of the management board will not, as such, be beneficial owners under this head. However, an individual who can manage at least 25 per cent of the funds other than through the normal management of the entity must be identified and verified as a beneficial owner.

As with the other categories of beneficial owners, the Law Society's Practice Note gives guidance on verification. It suggests that this may be undertaken by:

• asking the client and receiving assurances as to the existence and identity of beneficial owners;

- asking other regulated persons more closely involved with the client (particularly in other jurisdictions) and receiving assurances as to the existence and identity of beneficial owners;
- reviewing the documentation setting up the entity or arrangement such as its constitution or rules.

Estates of deceased persons

Regulation 6(8) deals with the definition of a beneficial owner in the context of an estate of a deceased person in the course of administration. A beneficial owner is defined as 'the executor, original or by representation, or administrator for the time being of a deceased person'. Since in most estate administration retainers a solicitor will be acting for the executor, the concept of a 'beneficial owner' during the administration of the estate will be irrelevant (the requirement to identify a beneficial owner under reg.5(b) (see above) only applies where there is a beneficial owner 'who is not the customer').

The beneficial owner may be relevant if a solicitor is simply acting for a beneficiary during the administration of the estate. In this situation, the executor would have to be identified and verified.

However, the main issue for estate practitioners will arise if there is continuing trust administration after the completion of the estate administration. Where this is the case, solicitors must identify and verify the trust's beneficial owners in accordance with reg.6(3) – see above.

Agency

Regulation 6(9) states that in any other case (i.e. in any other case than the five situations giving rise to beneficial ownership noted above) a beneficial owner means the individual who ultimately owns or controls the customer or on whose behalf a transaction is being conducted.

The requirement to identify and verify a beneficial owner in this category is not dissimilar to the requirement contained in the 2003 Regulations which required that where a client appeared to be acting for another person, measures had to be taken to establish the identity of that other person.

Consequently, this provision should not impose hugely different obligations on firms of solicitors. The Law Society's Practice Note gives some examples of where a client may be acting on behalf of another and gives guidance on how the identity could be verified:

- Exercising a power of attorney: the document granting power of attorney may be sufficient to verify the beneficial owner's identity.
- Acting as the deputy, administrator or insolvency practitioner: appointment documents may be sufficient to verify the beneficial owner's identity.

- An appointed broker or other agent to conduct a transaction: a signed letter of appointment may be sufficient to verify the beneficial owner's identity.

9.3.3   Obtaining information on the purpose

The third element of CDD is the requirement contained in reg.5(c) to obtain information on the purpose and intended nature of the business relationship. Whilst this is as important as the first two elements (identification and verification of the client and beneficial owner) this requirement does not, generally, impose an additional burden on solicitors. As a result of Rule 2.02 of the Solicitors' Code of Conduct 2007 (Client Care) solicitors must:

> identify clearly the client's objectives in relation to the work to be done for the client;

Compliance with the Client Care rule should ensure compliance with the Regulations. However, where a high risk client has been identified additional enquiries may need to be made regarding the underlying purpose of the client's retainer.

9.3.4   Timing of CDD

Regulation 7 requires a relevant person to apply CDD when that person:

(a)   establishes a business relationship;
(b)   carries out an occasional transaction;
(c)   suspects money laundering or terrorist financing; or
(d)   doubts the veracity or adequacy of documents, data or information previously obtained for the purposes of identification or verification.

Each of these will be dealt with in turn.

Business relationships

A 'business relationship' is defined in reg.2(1) as meaning:

> a business, professional or commercial relationship between a relevant person and a customer, which is expected by the relevant person, at the time when contact is established, to have an element of duration

This is different from the definition of the same term contained in the 2003 Regulations. The 2003 Regulations defined the term by reference to arrangements facilitating the carrying out of transactions on a 'frequent, habitual or regular basis'. The 2003 Regulations also required, as part of the definition, that the total to be paid was unknown or not capable of being ascertained.

Thus, single retainers with clients where the amount of money involved was known would not be 'business relationships' under the 2003 Regulations unless the retainer was part of a general retainer the solicitor had with the client.

However, the new definition, which only requires an 'element of duration', would cover most single retainers. There is an advantage in treating retainers as a 'business relationship' when it comes to timing. Regulation 9(2) requires relevant persons to verify the identity of the client and any beneficial owner before the establishment of a business relationship. Under the 2003 Regulations, the obligation to identity the client was to do so as soon as reasonably practicable after first contact was made between the solicitor and client. The 2007 Regulations suggest that solicitors cannot establish a relationship unless the CDD requirements relating to identification have been completed. Indeed, reg.11 states that where a relevant person is unable to carry out CDD measures in accordance with the Regulations, that person:

(a) must not carry out a transaction with or for the customer through a bank account;
(b) must not establish a business relationship or carry out an occasional transaction with the customer;
(c) must terminate any existing business relationship with the customer;
(d) must consider whether he is required to make a disclosure by Part 7 of the Proceeds of Crime Act 2002 or Part 3 of the Terrorism Act 2000.

However, reg.9(3) provides an exception to the obligations to undertake CDD before the establishment of a business relationship. The exception only applies where there is a business relationship (it does not apply where there is an occasional transaction) and permits a solicitor to complete the verification process during the establishment of a business relationship if two conditions are satisfied:

(a) it must be necessary not to interrupt the normal conduct of business; and
(b) there must be little risk of money laundering or terrorist financing occurring,

Where the exception applies, the verification must be completed as soon as practicable after contact is first established.

Providing solicitors are satisfied that they can comply with the two conditions, the timing requirements for verification remain the same as under the 2003 Regulations.

The Regulations do not define what is reasonably practicable. However, the Money Laundering Regulations 1993, SI 1993/1933 contained a similar requirement – requiring evidence of identity to be obtained as soon as is reasonably practicable after contact is first made. Those Regulations provided supplementary provisions relating to this phrase – there is no reason why these supplementary provisions should not be used as guidance in the interpretation of the phrase in the 2007 Regulations. The relevant 1993 regulation provided (reg.11(2)):

> In determining . . . the time span in which satisfactory evidence of a person's identity has to be obtained, in relation to any particular business relationship . . . all the circumstances shall be taken into account including, in particular –
>
> (a)　the nature of the business relationship . . .;
> (b)　the geographical locations of the parties;
> (c)　whether it is practical to obtain the evidence before commitments are entered into between the parties or before money passes . . .

Many firms will link the identification and verification procedures to their new file opening procedures. In some cases firms will adopt policies which will not allow a file to be formally opened (no file number or reference is allocated to the client) until satisfactory identity procedures have been carried out. In all cases, it makes sense to adopt a policy which requires completion of the identification and verification procedures before significant sums are accepted into client account.

One further important matter must be considered at this point. If, for any reason, a solicitor cannot verify a client's or beneficial owner's identity in accordance with the Regulations, this failure might give rise to suspicion that the client or another is involved in money laundering. The requirements of PoCA 2002, ss.327–329 (the money laundering offences), s.330 (failure to disclose), and ss.333A (tipping off) or 342 (prejudicing an investigation) might be relevant.

Occasional transactions

An 'occasional transaction' is defined in reg.2(1) as meaning:

> a transaction (carried out other than as part of a business relationship) amounting to 15,000 euro or more, whether the transaction is carried out in a single operation or several operations which appear to be linked

Consequently, 'business relationships' and 'occasional transactions' are mutually exclusive. Given the new definition of a 'business relationship' which only requires 'an element of duration' solicitors are unlikely to be regularly involved in 'occasional transactions'. As mentioned above, the exceptions to the timing requirements for CDD do not apply to occasional transactions. Consequently, in most cases, it will be to a solicitor's advantage to categorise the retainer as a 'business relationship'.

However, where there is a genuine 'occasional transaction' the Regulations provide for a financial test of 15,000 euro or more – transactions under this value will not be subject to the Regulations. However, the proviso to the definition ensures that single transactions of less than 15,000 euro can be 'linked' in order satisfy the definition.

Suspicion of money laundering and terrorist financing

CDD must be undertaken whenever the Regulations apply and there is a suspicion of money laundering or terrorist financing (even if the transaction is an occasional transaction). This is a requirement new to the 2007 Regulations. The firm's system must ensure that where a report is made to the MLRO by a member of the firm, in addition to complying with the requirements under Part 7 of POCA 2002, consideration is given to the obligation to undertake further CDD checks. This obligation would mean revisiting the verification of the client's identity, and where necessary updating documents used for verification purposes, revisiting the verification of beneficial owners and making further checks on the purpose and intended nature of the business.

Where necessary, these further checks should be carried out using independent and reliable sources. In all cases, a solicitor must avoid the 'tipping off' offences in POCA 2002, s.333A (see **Chapter 7**).

Evidence of these additional checks should be recorded (for details of the record-keeping obligations under the Regulations, see below).

Doubts over the veracity or adequacy of documents, etc.

The fourth occasion where reg.7(1) requires CDD to be carried out is where there is doubt over the veracity or adequacy of documents, data or information previously obtained for the purposes of identification or verification. Fee earners must be alert to information acquired during the course of acting for a client which might suggest that documents, etc. used for CDD purposes are false or inadequate. New fee earners acting on an existing business relationship should familiarise themselves with the documents used for CDD purposes in order to be able to comply with this requirement.

Where the obligation arises under this head, replacement evidence must be obtained (if the doubt relates to the veracity of the original documents) or additional evidence must be obtained (where the original evidence appears to be inadequate). In both cases, the extent of the evidence must be determined on a risk-sensitive basis. If such replacement or additional evidence is not forthcoming, reg.11 would require the existing business relationship to be terminated.

9.3.5 Ongoing monitoring

In addition to the obligation to undertake CDD where there is doubt over the veracity or adequacy of documents, etc. reg.8 imposes additional ongoing monitoring obligations where there is a business relationship. The regulation defines 'ongoing monitoring' for these purposes as:

(a) scrutiny of transactions undertaken throughout the course of the relationship (including, where necessary, the source of funds) to ensure that the transactions are consistent with the relevant person's knowledge of the customer, his business and risk profile; and

(b) keeping the documents, data or information obtained for the purpose of applying customer due diligence measures up-to-date.

Each of these will be dealt with in turn.

Scrutiny of transactions

When CDD is first carried out at the outset of a retainer, a risk profile of the client and the matter should have been undertaken as part of that process. Fee earners working on the file should be aware of that profile and during the course of the transaction must ensure that there is consistency between the original assessment and the ongoing nature of the transaction.

If the nature of the transaction develops in such a way that there is a change in the risk profile of the client or matter, consideration should then be given to further CDD being undertaken as a result of reg.7(1) (see above). If the change in the risk profile means that the documents, data or information previously obtained for CDD purposes are now inadequate, additional evidence will have to be obtained.

Updating documents, etc.

Ongoing monitoring also means keeping documents, etc. obtained for CDD purposes up to date. Where a client returns and the firm wishes to rely upon the CDD undertaken for a previous retainer, a check should be made to ensure that the previously obtained material is still up-to-date. The Law Society's Practice Note states that this should particularly be the case where there has been a gap of over three years between instructions. The Practice Note also states:

You are not required to:
– conduct the whole CDD process again every few years
– conduct random audits of files
– suspend or terminate a business relationship until you have updated data, information or documents, as long as you are still satisfied you know who your client is, and keep under review any request for further verification material or processes to get that material
– use sophisticated computer analysis packages to review each new retainer for anomalies.

Regulation 8(3) requires the ongoing monitoring requirements to be determined using a risk-sensitive basis. Consequently, the nature of the obligations will depend on the circumstances.

9.3.6 Existing clients

There were two transitional provisions contained in the 2003 Regulations. The first allowed firms to avoid the need for identification procedures for clients who formed specified business relationships before 1 April 1994; the second for clients who formed specified business relationships before 1 March 2004. Neither of these provisions survives the 2007 Regulations. The firm must undertake appropriate CDD for all clients where the Regulations apply.

However, this does not mean that all client retainers existing on 15 December 2007 gave rise to a requirement to undertake CDD in accordance with the Regulations. Provided those clients were properly identified under the terms of the previous Regulations (or properly subject to the previous transitional provisions), there is no need to take further steps immediately on the coming into force of the 2007 Regulations. However, all the firm's clients are subject to reg.7 and as such CDD will have to be undertaken for pre-15 December 2007 retainers where money laundering or terrorist financing is suspected or where there are doubts over the veracity or adequacy of documents previously obtained for identification purposes. Where an existing client instructs the firm on a new matter (having previously been identified under the old Regulations) the Law Society's Practice Note (para.4.10) suggests the following may trigger the need for CDD:

- a gap in retainers of three years or more;
- a client instructing on a higher risk matter; or
- an existing high risk client.

Further, all clients (regardless of when the relationship was formed) will be subject to the ongoing monitoring requirements of reg.8.

9.4 RECORD-KEEPING

Regulation 19 requires a relevant person to keep records for a specified period of time. The records which must be kept are:

(a) a copy of, or the references to, the evidence of the client's identity obtained as a result of:

- reg.7 (the requirement to undertake CDD when establishing a business relationship; carrying out an occasional transaction; suspecting money laundering or terrorist financing; or when there are doubts over the veracity or adequacy of documents previously obtained for CDD purposes);

– reg.8 (ongoing monitoring requirements); or
– reg.14 (enhanced CDD and ongoing monitoring), and

(b) the supporting records in respect of a business relationship or occasional transaction which is subject to CDD measures or ongoing monitoring.

In respect of (a) above (evidence of client identity) the records must be kept for a period of five years beginning on the date when the business relationship ends or the occasional transaction is completed. In respect of (b) (supporting records) where the records relate to a particular transaction, the record must be kept for a period of five years beginning with date on which the transaction completes. In other cases the five-year period begins on the date on which the business relationship ends.

Given that the five-year period commences in all cases at the end of the relationship or transaction, firms must recognise that in some cases the period might extend beyond the normal file retention period or accounting record retention. It is important for procedures to be maintained to ensure the money laundering records are not destroyed before the end of the retention period.

Further, given that most firms will use the client files for reg.19 purposes (the supporting records), care must be taken at the end of a transaction not to hand over the client's file to the client or to a client's new solicitors without first creating a separate record of the transaction for reg.19 purposes.

Although the Regulations do not specify where the records must be kept, there are compelling reasons for considering a central record of client identification evidence. If client identification records are kept on a client file, at the end of the transaction the file may be sent to storage (this will still satisfy the retention requirements, provided the firm is able to recover the file from storage). However, if after say, three years, the client returns to the firm, it is useful to have access to a central record of client identities to allow a fee earner to consider what ongoing obligations arise, rather than to have to access a file in storage.

9.4.1 Client's identity

The records relating to the client's identity should be the original or copy documents or data or references to information obtained from a reliable and independent source in accordance with reg.5(a). A digitally scanned copy of an original document should suffice for record-keeping purposes.

To ensure that individual members of staff who are responsible for accepting evidence of identity are made fully aware of their responsibilities regarding CDD and record-keeping, many firms require members of staff personally to sign a statement confirming that they have seen the original of any document relied upon and that they are satisfied from the evidence that it is reasonably capable of establishing that the client is the person he claims to be. In the case of photographic evidence, the member of staff can be asked to certify the copy by way of confirming that the client appears to be the person shown in the photograph.

Where a passport is used for identification purposes, reference should be made to guidance from HMSO (Note 20) dated 5 December 2002 (amended in January 2007). The note confirms that passports are subject to Crown copyright and states:

Page 31 (the 'bio page') of the British Passport contains the personal details of the passport holder. Passport holders' identity and personal information are valuable. Criminals can find out an individual's personal details and use them to open bank accounts and get credit cards, loans, state benefits and documents such as passports and driving licences. If an identity is stolen, the individual may have difficulty getting loans, credit cards or a mortgage until the matter is sorted out. The Identity and Passport Service advises passport holders to only agree to the reproduction of the personal details page in the passport if they are satisfied that the person or organisation they are giving this to will protect it from unauthorised disclosure.

The Identity and Passport Service advises organisations who wish to retain a reproduction of the personal details in the passport that they should obtain the consent of the individual to do so. They also advise organisations to retain a record of the consent and to store the passport details securely.

If evidence is obtained from an electronic database, a printout of the evidence should be made and kept by way of evidence.

Since the Regulations do not specify what can and cannot be used as evidence of identity, firms may agree to accept personal knowledge of an individual partner or established member of staff as sufficient evidence of the identity of clients introduced by them. It would appear to be over zealous to demand a passport or other formal evidence of identity from a partner's long-established friend or family member.

The Law Society's Anti-money Laundering Practice Note states (paragraph 4.6.1) that evidence of identity can include 'assurances from persons within the regulated sector or those in your firm who have dealt with the person for some time'. However, in these circumstances, a record must still be retained in accordance with reg.19 – an appropriate written confirmation of the partner's or other member of staff's knowledge of the client's identity should be retained.

9.4.2 Other supporting records

In addition to records relating to the client's identity, the Money Laundering Regulations 2007 require a firm to keep supporting records in respect of any business relationship or occasional transaction which is subject to CDD measures or on-going monitoring The supporting records will cover the iden-tification and verification of any beneficial owner and the information relating to the purpose and intended nature of the business relationship. In most cases the obligations in respect of these records will be satisfied by maintaining a client file and appropriate accounting records in accordance with the Solicitors Accounts Rules.

In guidance applicable to the previous Money Laundering Regulations (which imposed similar record-keeping requirements) the Law Society recom-mended that firms should keep a record of the origin of funds paid by the client to the firm (and, where appropriate, details of cheques should be noted). Whilst the client file is likely to contain general details of the origin of any funds, specific details such as the bank address and sort code, account name and number from which funds have been drawn may not necessarily have been recorded on the file.

In the case of electronic fund transfers, since 1 January 2007, credit insti-tutions in all EU member states must provide the payer's name, address and account number (see EU Regulation 1781/2006). However, this regulation does not apply where payment is made by cheque. Consideration should be given to photocopying cheques before paying them into client account (if the volume of cheques makes this practicable). Alternatively, adjustments can be made to a firm's internal paying-in slip, used by fee earners to send cheques to the accounts department, requiring the paying bank's sort code and account number to be recorded.

9.5 POLICIES AND PROCEDURES

Regulation 20(1) provides:

> A relevant person must establish and maintain appropriate and risk-sensitive policies and procedures relating to –
> (a) customer due diligence measures and ongoing monitoring;
> (b) reporting;
> (c) record-keeping;
> (d) internal control;
> (e) risk assessment and management;
> (f) the monitoring and management of compliance with, and the internal communication of, such policies and procedures,
> in order to prevent activities related to money laundering and terrorist financing.

Failure to comply with reg.20 is a criminal offence rendering the relevant person, on summary conviction, to a fine not exceeding the statutory maximum or, on conviction on indictment, to imprisonment for a term not exceeding two years, to a fine or to both (reg.45(1)).

9.5.1 CDD and ongoing monitoring

The requirements relating to customer due diligence and ongoing monitoring have been dealt with above. Firms should, however, be able to demonstrate that appropriate systems have been adopted and, when called upon, satisfy the SRA that such systems exist. Regulation 7(3)(a) requires a relevant person to be able to demonstrate to his supervisory body (in the case of solicitors, the SRA) that the extent of the measures undertaken for CDD purposes is appropriate in view of the risks of money laundering and terrorist financing. The Law Society's Anti-money Laundering Practice Note suggests that the procedures for CDD may include:

- when CDD is to be undertaken;
- information to be recorded on client identity;
- information to be obtained to verify identity, either specifically or providing a range of options with a clear statement of who can exercise their discretion on the level of verification to be undertaken in any particular case;
- when simplified due diligence may occur;
- what steps need to be taken for enhanced due diligence;
- what steps need to be taken to ascertain whether the client is a PEP;
- when CDD needs to occur and under what circumstances delayed CDD is permitted;
- how to conduct CDD on existing clients; and
- what ongoing monitoring is required.

9.5.2 Reporting

Regulation 20(2)(d) sets out the reporting requirements under the Money Laundering Regulations 2007.

The first obligation in the regulation requires the firm to appoint someone as a nominated officer – i.e. the MLRO (reg.20(2)(d)(i)). The MLRO's role is to receive disclosures from members of the firm. The nominated officer does not have to be a partner (or, in an incorporated practice, an officer) but should be of sufficient seniority to have access to the firm's clients' files and other internal business records.

A sole practitioner who does not employ staff or acts in association with anyone else is not subject to reg.20(2)(d) and therefore does not have to appoint a nominated officer. Regulation 20(3) provides: 'Paragraph (2)(d) does not apply where the relevant person is an individual who neither employs nor acts in association with any other person.'

Larger firms may wish to appoint deputy nominated officers who may undertake some of the functions of the nominated officer, subject to the nominated officer's overall supervision. All firms, whatever their size, should make arrangements covering the absence of the nominated officer as a result of holidays, sick leave or other reason.

Firms authorised under the Financial Services and Markets Act 2000 will have to seek approval of the FSA to the appointment of the nominated officer.

The second obligation, imposed by reg.20(2)(d)(ii), requires anyone in a firm to whom information comes in the course of business as a result of which they know or suspect (or have reasonable grounds for knowing or suspecting) that another is engaged in money laundering or terrorist financing to comply with the appropriate provisions of PoCA 2002 or the Terrorism Act 2000.

This provision effectively replicates PoCA 2002, s.330 and the Terrorism Act 2000, s.21A (see **Chapter 5**), since the scope of the Money Laundering Regulations 2007 mirrors the definition of the regulated sector. Like PoCA 2002, s.330, and the Terrorism Act 2000, s.21A, reg.20(2)(d)(ii) applies an objective test of knowledge or suspicion. The regulation requires a disclosure to be made to the firm's nominated officer or to SOCA, although most firms will require members to disclose internally.

Regulation 20(2)(d)(iii) requires a nominated officer (where the disclosure is made to such a person) to consider any disclosures made by members of the firm in the light of all relevant information available in the firm – hence the requirement for the nominated officer to be of sufficient seniority to gain access to this information. The Regulations do not specifically require the nominated officer to keep a record of this consideration but it would be good practice to do so. The information recorded can include:

(a)   the name of the member of staff making the disclosure;
(b)   the details of, and reasons for, the disclosure;
(c)   the other relevant information taken into account by the nominated officer in making his determination;
(d)   the decision whether or not to report to SOCA and the reason for that decision.

If the firm requires internal reports to be submitted to the nominated officer on specified forms, retention of these forms would satisfy the record-keeping requirements of (a) and (b) above although additional records would have to be kept to satisfy (c) and (d).

9.5.3   Record-keeping

The requirement to keep records under reg.19 has been dealt with above.

9.5.4 Internal control

The need for policies and procedures relating to 'internal control' is expanded in reg.20(2). This regulation requires firms to include procedures providing for the identification and scrutiny of:

- complex or unusually large transactions;
- unusual patterns of transactions suggesting no apparent economic or lawful purpose;
- other activities likely to be related to money laundering or terrorist financing;
- PEPs;
- transactions which favour anonymity.

The procedures should deal with the steps to be taken when fee earners identify transactions which fall into any of the above categories. The Law Society's Anti-money Laundering Practice Note provides some examples of issues which could be covered by an internal controls system. These include:

- the level of personnel permitted to exercise discretion on the risk-based application of the Regulations, and under what circumstances;
- CDD requirements to be met for simplified, standard and enhanced due diligence;
- when outsourcing of CDD obligations or reliance will be permitted, and on what conditions;
- how to restrict work being conducted on a file where CDD has not been completed;
- the circumstances in which delayed CDD is permitted;
- when cash payments will be accepted;
- when payments will be accepted from or made to third parties; and
- the manner in which disclosures are to be made to the nominated officer.

9.5.5 Risk assessment and management

The Money Laundering Regulations 2007 require risk-sensitive policies and thus risk assessment must be undertaken. Rule 5.01(1)(l) of the Solicitors' Code of Conduct 2007 provides that firms must make arrangements for the effective management of the firm as a whole, and in particular the 'management of risk'. Accordingly, firms should already have in place arrangements for the assessment of risks attaching to the common areas of their practice. The guidance notes to the Code of Conduct suggest that risk management arrangements are unlikely to be adequate unless they include periodic reviews of the firm's risk profile. The firm's procedures must be extended to cover money laundering and terrorist financing. Whilst the exact nature of the procedures required will depend upon the size of the firm and the nature of the firm's business, the Law Society's Practice Note indicates the following issues may be covered in a risk assessment system:

- the firm's current risk profile;
- how AML/CTF risks will be assessed, and processes for re-assessment and updating of the firm's risk profile;
- internal controls to be implemented to mitigate the risks;
- which firm personnel have authority to make risk-based decisions on compliance on individual files;
- how compliance will be monitored and how the effectiveness of internal controls will be reviewed.

9.5.6 Managing, monitoring and communication of policies and procedures

Managing and monitoring of the firm's procedures is vital. This can be undertaken by random file checks and the use of file checklists. Regular reports from the firm's nominated officer should be made to the firm's senior management. These reports should include statistics on the internal reports and queries made by members of staff, the identification of common issues arising and recommendations for any changes necessary to the firm's procedures.

9.6 TRAINING

Regulation 21 states:

> A relevant person must take appropriate measures so that all relevant employees of his are –
>
> (a) made aware of the law relating to money laundering and terrorist financing; and
> (b) regularly given training in how to recognise and deal with transactions and other activities which may be related to money laundering or terrorist financing.

There is no specification of what amounts to training for these purposes. Certainly, it does not require firms to provide face-to-face training with a tutor. The training obligations can be complied with by handouts, manuals, video and computer and web-based training. It is, however, important that firms design their training for all relevant staff and that the training is at an appropriate level for individual members of staff.

Fee earners (particularly those involved in higher risk areas of practice) will require full training on the substantive law, the firm's procedures and on recognition of transactions which may be related to money laundering. This training should be updated at frequent intervals.

Members of the accounts staff should also receive training since they will be handling client and other money. Secretaries and receptionists should receive training if they are likely to be in contact with clients. For example, if a fee earner makes an authorised disclosure to the firm's nominated officer as a result of suspicious circumstances and the firm's nominated officer then discloses to SOCA, the seven-working day period will start to run during which limited work only on the relevant file can be undertaken (for details, see **Chapter 4**). During that seven-day period, it might not be possible to explain to the client why nothing is being done on the file subject to the risk of tipping off unless the legal professional adviser defence applies (see **Chapter 7**). Consequently, a fee earner may need to ask a secretary to field calls from the client or other party – the client might even turn up at reception to ascertain what is going on. In both cases, the secretary and/or receptionist needs to be aware of the risks in communicating with the client or other side.

New members of staff should receive induction training relating to the firm's procedures. Even if new members of staff have received money laundering training at their previous employers, each firm will have its own internal procedures and it is vital for all members of staff to be aware of these procedures.

The obligation to comply with the procedures laid down in the Money Laundering Regulations 2007 is imposed upon the partners, in a partnership or the sole practitioner in a sole practice, or an officer in an incorporated practice. It is, therefore, important that the firm maintains a record of compliance with the training obligations. An attendance sheet should be kept of all face-to-face training. Where other methods of training are used, appropriate records should also be kept.

9.7   PENALTIES

Regulation 45(1) sets out the offences under the Money Laundering Regulations 2007. The following offences are of particular relevance to solicitors.

Failure to comply with any of the requirements in the following regulations will be an offence:

- reg.7 (application of CDD measures);
- reg.8 (ongoing monitoring);
- reg.9(2) (timing of verification);
- reg.11 (requirement to cease transaction);
- reg.14(1) (requirements for enhanced CDD and ongoing monitoring);
- reg.19 (record-keeping);
- reg.20 (policies and procedures);
- reg.21 (training).

In all cases, a person who commits an offence is liable:

(a) on conviction on indictment, to imprisonment for a term not exceeding 2 years, to a fine or to both;

(b) on summary conviction, to a fine not exceeding the statutory maximum.

Regulation 45(2) states:

In deciding whether a person has committed an offence under paragraph (1), the court must consider whether he followed any relevant guidance which was at the time –

(a) issued by a supervisory authority or any other appropriate body;

(b) approved by the Treasury; and

(c) published in a manner approved by the Treasury as suitable in their opinion to bring the guidance to the attention of persons likely to be affected by it.

A supervisory body is defined in reg.23(1) and the term includes the Law Society.

The Law Society initially issued Guidance on PoCA 2002 and related matters to the solicitors' profession ('Money Laundering Guidance: Professional Ethics', Pilot Edition) in January 2004. The Guidance was significantly amended in the light of *Bowman* v. *Fels* by the replacement of the original Annex 3 to the Guidance. On 3 September 2007, the Law Society replaced this Guidance with a Practice Note (the Anti-money Laundering Practice Note), and the latest version of the Practice Note is dated 22 February 2008. The Law Society is seeking Treasury approval of the Practice Note. Extracts from the Practice Note appear throughout the text of this book, and the full text of the Practice Note is available at **Appendix B1** and on the Law Society website (**www.lawsociety.org.uk**).

Further, reg.47 provides that where it is shown that an offence under reg.45 has been committed by a body corporate or partnership with the consent of or the connivance of an officer (in the case of an incorporated practice) or a partner (in the case of a partnership) or to be attributable to any neglect on their part, the officer as well as the body corporate or the partner as well as the partnership is guilty of an offence and liable to be proceeded against and punished accordingly. Partners and principals should note that personal liability can therefore arise where there is a failure to comply with the Regulations.

PART II

Practical Guidance

CHAPTER 10

Reporting suspicions

10.1 INTRODUCTION

The substantive law and the Money Laundering Regulations 2007 require disclosure of knowledge or suspicion of money laundering by way of defence and/or by way of obligation. In both cases, the disclosure can be internal (to the firm's nominated officer) or external. External authorised and protected disclosures need to be made to a constable, or an officer of HMRC. Other external disclosures are made to a person authorised by the Director General of the Serious Organised Crime Agency (SOCA). In practice, this means that all external disclosures are made to SOCA.

10.2 INTERNAL DISCLOSURES

Firms can decide themselves on the manner of internal disclosures. Although the Proceeds of Crime Act 2002 (PoCA 2002), s.339 provides that the form of disclosures (both internal and external) can be prescribed by order of the Secretary of State (see **Chapter 4**), at the time of writing no such order has been made. For internal disclosures, it is recommended that firms use an appropriate written form of disclosure. The consequences of making a disclosure are such that it is vital for firms to be able to recognise when a formal disclosure has been made internally – distinguishing this from an informal discussion with a more senior member of the firm. A precedent (which may be adapted depending upon the size and nature of the firm) can be found in **Appendix C3**.

As noted in **Chapter 9**, it is also recommended that nominated officers keep a record of internal disclosures and the steps taken by them in the light of such disclosures. This is particularly important where the decision is made not to report to SOCA.

If firms use an internal reporting form, it is vital that a copy of this form is not kept on the client's file. At the end of a transaction (or during a transaction, if a client chooses to change solicitors) and on the payment of a solicitor's costs, the client may require the firm to hand over the file (either to himself or to his new solicitors). If details of the internal disclosure remain, inadvertently, on the file, in extreme circumstances this could lead to a conviction for tipping off. (For details of the offence of tipping off, see **Chapter 7**.)

10.3   EXTERNAL DISCLOSURES

External disclosures by members of staff to SOCA should not be encouraged by way of a defence or compliance with an obligation. Members of staff will obtain the necessary defence or fulfil any obligation by making an internal disclosure to the firm's nominated officer. Complex questions of confidentiality and LPP can more easily be dealt with where the disclosure is internal. External reporting should be limited to the firm's nominated officer and will arise where the officer's obligations under PoCA 2002, ss.331 or 332 or reg.20 of the Money Laundering Regulations 2007 apply. (For details of PoCA 2002, ss.331 and 332, see **Chapter 5**; for details of reg.20, see **Chapter 9**.)

Disclosures by a nominated officer can be to SOCA using the form, available for downloading from the SOCA website (**www.soca.gov.uk**). There are two forms available: one for standard disclosures (the standard report form) and one for limited intelligence disclosure reports. Full guidance notes on how to complete the forms are provided on the website. The forms for disclosure are reproduced in **Appendix C4** together with the guidance for their completion. SOCA's preferred method for reporting is for these forms to be submitted electronically, but hard copy versions can be printed using the templates found on the SOCA website. A new web-based reporting mechanism was introduced in April 2006 and can be used by anyone with access to the Internet at the SOCA website by following the links to 'SAR Online System'.

10.3.1   Standard Suspicious Activity Report (SAR) form

The standard report form (SAR) should be used where firms are making protected or authorised disclosures under PoCA 2002, ss.337 and 338. The form can also be used where it is necessary to make a disclosure as a result of the Terrorism Act 2000.

SOCA guidance states that although these forms are not mandatory, they are the preferred format and have been designed to facilitate the efficient and effective handling of disclosures by SOCA. The downloaded version of the report can be completed on the firm's own computer, but SOCA have advised that this version must not be used for handwritten reports. Handwritten reports should only be completed on a special version of the form available by telephoning 020 7238 8282.

Where firms are using a computer-completed form (downloaded from the SOCA website) it will be necessary for the form to be printed and submitted by post or fax. The form cannot be submitted through the Internet. Forms should be faxed to 020 7238 8286 or sent by post to UK FIU, PO Box 8000, London SE11 5EN.

The downloaded version is available in PDF format. Unless firms have the commercial version of the Acrobat Reader, the completed form cannot be saved to firms' computer files as a PDF document. It can, however, be printed and a hard copy retained. If firms wish to retain an electronic version, the completed PDF format document can be copied into a Word document and saved.

The standard form consists of six sheets and these can be submitted in different combinations depending upon the information disclosed. Since the form has been designed to be read by Image Character Recognition technology, amendments or additions outside the structure of the form will hamper the capability of SOCA to process the form efficiently. The six sheets consist of:

- **Sheet 1: Report details**. SOCA state that it is necessary for this sheet to be clearly completed enabling SOCA to check that it has received the correct number of sheets.
- **Sheet 2: Subject details**. This sets out the details of the subject of the report (victim or suspect).
- **Sheet 3: Additional details**. This sets out addresses of the subject.
- **Sheet 4: Transaction details**. This sets out the type of transaction and the amounts involved.
- **Sheet 5: Reasons for suspicion**. These must be set out in full.
- **Sheet 6: Reason for suspicion continuation**.

In addition, the first time a firm submits a disclosure to SOCA or when the firm's contact details have changed, it will be necessary to submit the Source Registration Document.

10.3.2   Limited intelligence value/suspicious activity reports

Dame Elizabeth Butler-Sloss in her judgment in *P* v. *P* stated:

> It is important for the legal profession to take into account . . . that the Act [PoCA 2002] makes no distinction between degrees of criminal property. An illegally obtained sum of £10 is no less susceptible to the definition of 'criminal property' than a sum of £1 million. Parliament clearly intended this to be the case. Whatever may be the resource implications, the legal profession would appear to be bound by the provisions of the Act in all cases, however big or small. If this approach is scrupulously followed by the legal advisers, the result is likely to have a considerable and adverse impact upon NCIS [now SOCA] . . .

Acknowledging the problem, SOCA has provided a limited intelligence value report (LIVR) for use in certain specified circumstances. As with the SAR, the form of this report can be downloaded from the SOCA website and completed on the solicitor's own computer (see above for further details). Special versions of the form are available where the solicitor wishes to complete the form by hand. The form must be submitted by fax or post, and the contact fax number and address is the same as used to submit the standard form (see **paragraph 10.3.1**).

The form itself is a single sheet. A copy, together with the guidance notes for completion, can be found in **Appendix C4**.

SOCA has issued guidance on the types of circumstances that are appropriate for abbreviated information to be provided in this form. It accepts that the provisions of PoCA 2002 mean that solicitors may be required to make disclosures but the information is likely to be of limited intelligence value to law enforcement agencies. However, SOCA reserves the right to ask solicitors to submit details on a standard form if it believes this is necessary. The Law Society's Practice Note (para.8.34) suggests that LIVRs may be appropriate where the solicitor knows that a law enforcement agency already has an interest in the matter.

The circumstances where an LIVR is appropriate can be found in the table included in the guidance notes at **Appendix C4**. LIVRs can only be used for reports made under PoCA 2002 – all reports made under the Terrorism Act 2000 must be in the standard form format.

10.3.3 Consent report

As noted in **Chapter 4**, on occasions solicitors may be under time constraints (e.g. completion of the transaction may be set for two or three days' time). In these circumstances, if an authorised disclosure is made, no further action which might facilitate the acquisition, retention, use or control of criminal property can be undertaken without appropriate consent. If the disclosure has been made internally, the firm's nominated officer cannot give appropriate consent unless SOCA has been notified and it has either consented to the action proposed or seven working days have elapsed during which SOCA has not given notice of refusal to act. (For details of these provisions, see **Chapter 3**.)

Where time is important the nominated officer should make the disclosure electronically or by fax (020 7238 8286) indicating that the matter is urgent and giving details of the time critical issues so that consent can be given quickly. In most cases there is no need to telephone the duty desk at SOCA first to explain the urgency (tel: 020 7238 8282). The 'consent required' box should be marked on the standard form. Details of the timescale and the impact of a delayed response should be included in the report.

Where a consent request is submitted the Consent Team will contact the person making the report by telephone with a decision. Written confirmation will subsequently be posted to the firm.

10.3.4 Law Society guidance

The Law Society has given guidance on making a disclosure. This can be found in Chapter 8 of the Anti-money Laundering Practice Note (see **Appendix B1**).

CHAPTER 11

Management of money laundering procedures

11.1 INTRODUCTION

This chapter provides guidance on how firms can organise their management and administration of money laundering procedures to promote compliance with the Money Laundering Regulations 2007 and to avoid risking inadvertent involvement in money laundering offences. The dangers from the legislation of undertaking any legal services on behalf of clients are such that it is vital for even the smallest of firms to adopt anti-money laundering systems and policies.

11.2 POLICY DECISIONS

Firms should make a number of policy decisions in respect of their anti-money laundering procedures. It is vital to undertake all areas of practice within a framework of positive policy decisions rather than allowing the organisation to develop procedures in an unstructured way. Clear policy decisions allow all those involved in relevant business within the firm and those involved in other risk areas of the practice to understand their responsibilities and obligations. A senior partner (or officer) should be responsible for ensuring business decisions on anti-money laundering procedures. This partner (or officer) will frequently be the firm's nominated officer although where the nominated officer is not a partner (or officer) overall responsibility for the firm's policies should rest with a partner or officer.

The policy decisions required to be taken by the firm are listed below. This may not be an exhaustive list. Further details are provided on each heading in the paragraphs which follow. The policies include:

- appointment of a nominated officer;
- risk assessment;
- amendments to the firm's terms of business;
- internal reporting procedures;
- customer due diligence procedures;

- record-keeping procedures;
- branch or overseas offices; and
- staff training.

11.2.1 Appointment of a nominated officer

Regulation 20 of the Money Laundering Regulations 2007 requires firms to nominate a person to receive disclosures of knowledge or suspicion of money laundering. If the firm is a relevant person, it is mandatory for such an officer to be appointed in accordance with reg.20. A failure to do so will amount to a criminal offence under the terms of reg.45.

However, even if the firm is not undertaking any business which brings it within the definition of a relevant person (in the light of the current definition, this is likely to apply to a very small number of firms) the appointment of a nominated officer is still good practice. The substantive law contained in the Proceeds of Crime Act 2002 (PoCA 2002) and the Terrorism Act 2000 does not oblige firms to appoint a nominated officer, however, without the appointment, authorised or protected disclosures could only be made to SOCA. The appointment of a nominated officer ensures that internal disclosures can be made. (The fact that a firm is not a relevant person under the Money Laundering Regulations 2007 does not avoid the risk that members of the firm may commit offences under PoCA 2002 or the Terrorism Act 2000.)

Most firms will appoint a partner to the role and this partner can then be made responsible for the overall anti-money laundering policies of the firm. However, there is no requirement that the nominated officer be a partner. The requirement in reg.20 that the nominated officer should consider reports from members of staff 'in the light of any relevant information' which is available in the firm means the nominated officer should be of sufficient seniority to have access to this information.

The role is an important and onerous one. A nominated officer will be subject to PoCA 2002, ss.331 and 332 (see **Chapter 6**) which give rise to criminal offences if the nominated officer fails to follow the requirements of the sections. Further criminal offences can arise under reg.45 of the Money Laundering Regulations 2007. Consequently, individuals should be prepared to accept the role only if they are able to take on the responsibilities, which in many cases will be time consuming. Thought might be given to the role rotating between specified partners, with each individual partner undertaking the role for a period of, say, six months, provided those undertaking the role have sufficient knowledge.

One important part of the role is the ability to provide detailed advice to members of the firm on their responsibilities and compliance with the firm's procedures. Nominated officers will need to keep up to date with developments in this area making the necessary amendments to the firm's procedures.

Larger firms will frequently appoint deputy officers to whom certain duties can be delegated. The nominated officer should, however, remain in overall control and will be the person ultimately responsible for complying with the legal obligations of an officer.

All firms must ensure that temporary cover is provided when the nominated officer is absent from the firm, for whatever reason.

11.2.2 Risk assessment

There is probably no area of practice which is not at risk, to some extent, from involvement in money laundering activities. However, some areas of practice are undoubtedly at more risk than others and firms need to identify the high-risk areas to ensure proper risk management procedures are put in place for the fee earners and others operating in these areas. The Money Laundering Regulations 2007 require the determination of the extent of CDD measures on a risk-sensitive basis depending upon the type of client, business relationship and transaction. For details, see **Chapter 9** and the Law Society's Anti-money Laundering Practice Note (see **Appendix B1**). Details of individual practice areas and the common risks are contained in **Chapter 12**.

11.2.3 Terms of business

The firm's terms of business should be reconsidered in the light of the substantive law and money laundering regulations. It will not be tipping off or the offence of prejudicing an investigation for firms to amend their standard terms of business, thereby explaining to clients the basis on which the money laundering requirements apply to all retainers. The Law Society have published some examples of possible terms to be used in client care letters regarding money laundering. These are to be found on the Law Society's website (**www.lawsociety.org.uk**) incorporated into the Client Care Letters Practice Note. Clauses to consider might include some or all of the following:

- **Client identification**. This term can be to the effect that government regulations require firms to obtain details of clients' identity before acting for them and in the absence of satisfactory evidence of identity the firm will not be able to act or continue to act for the client.
- **Reporting obligations**. This term can indicate that the firm has an obligation to report knowledge or suspicion of certain criminal activities to the authorities and that in many cases this must be done without reference to, or the consent of, the client.
- **Terminating the retainer**. This term can indicate that, in extreme cases, the firm might have to terminate the client's instructions in circumstances where the firm may not be able to communicate the reason for the termination to the client. (This could be relevant where an authorised disclo-

sure is made to SOCA and the firm receives notice of refusal of consent to the firm continuing to act. The fee earner could be tipping off if the reason for the termination was communicated to the client.)

- **Limitation of liability**. Theoretically, solicitors could be liable in civil law to clients (and others who might be victims of criminal activities). The Law Society's Anti-money Laundering Practice Note provides an excellent and comprehensive statement of the law on civil liability arising in the context of money laundering and offers practical guidance on how to reduce the risk of liability. Its guidance on this topic can be found in Chapter 10 of the Practice Note (see **Appendix B1**).

Although an exclusion clause will not assist a solicitor where a victim who is not a client makes a civil claim, such a clause may assist in relation to claims by clients. If a completion is delayed as a result of an authorised disclosure and the client is consequently in breach of contract, the client may seek to obtain damages from the solicitor, particularly if it turns out that the suspected criminal conduct did not exist. A clause which seeks to limit liability from civil claims arising from a decision by a solicitor relating to his money laundering obligations may be helpful. Any such clause is likely to be subject to the reasonableness test in s.2(2) of the Unfair Contract Terms Act 1977. The Solicitors Regulation Authority's requirements on limitation of liability by contract are contained in Rule 2.07 of the Solicitors' Code of Conduct 2007. Rule 2.07 states:

> If you are a principal in a firm you must not exclude or attempt to exclude by contract all liability to your clients. However, you may limit civil liability, provided that such limitation is not below the minimum level of cover required by the Solicitors' Indemnity Insurance Rules for a policy of qualifying insurance, and the agreement is in writing.

(The current minimum level of cover is £2 million for unincorporated practices, £3 million for most incorporated practices).

- **Source of funds**. This term may specify that, as a result of Government regulations, the firm must have regard to the source of any funds to be used by the client in any transaction and that, consequently, the firm will require clients to fully disclose details of the source of funds. Failure to do may lead to the firm terminating the retainer.

Where funds are sourced from abroad, consideration might be given to a requirement that such funds are brought into the UK through a UK clearing bank rather that directly into the solicitor's client account. In this way some comfort can be obtained from the bank's anti-money laundering procedures. However, it must be acknowledged that the use of a UK bank in these circumstances will not completely avoid any risks on the part of the solicitor. The solicitor may have information obtained in the course of acting which the bank does not have and which gives rise to suspicion or knowledge of criminal intent.

11.2.4 Internal reporting procedures

A key decision to be taken by firms is how members of staff should report their knowledge or suspicion of money laundering matters. For most firms, the decision will be that all members of staff should use the internal reporting procedures rather than external reporting. The name of the nominated officer together with the name of the deputy and/or alternative should be made known to all members of staff. Firms should consider using a standard form for internal reporting purposes, allowing for a clear distinction to be made between informal discussions with the nominated officer and formal disclosures.

A clear policy for post-disclosure requirements must be adopted and communicated. This policy should be that once an internal disclosure has been made:

- No further work should be undertaken on the file without the consent of the nominated officer. Failure to abide by this requirement could lead to the loss of any defence afforded by an authorised disclosure (see **Chapter 4**). Whilst in practice it may be possible for a limited amount of preparatory work to be undertaken on the file (i.e. work which does not facilitate the acquisition, retention, use or control of criminal property) it is dangerous to allow individual fee earners to make a decision as to what might be possible and what activities might negate any defence. The nominated officer should take this decision, after careful consideration of the facts.
- No communication should be made to anyone concerning the disclosure, without the consent of the nominated officer. Failure to comply with this requirement may lead to tipping off and/or the offence of prejudicing an investigation (see **Chapter 7**). Again, it makes sense to keep control of any subsequent communications centrally rather than to allow individual members of staff to make their own decisions. This restriction on communicating should be absolute. In other words, those making the disclosure should not communicate details to anyone, including other members of staff.

One problem arising from these policies (particularly the policy of restricting communications regarding the disclosure) is that if a fee earner leaves the firm or otherwise ceases to act on a file, any new fee earner may not be aware that concerns have been expressed regarding money laundering and that an authorised disclosure may have been made internally. To overcome this problem some firms operate a black book system. The nominated officer enters all reports (formal or otherwise) in a black book which is kept confidential.

New fee earners can make a black book search by approaching the nominated officer who can simply confirm if any entry regarding that file has been made. Files which have given rise to a report could be tagged (extra number/letter on file reference) which would then indicate to any fee earner coming to the file that a black book search should be made. Tagging using a discreet indication should not give rise to any risk of tipping off where the client requires access to the file.

This system may be of particular relevance where a litigation matter is conducted with knowledge or suspicion that the funds or property involved might be criminal property. Although *Bowman* v. *Fels* excludes litigation from the effects of the money laundering offences (PoCA 2002, ss.327–329), the litigation process does not 'clean' the criminal property. Recording knowledge or suspicion in these circumstances allows fee earners to consider whether any future transaction matter undertaken on behalf of the client might have to be reported to the authorities.

11.2.5 Client identification procedures (customer due diligence)

In addition to deciding exactly what evidence of identity is acceptable for different categories of client (for details see **Chapter 9** and **Appendix B1**) a policy decision must be taken specifying which clients are subject to CDD.

If firms wish to apply the Money Laundering Regulations 2007 strictly, a complex new file opening procedure will have to be adopted which will have to be capable of ascertaining:

- Whether the firm is a relevant person for the purposes of the retainer.
- If so, whether it is a business relationship or an occasional transaction.
- If it appears to be an occasional transaction, whether the amount involved is 15,000 or more.
- Whether there is knowledge or suspicion of money laundering.

Even if, in the light of this complex checklist, a decision is taken that no CDD procedures are necessary, the firm's procedures must be able to identify when an occasional transaction (which initially did not require identification) becomes a business relationship or when a transaction which starts with the firm not being a relevant person becomes subject to the Regulations (for example a litigation matter where tax advice is being sought and given).

There is a lot to be said for applying CDD procedures to all clients regardless of the type of business. The firm should also adopt a clear policy on what can and cannot be undertaken on behalf of clients before satisfactory evidence of identity is obtained. This should include reference to the holding of client money (see **Chapter 9** for further detail).

11.2.6 Record-keeping requirements

Details of the formal records required under the Money Laundering Regulations 2007 are contained in **Chapter 9**. However, the firm should consider keeping records (possibly using internally agreed forms) covering the following areas:

- Record of the evidence of the client's and, if relevant, beneficial owner's identity (as required by the Regulations).
- Record of the transaction (as required by the Regulations). In many cases this record can be satisfied by reference to the contents of the client file and accounting records.
- Copy of the client/beneficial owner verification forms (for an example, see **Appendix C1**).
- Details of the client's source of funds.
- Record of internal disclosures.
- Record of the nominated officer's consideration and determination regarding internal disclosures.
- Record of external disclosures.
- Record of staff training.

11.2.7 Branch or overseas offices

Where a firm has a branch and/or an overseas office, firms should consider how best to ensure compliance by those offices with their anti-money laundering procedures. If the firm has a branch office in England and Wales, staff at the branch office will be subject to the same obligations as those working in the main office. Effective control procedures must be devised in accordance with the firm's general procedures. Deputy nominated officers may be appointed in each branch office.

Overseas offices will not, strictly, be subject to UK law or to the Money Laundering Regulations 2007. However, many overseas jurisdictions impose similar anti-money laundering requirements on local practitioners. EU countries will be subject to the Third EU Money Laundering Directive and, as such, should have introduced similar provisions to the UK Regulations. As a general rule, however, it appears that the UK's legislation and money laundering regulations impose a greater obligation upon practitioners compared with some overseas jurisdictions (indeed, at the time of writing not all EU countries have implemented or fully implemented the Third Directive). Consequently, many English and Welsh firms with overseas offices have adopted a policy that their overseas offices should comply with the UK requirements to enable a common set of procedures throughout the firm's offices. Local nominated officers can be appointed in each office with similar roles to the nominated officer in the UK.

11.2.8 Staff training

The training requirements are contained in reg.21 of the Money Laundering Regulations 2007 and are dealt with in **Chapter 9**.

Firms should determine their training policies so as to ensure that all relevant members of staff receive training in the substantive law, the Regulations, the firm's own procedures and in the recognition and dealing with transactions which may involve money laundering.

The firm's compliance manual (see **paragraph 11.3**) should be distributed to all relevant members of staff and, if appropriate, members of staff should be asked to sign a declaration that they have read and understood its contents.

Training should be a rolling programme, with regular updating sessions and sessions for newly joined members of staff. It should cover all members of staff, fee earning as well as support staff, but should be tailored to individual group requirements.

11.3 THE COMPLIANCE MANUAL

The Terrorism Act 2000, PoCA 2002, and the Money Laundering Regulations 2007 require firms to comply with a fairly complex framework of rules. Full compliance with these requirements is essential.

Poor compliance in some circumstances can lead to a criminal conviction and the possibility of disciplinary action being taken against members of the firm. The firm's procedures for compliance with the requirements must therefore be given attention by high-level management within the firm. Once determined, the firm's policies and procedures must be communicated to all personnel who at any time may be involved in financial transactions.

The most satisfactory method of recording and communicating the firm's procedures is by the use of a compliance manual. The manual should be in an easily readable form and should not attempt to reiterate all the provisions of PoCA 2002, the Terrorism Act 2000 or the Money Laundering Regulations 2007. Instead, it should seek to provide practical explanations and instructions in respect of the anti-money laundering procedures adopted by the firm. The manual should be arranged in suitable sections. It is essential that the manual is kept up to date.

The contents of the manual will vary from firm to firm. It is suggested that the following should be included in the manual:

- **Policy decisions.** The policies which have been determined by the firm should be clearly stated. The names of the nominated officer, deputies and alternative officer should be stated.
- **Brief explanation and illustration of the Acts and the Regulations as they apply to the firm.** The manual should not seek to reiterate all the

provisions of PoCA 2002 or the Terrorism Act 2000 and other material. However, the emphasis should be on explanation and illustration of how the Acts and Regulations apply to the firm's business.

- **The firm's procedures for compliance.** The firm's procedures should be recorded to ensure that all personnel understand how clients must be identified, how internal reports should be made and which records need to be maintained and where they are held.
- **Specimen forms.** All forms relating to the firm's anti-money laundering procedures should be included with instructions for their use.
- **Instructions to departments of the firm on procedures which relate specifically to work undertaken in those departments.** Procedures to be followed when dealing with clients of the various departments should be recorded where possible using one subsection per department. The procedures should, of course, be consistent with the policy decisions made on the type and extent of any risk and the possibility of the work involving activities in the regulated sector.
- **A list of warnings.** A simple list of warnings could be included to inform staff when they are stepping outside the firm's policies or their individual authority.
- **Help.** No matter how well written the manual is, the Acts and the Regulations can present a considerable compliance problem. The manual should give clear instructions on how to obtain assistance and advice from within the firm. A call for help at a crucial point by a fee earner could prevent a breach of the firm's internal policies and prevent the inadvertent commission of a crime.

CHAPTER 12

How to spot money laundering activities in a solicitor's practice

12.1 INTRODUCTION

It should be clear from the previous chapters in this book that almost all areas of a solicitor's practice are at risk from possible involvement in money laundering transactions. This chapter identifies specific practice areas and highlights the activities within those areas that could give rise to the risk.

It is impossible to define what amounts to a suspicion of involvement in criminal activities. Some parts of PoCA 2002 (e.g. the money laundering offences in ss.327–329) require the test of whether the accused had knowledge or suspicion to be satisfied on a subjective basis. In other parts of PoCA 2002 (notably failure to report, s.330) the test is a subjective and objective test. Some individuals are more suspicious than others, so in applying a subjective test, different results can be obtained using the same facts. Firms must encourage their staff to err on the side of caution; staff must be encouraged to consult with more senior members of the firm and, if necessary, with the firm's nominated officer. The Law Society's Anti-money Laundering Practice Note provides some further guidance on the term 'suspicion'. It says:

> The term 'suspects' is one which the court has historically avoided defining; however because of its importance in English criminal law, some general guidance has been given. In the case of *Da Silva* [1996] EWCA Crim 1654, which was prosecuted under the previous money laundering legislation, Longmore LJ stated:
>
> > 'It seems to us that the essential element in the word "suspect" and its affiliates, in this context, is that the defendant must think that there is a possibility, which is more than fanciful, that the relevant facts exist. A vague feeling of unease would not suffice.'
>
> There is no requirement for the suspicion to be clear or firmly grounded on specific facts, but there must be a degree of satisfaction, not necessarily amounting to belief, but at least extending beyond speculation . . .
>
> If you think a transaction is suspicious, you are not expected to know the exact nature of the criminal offence or that particular funds were definitely those arising from the crime. You may have noticed something unusual or unexpected and after making enquiries, the facts do not seem normal or make commercial sense. You do not have to have evidence that money laundering is taking place to have suspicion.

Knowledge means actual knowledge. There is some authority for the view that in the criminal law 'knowledge' includes 'wilfully shutting one's eyes to the truth': see, e.g. per Lord Reid in *Warner* v. *Metropolitan Police Commr* [1969] 2 AC 256 at 279, HL; *Atwal* v. *Massey*, 56 Cr App R 6, DC. However, such a proposition must be treated with great caution. The clear view of the courts at present is that this is a matter of evidence, and that nothing short of actual knowledge will suffice.

12.2 CORPORATE DEPARTMENT

Activities in a firm's corporate department can give rise to a high risk of involvement in possible money laundering. Company formation services and financial transactions involving corporate clients will be within both the regulated sector for the purposes of the offence of failure to report (PoCA 2002, s.330) and within the definition of relevant business for the purposes of the Money Laundering Regulations 2007.

Consequently, corporate clients (and where appropriate, beneficial owners) should be subject to CDD at the outset of new instructions. Further, members of staff will be required to report their knowledge or suspicion of criminal activities (under PoCA 2002, s.330) even if the retainer does not involve an arrangement which facilitates the acquisition, retention, use or control of criminal property or involve the holding in client account of possible criminal funds.

The following are specific areas of concern.

12.2.1 Formation of companies without any apparent commercial or other purpose

HM Treasury have identified front or shell companies as being a factor in many complex money laundering operations. Solicitors must be satisfied as to the commercial reason for a company formation transaction. They must understand why the client has come to the solicitor for assistance. In most cases, solicitors will be used because there will be an underlying legal service being provided along with the actual company formation: advising on the structure of the shareholding, the rights of shareholders, the constitution of the company, etc. Instructions where a client (particularly one unknown to the firm) simply asks the firm to form a company should be treated with a degree of suspicion.

12.2.2 Formation of subsidiaries in circumstances where there appears to be no commercial or other purpose (particularly overseas subsidiaries)

For the same reason, formation of subsidiary companies should be treated with care where there appears to be no commercial or other proper purpose.

Any corporate transaction in an overseas jurisdiction should be considered carefully, particularly if the overseas jurisdiction is a country on the FATF's (Financial Action Task Force on Money Laundering) list of Non-Cooperative Countries and Territories (NCCTs). The FATF seeks to identify non-cooperative countries in the worldwide fight against money laundering. At the time of writing there are no NCCTs. However, solicitors can check the position by accessing the FATF's website (**www.fatf-gafi.org**). On 16 October 2008, the FATF warned of higher risks of money laundering and terrorist financing by deficiencies in the systems in Iran, Uzbekistan, Turkmenistan, Pakistan, São Tomé and Northern Cyprus. Transactions with these countries can present a higher risk of money laundering. Further, the International Bar Association provides a summary of money laundering legislation around the world (**www.anti-moneylaundering.org**).

12.2.3 Appointment of solicitors as directors with little or no commercial involvement

It might be flattering for a solicitor to be asked to serve as a director of a client company and in many cases there may be compelling commercial reasons for such an appointment. However, those involved in money laundering will wish to project any company they use as a legitimate concern and having a reputable solicitor on the board of directors will assist in this aim. Solicitors must consider the possibility of involvement in money laundering before accepting any board appointment.

12.2.4 Purchase of private company using suspect funds

The purchase (or sale) of any asset can involve a money laundering transaction. The funds used to purchase the asset may fall within the definition of criminal property (see **Chapter 2**). Because of the wide definition, company shares may have been purchased in the past using criminal funds meaning that the shares could represent a person's benefit from criminal conduct and thus be criminal property. As with the purchase of any asset, solicitors should be concerned about the source of funds and/or the legitimacy of any asset.

12.2.5 Large payments for unspecified services to consultants, related parties, employees, etc

In the course of acting for a corporate client, solicitors are likely to become aware of many facts relating to the running of the company. Some of these facts (such as large payments for unspecified services or suspected tax evasion) may give rise to knowledge or suspicion of money laundering. Other examples might include the discovery of unauthorised transactions or improperly recorded transactions (particularly where the company has poor/inadequate accounting systems).

Even if the solicitor is not involved in a transaction relating to these payments, the fact that corporate work is likely to be within the regulated sector means that knowledge or suspicion of these matters could give rise to an obligation to report.

12.2.6 Unusual transactions (including purchase/sale transactions significantly above/below market price)

Transactions may be unusual in themselves or because they are unusual by reference to the normal type of work done by the firm or for the particular client.

Fee earners should not act outside their normal range of expertise. Undoubtedly, money launderers play on the fact that firms might be persuaded to accept instructions (frequently at an attractive fee) in circumstances where the firm or fee earner has no in-depth knowledge of the type of transaction involved. In this way the money launderers will avoid detailed questions from the firm concerning the transaction.

Firms should be aware of the normal transactions their clients have been involved in over recent years. The most difficult transaction to identify involving money laundering is where the client has been a good client providing the firm with legitimate business over a number of years. Such clients who suddenly go rogue can be very difficult to identify as money launderers. Enquiries should be made where established clients instruct the firm in unusual circumstances.

Transactions which are unusual in themselves obviously give rise to concern and these will include any transaction which appears to be significantly over- or under-valued.

12.2.7 Long delays over the production of company accounts

Those using companies for unlawful purposes are unlikely to want to make public financial disclosures by filing accounts for the company. The penalties for late filing of company accounts are unlikely to concern the individuals behind the company – they will hope to have achieved their object and be well away before steps are taken to enforce the filing requirements.

12.2.8 Dubious businesses often use more than one set of professional advisers. Ask 'why me?'

Solicitors should be particularly concerned where they discover that a particular corporate client has instructed another firm of solicitors in similar circumstances, where, for example, there appears to be a parallel deal involving different advisers. One common approach used by money launderers is to split up a complex transaction into a number of smaller transactions, using different professional advisers in each of the smaller transactions. In this way, no one firm sees the overall picture. However, firms should be suspicious if the facts of a case suggest that this is what is going on. (An illustration of this method, where a corporate client uses a number of solicitors in a conveyancing transaction, is given in **paragraph 12.3.4**.)

12.2.8 Private equity/collective investment schemes

The Law Society's Anti-money Laundering Practice Note provided detailed guidance on the risks associated with the establishment of a private equity business, the formation of private equity funds, the ongoing legal issues connected with such work and work involving collective investment schemes. This guidance can be found in Chapter 11 of the Practice Note (see **Appendix B1**).

12.3 PROPERTY DEPARTMENT

Activities in a firm's property department also give rise to a high risk of involvement in possible money laundering. Real property transactions will be within both the regulated sector for the purposes of the offence of failure to report (PoCA 2002, s.330) and within the definition of relevant business for the purposes of the Money Laundering Regulations 2007.

Guidance can be found in the Law Society's Practice Note, Chapter 11 (see **Appendix B3**).

Property clients should be subject to CDD at the outset of new instructions. Further, members of staff will be required to report their knowledge or suspicion of criminal activities (under PoCA 2002 s.330) even if the retainer does not involve an arrangement which facilitates the acquisition, retention, use or control of criminal property or involve the holding in client account of possible criminal funds.

The following are specific areas of concern.

12.3.1 Fictitious buyers (introduced by third party) and not known to the solicitor

Criminals commonly used the fictitious buyer scam to obtain mortgage advances by deception. Frequently, this involves individuals who claim to represent a large numbers of clients all of whom have suddenly decided to purchase houses and most of whom can never find time to meet the solicitor.

Mortgage applications would be made in fictitious names to many financial institutions (often using the same properties) using a number of innocent solicitors. The mortgage advance would clearly amount to criminal property (having been obtained by deception) and solicitors would clearly be at risk of involvement in money laundering activities. Any arrangement in which the solicitor was concerned (typically, the completion of the mortgage) would facilitate the acquisition, retention, use or control of criminal property. This could apply where the client was involved in the criminal activity or where the solicitor was acting for the financial institution and another firm represented the perpetrator of the crime. Holding and/or dealing with the mortgage advance money in these circumstances could also give rise to the offence of acquisition, use or possession (PoCA 2002, s.329) or possibly the offence of concealing (PoCA 2002, s.327).

Whilst it is fair to say that the requirements for obtaining verification of the client's identity have undoubtedly reduced the number of frauds using this particular scam, solicitors must nonetheless be vigilant – this illustrates the importance of adopting proper and effective client identification procedures.

12.3.2 Payment of deposit directly to vendor (particularly where the deposit paid is excessive)

Another typical method of defrauding mortgage providers is to misrepresent the purchase price – using a price which appears to suggest that the value of the security is greater than it is in reality. Often this scam is achieved by a direct payment to the vendor by the purchaser, rather than making the payment through the solicitors.

By way of illustration, a client is purchasing property at an agreed price of £400,000. The client's building society agrees a maximum mortgage advance of 80 per cent of the purchase price, i.e. £320,000. Because of a poor survey report, the vendor agrees with the purchaser to reduce the price to £350,000. This would have the effect of reducing the mortgage advance if it came to the knowledge of the building society. The vendor and purchaser decide not to notify their own solicitors or the building society of the reduction. On exchange of contracts, the purchaser informs his solicitor that he has paid a deposit of £50,000 directly to the purchaser, leaving only £350,000 to be paid on completion. Of course, no deposit has been paid and the property is purchased at a price of £350,000 albeit the paperwork shows a price of £400,000. The payment of a direct deposit (greater than the normal 10 per cent of the purchase price) should put the purchaser's solicitor on notice that the transaction needs to be considered with care.

12.3.3   Purchase of property using suspect funds

The purchase (or sale) of property can involve a money laundering transaction. The funds used to purchase the property may fall within the definition of criminal property (see **Chapter 2**). Further, because of the wide definition, property may have been purchased in the past using criminal funds meaning that the property could represent a person's benefit from criminal conduct and thus be criminal property. As with the purchase of any asset, solicitors should be concerned at the source of funds and/or the legitimacy of any asset.

12.3.4   Purchase of property using a corporate vehicle where there is no good commercial or other reason

As noted above, corporate vehicles are frequently used in money laundering transactions. It is sometimes easier to split complex transactions into smaller matters where companies are used. Firms must be satisfied that there are good commercial or legal reasons for using a company.

A group of criminal individuals intend purchasing a chain of 12 hotels. The total purchase price amounts to, say, £15 million. However, the individuals (perhaps using a crooked surveyor) intend applying for finance of £20 million using the hotels as security. To do this they will represent the value of the hotels as being in the region of £25 million.

The original purchase will go through at the legitimate price: £15 million. Rather than purchasing the group in the names of the individuals (or by way of a share purchase), the transaction will be an asset purchase, transferring the title to the 12 hotels into the name of a company (possibly an overseas company created using nominees for the individuals). This transaction will appear to be legitimate (although the purchase in the name of an off-shore company held by nominees might give rise to suspicion on the part of the purchaser's solicitor). Indeed, at this stage, it appears that no criminal activity has been undertaken. To avoid any further suspicion at the next stage (which will amount to criminal activity) the individuals are likely to instruct 12 different firms of solicitors, each of whom will be asked to act for the off-shore company on the sale of a single hotel to individuals (or other companies connected with them). The purchasers will also instruct 12 different firms of solicitors to act on their behalf. The total purchase price for these 12 transactions will be shown at £25 million, financed by loans of, in total, £20 million.

All solicitors acting in this scenario could be involved in an arrangement contrary to PoCA 2002, s.328 and guilty of a criminal offence if they knew or suspected that the arrangement facilitated the acquisition, retention, use or control of criminal property. The use of a company in the original transaction (solicitors acting on the second stage will be made aware that the individual hotels had been recently purchased by the off-shore company) and the possible knowledge that other professionals were involved in similar transactions could be sufficient to put the firms involved on notice that the circumstances were suspicious.

12.3.5 Tax issues

Tax evasion by a client or third party can lead to money laundering – facilitating such evasion can be an offence under PoCA 2002 s.328 (arrangements). Knowledge of another person's tax evasion may have to be disclosed where PoCA 2002 s.330 (failure to disclose) applies. In property work the danger arises from abuse of Stamp Duty Land Tax. Any attempt to avoid this improperly will be tax evasion, and subject to LPP, a disclosure should be made.

12.4 PRIVATE CLIENT DEPARTMENT

Activities in a firm's trust department can give rise to a high risk of involvement in possible money laundering. Probate work is less likely to give rise to a high risk of involvement but, nonetheless, since assets of various categories are involved, money laundering cannot be ruled out completely. Both trust administration and probate transactions are likely to be within both the regulated sector for the purposes of the offence of failure to report (PoCA 2002, s.330) and within the definition of relevant business for the purposes of the Money Laundering Regulations 2007.

Law Society's guidance on this topic is contained in Chapter 11 of the Anti-money Laundering Practice Note (see **Appendix B1**).

In trust administration, the client will usually be the trustee(s). Trustees should be subject to CDD procedures at the outset of new instructions using the procedures for individual clients (or, if the trustee is a trust corporation, for companies). However, in all circumstances solicitors must consider the requirements relating to beneficial owners and take the necessary steps to verify their identity (for details, see **Chapter 7**). In probate matters, the client is the executor(s) or administrator(s) and again their identity should be established using the procedures for individuals or companies. The beneficial owner will also be the executor(s) or administrator(s) during the period of administration. Consequently, no further identification procedures will be necessary unless there is a will trust and the solicitor continues, after the administration of the estate, to administer the will trust. Here it will be necessary to undertake CDD on the beneficial owners.

If the trust or estate administration work involves financial or real property transactions, tax advice, advice and arrangements relating to the purchase or sale of specified investments or acting on the formation, operation or management of a trust, the work will be in the regulated sector. This means that members of staff will be required to report their knowledge or suspicion of criminal activities even if the retainer does not involve an arrangement which facilitates the acquisition, retention, use or control of criminal property or involve the holding in client account of possible criminal funds.

The following are specific areas of concern.

12.4.1 The formation of trusts with no apparent commercial or other purpose

HM Treasury have identified trust funds as being a factor in many complex money laundering operations. Solicitors must be satisfied as to the commercial reason for a trust formation. They must understand why the client has come to the solicitor for assistance. In most cases, solicitors will be used because there will be an underlying legal service being provided along with the actual trust formation: administering the trust, or giving tax advice on the use of the trust. Instructions where a client (particularly one unknown to the firm) simply asks the firm to form a trust should be treated with a degree of suspicion. This is particularly so where the trust is intended to be an off-shore trust. Sometimes, the identity of off-shore trustees may be difficult to ascertain. Fee earners must be reminded that, where the firm is undertaking trust work in the UK which is subject to the Money Laundering Regulations 2007 and satisfactory evidence of identification (of the trustees or the beneficial owners) cannot be obtained, the business retainer must not proceed further.

If the intended trust fund is to be established in an overseas jurisdiction, particular care must be taken to ensure the identity of the trustees and the beneficial owners and the legitimacy of the trust fund.

12.4.2 The appointment of solicitors as trustees with little or no commercial involvement

As with the appointment of a solicitor as a director of a corporate client, it can be flattering for a solicitor to be asked by a settlor to act as a trustee of a trust. In many cases there may be compelling commercial or legal reasons for such an appointment. However, those involved in money laundering will wish to project any trust fund they use as a legitimate fund and having a reputable solicitor as a trustee will assist in this aim. Solicitors must consider the possibility of involvement in money laundering before accepting any trust appointment.

12.4.3 The receipt of suspect funds into the trust fund

The purchase (or sale) of any asset held in a trust fund can involve a money laundering transaction. The funds used to purchase the asset may fall within the definition of criminal property (see **Chapter 2**). Further, because of the wide definition, assets or investments held in the fund may have been purchased in the past using criminal funds meaning that those assets could represent a person's benefit from criminal conduct and thus be criminal property. As with the purchase of any asset, solicitors should be concerned at the source of funds and/or the legitimacy of any asset.

12.4.4 Administration of estates

Whilst probate work is a relatively low risk area for money laundering issues, particular care should be taken when dealing with overseas assets – the definition of criminal property arising from overseas activities is wide (see **Chapter 2**). Further concerns may arise (giving rise to suspicion) if the deceased, to the solicitor's knowledge, had been convicted of acquisitive criminal conduct during his lifetime.

Where a solicitor knows or suspects that the assets in the estate include (or might include) criminal property, steps must be taken to avoid committing an offence under PoCA 2002. This might occur where there is knowledge or suspicion that the deceased person had improperly claimed welfare benefits or evaded tax during his lifetime. There is no requirement that the deceased was convicted of such offences – if the solicitor knows or suspects that this is the case, there is knowledge or suspicion that the estate includes criminal property and this must be acted on accordingly.

12.5 TAXATION ADVICE

The provision by way of business advice about the tax affairs of another will fall within the scope of the Money Laundering Regulations 2007 and is within the regulated sector for the purposes of the offence of failure to report (PoCA 2002, s.330). Consequently, in any practice area where tax advice is given, clients should be subject to CDD procedures at the outset of new instructions even if the practice area itself would not involve relevant business. For example, drafting a will, or giving employment advice, will not be within the scope of the Money Laundering Regulations 2007. However, if in the course of will drafting, advice is given on inheritance tax planning, this advice will be sufficient to bring the matter within the scope of the Regulations. Similarly, if in the course of employment advice, tax advice is given, this matter will also require compliance with the Regulations.

Because tax advice will amount to business in the regulated sector, members of staff will be required to report their knowledge or suspicion of criminal activities even if the retainer does not involve an arrangement which facilitates the acquisition, retention, use or control of criminal property or involve the holding in client account of possible criminal funds.

Where a client admits tax evasion to a solicitor, that client is likely to be engaged in money laundering, i.e. the client is in possession of criminal property, money or assets that represent money that should have been paid to HMRC authorities. If the solicitor's transaction will involve any part of these funds or assets, the solicitor is in danger of being involved in an arrangement that will facilitate the retention, use or control of criminal property. It is likely that an authorised disclosure must be made. Even if the particular funds are not going to be used as part of a transaction, a report under PoCA 2002, s.330 will have to be made unless one of the appropriate defences applies (in particular, the information may have been passed on to the solicitor in privileged circumstances). Careful consideration must be given to the facts of the transaction.

There is a narrow dividing line between the concepts of tax evasion (which is a criminal offence) and tax avoidance (which is legitimate). Solicitors giving tax advice must take care not to cross that line so that the advice leads to tax evasion. The advice in these circumstances could amount to an arrangement which facilitates the acquisition of criminal property.

12.6 TRANSACTIONAL MATTERS – GENERAL

The Law Society has issued a number of flowcharts as part of its Anti-money Laundering Practice Note (see Chapter 12 of the Practice Note (see **Appendix B1**)). These provide a helpful step-by-step guide to the approach to take in transactional matters where there is knowledge or suspicion of money laundering. They cover questions of whether there is knowledge of a principal offence and the defences available.

12.7 LITIGATION DEPARTMENT

The Court of Appeal's decision in *Bowman* v. *Fels* (see **Chapter 2**) means that litigation activities are unlikely to involve solicitors in any of the money laundering offences (PoCA 2002, ss.327–329). Further, litigation, in itself, is not in the regulated sector and thus will not give rise to an obligation to disclose under s.330 (see **Chapter 5**). However, as noted in **Chapter 2**, care must be taken if any criminal property comes into the possession of a solicitor following litigation. The litigation has not 'cleaned' the criminal property and subsequent transactions involving the property may well give rise to money laundering implications.

12.8 CONCLUSION

In whatever practice area a solicitor works, there will be some element of risk from involvement in money laundering. Ensure that you have the latest version of the Law Society's Anti-money Laundering Practice Note (available online from the Law Society website) and consider keeping up-to-date by subscribing to the Law Society's monthly 'Money Laundering Update' (emailed, free of cost, to those solicitors subscribing for it). Finally, note the following from the Practice Note:

> Solicitors are key professionals in the business and financial world, facilitating vital transactions that underpin the UK economy. As such, they have a significant role to play in ensuring their services are not used to further a criminal purpose. As professionals, solicitors must act with integrity and uphold the law, and they must not engage in criminal activity.

PART III

Appendices

A1

Extracts from the Proceeds of Crime Act 2002 (as amended at August 2008)

PART 7   MONEY LAUNDERING

Offences

327 Concealing etc

(1)   A person commits an offence if he–

    (a)   conceals criminal property;
    (b)   disguises criminal property;
    (c)   converts criminal property;
    (d)   transfers criminal property;
    (e)   removes criminal property from England and Wales or from Scotland or from Northern Ireland.

(2)   But a person does not commit such an offence if–

    (a)   he makes an authorised disclosure under section 338 and (if the disclosure is made before he does the act mentioned in subsection (1)) he has the appropriate consent;
    (b)   he intended to make such a disclosure but had a reasonable excuse for not doing so;
    (c)   the act he does is done in carrying out a function he has relating to the enforcement of any provision of this Act or of any other enactment relating to criminal conduct or benefit from criminal conduct.

(2A) Nor does a person commit an offence under subsection (1) if–

    (a)   he knows, or believes on reasonable grounds, that the relevant criminal conduct occurred in a particular country or territory outside the United Kingdom, and
    (b)   the relevant criminal conduct–

        (i)   was not, at the time it occurred, unlawful under the criminal law then applying in that country or territory, and
        (ii)   is not of a description prescribed by an order made by the Secretary of State.

(2B) In subsection (2A) 'the relevant criminal conduct' is the criminal conduct by reference to which the property concerned is criminal property.

(2C) A deposit-taking body that does an act mentioned in paragraph (c) or (d) of subsection (1) does not commit an offence under that subsection if–

(a) it does the act in operating an account maintained with it, and

(b) the value of the criminal property concerned is less than the threshold amount determined under section 339A for the act.

(3) Concealing or disguising criminal property includes concealing or disguising its nature, source, location, disposition, movement or ownership or any rights with respect to it.

328 Arrangements

(1) A person commits an offence if he enters into or becomes concerned in an arrangement which he knows or suspects facilitates (by whatever means) the acquisition, retention, use or control of criminal property by or on behalf of another person.

(2) But a person does not commit such an offence if–

(a) he makes an authorised disclosure under section 338 and (if the disclosure is made before he does the act mentioned in subsection (1)) he has the appropriate consent;

(b) he intended to make such a disclosure but had a reasonable excuse for not doing so;

(c) the act he does is done in carrying out a function he has relating to the enforcement of any provision of this Act or of any other enactment relating to criminal conduct or benefit from criminal conduct.

(3) Nor does a person commit an offence under subsection (1) if–

(a) he knows, or believes on reasonable grounds, that the relevant criminal conduct occurred in a particular country or territory outside the United Kingdom, and

(b) the relevant criminal conduct–

(i) was not, at the time it occurred, unlawful under the criminal law then applying in that country or territory, and

(ii) is not of a description prescribed by an order made by the Secretary of State.

(4) In subsection (3) 'the relevant criminal conduct' is the criminal conduct by reference to which the property concerned is criminal property.

(5) A deposit-taking body that does an act mentioned in subsection (1) does not commit an offence under that subsection if–

(a) it does the act in operating an account maintained with it, and

(b) the arrangement facilitates the acquisition, retention, use or control of criminal property of a value that is less than the threshold amount determined under section 339A for the act.

329 Acquisition, use and possession

(1) A person commits an offence if he–

(a) acquires criminal property;

(b) uses criminal property;

(c) has possession of criminal property.

(2) But a person does not commit such an offence if–

(a) he makes an authorised disclosure under section 338 and (if the disclosure is made before he does the act mentioned in subsection (1)) he has the appropriate consent;

(b) he intended to make such a disclosure but had a reasonable excuse for not doing so;

(c) he acquired or used or had possession of the property for adequate consideration;

(d) the act he does is done in carrying out a function he has relating to the enforcement of any provision of this Act or of any other enactment relating to criminal conduct or benefit from criminal conduct.

(2A) Nor does a person commit an offence under subsection (1) if–

(a) he knows, or believes on reasonable grounds, that the relevant criminal conduct occurred in a particular country or territory outside the United Kingdom, and

(b) the relevant criminal conduct–

(i) was not, at the time it occurred, unlawful under the criminal law then applying in that country or territory, and

(ii) is not of a description prescribed by an order made by the Secretary of State.

(2B) In subsection (2A) 'the relevant criminal conduct' is the criminal conduct by reference to which the property concerned is criminal property.

(2C) A deposit-taking body that does an act mentioned in subsection (1) does not commit an offence under that subsection if–

(a) it does the act in operating an account maintained with it, and

(b) the value of the criminal property concerned is less than the threshold amount determined under section 339A for the act.

(3) For the purposes of this section–

(a) a person acquires property for inadequate consideration if the value of the consideration is significantly less than the value of the property;

(b) a person uses or has possession of property for inadequate consideration if the value of the consideration is significantly less than the value of the use or possession;

(c) the provision by a person of goods or services which he knows or suspects may help another to carry out criminal conduct is not consideration.

330 Failure to disclose: regulated sector

(1) A person commits an offence if [the conditions in subsections (2) to (4) are satisfied].

(2) The first condition is that he–

(a) knows or suspects, or

(b) has reasonable grounds for knowing or suspecting,

that another person is engaged in money laundering.

(3) The second condition is that the information or other matter–

(a) on which his knowledge or suspicion is based, or

(b) which gives reasonable grounds for such knowledge or suspicion,

came to him in the course of a business in the regulated sector.

(3A) The third condition is–

    (a)   that he can identify the other person mentioned in subsection (2) or the whereabouts of any of the laundered property, or

    (b)   that he believes, or it is reasonable to expect him to believe, that the information or other matter mentioned in subsection (3) will or may assist in identifying that other person or the whereabouts of any of the laundered property.

(4)   The fourth condition is that he does not make the required disclosure to–

    (a)   a nominated officer, or

    (b)   a person authorised for the purposes of this Part by the Director General of SOCA,

as soon as is practicable after the information or other matter mentioned in subsection (3) comes to him.

(5)   The required disclosure is a disclosure of–

    (a)   the identity of the other person mentioned in subsection (2), if he knows it,

    (b)   the whereabouts of the laundered property, so far as he knows it, and

    (c)   the information or other matter mentioned in subsection (3).

(5A) The laundered property is the property forming the subject-matter of the money laundering that he knows or suspects, or has reasonable grounds for knowing or suspecting, that other person to be engaged in.

(6)   But he does not commit an offence under this section if–

    (a)   he has a reasonable excuse for not making the required disclosure,

    (b)   he is a professional legal adviser or relevant professional adviser and–

        (i)   if he knows either of the things mentioned in subsection (5)(a) and (b), he knows the thing because of information or other matter that came to him in privileged circumstances, or

        (ii)   the information or other matter mentioned in subsection (3) came to him in privileged circumstances, or

    (c)   subsection (7) or (7B) applies to him.

(7)   This subsection applies to a person if–

    (a)   he does not know or suspect that another person is engaged in money laundering, and

    (b)   he has not been provided by his employer with such training as is specified by the Secretary of State by order for the purposes of this section.

(7A) Nor does a person commit an offence under this section if–

    (a)   he knows, or believes on reasonable grounds, that the money laundering is occurring in a particular country or territory outside the United Kingdom, and

    (b)   the money laundering–

        (i)   is not unlawful under the criminal law applying in that country or territory, and

        (ii)   is not of a description prescribed in an order made by the Secretary of State.

(7B) This subsection applies to a person if–

(a) he is employed by, or is in partnership with, a professional legal adviser or a relevant professional adviser to provide the adviser with assistance or support,

(b) the information or other matter mentioned in subsection (3) comes to the person in connection with the provision of such assistance or support, and

(c) the information or other matter came to the adviser in privileged circumstances.

(8) In deciding whether a person committed an offence under this section the court must consider whether he followed any relevant guidance which was at the time concerned–

(a) issued by a supervisory authority or any other appropriate body,

(b) approved by the Treasury, and

(c) published in a manner it approved as appropriate in its opinion to bring the guidance to the attention of persons likely to be affected by it.

(9) A disclosure to a nominated officer is a disclosure which–

(a) is made to a person nominated by the alleged offender's employer to receive disclosures under this section, and

(b) is made in the course of the alleged offender's employment.

(9A) But a disclosure which satisfies paragraphs (a) and (b) of subsection (9) is not to be taken as a disclosure to a nominated officer if the person making the disclosure–

(a) is a professional legal adviser or other relevant professional adviser,

(b) makes it for the purpose of obtaining advice about making a disclosure under this section, and

(c) does not intend it to be a disclosure under this section.

(10) Information or other matter comes to a professional legal adviser or relevant professional adviser in privileged circumstances if it is communicated or given to him–

(a) by (or by a representative of) a client of his in connection with the giving by the adviser of legal advice to the client,

(b) by (or by a representative of) a person seeking legal advice from the adviser, or

(c) by a person in connection with legal proceedings or contemplated legal proceedings.

(11) But subsection (10) does not apply to information or other matter which is communicated or given with the intention of furthering a criminal purpose.

(12) Schedule 9 has effect for the purpose of determining what is–

(a) a business in the regulated sector;

(b) a supervisory authority.

(13) An appropriate body is any body which regulates or is representative of any trade, profession, business or employment carried on by the alleged offender.

(14) A relevant professional adviser is an accountant, auditor or tax adviser who is a member of a professional body which is established for accountants, auditors or tax advisers (as the case may be) and which makes provision for–

(a) testing the competence of those seeking admission to membership of such a body as a condition for such admission; and

(b) imposing and maintaining professional and ethical standards for its members, as well as imposing sanctions for non-compliance with those standards.

331 Failure to disclose: nominated officers in the regulated sector

(1) A person nominated to receive disclosures under section 330 commits an offence if the conditions in subsections (2) to (4) are satisfied.

(2) The first condition is that he–

(a) knows or suspects, or
(b) has reasonable grounds for knowing or suspecting,

that another person is engaged in money laundering.

(3) The second condition is that the information or other matter–

(a) on which his knowledge or suspicion is based, or
(b) which gives reasonable grounds for such knowledge or suspicion,

came to him in consequence of a disclosure made under section 330.

(3A) The third condition is–

(a) that he knows the identity of the other person mentioned in subsection (2), or the whereabouts of any of the laundered property, in consequence of a disclosure made under section 330,
(b) that that other person, or the whereabouts of any of the laundered property, can be identified from the information or other matter mentioned in subsection (3), or
(c) that he believes, or it is reasonable to expect him to believe, that the information or other matter will or may assist in identifying that other person or the whereabouts of any of the laundered property.

(4) The fourth condition is that he does not make the required disclosure to a person authorised for the purposes of this Part by the Director General of SOCA as soon as is practicable after the information or other matter mentioned in subsection (3) comes to him.

(5) The required disclosure is a disclosure of–

(a) the identity of the other person mentioned in subsection (2), if disclosed to him under section 330,
(b) the whereabouts of the laundered property, so far as disclosed to him under section 330, and
(c) the information or other matter mentioned in subsection (3).

(5A) The laundered property is the property forming the subject-matter of the money laundering that he knows or suspects, or has reasonable grounds for knowing or suspecting, that other person to be engaged in.

(6) But he does not commit an offence under this section if he has a reasonable excuse for not making the required disclosure.

(6A) Nor does a person commit an offence under this section if–

(a) he knows, or believes on reasonable grounds, that the money laundering is occurring in a particular country or territory outside the United Kingdom, and
(b) the money laundering–

      (i)   is not unlawful under the criminal law applying in that country or territory, and

      (ii)   is not of a description prescribed in an order made by the Secretary of State.

(7)   In deciding whether a person committed an offence under this section the court must consider whether he followed any relevant guidance which was at the time concerned–

    (a)   issued by a supervisory authority or any other appropriate body,

    (b)   approved by the Treasury, and

    (c)   published in a manner it approved as appropriate in its opinion to bring the guidance to the attention of persons likely to be affected by it.

(8)   Schedule 9 has effect for the purpose of determining what is a supervisory authority.

(9)   An appropriate body is a body which regulates or is representative of a trade, profession, business or employment.

332   Failure to disclose: other nominated officers

(1)   A person nominated to receive disclosures under section 337 or 338 commits an offence if the conditions in subsections (2) to (4) are satisfied.

(2)   The first condition is that he knows or suspects that another person is engaged in money laundering.

(3)   The second condition is that the information or other matter on which his knowledge or suspicion is based came to him in consequence of a disclosure made under the applicable section.

(3A) The third condition is–

    (a)   that he knows the identity of the other person mentioned in subsection (2), or the whereabouts of any of the laundered property, in consequence of a disclosure made under the applicable section,

    (b)   that that other person, or the whereabouts of any of the laundered property, can be identified from the information or other matter mentioned in subsection (3), or

    (c)   that he believes, or it is reasonable to expect him to believe, that the information or other matter will or may assist in identifying that other person or the whereabouts of any of the laundered property.

(4)   The fourth condition is that he does not make the required disclosure to a person authorised for the purposes of this Part by the Director General of SOCA as soon as is practicable after the information or other matter mentioned in subsection (3) comes to him.

(5)   The required disclosure is a disclosure of–

    (a)   the identity of the other person mentioned in subsection (2), if disclosed to him under the applicable section,

    (b)   the whereabouts of the laundered property, so far as disclosed to him under the applicable section, and

    (c)   the information or other matter mentioned in subsection (3).

(5A) The laundered property is the property forming the subject-matter of the money laundering that he knows or suspects that other person to be engaged in.

(5B) The applicable section is section 337 or, as the case may be, section 338.

(6)   But he does not commit an offence under this section if he has a reasonable excuse for not making the required disclosure.

(7) Nor does a person commit an offence under this section if–

   (a) he knows, or believes on reasonable grounds, that the money laundering is occurring in a particular country or territory outside the United Kingdom, and

   (b) the money laundering–

      (i) is not unlawful under the criminal law applying in that country or territory, and

      (ii) is not of a description prescribed in an order made by the Secretary of State.

333 ...

...

333A Tipping off: regulated sector

(1) A person commits an offence if–

   (a) the person discloses any matter within subsection (2);

   (b) the disclosure is likely to prejudice any investigation that might be conducted following the disclosure referred to in that subsection; and

   (c) the information on which the disclosure is based came to the person in the course of a business in the regulated sector.

(2) The matters are that the person or another person has made a disclosure under this Part–

   (a) to a constable,

   (b) to an officer of Revenue and Customs,

   (c) to a nominated officer, or

   (d) to a member of staff of the Serious Organised Crime Agency authorised for the purposes of this Part by the Director General of that Agency,

of information that came to that person in the course of a business in the regulated sector.

(3) A person commits an offence if–

   (a) the person discloses that an investigation into allegations that an offence under this Part has been committed is being contemplated or is being carried out;

   (b) the disclosure is likely to prejudice that investigation; and

   (c) the information on which the disclosure is based came to the person in the course of a business in the regulated sector.

(4) A person guilty of an offence under this section is liable–

   (a) on summary conviction to imprisonment for a term not exceeding three months, or to a fine not exceeding level 5 on the standard scale, or to both;

   (b) on conviction on indictment to imprisonment for a term not exceeding two years, or to a fine, or to both.

(5) This section is subject to–

   (a) section 333B (disclosures within an undertaking or group etc),

   (b) section 333C (other permitted disclosures between institutions etc), and

(c)   section 333D (other permitted disclosures etc).

333B   Disclosures within an undertaking or group etc

(1)   An employee, officer or partner of an undertaking does not commit an offence under section 333A if the disclosure is to an employee, officer or partner of the same undertaking.

(2)   A person does not commit an offence under section 333A in respect of a disclosure by a credit institution or a financial institution if–

(a)   the disclosure is to a credit institution or a financial institution,

(b)   the institution to whom the disclosure is made is situated in an EEA State or in a country or territory imposing equivalent money laundering requirements, and

(c)   both the institution making the disclosure and the institution to whom it is made belong to the same group.

(3)   In subsection (2) 'group' has the same meaning as in Directive 2002/87/EC of the European Parliament and of the Council of 16th December 2002 on the supplementary supervision of credit institutions, insurance undertakings and investment firms in a financial conglomerate.

(4)   A professional legal adviser or a relevant professional adviser does not commit an offence under section 333A if–

(a)   the disclosure is to a professional legal adviser or a relevant professional adviser,

(b)   both the person making the disclosure and the person to whom it is made carry on business in an EEA State or in a country or territory imposing equivalent money laundering requirements, and

(c)   those persons perform their professional activities within different under-takings that share common ownership, management or control.

333C   Other permitted disclosures between institutions etc

(1)   This section applies to a disclosure–

(a)   by a credit institution to another credit institution,

(b)   by a financial institution to another financial institution,

(c)   by a professional legal adviser to another professional legal adviser, or

(d)   by a relevant professional adviser of a particular kind to another relevant professional adviser of the same kind.

(2)   A person does not commit an offence under section 333A in respect of a disclosure to which this section applies if–

(a)   the disclosure relates to–

(i)   a client or former client of the institution or adviser making the disclosure and the institution or adviser to whom it is made,

(ii)   a transaction involving them both, or

(iii)   the provision of a service involving them both;

(b)   the disclosure is for the purpose only of preventing an offence under this Part of this Act;

(c)   the institution or adviser to whom the disclosure is made is situated in an EEA State or in a country or territory imposing equivalent money laundering requirements; and

(d) the institution or adviser making the disclosure and the institution or adviser to whom it is made are subject to equivalent duties of professional confidentiality and the protection of personal data (within the meaning of section 1 of the Data Protection Act 1998).

333D Other permitted disclosures etc

(1) A person does not commit an offence under section 333A if the disclosure is–

(a) to the authority that is the supervisory authority for that person by virtue of the Money Laundering Regulations 2007 (SI 2007/2157); or

(b) for the purpose of–

(i) the detection, investigation or prosecution of a criminal offence (whether in the United Kingdom or elsewhere),

(ii) an investigation under this Act, or

(iii) the enforcement of any order of a court under this Act.

(2) A professional legal adviser or a relevant professional adviser does not commit an offence under section 333A if the disclosure–

(a) is to the adviser's client, and

(b) is made for the purpose of dissuading the client from engaging in conduct amounting to an offence.

(3) A person does not commit an offence under section 333A(1) if the person does not know or suspect that the disclosure is likely to have the effect mentioned in section 333A(1)(b).

(4) A person does not commit an offence under section 333A(3) if the person does not know or suspect that the disclosure is likely to have the effect mentioned in section 333A(3)(b).

333E Interpretation of sections 333A to 333D

(1) For the purposes of sections 333A to 333D, Schedule 9 has effect for determining–

(a) what is a business in the regulated sector, and

(b) what is a supervisory authority.

(2) In those sections–

'credit institution' has the same meaning as in Schedule 9;

'financial institution' means an undertaking that carries on a business in the regulated sector by virtue of any of paragraphs (b) to (i) of paragraph 1(1) of that Schedule.

(3) References in those sections to a disclosure by or to a credit institution or a financial institution include disclosure by or to an employee, officer or partner of the institution acting on its behalf.

(4) For the purposes of those sections a country or territory imposes 'equivalent money laundering requirements' if it imposes requirements equivalent to those laid down in Directive 2005/60/EC of the European Parliament and of the Council of 26th October 2005 on the prevention of the use of the financial system for the purpose of money laundering and terrorist financing.

(5) In those sections 'relevant professional adviser' means an accountant, auditor or tax adviser who is a member of a professional body which is established for accountants, auditors or tax advisers (as the case may be) and which makes provision for–

   (a)   testing the competence of those seeking admission to membership of such a body as a condition for such admission; and

   (b)   imposing and maintaining professional and ethical standards for its members, as well as imposing sanctions for non-compliance with those standards.

334 Penalties

(1)   A person guilty of an offence under section 327, 328 or 329 is liable–

   (a)   on summary conviction, to imprisonment for a term not exceeding six months or to a fine not exceeding the statutory maximum or to both, or

   (b)   on conviction on indictment, to imprisonment for a term not exceeding 14 years or to a fine or to both.

(2)   A person guilty of an offence under section 330, 331 or 332 is liable–

   (a)   on summary conviction, to imprisonment for a term not exceeding six months or to a fine not exceeding the statutory maximum or to both, or

   (b)   on conviction on indictment, to imprisonment for a term not exceeding five years or to a fine or to both.

(3)   A person guilty of an offence under section 339(1A) is liable on summary conviction to a fine not exceeding level 5 on the standard scale.

Consent

335 Appropriate consent

(1)   The appropriate consent is–

   (a)   the consent of a nominated officer to do a prohibited act if an authorised disclosure is made to the nominated officer;

   (b)   the consent of a constable to do a prohibited act if an authorised disclosure is made to a constable;

   (c)   the consent of a customs officer to do a prohibited act if an authorised disclosure is made to a customs officer.

(2)   A person must be treated as having the appropriate consent if–

   (a)   he makes an authorised disclosure to a constable or a customs officer, and

   (b)   the condition in subsection (3) or the condition in subsection (4) is satisfied.

(3)   The condition is that before the end of the notice period he does not receive notice from a constable or customs officer that consent to the doing of the act is refused.

(4)   The condition is that–

   (a)   before the end of the notice period he receives notice from a constable or customs officer that consent to the doing of the act is refused, and

   (b)   the moratorium period has expired.

(5)   The notice period is the period of seven working days starting with the first working day after the person makes the disclosure.

(6)   The moratorium period is the period of 31 days starting with the day on which the person receives notice that consent to the doing of the act is refused.

(7) A working day is a day other than a Saturday, a Sunday, Christmas Day, Good Friday or a day which is a bank holiday under the Banking and Financial Dealings Act 1971 (c 80) in the part of the United Kingdom in which the person is when he makes the disclosure.

(8) References to a prohibited act are to an act mentioned in section 327(1), 328(1) or 329(1) (as the case may be).

(9) A nominated officer is a person nominated to receive disclosures under section 338.

(10) Subsections (1) to (4) apply for the purposes of this Part.

336 Nominated officer: consent

(1) A nominated officer must not give the appropriate consent to the doing of a prohibited act unless the condition in subsection (2), the condition in subsection (3) or the condition in subsection (4) is satisfied.

(2) The condition is that–

    (a) he makes a disclosure that property is criminal property to a person authorised for the purposes of this Part by the Director General of SOCA, and

    (b) such a person gives consent to the doing of the act.

(3) The condition is that–

    (a) he makes a disclosure that property is criminal property to a person authorised for the purposes of this Part by the Director General of SOCA, and

    (b) before the end of the notice period he does not receive notice from such a person that consent to the doing of the act is refused.

(4) The condition is that–

    (a) he makes a disclosure that property is criminal property to a person authorised for the purposes of this Part by the Director General of SOCA,

    (b) before the end of the notice period he receives notice from such a person that consent to the doing of the act is refused, and

    (c) the moratorium period has expired.

(5) A person who is a nominated officer commits an offence if–

    (a) he gives consent to a prohibited act in circumstances where none of the conditions in subsections (2), (3) and (4) is satisfied, and

    (b) he knows or suspects that the act is a prohibited act.

(6) A person guilty of such an offence is liable–

    (a) on summary conviction, to imprisonment for a term not exceeding six months or to a fine not exceeding the statutory maximum or to both, or

    (b) on conviction on indictment, to imprisonment for a term not exceeding five years or to a fine or to both.

(7) The notice period is the period of seven working days starting with the first working day after the nominated officer makes the disclosure.

(8) The moratorium period is the period of 31 days starting with the day on which the nominated officer is given notice that consent to the doing of the act is refused.

(9) A working day is a day other than a Saturday, a Sunday, Christmas Day, Good Friday or a day which is a bank holiday under the Banking and Financial Dealings Act 1971 (c 80) in the part of the United Kingdom in which the nominated officer is when he gives the appropriate consent.

(10) References to a prohibited act are to an act mentioned in section 327(1), 328(1) or 329(1) (as the case may be).

(11) A nominated officer is a person nominated to receive disclosures under section 338.

Disclosures

337 Protected disclosures

(1) A disclosure which satisfies the following three conditions is not to be taken to breach any restriction on the disclosure of information (however imposed).

(2) The first condition is that the information or other matter disclosed came to the person making the disclosure (the discloser) in the course of his trade, profession, business or employment.

(3) The second condition is that the information or other matter–

(a) causes the discloser to know or suspect, or
(b) gives him reasonable grounds for knowing or suspecting,

that another person is engaged in money laundering.

(4) The third condition is that the disclosure is made to a constable, a customs officer or a nominated officer as soon as is practicable after the information or other matter comes to the discloser.

(4A) Where a disclosure consists of a disclosure protected under subsection (1) and a disclosure of either or both of–

(a) the identity of the other person mentioned in subsection (3), and
(b) the whereabouts of property forming the subject-matter of the money laundering that the discloser knows or suspects, or has reasonable grounds for knowing or suspecting, that other person to be engaged in,

the disclosure of the thing mentioned in paragraph (a) or (b) (as well as the disclosure protected under subsection (1)) is not to be taken to breach any restriction on the disclosure of information (however imposed).

(5) A disclosure to a nominated officer is a disclosure which–

(a) is made to a person nominated by the discloser's employer to receive disclosures under section 330 or this section, and
(b) is made in the course of the discloser's employment.

338 Authorised disclosures

(1) For the purposes of this Part a disclosure is authorised if–

(a) it is a disclosure to a constable, a customs officer or a nominated officer by the alleged offender that property is criminal property,
(b) ... and
(c) the first, second or third condition set out below is satisfied.

(2) The first condition is that the disclosure is made before the alleged offender does the prohibited act.

(2A) The second condition is that–

    (a)   the disclosure is made while the alleged offender is doing the prohibited act,

    (b)   he began to do the act at a time when, because he did not then know or suspect that the property constituted or represented a person's benefit from criminal conduct, the act was not a prohibited act, and

    (c)   the disclosure is made on his own initiative and as soon as is practicable after he first knows or suspects that the property constitutes or represents a person's benefit from criminal conduct.

(3)   The third condition is that–

    (a)   the disclosure is made after the alleged offender does the prohibited act,

    (b)   he has a reasonable excuse for his failure to make the disclosure before he did the act, and

    (c)   the disclosure is made on his own initiative and as soon as it is practicable for him to make it.

(4)   An authorised disclosure is not to be taken to breach any restriction on the disclosure of information (however imposed).

(5)   A disclosure to a nominated officer is a disclosure which–

    (a)   is made to a person nominated by the alleged offender's employer to receive authorised disclosures, and

    (b)   is made in the course of the alleged offender's employment . . ..

(6)   References to the prohibited act are to an act mentioned in section 327(1), 328(1) or 329(1) (as the case may be).

339   Form and manner of disclosures

(1)   The Secretary of State may by order prescribe the form and manner in which a disclosure under section 330, 331, 332 or 338 must be made.

(1A) A person commits an offence if he makes a disclosure under section 330, 331, 332 or 338 otherwise than in the form prescribed under subsection (1) or otherwise than in the manner so prescribed.

(1B) But a person does not commit an offence under subsection (1A) if he has a reasonable excuse for making the disclosure otherwise than in the form prescribed under subsection (1) or (as the case may be) otherwise than in the manner so prescribed.

(2)   The power under subsection (1) to prescribe the form in which a disclosure must be made includes power to provide for the form to include a request to a person making a disclosure that the person provide information specified or described in the form if he has not provided it in making the disclosure.

(3)   Where under subsection (2) a request is included in a form prescribed under subsection (1), the form must–

    (a)   state that there is no obligation to comply with the request, and

    (b)   explain the protection conferred by subsection (4) on a person who complies with the request.

(4)   A disclosure made in pursuance of a request under subsection (2) is not to be taken to breach any restriction on the disclosure of information (however imposed).

(5)   . . .

(6) . . .

(7) Subsection (2) does not apply to a disclosure made to a nominated officer.

339ZA Disclosures to SOCA

Where a disclosure is made under this Part to a constable or an officer of Revenue and Customs, the constable or officer of Revenue and Customs must disclose it in full to a person authorised for the purposes of this Part by the Director General of the Serious Organised Crime Agency as soon as practicable after it has been made.

Threshold amounts

339A Threshold amounts

(1) This section applies for the purposes of sections 327(2C), 328(5) and 329(2C).

(2) The threshold amount for acts done by a deposit-taking body in operating an account is £250 unless a higher amount is specified under the following provisions of this section (in which event it is that higher amount).

(3) An officer of Revenue and Customs, or a constable, may specify the threshold amount for acts done by a deposit-taking body in operating an account–

   (a) when he gives consent, or gives notice refusing consent, to the deposit-taking body's doing of an act mentioned in section 327(1), 328(1) or 329(1) in opening, or operating, the account or a related account, or

   (b) on a request from the deposit-taking body.

(4) Where the threshold amount for acts done in operating an account is specified under subsection (3) or this subsection, an officer of Revenue and Customs, or a constable, may vary the amount (whether on a request from the deposit-taking body or otherwise) by specifying a different amount.

(5) Different threshold amounts may be specified under subsections (3) and (4) for different acts done in operating the same account.

(6) The amount specified under subsection (3) or (4) as the threshold amount for acts done in operating an account must, when specified, not be less than the amount specified in subsection (2).

(7) The Secretary of State may by order vary the amount for the time being specified in subsection (2).

(8) For the purposes of this section, an account is related to another if each is maintained with the same deposit-taking body and there is a person who, in relation to each account, is the person or one of the persons entitled to instruct the body as respects the operation of the account.

Interpretation

340 Interpretation

(1) This section applies for the purposes of this Part.

(2) Criminal conduct is conduct which–

   (a) constitutes an offence in any part of the United Kingdom, or

   (b) would constitute an offence in any part of the United Kingdom if it occurred there.

(3) Property is criminal property if–

    (a) it constitutes a person's benefit from criminal conduct or it represents such a benefit (in whole or part and whether directly or indirectly), and

    (b) the alleged offender knows or suspects that it constitutes or represents such a benefit.

(4) It is immaterial–

    (a) who carried out the conduct;

    (b) who benefited from it;

    (c) whether the conduct occurred before or after the passing of this Act.

(5) A person benefits from conduct if he obtains property as a result of or in connection with the conduct.

(6) If a person obtains a pecuniary advantage as a result of or in connection with conduct, he is to be taken to obtain as a result of or in connection with the conduct a sum of money equal to the value of the pecuniary advantage.

(7) References to property or a pecuniary advantage obtained in connection with conduct include references to property or a pecuniary advantage obtained in both that connection and some other.

(8) If a person benefits from conduct his benefit is the property obtained as a result of or in connection with the conduct.

(9) Property is all property wherever situated and includes–

    (a) money;

    (b) all forms of property, real or personal, heritable or moveable;

    (c) things in action and other intangible or incorporeal property.

(10) The following rules apply in relation to property–

    (a) property is obtained by a person if he obtains an interest in it;

    (b) references to an interest, in relation to land in England and Wales or Northern Ireland, are to any legal estate or equitable interest or power;

    (c) references to an interest, in relation to land in Scotland, are to any estate, interest, servitude or other heritable right in or over land, including a heritable security;

    (d) references to an interest, in relation to property other than land, include references to a right (including a right to possession).

(11) Money laundering is an act which–

    (a) constitutes an offence under section 327, 328 or 329,

    (b) constitutes an attempt, conspiracy or incitement to commit an offence specified in paragraph (a),

    (c) constitutes aiding, abetting, counselling or procuring the commission of an offence specified in paragraph (a), or

    (d) would constitute an offence specified in paragraph (a), (b) or (c) if done in the United Kingdom.

(12) For the purposes of a disclosure to a nominated officer–

    (a) references to a person's employer include any body, association or organisation (including a voluntary organisation) in connection with whose activities the person exercises a function (whether or not for gain or reward), and

    (b) references to employment must be construed accordingly.

(13) References to a constable include references to a person authorised for the purposes of this Part by the Director General of SOCA.

(14) 'Deposit-taking body' means–

(a) a business which engages in the activity of accepting deposits, or

(b) the National Savings Bank.

PART 8   INVESTIGATIONS

Chapter 1
Introduction

341   Investigations

(1) For the purposes of this Part a confiscation investigation is an investigation into–

(a) whether a person has benefited from his criminal conduct, or

(b) the extent or whereabouts of his benefit from his criminal conduct.

(2) For the purposes of this Part a civil recovery investigation is an investigation into–

(a) whether property is recoverable property or associated property,

(b) who holds the property, or

(c) its extent or whereabouts.

(3) But an investigation is not a civil recovery investigation if–

(a) proceedings for a recovery order have been started in respect of the property in question,

(b) an interim receiving order applies to the property in question,

(c) an interim administration order applies to the property in question, or

(d) the property in question is detained under section 295.

(3A) For the purposes of this Part a detained cash investigation is–

(a) an investigation for the purposes of Chapter 3 of Part 5 into the derivation of cash detained under section 295 or a part of such cash, or

(b) an investigation for the purposes of Chapter 3 of Part 5 into whether cash detained under section 295, or a part of such cash, is intended by any person to be used in unlawful conduct.

(4) For the purposes of this Part a money laundering investigation is an investigation into whether a person has committed a money laundering offence.

342   Offences of prejudicing investigation

(1) This section applies if a person knows or suspects that an appropriate officer or (in Scotland) a proper person is acting (or proposing to act) in connection with a confiscation investigation, a civil recovery investigation, a detained cash investigation or a money laundering investigation which is being or is about to be conducted.

(2) The person commits an offence if–

(a) he makes a disclosure which is likely to prejudice the investigation, or

(b) he falsifies, conceals, destroys or otherwise disposes of, or causes or permits the falsification, concealment, destruction or disposal of, documents which are relevant to the investigation.

(3) A person does not commit an offence under subsection (2)(a) if–

    (a) he does not know or suspect that the disclosure is likely to prejudice the investigation,

    (b) the disclosure is made in the exercise of a function under this Act or any other enactment relating to criminal conduct or benefit from criminal conduct or in compliance with a requirement imposed under or by virtue of this Act,

    (ba) the disclosure is of a matter within section 333A(2) or (3)(a) (money laundering: tipping off) and the information on which the disclosure is based came to the person in the course of a business in the regulated sector, or

    (c) he is a professional legal adviser and the disclosure falls within subsection (4).

(4) A disclosure falls within this subsection if it is a disclosure–

    (a) to (or to a representative of) a client of the professional legal adviser in connection with the giving by the adviser of legal advice to the client, or

    (b) to any person in connection with legal proceedings or contemplated legal proceedings.

(5) But a disclosure does not fall within subsection (4) if it is made with the intention of furthering a criminal purpose.

(6) A person does not commit an offence under subsection (2)(b) if–

    (a) he does not know or suspect that the documents are relevant to the investigation, or

    (b) he does not intend to conceal any facts disclosed by the documents from any appropriate officer or (in Scotland) proper person carrying out the investigation.

(7) A person guilty of an offence under subsection (2) is liable–

    (a) on summary conviction, to imprisonment for a term not exceeding six months or to a fine not exceeding the statutory maximum or to both, or

    (b) on conviction on indictment, to imprisonment for a term not exceeding five years or to a fine or to both.

(8) For the purposes of this section–

    (a) 'appropriate officer' must be construed in accordance with section 378;

    (b) 'proper person' must be construed in accordance with section 412;

    (c) Schedule 9 has effect for determining what is a business in the regulated sector.

A2

Extracts from the Terrorism Act 2000 (as amended at August 2008)

Offences

15 Fund-raising

(1) A person commits an offence if he–

    (a) invites another to provide money or other property, and

    (b) intends that it should be used, or has reasonable cause to suspect that it may be used, for the purposes of terrorism.

(2) A person commits an offence if he–

    (a) receives money or other property, and

    (b) intends that it should be used, or has reasonable cause to suspect that it may be used, for the purposes of terrorism.

(3) A person commits an offence if he–

    (a) provides money or other property, and

    (b) knows or has reasonable cause to suspect that it will or may be used for the purposes of terrorism.

(4) In this section a reference to the provision of money or other property is a reference to its being given, lent or otherwise made available, whether or not for consideration.

16 Use and possession

(1) A person commits an offence if he uses money or other property for the purposes of terrorism.

(2) A person commits an offence if he–

    (a) possesses money or other property, and

    (b) intends that it should be used, or has reasonable cause to suspect that it may be used, for the purposes of terrorism.

17 Funding arrangements

A person commits an offence if–

    (a) he enters into or becomes concerned in an arrangement as a result of which money or other property is made available or is to be made available to another, and

(b) he knows or has reasonable cause to suspect that it will or may be used for the purposes of terrorism.

18   Money laundering

(1) A person commits an offence if he enters into or becomes concerned in an arrangement which facilitates the retention or control by or on behalf of another person of terrorist property–

    (a) by concealment,
    (b) by removal from the jurisdiction,
    (c) by transfer to nominees, or
    (d) in any other way.

(2) It is a defence for a person charged with an offence under subsection (1) to prove that he did not know and had no reasonable cause to suspect that the arrangement related to terrorist property.

. . .

21A   Failure to disclose: regulated sector

(1) A person commits an offence if each of the following three conditions is satisfied.

(2) The first condition is that he–

    (a) knows or suspects, or
    (b) has reasonable grounds for knowing or suspecting,
that another person has committed [or attempted to commit] an offence under any of sections 15 to 18.

(3) The second condition is that the information or other matter–

    (a) on which his knowledge or suspicion is based, or
    (b) which gives reasonable grounds for such knowledge or suspicion,
came to him in the course of a business in the regulated sector.

(4) The third condition is that he does not disclose the information or other matter to a constable or a nominated officer as soon as is practicable after it comes to him.

(5) But a person does not commit an offence under this section if–

    (a) he has a reasonable excuse for not disclosing the information or other matter;
    (b) he is a professional legal adviser or relevant professional adviser and the information or other matter came to him in privileged circumstances; or
    (c) subsection (5A) applies to him.

(5A) This subsection applies to a person if–

    (a) the person is employed by, or is in partnership with, a professional legal adviser or relevant professional adviser to provide the adviser with assistance or support,
    (b) the information or other matter comes to the person in connection with the provision of such assistance or support, and
    (c) the information or other matter came to the adviser in privileged circumstances.

(6)   In deciding whether a person committed an offence under this section the court must consider whether he followed any relevant guidance which was at the time concerned–

(a)   issued by a supervisory authority or any other appropriate body,

(b)   approved by the Treasury, and

(c)   published in a manner it approved as appropriate in its opinion to bring the guidance to the attention of persons likely to be affected by it.

(7)   A disclosure to a nominated officer is a disclosure which–

(a)   is made to a person nominated by the alleged offender's employer to receive disclosures under this section, and

(b)   is made in the course of the alleged offender's employment and in accordance with the procedure established by the employer for the purpose.

(8)   Information or other matter comes to a professional legal adviser or relevant professional adviser in privileged circumstances if it is communicated or given to him–

(a)   by (or by a representative of) a client of his in connection with the giving by the adviser of legal advice to the client,

(b)   by (or by a representative of) a person seeking legal advice from the adviser, or

(c)   by a person in connection with legal proceedings or contemplated legal proceedings.

(9)   But subsection (8) does not apply to information or other matter which is communicated or given with a view to furthering a criminal purpose.

(10) Schedule 3A has effect for the purpose of determining what is–

(a)   a business in the regulated sector;

(b)   a supervisory authority.

(11) For the purposes of subsection (2) a person is to be taken to have committed an offence there mentioned if–

(a)   he has taken an action or been in possession of a thing, and

(b)   he would have committed the offence if he had been in the United Kingdom at the time when he took the action or was in possession of the thing.

(12) A person guilty of an offence under this section is liable–

(a)   on conviction on indictment, to imprisonment for a term not exceeding five years or to a fine or to both;

(b)   on summary conviction, to imprisonment for a term not exceeding six months or to a fine not exceeding the statutory maximum or to both.

(13) An appropriate body is any body which regulates or is representative of any trade, profession, business or employment carried on by the alleged offender.

(14) The reference to a constable includes a reference to a member of the staff of the Serious Organised Crime Agency authorised for the purposes of this section by the Director General of that Agency.

(15) In this section 'relevant professional adviser' means an accountant, auditor or tax adviser who is a member of a professional body which is established for accountants, auditors or tax advisers (as the case may be) and which makes provision for–

(a) testing the competence of those seeking admission to membership of such a body as a condition for such admission; and

(b) imposing and maintaining professional and ethical standards for its members, as well as imposing sanctions for non-compliance with those standards.

Money Laundering Regulations 2007, SI 2007/2157

1 Citation, commencement etc

(1) These Regulations may be cited as the Money Laundering Regulations 2007 and come into force on 15th December 2007.
(2) These Regulations are prescribed for the purposes of sections 168(4)(b) (appointment of persons to carry out investigations in particular cases) and 402(1)(b) (power of the Authority to institute proceedings for certain other offences) of the 2000 Act.
(3) The Money Laundering Regulations 2003 are revoked.

2 Interpretation

(1) In these Regulations–

'the 2000 Act' means the Financial Services and Markets Act 2000;
'Annex I financial institution' has the meaning given by regulation 22(1);
'auditor', except in regulation 17(2)(c) and (d), has the meaning given by regulation 3(4) and (5);
'authorised person' means a person who is authorised for the purposes of the 2000 Act;
'the Authority' means the Financial Services Authority;
'the banking consolidation directive' means Directive 2006/48/EC of the European Parliament and of the Council of 14th June 2006 relating to the taking up and pursuit of the business of credit institutions;
'beneficial owner' has the meaning given by regulation 6;
'business relationship' means a business, professional or commercial relationship between a relevant person and a customer, which is expected by the relevant person, at the time when contact is established, to have an element of duration;
'cash' means notes, coins or travellers' cheques in any currency;
'casino' has the meaning given by regulation 3(13);
'the Commissioners' means the Commissioners for Her Majesty's Revenue and Customs;
'consumer credit financial institution' has the meaning given by regulation 22(1);
'credit institution' has the meaning given by regulation 3(2);
'customer due diligence measures' has the meaning given by regulation 5;

'DETI' means the Department of Enterprise, Trade and Investment in Northern Ireland;

'the electronic money directive' means Directive 2000/46/EC of the European Parliament and of the Council of 18th September 2000 on the taking up, pursuit and prudential supervision of the business of electronic money institutions;

'estate agent' has the meaning given by regulation 3(11);

'external accountant' has the meaning given by regulation 3(7);

'financial institution' has the meaning given by regulation 3(3);

'firm' means any entity, whether or not a legal person, that is not an individual and includes a body corporate and a partnership or other unincorporated association;

'high value dealer' has the meaning given by regulation 3(12);

'the implementing measures directive' means Commission Directive 2006/70/EC of 1st August 2006 laying down implementing measures for the money laundering directive;

'independent legal professional' has the meaning given by regulation 3(9);

'insolvency practitioner', except in regulation 17(2)(c) and (d), has the meaning given by regulation 3(6);

'the life assurance consolidation directive' means Directive 2002/83/EC of the European Parliament and of the Council of 5th November 2002 concerning life assurance;

'local weights and measures authority' has the meaning given by section 69 of the Weights and Measures Act 1985 (local weights and measures authorities);

'the markets in financial instruments directive' means Directive 2004/39/EC of the European Parliament and of the Council of 12th April 2004 on markets in financial instruments;

'money laundering' means an act which falls within section 340(11) of the Proceeds of Crime Act 2002;

'the money laundering directive' means Directive 2005/60/EC of the European Parliament and of the Council of 26th October 2005 on the prevention of the use of the financial system for the purpose of money laundering and terrorist financing;

'money service business' means an undertaking which by way of business operates a currency exchange office, transmits money (or any representations of monetary value) by any means or cashes cheques which are made payable to customers;

'nominated officer' means a person who is nominated to receive disclosures under Part 7 of the Proceeds of Crime Act 2002 (money laundering) or Part 3 of the Terrorism Act 2000 (terrorist property);

'non-EEA state' means a state that is not an EEA state;

'notice' means a notice in writing;

'occasional transaction' means a transaction (carried out other than as part of a business relationship) amounting to 15,000 euro or more, whether the transaction is carried out in a single operation or several operations which appear to be linked;

'the OFT' means the Office of Fair Trading;

'ongoing monitoring' has the meaning given by regulation 8(2);

'regulated market'–

(a) within the EEA, has the meaning given by point 14 of Article 4(1) of the markets in financial instruments directive; and

(b) outside the EEA, means a regulated financial market which subjects companies whose securities are admitted to trading to disclosure obligations which are contained in international standards and are equivalent to the specified disclosure obligations;

'relevant person' means a person to whom, in accordance with regulations 3 and 4, these Regulations apply;

'the specified disclosure obligations' means disclosure requirements consistent with–

(a) Article 6(1) to (4) of Directive 2003/6/EC of the European Parliament and of the Council of 28th January 2003 on insider dealing and market manipulation;

(b) Articles 3, 5, 7, 8, 10, 14 and 16 of Directive 2003/71/EC of the European Parliament and of the Council of 4th November 2003 on the prospectuses to be published when securities are offered to the public or admitted to trading;

(c) Articles 4 to 6, 14, 16 to 19 and 30 of Directive 2004/109/EC of the European Parliament and of the Council of 15th December 2004 relating to the harmonisation of transparency requirements in relation to information about issuers whose securities are admitted to trading on a regulated market; or

(d) Community legislation made under the provisions mentioned in sub-paragraphs (a) to (c);

'supervisory authority' in relation to any relevant person means the supervisory authority specified for such a person by regulation 23;

'tax adviser' (except in regulation 11(3)) has the meaning given by regulation 3(8);

'terrorist financing' means an offence under–

(a) section 15 (fund-raising), 16 (use and possession), 17 (funding arrangements), 18 (money laundering) or 63 (terrorist finance: jurisdiction) of the Terrorism Act 2000;

(b) paragraph 7(2) or (3) of Schedule 3 to the Anti-Terrorism, Crime and Security Act 2001 (freezing orders);

(c) article 7, 8 or 10 of the Terrorism (United Nations Measures) Order 2006; or

(d) article 7, 8 or 10 of the Al-Qaida and Taliban (United Nations Measures) Order 2006;

'trust or company service provider' has the meaning given by regulation 3(10).

(2) In these Regulations, references to amounts in euro include references to equivalent amounts in another currency.

(3) Unless otherwise defined, expressions used in these Regulations and the money laundering directive have the same meaning as in the money laundering directive and expressions used in these Regulations and in the implementing measures directive have the same meaning as in the implementing measures directive.

3 Application of the Regulations

(1) Subject to regulation 4, these Regulations apply to the following persons acting in the course of business carried on by them in the United Kingdom ('relevant persons')–

(a) credit institutions;
(b) financial institutions;
(c) auditors, insolvency practitioners, external accountants and tax advisers;
(d) independent legal professionals;
(e) trust or company service providers;
(f) estate agents;
(g) high value dealers;
(h) casinos.

(2) 'Credit institution' means–

(a) a credit institution as defined in Article 4(1)(a) of the banking consolidation directive; or
(b) a branch (within the meaning of Article 4(3) of that directive) located in an EEA state of an institution falling within sub-paragraph (a) (or an equivalent institution whose head office is located in a non-EEA state) wherever its head office is located,

when it accepts deposits or other repayable funds from the public or grants credits for its own account (within the meaning of the banking consolidation directive).

(3) 'Financial institution' means–

(a) an undertaking, including a money service business, when it carries out one or more of the activities listed in points 2 to 12 and 14 of Annex 1 to the banking consolidation directive (the relevant text of which is set out in Schedule 1 to these Regulations), other than–

(i) a credit institution;
(ii) an undertaking whose only listed activity is trading for own account in one or more of the products listed in point 7 of Annex 1 to the banking consolidation directive where the undertaking does not have a customer,

and, for this purpose, 'customer' means a third party which is not a member of the same group as the undertaking;

(b) an insurance company duly authorised in accordance with the life assurance consolidation directive, when it carries out activities covered by that directive;
(c) a person whose regular occupation or business is the provision to other persons of an investment service or the performance of an investment activity on a professional basis, when providing or performing investment services or activities (within the meaning of the markets in financial instruments directive), other than a person falling within Article 2 of that directive;
(d) a collective investment undertaking, when marketing or otherwise offering its units or shares;
(e) an insurance intermediary as defined in Article 2(5) of Directive 2002/92/EC of the European Parliament and of the Council of 9th December 2002 on insurance mediation, with the exception of a tied insurance intermediary as mentioned in Article 2(7) of that Directive, when it acts in respect of contracts of long-term insurance within the meaning given by article 3(1) of, and Part II of Schedule 1 to, the Financial Services and Markets Act 2000 (Regulated Activities) Order 2001;

(f) a branch located in an EEA state of a person referred to in sub-paragraphs (a) to (e) (or an equivalent person whose head office is located in a non-EEA state), wherever its head office is located, when carrying out any activity mentioned in sub-paragraphs (a) to (e);

(g) the National Savings Bank;

(h) the Director of Savings, when money is raised under the auspices of the Director under the National Loans Act 1968.

(4) 'Auditor' means any firm or individual who is a statutory auditor within the meaning of Part 42 of the Companies Act 2006 (statutory auditors), when carrying out statutory audit work within the meaning of section 1210 of that Act.

(5) Before the entry into force of Part 42 of the Companies Act 2006 the reference in paragraph (4) to–

(a) a person who is a statutory auditor shall be treated as a reference to a person who is eligible for appointment as a company auditor under section 25 of the Companies Act 1989 (eligibility for appointment) or article 28 of the Companies (Northern Ireland) Order 1990; and

(b) the carrying out of statutory audit work shall be treated as a reference to the provision of audit services.

(6) 'Insolvency practitioner' means any person who acts as an insolvency practitioner within the meaning of section 388 of the Insolvency Act 1986 (meaning of 'act as insolvency practitioner') or article 3 of the Insolvency (Northern Ireland) Order 1989.

(7) 'External accountant' means a firm or sole practitioner who by way of business provides accountancy services to other persons, when providing such services.

(8 'Tax adviser' means a firm or sole practitioner who by way of business provides advice about the tax affairs of other persons, when providing such services.

(9) 'Independent legal professional' means a firm or sole practitioner who by way of business provides legal or notarial services to other persons, when participating in financial or real property transactions concerning–

(a) the buying and selling of real property or business entities;

(b) the managing of client money, securities or other assets;

(c) the opening or management of bank, savings or securities accounts;

(d) the organisation of contributions necessary for the creation, operation or management of companies; or

(e) the creation, operation or management of trusts, companies or similar structures,

and, for this purpose, a person participates in a transaction by assisting in the planning or execution of the transaction or otherwise acting for or on behalf of a client in the transaction.

(10) 'Trust or company service provider' means a firm or sole practitioner who by way of business provides any of the following services to other persons–

(a) forming companies or other legal persons;

(b) acting, or arranging for another person to act–

(i) as a director or secretary of a company;

(ii) as a partner of a partnership; or

(iii) in a similar position in relation to other legal persons;

    (c)   providing a registered office, business address, correspondence or administrative address or other related services for a company, partnership or any other legal person or arrangement;

    (d)   acting, or arranging for another person to act, as–

        (i)   a trustee of an express trust or similar legal arrangement; or

        (ii)   a nominee shareholder for a person other than a company whose securities are listed on a regulated market,

    when providing such services.

(11)   'Estate agent' means–

    (a)   a firm; or

    (b)   sole practitioner,

who, or whose employees, carry out estate agency work (within the meaning given by section 1 of the Estate Agents Act 1979 (estate agency work)), when in the course of carrying out such work.

(12)   'High value dealer' means a firm or sole trader who by way of business trades in goods (including an auctioneer dealing in goods), when he receives, in respect of any transaction, a payment or payments in cash of at least 15,000 euros in total, whether the transaction is executed in a single operation or in several operations which appear to be linked.

(13)   'Casino' means the holder of a casino operating licence and, for this purpose, a 'casino operating licence' has the meaning given by section 65(2) of the Gambling Act 2005 (nature of licence).

(14)   In the application of this regulation to Scotland, for 'real property' in paragraph (9) substitute 'heritable property'.

4   Exclusions

(1)   These Regulations do not apply to the following persons when carrying out any of the following activities–

    (a)   a society registered under the Industrial and Provident Societies Act 1965, when it–

        (i)   issues withdrawable share capital within the limit set by section 6 of that Act (maximum shareholding in society); or

        (ii)   accepts deposits from the public within the limit set by section 7(3) of that Act (carrying on of banking by societies);

    (b)   a society registered under the Industrial and Provident Societies Act (Northern Ireland) 1969, when it–

        (i)   issues withdrawable share capital within the limit set by section 6 of that Act (maximum shareholding in society); or

        (ii)   accepts deposits from the public within the limit set by section 7(3) of that Act (carrying on of banking by societies);

    (c)   a person who is (or falls within a class of persons) specified in any of paragraphs 2 to 23, 25 to 38 or 40 to 49 of the Schedule to the Financial Services and Markets Act 2000 (Exemption) Order 2001, when carrying out any activity in respect of which he is exempt;

    (d)   a person who was an exempted person for the purposes of section 45 of the Financial Services Act 1986 (miscellaneous exemptions) immediately before its repeal, when exercising the functions specified in that section;

(e)   a person whose main activity is that of a high value dealer, when he engages in financial activity on an occasional or very limited basis as set out in paragraph 1 of Schedule 2 to these Regulations; or

(f)   a person, when he prepares a home information pack or a document or information for inclusion in a home information pack.

(2)   These Regulations do not apply to a person who falls within regulation 3 solely as a result of his engaging in financial activity on an occasional or very limited basis as set out in paragraph 1 of Schedule 2 to these Regulations.

(3)   Parts 2 to 5 of these Regulations do not apply to–

(a)   the Auditor General for Scotland;

(b)   the Auditor General for Wales;

(c)   the Bank of England;

(d)   the Comptroller and Auditor General;

(e)   the Comptroller and Auditor General for Northern Ireland;

(f)   the Official Solicitor to the Supreme Court, when acting as trustee in his official capacity;

(g)   the Treasury Solicitor.

(4)   In paragraph (1)(f), 'home information pack' has the same meaning as in Part 5 of the Housing Act 2004 (home information packs).

Part 2
Customer Due Diligence

5 Meaning of customer due diligence measures

'Customer due diligence measures' means–

(a)   identifying the customer and verifying the customer's identity on the basis of documents, data or information obtained from a reliable and independent source;

(b)   identifying, where there is a beneficial owner who is not the customer, the beneficial owner and taking adequate measures, on a risk-sensitive basis, to verify his identity so that the relevant person is satisfied that he knows who the beneficial owner is, including, in the case of a legal person, trust or similar legal arrangement, measures to understand the ownership and control structure of the person, trust or arrangement; and

(c)   obtaining information on the purpose and intended nature of the business relationship.

6 Meaning of beneficial owner

(1)   In the case of a body corporate, 'beneficial owner' means any individual who–

(a)   as respects any body other than a company whose securities are listed on a regulated market, ultimately owns or controls (whether through direct or indirect ownership or control, including through bearer share holdings) more than 25% of the shares or voting rights in the body; or

(b)   as respects any body corporate, otherwise exercises control over the management of the body.

(2)   In the case of a partnership (other than a limited liability partnership), 'beneficial owner' means any individual who–

(a) ultimately is entitled to or controls (whether the entitlement or control is direct or indirect) more than a 25% share of the capital or profits of the partnership or more than 25% of the voting rights in the partnership; or

(b) otherwise exercises control over the management of the partnership.

(3) In the case of a trust, 'beneficial owner' means–

(a) any individual who is entitled to a specified interest in at least 25% of the capital of the trust property;

(b) as respects any trust other than one which is set up or operates entirely for the benefit of individuals falling within sub-paragraph (a), the class of persons in whose main interest the trust is set up or operates;

(c) any individual who has control over the trust.

(4) In paragraph (3)–

'specified interest' means a vested interest which is–

(a) in possession or in remainder or reversion (or, in Scotland, in fee); and

(b) defeasible or indefeasible;

'control' means a power (whether exercisable alone, jointly with another person or with the consent of another person) under the trust instrument or by law to–

(a) dispose of, advance, lend, invest, pay or apply trust property;

(b) vary the trust;

(c) add or remove a person as a beneficiary or to or from a class of beneficiaries;

(d) appoint or remove trustees;

(e) direct, withhold consent to or veto the exercise of a power such as is mentioned in sub-paragraph (a), (b), (c) or (d).

(5) For the purposes of paragraph (3)–

(a) where an individual is the beneficial owner of a body corporate which is entitled to a specified interest in the capital of the trust property or which has control over the trust, the individual is to be regarded as entitled to the interest or having control over the trust; and

(b) an individual does not have control solely as a result of–

(i) his consent being required in accordance with section 32(1)(c) of the Trustee Act 1925 (power of advancement);

(ii) any discretion delegated to him under section 34 of the Pensions Act 1995 (power of investment and delegation);

(iii) the power to give a direction conferred on him by section 19(2) of the Trusts of Land and Appointment of Trustees Act 1996 (appointment and retirement of trustee at instance of beneficiaries); or

(iv) the power exercisable collectively at common law to vary or extinguish a trust where the beneficiaries under the trust are of full age and capacity and (taken together) absolutely entitled to the property subject to the trust (or, in Scotland, have a full and unqualified right to the fee).

(6) In the case of a legal entity or legal arrangement which does not fall within paragraph (1), (2) or (3), 'beneficial owner' means–

(a) where the individuals who benefit from the entity or arrangement have been determined, any individual who benefits from at least 25% of the property of the entity or arrangement;

(b) where the individuals who benefit from the entity or arrangement have yet to be determined, the class of persons in whose main interest the entity or arrangement is set up or operates;

(c) any individual who exercises control over at least 25% of the property of the entity or arrangement.

(7) For the purposes of paragraph (6), where an individual is the beneficial owner of a body corporate which benefits from or exercises control over the property of the entity or arrangement, the individual is to be regarded as benefiting from or exercising control over the property of the entity or arrangement.

(8) In the case of an estate of a deceased person in the course of administration, 'beneficial owner' means–

(a) in England and Wales and Northern Ireland, the executor, original or by representation, or administrator for the time being of a deceased person;

(b) in Scotland, the executor for the purposes of the Executors (Scotland) Act 1900.

(9) In any other case, 'beneficial owner' means the individual who ultimately owns or controls the customer or on whose behalf a transaction is being conducted.

(10) In this regulation–

'arrangement', 'entity' and 'trust' means an arrangement, entity or trust which administers and distributes funds;

'limited liability partnership' has the meaning given by the Limited Liability Partnerships Act 2000.

7 Application of customer due diligence measures

(1) Subject to regulations 9, 10, 12, 13, 14, 16(4) and 17, a relevant person must apply customer due diligence measures when he–

(a) establishes a business relationship;

(b) carries out an occasional transaction;

(c) suspects money laundering or terrorist financing;

(d) doubts the veracity or adequacy of documents, data or information previously obtained for the purposes of identification or verification.

(2) Subject to regulation 16(4), a relevant person must also apply customer due diligence measures at other appropriate times to existing customers on a risk-sensitive basis.

(3) A relevant person must–

(a) determine the extent of customer due diligence measures on a risk-sensitive basis depending on the type of customer, business relationship, product or transaction; and

(b) be able to demonstrate to his supervisory authority that the extent of the measures is appropriate in view of the risks of money laundering and terrorist financing.

(4) Where–

(a) a relevant person is required to apply customer due diligence measures in the case of a trust, legal entity (other than a body corporate) or a legal arrangement (other than a trust); and

(b)   the class of persons in whose main interest the trust, entity or arrangement is set up or operates is identified as a beneficial owner,

the relevant person is not required to identify all the members of the class.

(5)   Paragraph (3)(b) does not apply to the National Savings Bank or the Director of Savings.

8   Ongoing monitoring

(1)   A relevant person must conduct ongoing monitoring of a business relationship.
(2)   'Ongoing monitoring' of a business relationship means–

(a)   scrutiny of transactions undertaken throughout the course of the relationship (including, where necessary, the source of funds) to ensure that the transactions are consistent with the relevant person's knowledge of the customer, his business and risk profile; and
(b)   keeping the documents, data or information obtained for the purpose of applying customer due diligence measures up-to-date.

(3)   Regulation 7(3) applies to the duty to conduct ongoing monitoring under paragraph (1) as it applies to customer due diligence measures.

9   Timing of verification

(1)   This regulation applies in respect of the duty under regulation 7(1)(a) and (b) to apply the customer due diligence measures referred to in regulation 5(a) and (b).
(2)   Subject to paragraphs (3) to (5) and regulation 10, a relevant person must verify the identity of the customer (and any beneficial owner) before the establishment of a business relationship or the carrying out of an occasional transaction.
(3)   Such verification may be completed during the establishment of a business relationship if–

(a)   this is necessary not to interrupt the normal conduct of business; and
(b)   there is little risk of money laundering or terrorist financing occurring,

provided that the verification is completed as soon as practicable after contact is first established.

(4)   The verification of the identity of the beneficiary under a life insurance policy may take place after the business relationship has been established provided that it takes place at or before the time of payout or at or before the time the beneficiary exercises a right vested under the policy.
(5)   The verification of the identity of a bank account holder may take place after the bank account has been opened provided that there are adequate safeguards in place to ensure that–

(a)   the account is not closed; and
(b)   transactions are not carried out by or on behalf of the account holder (including any payment from the account to the account holder),

before verification has been completed.

10   Casinos

(1)   A casino must establish and verify the identity of–

(a)   all customers to whom the casino makes facilities for gaming available–

    (i)   before entry to any premises where such facilities are provided; or

    (ii)   where the facilities are for remote gaming, before access is given to such facilities; or

(b)   if the specified conditions are met, all customers who, in the course of any period of 24 hours–

    (i)   purchase from, or exchange with, the casino chips with a total value of 2,000 euro or more;

    (ii)   pay the casino 2,000 euro or more for the use of gaming machines; or

    (iii) pay to, or stake with, the casino 2,000 euro or more in connection with facilities for remote gaming.

(2)   The specified conditions are–

(a)   the casino verifies the identity of each customer before or immediately after such purchase, exchange, payment or stake takes place, and

(b)   the Gambling Commission is satisfied that the casino has appropriate procedures in place to monitor and record–

    (i)   the total value of chips purchased from or exchanged with the casino;

    (ii)   the total money paid for the use of gaming machines; or

    (iii) the total money paid or staked in connection with facilities for remote gaming,

by each customer.

(3)   In this regulation–

'gaming', 'gaming machine', 'remote operating licence' and 'stake' have the meanings given by, respectively, sections 6(1) (gaming & game of chance), 235 (gaming machine), 67 (remote gambling) and 353(1) (interpretation) of the Gambling Act 2005;

'premises' means premises subject to–

(a)   a casino premises licence within the meaning of section 150(1)(a) of the Gambling Act 2005 (nature of licence); or

(b)   a converted casino premises licence within the meaning of paragraph 65 of Part 7 of Schedule 4 to the Gambling Act 2005 (Commencement No 6 and Transitional Provisions) Order 2006;

'remote gaming' means gaming provided pursuant to a remote operating licence.

11   Requirement to cease transactions etc

(1)   Where, in relation to any customer, a relevant person is unable to apply customer due diligence measures in accordance with the provisions of this Part, he–

(a)   must not carry out a transaction with or for the customer through a bank account;

(b)   must not establish a business relationship or carry out an occasional transaction with the customer;

(c)   must terminate any existing business relationship with the customer;

(d)   must consider whether he is required to make a disclosure by Part 7 of the Proceeds of Crime Act 2002 or Part 3 of the Terrorism Act 2000.

(2)   Paragraph (1) does not apply where a lawyer or other professional adviser is in the course of ascertaining the legal position for his client or performing his task

of defending or representing that client in, or concerning, legal proceedings, including advice on the institution or avoidance of proceedings.

(3) In paragraph (2), 'other professional adviser' means an auditor, accountant or tax adviser who is a member of a professional body which is established for any such persons and which makes provision for–

    (a) testing the competence of those seeking admission to membership of such a body as a condition for such admission; and

    (b) imposing and maintaining professional and ethical standards for its members, as well as imposing sanctions for non-compliance with those standards.

12 Exception for trustees of debt issues

(1) A relevant person–

    (a) who is appointed by the issuer of instruments or securities specified in paragraph (2) as trustee of an issue of such instruments or securities; or

    (b) whose customer is a trustee of an issue of such instruments or securities,

is not required to apply the customer due diligence measure referred to in regulation 5(b) in respect of the holders of such instruments or securities.

(2) The specified instruments and securities are–

    (a) instruments which fall within article 77 of the Financial Services and Markets Act 2000 (Regulated Activities) Order 2001; and

    (b) securities which fall within article 78 of that Order.

13 Simplified due diligence

(1) A relevant person is not required to apply customer due diligence measures in the circumstances mentioned in regulation 7(1)(a), (b) or (d) where he has reasonable grounds for believing that the customer, transaction or product related to such transaction, falls within any of the following paragraphs.

(2) The customer is–

    (a) a credit or financial institution which is subject to the requirements of the money laundering directive; or

    (b) a credit or financial institution (or equivalent institution) which–

        (i) is situated in a non-EEA state which imposes requirements equivalent to those laid down in the money laundering directive; and

        (ii) is supervised for compliance with those requirements.

(3) The customer is a company whose securities are listed on a regulated market subject to specified disclosure obligations.

(4) The customer is an independent legal professional and the product is an account into which monies are pooled, provided that–

    (a) where the pooled account is held in a non-EEA state–

        (i) that state imposes requirements to combat money laundering and terrorist financing which are consistent with international standards; and

        (ii) the independent legal professional is supervised in that state for compliance with those requirements; and

    (b)   information on the identity of the persons on whose behalf monies are held in the pooled account is available, on request, to the institution which acts as a depository institution for the account.

(5)   The customer is a public authority in the United Kingdom.

(6)   The customer is a public authority which fulfils all the conditions set out in paragraph 2 of Schedule 2 to these Regulations.

(7)   The product is–

    (a)   a life insurance contract where the annual premium is no more than 1,000 euro or where a single premium of no more than 2,500 euro is paid;

    (b)   an insurance contract for the purposes of a pension scheme where the contract contains no surrender clause and cannot be used as collateral;

    (c)   a pension, superannuation or similar scheme which provides retirement benefits to employees, where contributions are made by an employer or by way of deduction from an employee's wages and the scheme rules do not permit the assignment of a member's interest under the scheme (other than an assignment permitted by section 44 of the Welfare Reform and Pensions Act 1999 (disapplication of restrictions on alienation) or section 91(5)(a) of the Pensions Act 1995 (inalienability of occupational pension)); or

    (d)   electronic money, within the meaning of Article 1(3)(b) of the electronic money directive, where–

        (i)   if the device cannot be recharged, the maximum amount stored in the device is no more than 150 euro; or

        (ii)   if the device can be recharged, a limit of 2,500 euro is imposed on the total amount transacted in a calendar year, except when an amount of 1,000 euro or more is redeemed in the same calendar year by the bearer (within the meaning of Article 3 of the electronic money directive).

(8)   The product and any transaction related to such product fulfils all the conditions set out in paragraph 3 of Schedule 2 to these Regulations.

(9)   The product is a child trust fund within the meaning given by section 1(2) of the Child Trust Funds Act 2004.

14   Enhanced customer due diligence and ongoing monitoring

(1)   A relevant person must apply on a risk-sensitive basis enhanced customer due diligence measures and enhanced ongoing monitoring–

    (a)   in accordance with paragraphs (2) to (4);

    (b)   in any other situation which by its nature can present a higher risk of money laundering or terrorist financing.

(2)   Where the customer has not been physically present for identification purposes, a relevant person must take specific and adequate measures to compensate for the higher risk, for example, by applying one or more of the following measures–

    (a)   ensuring that the customer's identity is established by additional documents, data or information;

    (b)   supplementary measures to verify or certify the documents supplied, or requiring confirmatory certification by a credit or financial institution which is subject to the money laundering directive;

    (c)   ensuring that the first payment is carried out through an account opened in the customer's name with a credit institution.

(3) A credit institution ('the correspondent') which has or proposes to have a correspondent banking relationship with a respondent institution ('the respondent') from a non-EEA state must–

    (a) gather sufficient information about the respondent to understand fully the nature of its business;

    (b) determine from publicly-available information the reputation of the respondent and the quality of its supervision;

    (c) assess the respondent's anti-money laundering and anti-terrorist financing controls;

    (d) obtain approval from senior management before establishing a new correspondent banking relationship;

    (e) document the respective responsibilities of the respondent and correspondent; and

    (f) be satisfied that, in respect of those of the respondent's customers who have direct access to accounts of the correspondent, the respondent–

        (i) has verified the identity of, and conducts ongoing monitoring in respect of, such customers; and

        (ii) is able to provide to the correspondent, upon request, the documents, data or information obtained when applying customer due diligence measures and ongoing monitoring.

(4) A relevant person who proposes to have a business relationship or carry out an occasional transaction with a politically exposed person must–

    (a) have approval from senior management for establishing the business relationship with that person;

    (b) take adequate measures to establish the source of wealth and source of funds which are involved in the proposed business relationship or occasional transaction; and

    (c) where the business relationship is entered into, conduct enhanced ongoing monitoring of the relationship.

(5) In paragraph (4), 'a politically exposed person' means a person who is–

    (a) an individual who is or has, at any time in the preceding year, been entrusted with a prominent public function by–

        (i) a state other than the United Kingdom;

        (ii) a Community institution; or

        (iii) an international body,

    including a person who falls in any of the categories listed in paragraph 4(1)(a) of Schedule 2;

    (b) an immediate family member of a person referred to in sub-paragraph (a), including a person who falls in any of the categories listed in paragraph 4(1)(c) of Schedule 2; or

    (c) a known close associate of a person referred to in sub-paragraph (a), including a person who falls in either of the categories listed in paragraph 4(1)(d) of Schedule 2.

(6) For the purpose of deciding whether a person is a known close associate of a person referred to in paragraph (5)(a), a relevant person need only have regard to information which is in his possession or is publicly known.

15   Branches and subsidiaries

(1)   A credit or financial institution must require its branches and subsidiary under-takings which are located in a non-EEA state to apply, to the extent permitted by the law of that state, measures at least equivalent to those set out in these Regulations with regard to customer due diligence measures, ongoing monitoring and record-keeping.

(2)   Where the law of a non-EEA state does not permit the application of such equiv-alent measures by the branch or subsidiary undertaking located in that state, the credit or financial institution must–

  (a)   inform its supervisory authority accordingly; and
  (b)   take additional measures to handle effectively the risk of money laundering and terrorist financing.

(3)   In this regulation 'subsidiary undertaking'–

  (a)   except in relation to an incorporated friendly society, has the meaning given by section 1162 of the Companies Act 2006 (parent and subsidiary under-takings) and, in relation to a body corporate in or formed under the law of an EEA state other than the United Kingdom, includes an undertaking which is a subsidiary undertaking within the meaning of any rule of law in force in that state for purposes connected with implementation of the European Council Seventh Company Law Directive 83/349/EEC of 13th June 1983 on consolidated accounts;
  (b)   in relation to an incorporated friendly society, means a body corporate of which the society has control within the meaning of section 13(9)(a) or (aa) of the Friendly Societies Act 1992 (control of subsidiaries and other bodies corporate).

(4)   Before the entry into force of section 1162 of the Companies Act 2006 the refer-ence to that section in paragraph (3)(a) shall be treated as a reference to section 258 of the Companies Act 1985 (parent and subsidiary undertakings).

16   Shell banks, anonymous accounts etc

(1)   A credit institution must not enter into, or continue, a correspondent banking relationship with a shell bank.

(2)   A credit institution must take appropriate measures to ensure that it does not enter into, or continue, a corresponding banking relationship with a bank which is known to permit its accounts to be used by a shell bank.

(3)   A credit or financial institution carrying on business in the United Kingdom must not set up an anonymous account or an anonymous passbook for any new or existing customer.

(4)   As soon as reasonably practicable on or after 15th December 2007 all credit and financial institutions carrying on business in the United Kingdom must apply customer due diligence measures to, and conduct ongoing monitoring of, all anonymous accounts and passbooks in existence on that date and in any event before such accounts or passbooks are used.

(5)   A 'shell bank' means a credit institution, or an institution engaged in equivalent activities, incorporated in a jurisdiction in which it has no physical presence involving meaningful decision-making and management, and which is not part of a financial conglomerate or third-country financial conglomerate.

(6) In this regulation, 'financial conglomerate' and 'third-country financial conglomerate' have the meanings given by regulations 1(2) and 7(1) respectively of the Financial Conglomerates and Other Financial Groups Regulations 2004.

17 Reliance

(1) A relevant person may rely on a person who falls within paragraph (2) (or who the relevant person has reasonable grounds to believe falls within paragraph (2)) to apply any customer due diligence measures provided that–

    (a) the other person consents to being relied on; and

    (b) notwithstanding the relevant person's reliance on the other person, the relevant person remains liable for any failure to apply such measures.

(2) The persons are–

    (a) a credit or financial institution which is an authorised person;

    (b) a relevant person who is–

        (i) an auditor, insolvency practitioner, external accountant, tax adviser or independent legal professional; and

        (ii) supervised for the purposes of these Regulations by one of the bodies listed in Part 1 of Schedule 3;

    (c) a person who carries on business in another EEA state who is–

        (i) a credit or financial institution, auditor, insolvency practitioner, external accountant, tax adviser or independent legal professional;

        (ii) subject to mandatory professional registration recognised by law; and

        (iii) supervised for compliance with the requirements laid down in the money laundering directive in accordance with section 2 of Chapter V of that directive; or

    (d) a person who carries on business in a non-EEA state who is–

        (i) a credit or financial institution (or equivalent institution), auditor, insolvency practitioner, external accountant, tax adviser or independent legal professional;

        (ii) subject to mandatory professional registration recognised by law;

        (iii) subject to requirements equivalent to those laid down in the money laundering directive; and

        (iv) supervised for compliance with those requirements in a manner equivalent to section 2 of Chapter V of the money laundering directive.

(3) In paragraph (2)(c)(i) and (d)(i), 'auditor' and 'insolvency practitioner' includes a person situated in another EEA state or a non-EEA state who provides services equivalent to the services provided by an auditor or insolvency practitioner.

(4) Nothing in this regulation prevents a relevant person applying customer due diligence measures by means of an outsourcing service provider or agent provided that the relevant person remains liable for any failure to apply such measures.

(5) In this regulation, 'financial institution' excludes money service businesses.

18   Directions where Financial Action Task Force applies counter-measures

The Treasury may direct any relevant person–

(a)   not to enter into a business relationship;
(b)   not to carry out an occasional transaction; or
(c)   not to proceed any further with a business relationship or occasional transaction,

with a person who is situated or incorporated in a non-EEA state to which the Financial Action Task Force has decided to apply counter-measures.

Part 3
Record-Keeping, Procedures and Training

19   Record-keeping

(1)   Subject to paragraph (4), a relevant person must keep the records specified in paragraph (2) for at least the period specified in paragraph (3).

(2)   The records are–

   (a)   a copy of, or the references to, the evidence of the customer's identity obtained pursuant to regulation 7, 8, 10, 14 or 16(4);
   (b)   the supporting records (consisting of the original documents or copies) in respect of a business relationship or occasional transaction which is the subject of customer due diligence measures or ongoing monitoring.

(3)   The period is five years beginning on–

   (a)   in the case of the records specified in paragraph (2)(a), the date on which–

      (i)   the occasional transaction is completed; or
      (ii)   the business relationship ends; or

   (b)   in the case of the records specified in paragraph (2)(b)–

      (i)   where the records relate to a particular transaction, the date on which the transaction is completed;
      (ii)   for all other records, the date on which the business relationship ends.

(4)   A relevant person who is relied on by another person must keep the records specified in paragraph (2)(a) for five years beginning on the date on which he is relied on for the purposes of regulation 7, 10, 14 or 16(4) in relation to any business relationship or occasional transaction.

(5)   A person referred to in regulation 17(2)(a) or (b) who is relied on by a relevant person must, if requested by the person relying on him within the period referred to in paragraph (4)–

   (a)   as soon as reasonably practicable make available to the person who is relying on him any information about the customer (and any beneficial owner) which he obtained when applying customer due diligence measures; and
   (b)   as soon as reasonably practicable forward to the person who is relying on him copies of any identification and verification data and other relevant documents on the identity of the customer (and any beneficial owner) which he obtained when applying those measures.

(6)   A relevant person who relies on a person referred to in regulation 17(2)(c) or (d) (a 'third party') to apply customer due diligence measures must take steps to

ensure that the third party will, if requested by the relevant person within the period referred to in paragraph (4)–

(a) as soon as reasonably practicable make available to him any information about the customer (and any beneficial owner) which the third party obtained when applying customer due diligence measures; and

(b) as soon as reasonably practicable forward to him copies of any identification and verification data and other relevant documents on the identity of the customer (and any beneficial owner) which the third party obtained when applying those measures.

(7) Paragraphs (5) and (6) do not apply where a relevant person applies customer due diligence measures by means of an outsourcing service provider or agent.

(8) For the purposes of this regulation, a person relies on another person where he does so in accordance with regulation 17(1).

20 Policies and procedures

(1) A relevant person must establish and maintain appropriate and risk-sensitive policies and procedures relating to–

(a) customer due diligence measures and ongoing monitoring;

(b) reporting;

(c) record-keeping;

(d) internal control;

(e) risk assessment and management;

(f) the monitoring and management of compliance with, and the internal communication of, such policies and procedures,

in order to prevent activities related to money laundering and terrorist financing.

(2) The policies and procedures referred to in paragraph (1) include policies and procedures–

(a) which provide for the identification and scrutiny of–

(i) complex or unusually large transactions;

(ii) unusual patterns of transactions which have no apparent economic or visible lawful purpose; and

(iii) any other activity which the relevant person regards as particularly likely by its nature to be related to money laundering or terrorist financing;

(b) which specify the taking of additional measures, where appropriate, to prevent the use for money laundering or terrorist financing of products and transactions which might favour anonymity;

(c) to determine whether a customer is a politically exposed person;

(d) under which–

(i) an individual in the relevant person's organisation is a nominated officer under Part 7 of the Proceeds of Crime Act 2002 and Part 3 of the Terrorism Act 2000;

(ii) anyone in the organisation to whom information or other matter comes in the course of the business as a result of which he knows or suspects or has reasonable grounds for knowing or suspecting that a person is engaged in money laundering or terrorist financing is required to comply with Part 7 of the Proceeds of Crime Act 2002 or, as the case may be, Part 3 of the Terrorism Act 2000; and

      (iii)   where a disclosure is made to the nominated officer, he must consider it in the light of any relevant information which is available to the relevant person and determine whether it gives rise to knowledge or suspicion or reasonable grounds for knowledge or suspicion that a person is engaged in money laundering or terrorist financing.

(3)   Paragraph (2)(d) does not apply where the relevant person is an individual who neither employs nor acts in association with any other person.

(4)   A credit or financial institution must establish and maintain systems which enable it to respond fully and rapidly to enquiries from financial investigators accredited under section 3 of the Proceeds of Crime Act 2002 (accreditation and training), persons acting on behalf of the Scottish Ministers in their capacity as an enforcement authority under that Act, officers of Revenue and Customs or constables as to–

    (a)   whether it maintains, or has maintained during the previous five years, a business relationship with any person; and

    (b)   the nature of that relationship.

(5)   A credit or financial institution must communicate where relevant the policies and procedures which it establishes and maintains in accordance with this regulation to its branches and subsidiary undertakings which are located outside the United Kingdom.

(6)   In this regulation–

'politically exposed person' has the same meaning as in regulation 14(4);
'subsidiary undertaking' has the same meaning as in regulation 15.

21 Training

A relevant person must take appropriate measures so that all relevant employees of his are–

    (a)   made aware of the law relating to money laundering and terrorist financing; and

    (b)   regularly given training in how to recognise and deal with transactions and other activities which may be related to money laundering or terrorist financing.

Part 4
Supervision and Registration
Interpretation

22 Interpretation

(1)   In this Part–

'Annex I financial institution' means any undertaking which falls within regulation 3(3)(a) other than–

    (a)   a consumer credit financial institution;

    (b)   a money service business; or

    (c)   an authorised person;

'consumer credit financial institution' means any undertaking which falls within regulation 3(3)(a) and which requires, under section 21 of the Consumer Credit

Act 1974 (businesses needing a licence), a licence to carry on a consumer credit business, other than–

(a) a person covered by a group licence issued by the OFT under section 22 of that Act (standard and group licences);

(b) a money service business; or

(c) an authorised person.

(2) In paragraph (1), 'consumer credit business' has the meaning given by section 189(1) of the Consumer Credit Act 1974 (definitions) and, on the entry into force of section 23(a) of the Consumer Credit Act 2006 (definitions of 'consumer credit business' and 'consumer hire business'), has the meaning given by section 189(1) of the Consumer Credit Act 1974 as amended by section 23(a) of the Consumer Credit Act 2006.

Supervision

23 Supervisory authorities

(1) Subject to paragraph (2), the following bodies are supervisory authorities–

(a) the Authority is the supervisory authority for–

(i) credit and financial institutions which are authorised persons;

(ii) trust or company service providers which are authorised persons;

(iii) Annex I financial institutions;

(b) the OFT is the supervisory authority for–

(i) consumer credit financial institutions;

(ii) estate agents;

(c) each of the professional bodies listed in Schedule 3 is the supervisory authority for relevant persons who are regulated by it;

(d) the Commissioners are the supervisory authority for–

(i) high value dealers;

(ii) money service businesses which are not supervised by the Authority;

(iii) trust or company service providers which are not supervised by the Authority or one of the bodies listed in Schedule 3;

(iv) auditors, external accountants and tax advisers who are not supervised by one of the bodies listed in Schedule 3.

(e) the Gambling Commission is the supervisory authority for casinos;

(f) DETI is the supervisory authority for–

(i) credit unions in Northern Ireland;

(ii) insolvency practitioners authorised by it under article 351 of the Insolvency (Northern Ireland) Order 1989;

(g) the Secretary of State is the supervisory authority for insolvency practitioners authorised by him under section 393 of the Insolvency Act 1986 (grant, refusal and withdrawal of authorisation).

(2) Where under paragraph (1) there is more than one supervisory authority for a relevant person, the supervisory authorities may agree that one of them will act as the supervisory authority for that person.

(3) Where an agreement has been made under paragraph (2), the authority which has agreed to act as the supervisory authority must notify the relevant person or publish the agreement in such manner as it considers appropriate.

(4) Where no agreement has been made under paragraph (2), the supervisory authorities for a relevant person must cooperate in the performance of their functions under these Regulations.

24 Duties of supervisory authorities

(1) A supervisory authority must effectively monitor the relevant persons for whom it is the supervisory authority and take necessary measures for the purpose of securing compliance by such persons with the requirements of these Regulations.

(2) A supervisory authority which, in the course of carrying out any of its functions under these Regulations, knows or suspects that a person is or has engaged in money laundering or terrorist financing must promptly inform the Serious Organised Crime Agency.

(3) A disclosure made under paragraph (2) is not to be taken to breach any restriction, however imposed, on the disclosure of information.

(4) The functions of the Authority under these Regulations shall be treated for the purposes of Parts 1, 2 and 4 of Schedule 1 to the 2000 Act (the Financial Services Authority) as functions conferred on the Authority under that Act.

*Registration of high value dealers, money service businesses
and trust or company service providers*

25 Duty to maintain registers

(1) The Commissioners must maintain registers of–

 (a) high value dealers;
 (b) money service businesses for which they are the supervisory authority; and
 (c) trust or company service providers for which they are the supervisory authority.

(2) The Commissioners may keep the registers in any form they think fit.

(3) The Commissioners may publish or make available for public inspection all or part of a register maintained under this regulation.

26 Requirement to be registered

(1) A person in respect of whom the Commissioners are required to maintain a register under regulation 25 must not act as a–

 (a) high value dealer;
 (b) money service business; or
 (c) trust or company service provider,
 unless he is included in the register.

(2) Paragraph (1) and regulation 29 are subject to the transitional provisions set out in regulation 50.

27 Applications for registration in a register maintained under regulation 25

(1) An applicant for registration in a register maintained under regulation 25 must make an application in such manner and provide such information as the Commissioners may specify.

(2) The information which the Commissioners may specify includes–

(a) the applicant's name and (if different) the name of the business;

(b) the nature of the business;

(c) the name of the nominated officer (if any);

(d) in relation to a money service business or trust or company service provider–

(i) the name of any person who effectively directs or will direct the business and any beneficial owner of the business; and

(ii) information needed by the Commissioners to decide whether they must refuse the application pursuant to regulation 28.

(3) At any time after receiving an application and before determining it, the Commissioners may require the applicant to provide, within 21 days beginning with the date of being requested to do so, such further information as they reasonably consider necessary to enable them to determine the application.

(4) If at any time after the applicant has provided the Commissioners with any information under paragraph (1) or (3)–

(a) there is a material change affecting any matter contained in that information; or

(b) it becomes apparent to that person that the information contains a significant inaccuracy,

he must provide the Commissioners with details of the change or, as the case may be, a correction of the inaccuracy within 30 days beginning with the date of the occurrence of the change (or the discovery of the inaccuracy) or within such later time as may be agreed with the Commissioners.

(5) The obligation in paragraph (4) applies also to material changes or significant inaccuracies affecting any matter contained in any supplementary information provided pursuant to that paragraph.

(6) Any information to be provided to the Commissioners under this regulation must be in such form or verified in such manner as they may specify.

28 Fit and proper test

(1) The Commissioners must refuse to register an applicant as a money service business or trust or company service provider if they are satisfied that–

(a) the applicant;

(b) a person who effectively directs, or will effectively direct, the business or service provider;

(c) a beneficial owner of the business or service provider; or

(d) the nominated officer of the business or service provider,

is not a fit and proper person.

(2) For the purposes of paragraph (1), a person is not a fit and proper person if he–

(a) has been convicted of–

(i) an offence under the Terrorism Act 2000;

     (ii)   an offence under paragraph 7(2) or (3) of Schedule 3 to the Anti-Terrorism, Crime and Security Act 2001 (offences);

     (iii) an offence under the Terrorism Act 2006;

     (iv) an offence under Part 7 (money laundering) of, or listed in Schedule 2 (lifestyle offences: England and Wales), 4 (lifestyle offences: Scotland) or 5 (lifestyle offences: Northern Ireland) to, the Proceeds of Crime Act 2002;

     (v)   an offence under the Fraud Act 2006 or, in Scotland, the common law offence of fraud;

     (vi) an offence under section 72(1), (3) or (8) of the Value Added Tax Act 1994 (offences); or

     (vii) the common law offence of cheating the public revenue;

(b)   has been adjudged bankrupt or sequestration of his estate has been awarded and (in either case) he has not been discharged;

(c)   is subject to a disqualification order under the Company Directors Disqualification Act 1986;

(d)   is or has been subject to a confiscation order under the Proceeds of Crime Act 2002;

(e)   has consistently failed to comply with the requirements of these Regulations, the Money Laundering Regulations 2003 or the Money Laundering Regulations 2001;

(f)   has consistently failed to comply with the requirements of regulation 2006/1781/EC of the European Parliament and of the Council of 15th November 2006 on information on the payer accompanying the transfer of funds;

(g)   has effectively directed a business which falls within sub-paragraph (e) or (f);

(h)   is otherwise not a fit and proper person with regard to the risk of money laundering or terrorist financing.

(3) For the purposes of this regulation, a conviction for an offence listed in paragraph (2)(a) is to be disregarded if it is spent for the purposes of the Rehabilitation of Offenders Act 1974.

29 Determination of applications under regulation 27

(1) Subject to regulation 28, the Commissioners may refuse to register an applicant for registration in a register maintained under regulation 25 only if–

   (a) any requirement of, or imposed under, regulation 27 has not been complied with;

   (b) it appears to the Commissioners that any information provided pursuant to regulation 27 is false or misleading in a material particular; or

   (c) the applicant has failed to pay a charge imposed by them under regulation 35(1).

(2) The Commissioners must within 45 days beginning either with the date on which they receive the application or, where applicable, with the date on which they receive any further information required under regulation 27(3), give the applicant notice of–

   (a) their decision to register the applicant; or

   (b) the following matters–

   (i) their decision not to register the applicant;
   (ii) the reasons for their decision;
   (iii) the right to require a review under regulation 43; and
   (iv) the right to appeal under regulation 44(1)(a).

(3) The Commissioners must, as soon as practicable after deciding to register a person, include him in the relevant register.

30 Cancellation of registration in a register maintained under regulation 25

(1) The Commissioners must cancel the registration of a money service business or trust or company service provider in a register maintained under regulation 25(1) if, at any time after registration, they are satisfied that he or any person mentioned in regulation 28(1)(b), (c) or (d) is not a fit and proper person within the meaning of regulation 28(2).

(2) The Commissioners may cancel a person's registration in a register maintained by them under regulation 25 if, at any time after registration, it appears to them that they would have had grounds to refuse registration under regulation 29(1).

(3) Where the Commissioners decide to cancel a person's registration they must give him notice of–

  (a) their decision and, subject to paragraph (4), the date from which the cancellation takes effect;
  (b) the reasons for their decision;
  (c) the right to require a review under regulation 43; and
  (d) the right to appeal under regulation 44(1)(a).

(4) If the Commissioners–

  (a) consider that the interests of the public require the cancellation of a person's registration to have immediate effect; and
  (b) include a statement to that effect and the reasons for it in the notice given under paragraph (3),

the cancellation takes effect when the notice is given to the person.

Requirement to inform the authority

31 Requirement on authorised person to inform the Authority

(1) An authorised person whose supervisory authority is the Authority must, before acting as a money service business or a trust or company service provider or within 28 days of so doing, inform the Authority that he intends, or has begun, to act as such.

(2) Paragraph (1) does not apply to an authorised person who–

  (a) immediately before 15th December 2007 was acting as a money service business or a trust or company service provider and continues to act as such after that date; and
  (b) before 15th January 2008 informs the Authority that he is or was acting as such.

(3) Where an authorised person whose supervisory authority is the Authority ceases to act as a money service business or a trust or company service provider, he must immediately inform the Authority.

(4) Any requirement imposed by this regulation is to be treated as if it were a requirement imposed by or under the 2000 Act.

(5) Any information to be provided to the Authority under this regulation must be in such form or verified in such manner as it may specify.

Registration of Annex I financial institutions, estate agents etc

32 Power to maintain registers

(1) The supervisory authorities mentioned in paragraph (2), (3) or (4) may, in order to fulfil their duties under regulation 24, maintain a register under this regulation.

(2) The Authority may maintain a register of Annex I financial institutions.

(3) The OFT may maintain registers of–

(a) consumer credit financial institutions; and
(b) estate agents.

(4) The Commissioners may maintain registers of–

(a) auditors;
(b) external accountants; and
(c) tax advisers,

who are not supervised by the Secretary of State, DETI or any of the professional bodies listed in Schedule 3.

(5) Where a supervisory authority decides to maintain a register under this regulation, it must take reasonable steps to bring its decision to the attention of those relevant persons in respect of whom the register is to be established.

(6) A supervisory authority may keep a register under this regulation in any form it thinks fit.

(7) A supervisory authority may publish or make available to public inspection all or part of a register maintained by it under this regulation.

33 Requirement to be registered

Where a supervisory authority decides to maintain a register under regulation 32 in respect of any description of relevant persons and establishes a register for that purpose, a relevant person of that description may not carry on the business or profession in question for a period of more than six months beginning on the date on which the supervisory authority establishes the register unless he is included in the register.

34 Applications for and cancellation of registration in a register maintained under regulation 32

(1) Regulations 27, 29 (with the omission of the words 'Subject to regulation 28' in regulation 29(1)) and 30(2), (3) and (4) apply to registration in a register maintained by the Commissioners under regulation 32 as they apply to registration in a register maintained under regulation 25.

(2) Regulation 27 applies to registration in a register maintained by the Authority or the OFT under regulation 32 as it applies to registration in a register maintained under regulation 25 and, for this purpose, references to the Commissioners are to be treated as references to the Authority or the OFT, as the case may be.

(3)   The Authority and the OFT may refuse to register an applicant for registration in a register maintained under regulation 32 only if–

    (a)   any requirement of, or imposed under, regulation 27 has not been complied with;

    (b)   it appears to the Authority or the OFT, as the case may be, that any information provided pursuant to regulation 27 is false or misleading in a material particular; or

    (c)   the applicant has failed to pay a charge imposed by the Authority or the OFT, as the case may be, under regulation 35(1).

(4)   The Authority or the OFT, as the case may be, must, within 45 days beginning either with the date on which it receives an application or, where applicable, with the date on which it receives any further information required under regulation 27(3), give the applicant notice of–

    (a)   its decision to register the applicant; or

    (b)   the following matters–

        (i)   that it is minded not to register the applicant;

        (ii)   the reasons for being minded not to register him; and

        (iii)   the right to make representations to it within a specified period (which may not be less than 28 days).

(5)   The Authority or the OFT, as the case may be, must then decide, within a reasonable period, whether to register the applicant and it must give the applicant notice of–

    (a)   its decision to register the applicant; or

    (b)   the following matters–

        (i)   its decision not to register the applicant;

        (ii)   the reasons for its decision; and

        (iii)   the right to appeal under regulation 44(1)(b).

(6)   The Authority or the OFT, as the case may be, must, as soon as reasonably practicable after deciding to register a person, include him in the relevant register.

(7)   The Authority or the OFT may cancel a person's registration in a register maintained by them under regulation 32 if, at any time after registration, it appears to them that they would have had grounds to refuse registration under paragraph (3).

(8)   Where the Authority or the OFT proposes to cancel a person's registration, it must give him notice of–

    (a)   its proposal to cancel his registration;

    (b)   the reasons for the proposed cancellation; and

    (c)   the right to make representations to it within a specified period (which may not be less than 28 days).

(9)   The Authority or the OFT, as the case may be, must then decide, within a reasonable period, whether to cancel the person's registration and it must give him notice of–

    (a)   its decision not to cancel his registration; or

    (b)   the following matters–

        (i)   its decision to cancel his registration and, subject to paragraph (10), the date from which cancellation takes effect;

(ii)   the reasons for its decision; and

(iii)   the right to appeal under regulation 44(1)(b).

(10) If the Authority or the OFT, as the case may be–

(a)   considers that the interests of the public require the cancellation of a person's registration to have immediate effect; and

(b)   includes a statement to that effect and the reasons for it in the notice given under paragraph (9)(b),

the cancellation takes effect when the notice is given to the person.

(11) In paragraphs (3) and (4), references to regulation 27 are to be treated as references to that paragraph as applied by paragraph (2) of this regulation.

Financial provisions

35   Costs of supervision

(1)   The Authority, the OFT and the Commissioners may impose charges–

(a)   on applicants for registration;

(b)   on relevant persons supervised by them.

(2)   Charges levied under paragraph (1) must not exceed such amount as the Authority, the OFT or the Commissioners (as the case may be) consider will enable them to meet any expenses reasonably incurred by them in carrying out their functions under these Regulations or for any incidental purpose.

(3)   Without prejudice to the generality of paragraph (2), a charge may be levied in respect of each of the premises at which a person carries on (or proposes to carry on) business.

(4)   The Authority must apply amounts paid to it by way of penalties imposed under regulation 42 towards expenses incurred in carrying out its functions under these Regulations or for any incidental purpose.

(5)   In paragraph (2), 'expenses' in relation to the OFT includes expenses incurred by a local weights and measures authority or DETI pursuant to arrangements made for the purposes of these Regulations with the OFT–

(a)   by or on behalf of the authority; or

(b)   by DETI.

Part 5
Enforcement
Powers of designated authorities

36   Interpretation

In this Part–

'designated authority' means–

(a)   the Authority;

(b)   the Commissioners;

(c)   the OFT; and

(d)   in relation to credit unions in Northern Ireland, DETI;

'officer', except in regulations 40(3), 41 and 47 means–

(a) an officer of the Authority, including a member of the Authority's staff or an agent of the Authority;
(b) an officer of Revenue and Customs;
(c) an officer of the OFT;
(d) a relevant officer; or
(e) an officer of DETI acting for the purposes of its functions under these Regulations in relation to credit unions in Northern Ireland;

'recorded information' includes information recorded in any form and any document of any nature;

'relevant officer' means–

(a) in Great Britain, an officer of a local weights and measures authority;
(b) in Northern Ireland, an officer of DETI acting pursuant to arrangements made with the OFT for the purposes of these Regulations.

37 Power to require information from, and attendance of, relevant and connected persons

(1) An officer may, by notice to a relevant person or to a person connected with a relevant person, require the relevant person or the connected person, as the case may be–

(a) to provide such information as may be specified in the notice;
(b) to produce such recorded information as may be so specified; or
(c) to attend before an officer at a time and place specified in the notice and answer questions.

(2) For the purposes of paragraph (1), a person is connected with a relevant person if he is, or has at any time been, in relation to the relevant person, a person listed in Schedule 4 to these Regulations.

(3) An officer may exercise powers under this regulation only if the information sought to be obtained as a result is reasonably required in connection with the exercise by the designated authority for whom he acts of its functions under these Regulations.

(4) Where an officer requires information to be provided or produced pursuant to paragraph (1)(a) or (b)–

(a) the notice must set out the reasons why the officer requires the information to be provided or produced; and
(b) such information must be provided or produced–

(i) before the end of such reasonable period as may be specified in the notice; and
(ii) at such place as may be so specified.

(5) In relation to information recorded otherwise than in legible form, the power to require production of it includes a power to require the production of a copy of it in legible form or in a form from which it can readily be produced in visible and legible form.

(6) The production of a document does not affect any lien which a person has on the document.

(7) A person may not be required under this regulation to provide or produce information or to answer questions which he would be entitled to refuse to provide, produce or answer on grounds of legal professional privilege in proceedings in

the High Court, except that a lawyer may be required to provide the name and address of his client.

(8) Subject to paragraphs (9) and (10), a statement made by a person in compliance with a requirement imposed on him under paragraph (1)(c) is admissible in evidence in any proceedings, so long as it also complies with any requirements governing the admissibility of evidence in the circumstances in question.

(9) In criminal proceedings in which a person is charged with an offence to which this paragraph applies—

(a) no evidence relating to the statement may be adduced; and

(b) no question relating to it may be asked,

by or on behalf of the prosecution unless evidence relating to it is adduced, or a question relating to it is asked, in the proceedings by or on behalf of that person.

(10) Paragraph (9) applies to any offence other than one under—

(a) section 5 of the Perjury Act 1911 (false statements without oath);

(b) section 44(2) of the Criminal Law (Consolidation) (Scotland) Act 1995 (false statements and declarations); or

(c) Article 10 of the Perjury (Northern Ireland) Order 1979 (false unsworn statements).

(11) In the application of this regulation to Scotland, the reference in paragraph (7) to—

(a) proceedings in the High Court is to be read as a reference to legal proceedings generally; and

(b) an entitlement on grounds of legal professional privilege is to be read as a reference to an entitlement on the grounds of confidentiality of communications—

(i) between a professional legal adviser and his client; or

(ii) made in connection with or in contemplation of legal proceedings and for the purposes of those proceedings.

38 Entry, inspection without a warrant etc

(1) Where an officer has reasonable cause to believe that any premises are being used by a relevant person in connection with his business or professional activities, he may on producing evidence of his authority at any reasonable time—

(a) enter the premises;

(b) inspect the premises;

(c) observe the carrying on of business or professional activities by the relevant person;

(d) inspect any recorded information found on the premises;

(e) require any person on the premises to provide an explanation of any recorded information or to state where it may be found;

(f) in the case of a money service business or a high value dealer, inspect any cash found on the premises.

(2) An officer may take copies of, or make extracts from, any recorded information found under paragraph (1).

(3) Paragraphs (1)(d) and (e) and (2) do not apply to recorded information which the relevant person would be entitled to refuse to disclose on grounds of legal professional privilege in proceedings in the High Court, except that a lawyer may

be required to provide the name and address of his client and, for this purpose, regulation 37(11) applies to this paragraph as it applies to regulation 37(7).

(4) An officer may exercise powers under this regulation only if the information sought to be obtained as a result is reasonably required in connection with the exercise by the designated authority for whom he acts of its functions under these Regulations.

(5) In this regulation, 'premises' means any premises other than premises used only as a dwelling.

39   Entry to premises under warrant

(1) A justice may issue a warrant under this paragraph if satisfied on information on oath given by an officer that there are reasonable grounds for believing that the first, second or third set of conditions is satisfied.

(2) The first set of conditions is–

    (a) that there is on the premises specified in the warrant recorded information in relation to which a requirement could be imposed under regulation 37(1)(b); and

    (b) that if such a requirement were to be imposed–

        (i) it would not be complied with; or

        (ii) the recorded information to which it relates would be removed, tampered with or destroyed.

(3) The second set of conditions is–

    (a) that a person on whom a requirement has been imposed under regulation 37(1)(b) has failed (wholly or in part) to comply with it; and

    (b) that there is on the premises specified in the warrant recorded information which has been required to be produced.

(4) The third set of conditions is–

    (a) that an officer has been obstructed in the exercise of a power under regulation 38; and

    (b) that there is on the premises specified in the warrant recorded information or cash which could be inspected under regulation 38(1)(d) or (f).

(5) A justice may issue a warrant under this paragraph if satisfied on information on oath given by an officer that there are reasonable grounds for suspecting that–

    (a) an offence under these Regulations has been, is being or is about to be committed by a relevant person; and

    (b) there is on the premises specified in the warrant recorded information relevant to whether that offence has been, or is being or is about to be committed.

(6) A warrant issued under this regulation shall authorise an officer–

    (a) to enter the premises specified in the warrant;

    (b) to search the premises and take possession of any recorded information or anything appearing to be recorded information specified in the warrant or to take, in relation to any such recorded information, any other steps which may appear to be necessary for preserving it or preventing interference with it;

(c) to take copies of, or extracts from, any recorded information specified in the warrant;

(d) to require any person on the premises to provide an explanation of any recorded information appearing to be of the kind specified in the warrant or to state where it may be found;

(e) to use such force as may reasonably be necessary.

(7) Where a warrant is issued by a justice under paragraph (1) or (5) on the basis of information on oath given by an officer of the Authority, for 'an officer' in paragraph (6) substitute 'a constable'.

(8) In paragraphs (1), (5) and (7), 'justice' means–

(a) in relation to England and Wales, a justice of the peace;

(b) in relation to Scotland, a justice within the meaning of section 307 of the Criminal Procedure (Scotland) Act 1995 (interpretation);

(c) in relation to Northern Ireland, a lay magistrate.

(9) In the application of this regulation to Scotland, the references in paragraphs (1), (5) and (7) to information on oath are to be read as references to evidence on oath.

40 Failure to comply with information requirement

(1) If, on an application made by–

(a) a designated authority; or

(b) a local weights and measures authority or DETI pursuant to arrangements made with the OFT–

(i) by or on behalf of the authority; or

(ii) by DETI,

it appears to the court that a person (the 'information defaulter') has failed to do something that he was required to do under regulation 37(1), the court may make an order under this regulation.

(2) An order under this regulation may require the information defaulter–

(a) to do the thing that he failed to do within such period as may be specified in the order;

(b) otherwise to take such steps to remedy the consequences of the failure as may be so specified.

(3) If the information defaulter is a body corporate, a partnership or an unincorporated body of persons which is not a partnership, the order may require any officer of the body corporate, partnership or body, who is (wholly or partly) responsible for the failure to meet such costs of the application as are specified in the order.

(4) In this regulation, 'court' means–

(a) in England and Wales and Northern Ireland, the High Court or the county court;

(b) in Scotland, the Court of Session or the sheriff court.

41 Powers of relevant officers

(1) A relevant officer may only exercise powers under regulations 37 to 39 pursuant to arrangements made with the OFT–

(a) by or on behalf of the local weights and measures authority of which he is an officer ('his authority'); or

(b) by DETI.

(2) Anything done or omitted to be done by, or in relation to, a relevant officer in the exercise or purported exercise of a power in this Part shall be treated for all purposes as having been done or omitted to be done by, or in relation to, an officer of the OFT.

(3) Paragraph (2) does not apply for the purposes of any criminal proceedings brought against the relevant officer, his authority, DETI or the OFT, in respect of anything done or omitted to be done by the officer.

(4) A relevant officer shall not disclose to any person other than the OFT and his authority or, as the case may be, DETI information obtained by him in the exercise of such powers unless–

(a) he has the approval of the OFT to do so; or

(b) he is under a duty to make the disclosure.

Civil penalties, review and appeals

42 Power to impose civil penalties

(1) A designated authority may impose a penalty of such amount as it considers appropriate on a relevant person who fails to comply with any requirement in regulation 7(1), (2) or (3), 8(1) or (3), 9(2), 10(1), 11(1), 14(1), 15(1) or (2), 16(1), (2), (3) or (4), 19(1), (4), (5) or (6), 20(1), (4) or (5), 21, 26, 27(4) or 33 or a direction made under regulation 18 and, for this purpose, 'appropriate' means effective, proportionate and dissuasive.

(2) The designated authority must not impose a penalty on a person under paragraph (1) where there are reasonable grounds for it to be satisfied that the person took all reasonable steps and exercised all due diligence to ensure that the requirement would be complied with.

(3) In deciding whether a person has failed to comply with a requirement of these Regulations, the designated authority must consider whether he followed any relevant guidance which was at the time–

(a) issued by a supervisory authority or any other appropriate body;

(b) approved by the Treasury; and

(c) published in a manner approved by the Treasury as suitable in their opinion to bring the guidance to the attention of persons likely to be affected by it.

(4) In paragraph (3), an 'appropriate body' means any body which regulates or is representative of any trade, profession, business or employment carried on by the person.

(5) Where the Commissioners decide to impose a penalty under this regulation, they must give the person notice of–

(a) their decision to impose the penalty and its amount;

(b) the reasons for imposing the penalty;

(c) the right to a review under regulation 43; and

(d) the right to appeal under regulation 44(1)(a).

(6) Where the Authority, the OFT or DETI proposes to impose a penalty under this regulation, it must give the person notice of–

(a)   its proposal to impose the penalty and the proposed amount;

(b)   the reasons for imposing the penalty; and

(c)   the right to make representations to it within a specified period (which may not be less than 28 days).

(7)   The Authority, the OFT or DETI, as the case may be, must then decide, within a reasonable period, whether to impose a penalty under this regulation and it must give the person notice of–

(a)   its decision not to impose a penalty; or

(b)   the following matters–

(i)   its decision to impose a penalty and the amount;

(ii)   the reasons for its decision; and

(iii) the right to appeal under regulation 44(1)(b).

(8)   A penalty imposed under this regulation is payable to the designated authority which imposes it.

43   Review procedure

(1)   This regulation applies to decisions of the Commissioners made under–

(a)   regulation 29, to refuse to register an applicant;

(b)   regulation 30, to cancel the registration of a registered person; and

(c)   regulation 42, to impose a penalty.

(2)   Any person who is the subject of a decision to which this regulation applies may by notice to the Commissioners require them to review that decision.

(3)   The Commissioners need not review any decision unless the notice requiring the review is given within 45 days beginning with the date on which they first gave notice of the decision to the person requiring the review.

(4)   Where the Commissioners are required under this regulation to review any decision they must either–

(a)   confirm the decision; or

(b)   withdraw or vary the decision and take such further steps (if any) in consequence of the withdrawal or variation as they consider appropriate.

(5)   Where the Commissioners do not, within 45 days beginning with the date on which the review was required by a person, give notice to that person of their determination of the review, they are to be taken for the purposes of these Regulations to have confirmed the decision.

44   Appeals

(1)   A person may appeal from a decision by–

(a)   the Commissioners on a review under regulation 43; and

(b)   the Authority, the OFT or DETI under regulation 34 or 42.

(2)   An appeal from a decision by–

(a)   the Commissioners is to a VAT and duties tribunal;

(b)   the Authority is to the Financial Services and Markets Tribunal;

(c)   the OFT is to the Consumer Credit Appeals Tribunal; and

(d)   DETI is to the High Court.

(3) The provisions of Part 5 of the Value Added Tax Act 1994 (appeals), subject to the modifications set out in paragraph 1 of Schedule 5, apply in respect of appeals to a VAT and duties tribunal made under this regulation as they apply in respect of appeals made to such a tribunal under section 83 (appeals) of that Act.

(4) The provisions of Part 9 of the 2000 Act (hearings and appeals), subject to the modifications set out in paragraph 2 of Schedule 5, apply in respect of appeals to the Financial Services and Markets Tribunal made under this regulation as they apply in respect of references made to that Tribunal under that Act.

(5) Sections 40A (the Consumer Credit Appeals Tribunal), 41 (appeals to the Secretary of State under Part 3) and 41A (appeals from the Consumer Credit Appeals Tribunal) of the Consumer Credit Act 1974 apply in respect of appeals to the Consumer Credit Appeal Tribunal made under this regulation as they apply in respect of appeals made to that Tribunal under section 41 of that Act.

(6) A VAT and duties tribunal hearing an appeal under paragraph (2) has the power to–

(a) quash or vary any decision of the supervisory authority, including the power to reduce any penalty to such amount (including nil) as they think proper; and

(b) substitute their own decision for any decision quashed on appeal.

(7) Notwithstanding paragraph (2)(c), until the coming into force of section 55 of the Consumer Credit Act 2006 (the Consumer Credit Appeals Tribunal), an appeal from a decision by the OFT is to the Financial Services and Markets Tribunal and, for these purposes, the coming into force of that section shall not affect–

(a) the hearing and determination by the Financial Service and Markets Tribunal of an appeal commenced before the coming into force of that section ('the original appeal'); or

(b) any appeal against the decision of the Financial Services and Markets Tribunal with respect to the original appeal.

(8) The modifications in Schedule 5 have effect for the purposes of appeals made under this regulation.

Criminal offences

45 Offences

(1) A person who fails to comply with any requirement in regulation 7(1), (2) or (3), 8(1) or (3), 9(2), 10(1), 11(1)(a), (b) or (c), 14(1), 15(1) or (2), 16(1), (2), (3) or (4), 19(1), (4), (5) or (6), 20(1), (4) or (5), 21, 26, 27(4) or 33, or a direction made under regulation 18, is guilty of an offence and liable–

(a) on summary conviction, to a fine not exceeding the statutory maximum;

(b) on conviction on indictment, to imprisonment for a term not exceeding two years, to a fine or to both.

(2) In deciding whether a person has committed an offence under paragraph (1), the court must consider whether he followed any relevant guidance which was at the time–

(a) issued by a supervisory authority or any other appropriate body;

(b) approved by the Treasury; and

(c) published in a manner approved by the Treasury as suitable in their opinion to bring the guidance to the attention of persons likely to be affected by it.

(3) In paragraph (2), an 'appropriate body' means any body which regulates or is representative of any trade, profession, business or employment carried on by the alleged offender.

(4) A person is not guilty of an offence under this regulation if he took all reasonable steps and exercised all due diligence to avoid committing the offence.

(5) Where a person is convicted of an offence under this regulation, he shall not also be liable to a penalty under regulation 42.

46 Prosecution of offences

(1) Proceedings for an offence under regulation 45 may be instituted by–

    (a) the Director of Revenue and Customs Prosecutions or by order of the Commissioners;

    (b) the OFT;

    (c) a local weights and measures authority;

    (d) DETI;

    (e) the Director of Public Prosecutions; or

    (f) the Director of Public Prosecutions for Northern Ireland.

(2) Proceedings for an offence under regulation 45 may be instituted only against a relevant person or, where such a person is a body corporate, a partnership or an unincorporated association, against any person who is liable to be proceeded against under regulation 47.

(3) Where proceedings under paragraph (1) are instituted by order of the Commissioners, the proceedings must be brought in the name of an officer of Revenue and Customs.

(4) Where a local weights and measures authority in England or Wales proposes to institute proceedings for an offence under regulation 45 it must give the OFT notice of the intended proceedings, together with a summary of the facts on which the charges are to be founded.

(5) A local weights and measures authority must also notify the OFT of the outcome of the proceedings after they are finally determined.

(6) A local weights and measures authority must, whenever the OFT requires, report in such form and with such particulars as the OFT requires on the exercise of its functions under these Regulations.

(7) Where the Commissioners investigate, or propose to investigate, any matter with a view to determining–

    (a) whether there are grounds for believing that an offence under regulation 45 has been committed by any person; or

    (b) whether such a person should be prosecuted for such an offence,

that matter is to be treated as an assigned matter within the meaning of section 1(1) of the Customs and Excise Management Act 1979.

(8) Paragraphs (1) and (3) to (6) do not extend to Scotland.

(9) In its application to the Commissioners acting in Scotland, paragraph (7)(b) shall be read as referring to the Commissioners determining whether to refer the matter to the Crown Office and Procurator Fiscal Service with a view to the Procurator Fiscal determining whether a person should be prosecuted for such an offence.

47 Offences by bodies corporate etc

(1) If an offence under regulation 45 committed by a body corporate is shown–

(a) to have been committed with the consent or the connivance of an officer of the body corporate; or

(b) to be attributable to any neglect on his part,

the officer as well as the body corporate is guilty of an offence and liable to be proceeded against and punished accordingly.

(2) If an offence under regulation 45 committed by a partnership is shown–

(a) to have been committed with the consent or the connivance of a partner; or
(b) to be attributable to any neglect on his part,

the partner as well as the partnership is guilty of an offence and liable to be proceeded against and punished accordingly.

(3) If an offence under regulation 45 committed by an unincorporated association (other than a partnership) is shown–

(a) to have been committed with the consent or the connivance of an officer of the association; or

(b) to be attributable to any neglect on his part,

that officer as well as the association is guilty of an offence and liable to be proceeded against and punished accordingly.

(4) If the affairs of a body corporate are managed by its members, paragraph (1) applies in relation to the acts and defaults of a member in connection with his functions of management as if he were a director of the body.

(5) Proceedings for an offence alleged to have been committed by a partnership or an unincorporated association must be brought in the name of the partnership or association (and not in that of its members).

(6) A fine imposed on the partnership or association on its conviction of an offence is to be paid out of the funds of the partnership or association.

(7) Rules of court relating to the service of documents are to have effect as if the partnership or association were a body corporate.

(8) In proceedings for an offence brought against the partnership or association–

(a) section 33 of the Criminal Justice Act 1925 (procedure on charge of offence against corporation) and Schedule 3 to the Magistrates' Courts Act 1980 (corporations) apply as they do in relation to a body corporate;

(b) section 70 (proceedings against bodies corporate) of the Criminal Procedure (Scotland) Act 1995 applies as it does in relation to a body corporate;

(c) section 18 of the Criminal Justice (Northern Ireland) Act 1945 (procedure on charge) and Schedule 4 to the Magistrates' Courts (Northern Ireland) Order 1981 (corporations) apply as they do in relation to a body corporate.

(9) In this regulation–

'officer'–

(a) in relation to a body corporate, means a director, manager, secretary, chief executive, member of the committee of management, or a person purporting to act in such a capacity; and

(b) in relation to an unincorporated association, means any officer of the association or any member of its governing body, or a person purporting to act in such capacity; and

'partner' includes a person purporting to act as a partner.

Part 6
Miscellaneous

48 Recovery of charges and penalties through the court

Any charge or penalty imposed on a person by a supervisory authority under regulation 35(1) or 42(1) is a debt due from that person to the authority, and is recoverable accordingly.

49 Obligations on public authorities

(1) The following bodies and persons must, if they know or suspect or have reasonable grounds for knowing or suspecting that a person is or has engaged in money laundering or terrorist financing, as soon as reasonably practicable inform the Serious Organised Crime Agency–

(a) the Auditor General for Scotland;

(b) the Auditor General for Wales;

(c) the Authority;

(d) the Bank of England;

(e) the Comptroller and Auditor General;

(f) the Comptroller and Auditor General for Northern Ireland;

(g) the Gambling Commission;

(h) the OFT;

(i) the Official Solicitor to the Supreme Court;

(j) the Pensions Regulator;

(k) the Public Trustee;

(l) the Secretary of State, in the exercise of his functions under enactments relating to companies and insolvency;

(m) the Treasury, in the exercise of their functions under the 2000 Act;

(n) the Treasury Solicitor;

(o) a designated professional body for the purposes of Part 20 of the 2000 Act (provision of financial services by members of the professions);

(p) a person or inspector appointed under section 65 (investigations on behalf of Authority) or 66 (inspections and special meetings) of the Friendly Societies Act 1992;

(q) an inspector appointed under section 49 of the Industrial and Provident Societies Act 1965 (appointment of inspectors) or section 18 of the Credit Unions Act 1979 (power to appoint inspector);

(r) an inspector appointed under section 431 (investigation of a company on its own application), 432 (other company investigations), 442 (power to investigate company ownership) or 446 (investigation of share dealing) of the Companies Act 1985 or under Article 424, 425, 435 or 439 of the Companies (Northern Ireland) Order 1986;

(s) a person or inspector appointed under section 55 (investigations on behalf of Authority) or 56 (inspections and special meetings) of the Building Societies Act 1986;

(t) a person appointed under section 167 (appointment of persons to carry out investigations), 168(3) or (5) (appointment of persons to carry out investigations in particular cases), 169(1)(b) (investigations to support overseas regulator) or 284 (power to investigate affairs of a scheme) of the 2000 Act, or under regulations made under section 262(2)(k) (open-ended investment companies) of that Act, to conduct an investigation; and

(u) a person authorised to require the production of documents under section 447 of the Companies Act 1985 (Secretary of State's power to require production of documents), Article 440 of the Companies (Northern Ireland) Order 1986 or section 84 of the Companies Act 1989 (exercise of powers by officer).

(2) A disclosure made under paragraph (1) is not to be taken to breach any restriction on the disclosure of information however imposed.

50 Transitional provisions: requirement to be registered

(1) Regulation 26 does not apply to an existing money service business, an existing trust or company service provider or an existing high value dealer until–

(a) where it has applied in accordance with regulation 27 before the specified date for registration in a register maintained under regulation 25(1) (a 'new register')–

    (i) the date it is included in a new register following the determination of its application by the Commissioners; or

    (ii) where the Commissioners give it notice under regulation 29(2)(b) of their decision not to register it, the date on which the Commissioners state that the decision takes effect or, where a statement is included in accordance with paragraph (3)(b), the time at which the Commissioners give it such notice;

(b) in any other case, the specified date.

(2) The specified date is–

(a) in the case of an existing money service business, 1st February 2008;
(b) in the case of an existing trust or company service provider, 1st April 2008;
(c) in the case of an existing high value dealer, the first anniversary which falls on or after 1st January 2008 of the date of its registration in a register maintained under regulation 10 of the Money Laundering Regulations 2003.

(3) In the case of an application for registration in a new register made before the specified date by an existing money service business, an existing trust or company service provider or an existing high value dealer, the Commissioners must include in a notice given to it under regulation 29(2)(b)–

(a) the date on which their decision is to take effect; or
(b) if the Commissioners consider that the interests of the public require their decision to have immediate effect, a statement to that effect and the reasons for it.

(4) In the case of an application for registration in a new register made before the specified date by an existing money services business or an existing trust or company service provider, the Commissioners must give it a notice under regulation 29(2) by–

(a) in the case of an existing money service business, 1st June 2008;
(b) in the case of an existing trust or company service provider, 1st July 2008; or
(c) where applicable, 45 days beginning with the date on which they receive any further information required under regulation 27(3).

(5)   In this regulation–

'existing money service business' and an 'existing high value dealer' mean a money service business or a high value dealer which, immediately before 15th December 2007, was included in a register maintained under regulation 10 of the Money Laundering Regulations 2003;

'existing trust or company service provider' means a trust or company service provider carrying on business in the United Kingdom immediately before 15th December 2007.

51   Minor and consequential amendments

Schedule 6, which contains minor and consequential amendments to primary and secondary legislation, has effect.

Alan Campbell

Frank Roy
Two Lords Commissioners of Her Majesty's Treasury

24th July 2007

SCHEDULE 1

Activities Listed in Points 2 to 12 and 14 of Annex I to the Banking Consolidation Directive

Regulation 3(3)(a)

2   Lending including, inter alia: consumer credit, mortgage credit, factoring, with or without recourse, financing of commercial transactions (including forfeiting).

3   Financial leasing.

4   Money transmission services.

5   Issuing and administering means of payment (e.g. credit cards, travellers' cheques and bankers' drafts).

6   Guarantees and commitments.

7   Trading for own account or for account of customers in:

(a)   money market instruments (cheques, bills, certificates of deposit, etc);
(b)   foreign exchange;
(c)   financial futures and options;
(d)   exchange and interest-rate instruments; or
(e)   transferable securities.

8   Participation in securities issues and the provision of services related to such issues.

9   Advice to undertakings on capital structure, industrial strategy and related questions and advice as well as services relating to mergers and the purchase of undertakings.

10   Money broking.

11   Portfolio management and advice.

12 Safekeeping and administration of securities.

14 Safe custody services.

SCHEDULE 2

Financial Activity, Simplified Due Diligence and Politically Exposed Persons

Regulations 4(1)(e) and (2), 13(6) and (8) and 14(5)

Financial activity on an occasional or very limited basis

1   For the purposes of regulation 4(1)(e) and (2), a person is to be considered as engaging in financial activity on an occasional or very limited basis if all the following conditions are fulfilled–

    (a)   the person's total annual turnover in respect of the financial activity does not exceed £64,000;

    (b)   the financial activity is limited in relation to any customer to no more than one transaction exceeding 1,000 euro, whether the transaction is carried out in a single operation, or a series of operations which appear to be linked;

    (c)   the financial activity does not exceed 5% of the person's total annual turnover;

    (d)   the financial activity is ancillary and directly related to the person's main activity;

    (e)   the financial activity is not the transmission or remittance of money (or any representation of monetary value) by any means;

    (f)   the person's main activity is not that of a person falling within regulation 3(1)(a) to (f) or (h);

    (g)   the financial activity is provided only to customers of the person's main activity and is not offered to the public.

Simplified due diligence

2   For the purposes of regulation 13(6), the conditions are–

    (a)   the authority has been entrusted with public functions pursuant to the Treaty on the European Union, the Treaties on the European Communities or Community secondary legislation;

    (b)   the authority's identity is publicly available, transparent and certain;

    (c)   the activities of the authority and its accounting practices are transparent;

    (d)   either the authority is accountable to a Community institution or to the authorities of an EEA state, or otherwise appropriate check and balance procedures exist ensuring control of the authority's activity.

3   For the purposes of regulation 13(8), the conditions are–

    (a)   the product has a written contractual base;

    (b)   any related transaction is carried out through an account of the customer with a credit institution which is subject to the money laundering directive or with a credit institution situated in a non-EEA state which imposes requirements equivalent to those laid down in that directive;

    (c)   the product or related transaction is not anonymous and its nature is such that it allows for the timely application of customer due diligence measures where there is a suspicion of money laundering or terrorist financing;

(d) the product is within the following maximum threshold–

    (i) in the case of insurance policies or savings products of a similar nature, the annual premium is no more than 1,000 euro or there is a single premium of no more than 2,500 euro;

    (ii) in the case of products which are related to the financing of physical assets where the legal and beneficial title of the assets is not transferred to the customer until the termination of the contractual relationship (whether the transaction is carried out in a single operation or in several operations which appear to be linked), the annual payments do not exceed 15,000 euro;

    (iii) in all other cases, the maximum threshold is 15,000 euro;

(e) the benefits of the product or related transaction cannot be realised for the benefit of third parties, except in the case of death, disablement, survival to a predetermined advanced age, or similar events;

(f) in the case of products or related transactions allowing for the investment of funds in financial assets or claims, including insurance or other kinds of contingent claims–

    (i) the benefits of the product or related transaction are only realisable in the long term;

    (ii) the product or related transaction cannot be used as collateral; and

    (iii) during the contractual relationship, no accelerated payments are made, surrender clauses used or early termination takes place.

Politically exposed persons

4 (1) For the purposes of regulation 14(5)–

(a) individuals who are or have been entrusted with prominent public functions include the following–

    (i) heads of state, heads of government, ministers and deputy or assistant ministers;

    (ii) members of parliaments;

    (iii) members of supreme courts, of constitutional courts or of other high-level judicial bodies whose decisions are not generally subject to further appeal, other than in exceptional circumstances;

    (iv) members of courts of auditors or of the boards of central banks;

    (v) ambassadors, chargés d'affaires and high-ranking officers in the armed forces; and

    (vi) members of the administrative, management or supervisory bodies of state-owned enterprises;

(b) the categories set out in paragraphs (i) to (vi) of sub-paragraph (a) do not include middle-ranking or more junior officials;

(c) immediate family members include the following–

    (i) a spouse;

    (ii) a partner;

    (iii) children and their spouses or partners; and

    (iv) parents;

(d) persons known to be close associates include the following–

(i)   any individual who is known to have joint beneficial ownership of a legal entity or legal arrangement, or any other close business relations, with a person referred to in regulation 14(5)(a); and

(ii)   any individual who has sole beneficial ownership of a legal entity or legal arrangement which is known to have been set up for the benefit of a person referred to in regulation 14(5)(a).

(2)   In paragraph (1)(c), 'partner' means a person who is considered by his national law as equivalent to a spouse.

SCHEDULE 3

Professional Bodies

Regulations 17(2)(b), 23(1)(c) and 32(4)

Part 1

1   Association of Chartered Certified Accountants

2   Council for Licensed Conveyancers

3   Faculty of Advocates

4   General Council of the Bar

5   General Council of the Bar of Northern Ireland

6   Institute of Chartered Accountants in England and Wales

7   Institute of Chartered Accountants in Ireland

8   Institute of Chartered Accountants of Scotland

9   Law Society

10   Law Society of Scotland

11   Law Society of Northern Ireland

Part 2

12   Association of Accounting Technicians

13   Association of International Accountants

14   Association of Taxation Technicians

15   Chartered Institute of Management Accountants

16   Chartered Institute of Public Finance and Accountancy

17   Chartered Institute of Taxation

18   Faculty Office of the Archbishop of Canterbury

19   Insolvency Practitioners Association

20   Institute of Certified Bookkeepers

21   Institute of Financial Accountants

22   International Association of Book-keepers

SCHEDULE 4

Connected Persons

Regulation 37(2)

Corporate bodies

1   If the relevant person is a body corporate ('BC'), a person who is or has been–

(a)   an officer or manager of BC or of a parent undertaking of BC;

(b)   an employee of BC;

(c)   an agent of BC or of a parent undertaking of BC

Partnerships

2   If the relevant person is a partnership, a person who is or has been a member, manager, employee or agent of the partnership.

Unincorporated associations

3   If the relevant person is an unincorporated association of persons which is not a partnership, a person who is or has been an officer, manager, employee or agent of the association.

Individuals

4   If the relevant person is an individual, a person who is or has been an employee or agent of that individual.

SCHEDULE 5

Modifications in Relation to Appeals

Regulation 44(8)

Part 1
Primary Legislation

The Value Added Tax Act 1994 (c 23)

1   Part 5 of the Value Added Tax Act 1994 (appeals) is modified as follows–

(a)   omit section 84; and

(b)   in paragraphs (1)(a), (2)(a) and (3)(a) of section 87, omit ', or is recoverable as, VAT'.

The Financial Services and Markets Act 2000 (c 8)

2   Part 9 of the 2000 Act (hearings and appeals) is modified as follows–

(a)   in the application of section 133 and Schedule 13 to any appeal commenced before the coming into force of section 55 of the Consumer Credit Act

241

2006, for all the references to 'the Authority', substitute 'the Authority or the OFT (as the case may be)';

(b) in section 133(1)(a) for 'decision notice or supervisory notice in question' substitute 'notice under regulation 34(5) or (9) or 42(7) of the Money Laundering Regulations 2007';

(c) in section 133 omit subsections (6), (7), (8) and (12); and

(d) in section 133(9) for 'decision notice' in both places where it occurs substitute 'notice under regulation 34(5) or (9) or 42(7) of the Money Laundering Regulations 2007'.

Part 2
Secondary Legislation

The Financial Services and Markets Tribunal Rules 2001

3 In the application of the Financial Services and Markets Tribunal Rules 2001 to any appeal commenced before the coming into force of section 55 of the Consumer Credit Act 2006, for all the references to 'the Authority' substitute 'the Authority or the OFT (as the case may be)'.

SCHEDULE 6

Minor and Consequential Amendments

Regulation 51

Part 1
Primary Legislation

The Value Added Tax Act 1994 (c 23)

1 In section 83 of the Value Added Tax Act 1994 (appeals), omit paragraph (zz).

The Northern Ireland Act 1998 (c 47)

2 In paragraph 25 of Schedule 3 to the Northern Ireland Act 1998 (reserved matters), for '2003' substitute '2007'.

The Criminal Justice and Police Act 2001 (c 16)

3 In Part 1 of Schedule 1 to the Criminal Justice and Police Act 2001 (powers of seizure to which section 50 of the 2001 Act applies), after paragraph 73I insert–
'The Money Laundering Regulations 2007
73J
The power of seizure conferred by regulation 39(6) of the Money Laundering Regulations 2007 (entry to premises under warrant).'.

Part 2
Secondary Legislation

The Independent Qualified Conveyancers (Scotland) Regulations 1997

4   Regulation 28 of the Independent Qualified Conveyancers (Scotland) Regulations 1997 is revoked.

The Executry Practitioners (Scotland) Regulations 1997

5   Regulation 26 of the Executry Practitioners (Scotland) Regulations 1997 is revoked.

The Cross-Border Credit Transfers Regulations 1999

6   In regulation 12(2) of the Cross-Border Credit Transfers Regulations 1999, for '2003' substitute '2007'.

The Terrorism Act 2000 (Crown Servants and Regulators) Regulations 2001

7   In regulation 2 of the Terrorism Act 2000 (Crown Servants and Regulators) Regulations 2001, in the definition of 'relevant business', for 'has the meaning given by regulation 2(2) of the Money Laundering Regulations 2003' substitute 'means an activity carried on in the course of business by any of the persons listed in regulation 3(1)(a) to (h) of the Money Laundering Regulations 2007'.

The Representation of the People (England and Wales) Regulations 2001

8   In regulation 114(3)(b) of the Representation of the People (England and Wales) Regulations 2001, for '2003' substitute '2007'.

The Representation of the People (Scotland) Regulations 2001

9   In regulation 113(3)(b) of the Representation of the People (Scotland) Regulations 2001, for '2003' substitute '2007'.

The Financial Services and Markets Act 2000 (Regulated Activities) Order 2001

10   In article 72E(9) of the Financial Services and Markets Act 2000 (Regulated Activities) Order 2001, for '2003' substitute '2007'.

The Proceeds of Crime Act 2002 (Failure to Disclose Money Laundering: Specified Training) Order 2003

11   In article 2 of the Proceeds of Crime Act 2002 (Failure to Disclose Money Laundering: Specified Training) Order 2003, for 'regulation 3(1)(c)(ii) of the Money Laundering Regulations 2003' substitute 'regulation 21 of the Money Laundering Regulations 2007'.

The Public Contracts (Scotland) Regulations 2006

12   In regulation 23(1)(f) of the Public Contracts (Scotland) Regulations 2006, for '2003' substitute '2007'.

243

The Utilities Contracts (Scotland) Regulations 2006

13   In regulation 26(1)(f) of the Utilities Contracts (Scotland) Regulations 2006, for '2003' substitute '2007'.

The Public Contracts Regulations 2006

14   In regulation 23(1)(e) of the Public Contracts Regulations 2006, for '2003' substitute '2007'.

The Utilities Contracts Regulations 2006

15   In regulation 26(1)(e) of the Utilities Contracts Regulations 2006, for '2003' substitute '2007'.

EXPLANATORY NOTE

(This note is not part of the Regulations)

These Regulations replace the Money Laundering Regulations 2003 (SI 2003/3075) with updated provisions which implement in part Directive 2005/60/EC (OJ No L 309, 25.11.2005, p 15) of the European Parliament and of the Council on the prevention of the use of the financial system for the purpose of money laundering and terrorist financing. A Transposition Note setting out how the main elements of this directive will be transposed into UK law is available from the Financial Services Team, HM Treasury, 1 Horse Guards Road, London SW1A 2HQ. An impact assessment has also been prepared. Copies of both documents have been placed in the library of each House of Parliament and are available on HM Treasury's website (**www.hm-treasury.gov.uk**).

The Regulations provide for various steps to be taken by the financial services sector and other persons to detect and prevent money laundering and terrorist financing. Obligations are imposed on 'relevant persons' (defined in regulation 3 and subject to the exclusions in regulation 4), who are credit and financial institutions, auditors, accountants, tax advisers and insolvency practitioners, independent legal professionals, trust or company service providers, estate agents, high value dealers and casinos.

Relevant persons are required, when undertaking certain activities in the course of business, to apply customer due diligence measures where they establish a business relationship, carry out an occasional transaction, suspect money laundering or terrorist finance or doubt the accuracy of customer identification information (regulation 7). Customer due diligence measures (defined in regulation 5) consist of identifying and verifying the identity of the customer and any beneficial owner (defined in regulation 6) of the customer, and obtaining information on the purpose and intended nature of the business relationship. Relevant persons also have to undertake ongoing monitoring of their business relationships (regulation 8).

Regulation 9 sets out the general rule on the timing of the verification of the customer's identity and certain exceptions. Regulation 10 sets out when casinos must identify and verify their customers. Failure to apply such measures means that a person cannot establish or continue a business relationship with the customer concerned or undertake an occasional transaction (regulation 11). Regulation 12 provides an exception from the requirement to identify the beneficial owner for debt issues held in trust.

Relevant persons may apply simplified customer due diligence measures for the products, customers or transactions listed in regulation 13 and must apply enhanced measures in the four situations set out in regulation 14. Regulation 15 sets out the obligations on relevant persons in respect of their overseas branches and subsidiaries. Regulation 16 imposes obligations in respect of shell banks and anonymous accounts. Regulation 17 lists the persons on whom relevant persons can rely to perform customer due diligence measures. Regulation 18 provides for the Treasury to make directions where the Financial Action Task Force applies counter-measures to a non-EEA state.

Part 3 imposes obligations in respect of record-keeping (regulation 19), policies and procedures (regulation 20) and staff training (regulation 21).

Part 4 deals with supervision and registration. Regulation 23 allocates supervisory authorities for different relevant persons. Regulation 24 sets out the duties of supervisors. Money service businesses, high value dealers and trust or company service providers which are not otherwise registered are subject to a system of mandatory registration set out in regulations 25 to 30. Money service businesses and trust or company service providers must not be registered unless the business, its owners, its nominated officer and senior managers are fit and proper persons: regulation 28. Other sectors will only be required to register if the supervisor decides to maintain a register (regulations 33 and 34). Regulation 35 enables supervisors to impose charges on persons they supervise.

Part 5 provides enforcement powers for certain supervisors, including powers to obtain information and enter and inspect premises (regulations 37 to 41). Civil penalties may be imposed by these supervisors under regulation 42 on persons who fail to comply with the requirements of Parts 2, 3 and 4. Provision is made for reviews of and appeals against such penalties (regulations 43 and 44). Relevant persons who fail to comply with the requirements of Parts 2, 3 and 4 will also be guilty of a criminal offence: regulations 45 to 47. Persons convicted of a criminal offence may not also be liable to a civil penalty.

Part 6 contains provision for the recovery of penalties and charges through the court (regulation 48), imposes an obligation on certain public authorities to report suspicions of money laundering or terrorist financing (regulation 49) and makes transitional provision (regulation 50). Regulation 51 makes minor and consequential amendments to primary and secondary legislation.

B1

The Law Society's Anti-money Laundering Practice Note (22 February 2008)

DEFINITIONS AND GLOSSARY

Definitions

Beneficial owners	see – chapter 4.7
Business relationship	a business, professional or commercial relationship between a relevant person and a customer, which is expected by the relevant person at the time when contact is established to have an element of duration
Customer due diligence	see – chapter 4
Criminal conduct	conduct which constitutes an offence in any part of the UK or would constitute an offence in any part of the UK if it occurred there – see s340(2) of POCA
Criminal property	property which is, or represents, a person's benefit from criminal conduct, where the alleged offender knows or suspects that it is such – see also the definition of property
Disclosure	a report made to SOCA under the Proceeds of Crime Act 2002 – also referred to as a suspicious activity report (SAR)
Insolvency practitioner	any person who acts as an insolvency practitioner within the meaning of section 388 of the Insolvency Act 1986 (as amended) or article 3 of the Insolvency (Northern Ireland) Order 1989 (as amended)
Inter vivos trust	a trust which takes effect while a person is alive
Legal professional privilege	see – chapter 6.4
Nominated officer	a person nominated within the firm to make disclosures to SOCA under the Proceeds of Crime Act 2002 – also referred to as a money laundering reporting officer (MLRO)
Occasional transaction	a transaction (carried out other than as part of a business relationship) amounting to 15,000 euros or more, whether the transaction is carried out in a single operation or several operations which appear to be linked
Ongoing monitoring	see – chapter 4.4

Overseas criminal conduct	conduct which occurs overseas that would be a criminal offence if it occurred in the UK
	does not include conduct which occurred overseas where it is known or believed on reasonable grounds that the relevant conduct occurred in a particular country or territory outside the UK, and such conduct was in fact not unlawful under the criminal law then applying in that country or territory
	that exemption will not apply to overseas criminal conduct if it would attract a maximum sentence in excess of 12 months imprisonment were the conduct to have occurred in the UK
	will always be exempt if the overseas conduct is such that it would constitute an offence under the Gaming Act 1968, the Lotteries & Amusements Act 1976 or s23 or s35 of the Financial Services and Markets Act 2000
	see s102 of SOCPA
Politically exposed persons	see – chapter 4.9.2
Privileged circumstances	see – chapter 6.5
Property	all property whether situated in the UK or abroad, including money, real and personal property, things in action, intangible property and an interest in land or a right in relation to any other property.
Regulated sector	activities, professions and entities regulated for the purposes of AML/CTF obligations – see chapter 1
Tax adviser	a firm or sole practitioner who, by way of business, provides advice about the tax affairs of another person, when providing such services
Terrorist property	money or other property which is likely to be used for the purposes of terrorism, the proceeds of the commission of acts of terrorism and the proceeds of acts carried out for the purposes of terrorism
Trust or company service provider	a firm or sole practitioner who by way of business provides any of the following services to other persons –
	forming companies or other legal persons
	acting or arranging for another person to act
	as a director or secretary of a company;
	as a partner of a partnership; or
	in a similar position in relation to other legal persons;
	providing a registered office, business address, correspondence or administrative address or other related services for a company, partnership or any other legal person or arrangement;
	acting, or arranging for another person to act, as –
	a trustee of an express trust or similar legal arrangement; or
	a nominee shareholder for another person other than a company listed on a regulated market when providing such services.

Glossary

AIM	Alternative Investment Market
AML / CTF	Anti-money laundering / counter-terrorist financing
CDD	Customer due diligence
EEA	European Economic Area
FATF	Financial Action Task-force
FSA	Financial Services Authority
GRO	General Register Office
HMRC	Her Majesty's Revenue and Customs
IBA	International Bar Association
JMLSG	Joint Money Laundering Steering Group
LLP's	Limited Liability Partnerships
LPP	Legal professional privilege
PEPs	Politically exposed persons
POCA	Proceeds of Crime Act 2002
Regulations	Money Laundering Regulations 2007
SARs	Suspicious activity reports
SRA	Solicitors Regulation Authority
SOCA	Serious Organised Crime Agency
Terrorism Act	Terrorism Act 2000
Third directive	Third European Money Laundering Directive

CHAPTER 1 – INTRODUCTION

1.1 General comments

Solicitors are key professionals in the business and financial world, facilitating vital transactions that underpin the UK economy. As such, they have a significant role to play in ensuring their services are not used to further a criminal purpose. As professionals, solicitors must act with integrity and uphold the law, and they must not engage in criminal activity.

Money laundering and terrorist financing are serious threats to society, losing revenue and endangering life, and fuelling other criminal activity.

This practice note aims to assist solicitors in England and Wales to meet their obligations under the UK anti-money laundering and counter-terrorist financing (AML/CTF) regime.

1.2 Status of this practice note

This practice note replaces previous Law Society guidance and good practice information on complying with AML/CTF obligations.

The purpose of this practice note is to:

- outline the legal and regulatory framework of AML/CTF obligations for solicitors within the UK

- outline good practice on implementing the legal requirements
- outline good practice in developing systems and controls to prevent solicitors being used to facilitate money laundering and terrorist financing
- provide direction on applying the risk-based approach to compliance effectively

The Solicitors Regulation Authority (SRA) will take into account whether a solicitor has complied with this practice note when undertaking its role as regulator of professional conduct, and as a supervisory authority for the purposes of the regulations. This practice note is not mandatory but a solicitor may be asked by the SRA to justify a decision to deviate from it.

Some solicitors' firms are authorised and regulated by the FSA because they are involved in mainstream regulated activities, e.g. advising clients directly on investments such as stocks and shares. Those firms should also consider the Joint Money Laundering Steering Group's guidance.

This practice note is not a substitute for the law, and compliance with it, is not a defence to offences under POCA, the Terrorism Act or the regulations. However, courts will generally have regard to any good practice on a particular topic issued by a professional body when considering the standard of a professional's conduct and whether they acted reasonably, honestly and appropriately.

We are seeking Treasury approval of this practice note, which, in accordance with regulation 45(2), will require the court to consider compliance with its contents in assessing whether a person committed an offence or took all reasonable steps and exercised all due diligence to avoid committing the offence.

1.3 Definition of money laundering

Money laundering is generally defined as the process by which the proceeds of crime, and the true ownership of those proceeds, are changed so that the proceeds appear to come from a legitimate source. Under POCA, the definition is broader and more subtle. Money laundering can arise from small profits and savings from relatively minor crimes, such as regulatory breaches, minor tax evasion or benefit fraud. A deliberate attempt to obscure the ownership of illegitimate funds is not necessary.

There are three acknowledged phases to money laundering: placement, layering and integration. However, the broader definition of money laundering offences in POCA includes even passive possession of criminal property as money laundering.

1.3.1 Placement

Cash generated from crime is placed in the financial system. This is the point when proceeds of crime are most apparent and at risk of detection. Because banks and financial institutions have developed AML procedures, criminals look for other ways of placing cash within the financial system. You can be targeted because a solicitor's firm commonly deals with client money.

1.3.2 Layering

Once proceeds of crime are in the financial system, layering obscures their origins by passing the money through complex transactions. These often involve different entities like companies and trusts and can take place in multiple jurisdictions. You may be targeted at this stage and detection can be difficult.

1.3.3   Integration

Once the origin of the funds has been obscured, the criminal is able to make the funds reappear as legitimate funds or assets. They will invest funds in legitimate businesses or other forms of investment, often using you to buy a property, set up a trust, acquire a company, or even settle litigation, among other activities. This is the most difficult stage of money laundering to detect.

1.4   Legal framework

1.4.1   Financial Action Task Force (FATF)

This was created in 1989 by the G7 Paris summit, building on UN treaties on trafficking of illicit substances in 1988 and confiscating the proceeds of crime in 1990. In 1990, FATF released their 40 recommendations for fighting money laundering. Between October 2001 and October 2004 it released nine further special recommendations to prevent terrorist funding.

1.4.2   European Union directives

1991 – FIRST MONEY LAUNDERING DIRECTIVE

The European Commission issued this to comply with the FATF recommendations. It applied to financial institutions, and required member states to make money laundering a criminal offence. It was incorporated into UK law via the Criminal Justice Act 1991, the Drug Trafficking Act 1994 and the Money Laundering Regulations 1993.

2001 – SECOND MONEY LAUNDERING DIRECTIVE

This incorporated the amendments to the FATF recommendations. It extended anti-money laundering obligations to a defined set of activities provided by a number of service professionals, such as independent legal professionals, accountants, auditors, tax advisers and real estate agents. It was incorporated into UK law via the Proceeds of Crime Act 2002 and the Money Laundering Regulations 2003.

2005 – THIRD MONEY LAUNDERING DIRECTIVE

This extended due diligence measures to beneficial owners, recognising that such measures can be applied on a risk-based approach, and required enhanced due diligence to be undertaken in certain circumstances. It is incorporated into UK law by the Money Laundering Regulations 2007 and the Terrorism Act 2000 (Amendment) Regulations 2007 (TACT regulations 2007) and Proceeds of Crime Act 2002 (Amendment) Regulations 2007 (POCA regulations 2007) (the TACT Regulations 2007 and the POCA Regulations 2007).

1.4.3   Proceeds of Crime Act 2002 (POCA)

SCOPE

POCA, as amended, establishes a number of money laundering offences including:

• principal money laundering offences

- offences of failing to report suspected money laundering
- offences of tipping off about a money laundering disclosure, tipping off about a money laundering investigation and prejudicing money laundering investigations

The TACT Regulations 2007 and the POCA Regulations 2007 repealed the s333 POCA tipping off offence. It has been replaced by section 333A which creates two new offences. S342(1) has also been amended to reflect these new offences.

APPLICATION

POCA applies to all persons, although certain failure to report offences and the tipping off offences only apply to persons who are engaged in activities in the regulated sector.

The Proceeds of Crime Act 2002 (Business in the Regulated Sector and Supervisory Authorities) Order 2007 amended the Proceeds of Crime Act 2002, changing the definition of the regulated sector to bring it into line with the Money Laundering Regulations 2007.

Under Schedule 9 of POCA, key activities which may be relevant to you are the provision by way of business, in one of the following ways:

- advice about the tax affairs of another person by a firm or sole practitioner
- legal or notarial services by a firm or sole practitioner involving the participation in financial or real property transactions concerning
  - the buying and selling of real property or business entities
  - the managing of client money, securities or other assets
  - the opening or management of bank, savings or securities accounts
  - the organisation of contributions necessary for the creation, operation or management of companies
  - the creation, operation or management of trusts, companies or similar structures

Chapters 5, 6, and 8 of this practice note provide more details on your obligations under POCA.

1.4.4   Terrorism Act 2000

SCOPE

The Terrorism Act 2000, as amended, establishes several offences about engaging in or facilitating terrorism, as well as raising or possessing funds for terrorist purposes. It establishes a list of proscribed organisations the Secretary of State believes are involved in terrorism. The TACT and POCA Regulations 2007 entered into force on 26 December 2007 and introduced tipping off offences and defences to the principal terrorist property offences into the Terrorism Act 2000.

Read about these provisions in Chapter 7

APPLICATION

The Terrorism Act applies to all persons. There is also a failure to disclose offence and tipping off offences for those operating within the regulated sector.

The Terrorism Act 2000 (Business in the Regulated Sector and Supervisory Authorities) Order 2007 amended the Terrorism Act, changing the definition of the regulated sector to bring it into line with the Money Laundering Regulations 2007.

Chapters 7 and 8 provide more detail on your obligations under the Terrorism Act.

1.4.5 The Money Laundering Regulations 2007

SCOPE

The Money Laundering Regulations 2007 repeal and replace the Money Laundering Regulations 2003 and implement the third directive. They set administrative requirements for the anti-money laundering regime within the regulated sector and outline the scope of customer due diligence.

The regulations aim to limit the use of professional services for money laundering by requiring professionals to know their clients and monitor the use of their services by clients.

APPLICATION

Regulation 3 states that the regulations apply to persons acting in the course of businesses carried on in the UK in the following areas:

- credit institutions
- financial institutions
- auditors, insolvency practitioners, external accountants and tax advisers
- independent legal professionals
- trust or company service providers
- estate agents
- high value dealers
- casinos

INDEPENDENT LEGAL PROFESSIONAL

An independent legal professional includes a solicitor working in a firm or as a sole practitioner who by way of business provides legal or notarial services to other persons. It does not include solicitors employed by a public authority or working in-house.

The regulations only apply to certain solicitors' activities where there is a high risk of money laundering occurring. As such, they apply where solicitors participate in financial or real property transactions concerning:

- buying and selling of real property or business entities
- managing of client money, securities or other assets
- opening or management of bank, savings or securities accounts
- organisation of contributions necessary for the creation, operation or management of companies
- creation, operation or management of trusts, companies or similar structures

You will be participating in a transaction by assisting in the planning or execution of the transaction or otherwise acting for or on behalf of a client in the transaction.

ACTIVITIES COVERED BY THE REGULATIONS

In terms of the activities covered, note that:

- managing client money is narrower than handling it
- opening or managing a bank account is wider than simply opening a solicitor's client account. It would be likely to cover solicitors acting as a trustee, attorney or a receiver

ACTIVITIES NOT COVERED BY THE REGULATIONS

The Treasury has confirmed that the following would not generally be viewed as participation in financial transactions:

- preparing a home information pack or any document or information for inclusion in a HIP – it is specifically excluded under Regulation 4(1)(f)
- payment on account of costs to a solicitor or payment of a solicitor's bill
- provision of legal advice
- participation in litigation or a form of alternative dispute resolution
- will-writing, although you should consider whether any accompanying taxation advice is covered
- publicly-funded work

If you are uncertain whether the regulations apply to your work, seek legal advice on the individual circumstances of your practice or simply take the broadest of the possible approaches to compliance with the regulations.

WORKING ELSEWHERE IN THE REGULATED SECTOR

When deciding whether you are within the regulated sector for the purpose of the regulations, you also need to consider whether you offer services bringing you within the definitions of a tax adviser, insolvency practitioner, or trust or company service provider. You must also consider the full range of related services, such as tax planning.

You will also need to consider whether your firm undertakes activities falling within the definition of financial institution, particularly with respect to the list of operations covered by the banking consolidation directive, as contained in schedule 1 of the regulations. When considering those operations, you should note that a will is not a designated investment, so storing it is not a safe custody service, and is not covered by the regulations.

Being nominated as a trustee under a will does not amount to being a trust and company service provider, because the trust is not formed until the testator's death.

If you are an independent legal professional within the regulated sector and you also fall within an another category, such as work regulated by FSA, this may affect your supervision under these regulations. You should contact the SRA for advice on any supervisory arrangements that they may have in place with other supervisory authorities.

1.5 Other Law Society services

We provide a number of other services to assist you in meeting your AML/CTF obligations:

- a monthly e-newsletter, Gatekeeper, providing updates on legislation and case law, highlighting emerging warning signs and criminal methodologies and detailing training opportunities
- the Practice Advice Service, which can be contacted on 0870 606 2522 during office hours, which will help you to navigate the practice note and talk through general issues relating to compliance
- the AML directory listing solicitors willing to give other solicitors thirty minutes of free advice on legal issues relating to compliance
- training opportunities

All of the Law Society's AML/CTF services can be accessed from **www.lawsociety.org.uk/moneylaundering**.

1.6 Acknowledgements

Many have had input into the preparation of this practice note. The members of the Money Laundering Task Force and others mentioned below deserve particular acknowledgement for both the time and energy they have committed to the development of the guidance.

Task force

Robin Booth	BCL Burton Copeland
Alison Matthews	Irwin Mitchell
Christopher Murray	Kingsley Napley
Peter Burrell	Herbert Smith
Stephen Gentle	Kingsley Napley
Nicola Boulton	Byrne and Partners
Louise Delahunty	Simmons and Simmons
Nick Cray	Lovells
Peter Rodd	Boys and Maugham
Chris McNeil	Freshfields Bruckhaus Deringer

Law Society staff

Che Odlum	Policy Adviser
Emma Oettinger	Policy Adviser
James Richards	E-communications Manager

Others

Richard Bark-Jones	Morecrofts
Daren Allen	DLA Piper
Sarah de Gay	Slaughter and May
Clive Cutbill	Withers
Johanna Waritay	Clifford Chance
Suzie Ogilvey	Linklaters
Elizabeth Richards	SRA

The Law Society would also like to specifically thank the following people for the generous provision of their time and expertise in assisting the Law Society with its campaign to ensure that the requirements regarding identification of beneficial owners were sufficiently clear and workable:

Richard Bark-Jones	Morecrofts
Toby Graham	Farrer & Co
Rabinder Singh QC	Matrix Chambers
Alex Balin	Matrix Chambers
Michael Furness QC	Wilberforce Chambers
Nicholas Le Poidevin	Lincolns Inn
Nicholas Green QC	Brick Court Chambers
Martyn Frost	STEP
Keith Johnston	STEP
Jacob Rigg	STEP

CHAPTER 2 – THE RISK-BASED APPROACH

2.1 General comments

The possibility of being used to assist with money laundering and terrorist financing poses many risks for your firm, including:

- criminal and disciplinary sanctions for firms and individual solicitors
- civil action against the firm as a whole and individual partners
- damage to reputation leading to a loss of business

These risks must be identified, assessed and mitigated, just as you do for all business risks facing your firm. If you know your client well and understand your instructions thoroughly, you will be better placed to assess risks and spot suspicious activities. Applying the risk-based approach will vary between firms. While you can, and should, start from the premise that most of your clients are not launderers or terrorist financers, you must assess the risk level particular to your firm and implement reasonable and considered controls to minimise those risks.

No matter how thorough your risk assessment or how appropriate your controls, some criminals may still succeed in exploiting you for criminal purposes. But an effective, risk-based approach and documented, risk-based judgements on individual clients and retainers will enable your firm to justify your position on managing the risk to law enforcement, courts and professional supervisors (oversight bodies).

The risk-based approach means that you focus your resources on the areas of greatest risk. The resulting benefits of this approach include:

- more efficient and effective use of resources proportionate to the risks faced
- minimising compliance costs and burdens on clients
- greater flexibility to respond to emerging risks as laundering and terrorist financing methods change

2.2 Application

The Money Laundering Regulations 2007 permit a risk-based approach to compliance with customer due diligence obligations.

This approach does not apply to reporting suspicious activity, because POCA and the Terrorism Act lay down specific legal requirements not to engage in certain activities and to make reports of suspicious activities once a suspicion is held. [See chapters 5 and 7] The risk-based approach still applies to ongoing monitoring of clients and retainers which enables you to identify suspicions.

2.3 Assessing your firm's risk profile

This depends on your firm's size, type of clients, and the practice areas it engages in.
You should consider the following factors:

2.3.1 Client demographic

Your client demographic can affect the risk of money laundering or terrorist financing. Factors which may vary the risk level include whether you:

- have a high turnover of clients or a stable existing client base
- act for politically exposed persons (PEPs)
- act for clients without meeting them

- practice in locations with high levels of acquisitive crime or for clients who have convictions for acquisitive crimes, which increases the likelihood the client may possess criminal property
- act for clients affiliated to countries with high levels of corruption or where terrorist organisations operate
- act for entities that have a complex ownership structure
- are easily able to obtain details of beneficial owners of your client or not

2.3.2 Services and areas of law

Some services and areas of law could provide opportunities to facilitate money laundering or terrorist financing. For example:

- complicated financial or property transactions
- providing assistance in setting up trusts or company structures, which could be used to obscure ownership of property
- payments that are made to or received from third parties
- payments made by cash
- transactions with a cross-border element

Simply because a client or a retainer falls within a risk category does not mean that money laundering or terrorist financing is occurring. You need to ensure your internal controls are designed to address the identified risks and take appropriate steps to minimise and deal with these risks.

Chapter 11 provides more information on warning signs to be alert to when assessing risk.

2.4 Assessing individual risk

Determining the risks posed by a specific client or retainer will then assist in applying internal controls in a proportionate and effective manner.

You may consider whether:

- your client is within a high risk category
- you can be easily satisfied the CDD material for your client is reliable and allows you to identify the client and verify that identity
- you can be satisfied you understand their control and ownership structure
- the retainer involves an area of law at higher risk of laundering or terrorist financing
- your client wants you to handle funds without an underlying transaction, contrary to the Solicitors' Account Rules
- there are any aspects of the particular retainer which would increase or decrease the risks

This assessment helps you adjust your internal controls to the appropriate level of risk presented by the individual client or the particular retainer. Different aspects of your CDD controls will meet the different risks posed:

If you are satisfied you have verified the client's identity, but the retainer is high risk, you may require fee earners to monitor the transaction more closely, rather than seek further verification of identity.

If you have concerns about verifying a client's identity, but the retainer is low risk, you may expend greater resources on verification and monitor the transaction in the normal way.

Risk assessment is an ongoing process both for the firm generally and for each client, business relationship and retainer. In a solicitor's practice it is the overall information held by the firm gathered while acting for the client that will inform the risk assessment process, rather than sophisticated computer data analysis systems. The more you know your client and understand your instructions, the better placed you will be to assess risks and spot suspicious activities.

CHAPTER 3 – SYSTEMS, POLICIES AND PROCEDURES

3.1 General comments

Develop systems to meet your obligations and risk profile in a risk-based and proportionate manner. Policies and procedures supporting these systems mean that staff apply the systems consistently and firms can demonstrate to oversight bodies that processes facilitating compliance are in place.

3.2 Application

Regulation 20 of the Money Laundering Regulations 2007 requires the regulated sector to have certain systems in place. If you are in the regulated sector, failing to have those systems is an offence, punishable by a fine or up to two years' imprisonment. You must demonstrate your compliance to the SRA, as supervisor under the regulations.

If you are outside the regulated sector, you should still consider how these systems can assist you to comply with your obligations to report suspicious transactions in accordance with POCA and the Terrorism Act.

3.3 Nominated officers

3.3.1 Why have a nominated officer?

Regulation 20(2)(d)(i) requires that all firms within the regulated sector must have a nominated officer to receive disclosures under Part 7 of POCA and the Terrorism Act, and to make disclosures to SOCA.

Regulation 20(3) provides that there is no requirement to have a nominated officer in the regulated sector if you are an individual who provides regulated services but do not employ any people or act in association with anyone else.

Firms who do not provide services within the regulated sector should consider appointing a nominated officer, even though it is not required, because POCA and the Terrorism Act still apply. The Solicitors' Code of Conduct 2007 requires business management systems facilitating compliance with legal obligations.

3.3.2 Who should be a nominated officer?

Your nominated officer should be of sufficient seniority to make decisions on reporting which can impact your firm's business relations with your clients and your exposure to criminal, civil, regulatory and disciplinary sanctions. They should also be in a position of sufficient responsibility to enable them to have access to all of your firm's client files and business information to enable them to make the required decisions on the basis of all information held by the firm.

Firms authorised by the FSA will need to obtain the FSA's approval to the appointment of the nominated officer as this is a controlled function under section 59 of the Financial Services and Markets Act 2000.

3.3.3   Role of the nominated officer

Your nominated officer is responsible for ensuring that, when appropriate, the information or other matter leading to knowledge or suspicion, or reasonable grounds for knowledge or suspicion of money laundering is properly disclosed to the relevant authority. The decision to report, or not to report, must not be subject to the consent of anyone else. Your nominated officer will also liaise with SOCA or law enforcement on the issue of whether to proceed with a transaction or what information may be disclosed to clients or third parties.

The size and nature of some firms may lead to the nominated officer delegating certain duties regarding the firm's AML/CTF obligations. In some large firms, one or more permanent deputies of suitable seniority may be appointed. All firms will need to consider arrangements for temporary cover when the nominated officer is absent.

3.4   Risk assessment

You can extend your existing risk management systems to address AML and CTF risks. The detail and sophistication of these systems will depend on your firm's size and the complexity of the business it undertakes. Ways of incorporating your risk assessment of clients, business relationships and transactions into the overall risk assessment will be governed by the size of your firm and how regularly compliance staff and senior management are involved in day-to-day activities.

Issues which may be covered in a risk assessment system include:

- the firm's current risk profile
- how AML/CTF risks will be assessed, and processes for re-assessment and updating of the firm's risk profile
- internal controls to be implemented to mitigate the risks
- which firm personnel have authority to make risk-based decisions on compliance on individual files
- how compliance will be monitored and effectiveness of internal controls will be reviewed

3.5   Internal controls and monitoring compliance

The level of internal controls and extent to which monitoring needs to take place will be affected by:

- your firm's size
- the nature, scale and complexity of its practice
- its overall risk profile

Issues which may be covered in an internal controls system include:

- the level of personnel permitted to exercise discretion on the risk-based application of the regulations, and under what circumstances
- CDD requirements to be met for simplified, standard and enhanced due diligence
- when outsourcing of CDD obligations or reliance will be permitted, and on what conditions
- how you will restrict work being conducted on a file where CDD has not been completed
- the circumstances in which delayed CDD is permitted
- when cash payments will be accepted
- when payments will be accepted from or made to third parties
- the manner in which disclosures are to be made to the nominated officer

Monitoring compliance will assist you to assess whether the policies and procedures you have implemented are effective in forestalling money laundering and terrorist financing opportunities within your firm. Issues which may be covered in a compliance system include:

- procedures to be undertaken to monitor compliance, which may involve:
  - random file audits
  - file checklists to be completed before opening or closing a file
  - a nominated officer's log of situations brought to their attention, queries from staff and reports made
- reports to be provided from the nominated officer to senior management on compliance
- how to rectify lack of compliance, when identified
- how lessons learnt will be communicated back to staff and fed back into the risk profile of the firm

3.6 Customer due diligence

You are required to have a system outlining the CDD measures to be applied to specific clients. You should consider recording your firm's risk tolerances to be able to demonstrate to your supervisor that your CDD measures are appropriate.

Your CDD system may include:

- when CDD is to be undertaken
- information to be recorded on client identity
- information to be obtained to verify identity, either specifically or providing a range of options with a clear statement of who can exercise their discretion on the level of verification to be undertaken in any particular case
- when simplified due diligence may occur
- what steps need to be taken for enhanced due diligence
- what steps need to be taken to ascertain whether your client is a PEP
- when CDD needs to occur and under what circumstances delayed CDD is permitted
- how to conduct CDD on existing clients
- what ongoing monitoring is required

For suggested methods on how to conduct CDD see Chapter 4 of this practice note.

3.7 Disclosures

Firms, but not sole practitioners, need to have a system clearly setting out the requirements for making a disclosure under POCA and the Terrorism Act. These may include:

- the circumstances in which a disclosure is likely to be required
- how and when information is to be provided to the nominated officer or their deputies
- resources which can be used to resolve difficult issues around making a disclosure
- how and when a disclosure is to be made to SOCA
- how to manage a client when a disclosure is made while waiting for consent
- the need to be alert to tipping off issues

For details on when a disclosure needs to be made see chapters 5, 6 and 7 of this practice note. For details on how to make a disclosure see chapter 8 of this practice note.

3.8 Record keeping

Various records must be kept to comply with the regulations and defend any allegations against the firm in relation to money laundering and failure to report offences. A firm's records system must outline what records are to be kept, the form in which they should be kept and how long they should be kept.

Regulation 19 requires that firms keep records of CDD material and supporting evidence and records in respect of the relevant business relationship or occasional transaction. Adapt your standard archiving procedures for these requirements.

3.8.1 CDD material

You may keep either a copy of verification material, or references to it. Keep it for five years after the business relationship ends or the occasional transaction is completed. Consider holding CDD material separately from the client file for each retainer, as it may be needed by different practice groups in your firm.

Depending on the size and sophistication of your firm's record storage procedures you may wish to:

- scan the verification material and hold it electronically
- take photocopies of CDD material and hold it in hard copy with a statement that the original has been seen
- accept certified copies of CDD material and hold them in hard copy
- keep electronic copies or hard copies of the results of any electronic verification checks
- record reference details of the CDD material sighted

The option of merely recording reference details may be particularly useful when taking instructions from clients at their home or other locations away from your office. The types of details it would be useful to record include:

- any reference numbers on documents or letters
- any relevant dates, such as issue, expiry or writing
- details of the issuer or writer
- all identity details recorded on the document

Where you are relied upon by another person under Regulation 17 for the completion of CDD measures, you must keep the relevant documents for five years from the date on which you were relied upon.

3.8.2 Risk assessment notes

You should consider keeping records of decisions on risk assessment processes of what CDD was undertaken. This does not need to be in significant detail, but merely a note on the CDD file stating the risk level you attributed to a file and why you considered you had sufficient CDD information. For example:

This is a low risk client with no beneficial owners providing medium risk instructions. Standard CDD material was obtained and medium level ongoing monitoring is to occur.

Such an approach may assist firms to demonstrate they have applied a risk-based approach in a reasonable and proportionate manner. Notes taken at the time are better than justifications provided later.

Firms may choose standard categories of comment to apply to notes.

3.8.3   Supporting evidence and records

You must keep all original documents or copies admissible in court proceedings.

Records of a particular transaction, either as an occasional transaction or within a business relationship, must be kept for five years after the date the transaction is completed.

All other documents supporting records must be kept for five years after the completion of the business relationship.

3.8.4   Suspicions and disclosures

It is recommended that you keep comprehensive records of suspicions and disclosures because disclosure of a suspicious activity is a defence to criminal proceedings. Such records may include notes of:

- ongoing monitoring undertaken and concerns raised by fee earners and staff
- discussions with the nominated officer regarding concerns
- advice sought and received regarding concerns
- why the concerns did not amount to a suspicion and a disclosure was not made
- copies of any disclosures made
- conversations with SOCA, law enforcement, insurers, supervisory authorities etc regarding disclosures made
- decisions not to make a report to SOCA which may be important for the nominated officer to justify his position to law enforcement

You should ensure records are not inappropriately disclosed to the client or third parties to avoid offences of tipping off and prejudicing an investigation, and to maintain a good relationship with your clients. This may be achieved by maintaining a separate file, either for the client or for the practice area.

3.8.5   Data protection

The Data Protection Act 1998 applies to you and SOCA. It allows clients or others to make subject access requests for data held by them. Such requests could cover any disclosures made.

Section 29 of the Data Protection Act 1998 states you need not provide personal data where disclosure would be likely to prejudice the prevention or detection of crime, or the apprehension or prosecution of offenders.

HM Treasury and the Information Commissioner have issued guidance which essentially provides that the Section 29 exception would apply where granting access would amount to tipping off. This may extend to suspicions only reported internally within the firm.

If you decide the Section 29 exception applies, document steps taken to assess this, to respond to any enquiries by the Information Commissioner.

Note the definition of personal data.

3.9   Communication and training

Your staff members are the most effective defence against launderers and terrorist financers who would seek to abuse the services provided by your firm.

Regulation 20 requires that you communicate your AML/CTF obligations to your staff, while regulation 21 requires that you provide staff with appropriate training on their legal obligations and information on how to recognise and deal with money laundering and terrorist financing risks.

Rule 5 of the Solicitors' Code of Conduct also requires you to train your staff to a level appropriate to their work and level of responsibility.

3.9.1 Criminal sanctions and defences

Receiving insufficient training is a defence for individual staff members who fail to report a suspicion of money laundering. However, it is not a defence to terrorist funding charges, and leaves your firm vulnerable to sanctions under the regulations for failing to properly train your staff.

3.9.2 Who should be trained?

When setting up a training and communication system you should consider:

- which staff require training
- what form the training will take
- how often training should take place
- how staff will be kept up-to-date with emerging risk factors for the firm

Assessments of who should receive training should include who deals with clients in areas of practice within the regulated sector, handles funds or otherwise assists with compliance. Consider fee earners, reception staff, administration staff and finance staff, because they will each be differently involved in compliance and so have different training requirements.

Training can take many forms and may include:

- face-to-face training seminars
- completion of online training sessions
- attendance at AML/CTF conferences
- participation in dedicated AML/CTF forums
- review of publications on current AML/CTF issues
- firm or practice group meetings for discussion of AML/CTF issues and risk factors

Providing an AML/CTF policy manual is useful to raise staff awareness and can be a continual reference source between training sessions.

3.9.3 How often?

You are required to provide training at regular and appropriate intervals. In determining whether your training programme meets this requirement, you should have regard to the firm's risk profile and the level of involvement certain staff have in ensuring compliance.

You should consider retaining evidence of your assessment of training needs and steps taken to meet such needs.

You should also consider:

- criminal sanctions and reputational risks of non-compliance
- developments in the common law
- changing criminal methodologies

Some type of training for all relevant staff every two years is preferable.

3.9.4   Communicating with your clients

While not specifically required by the regulations, we consider it useful for you to tell your client about your AML/CTF obligations. Clients are then generally more willing to provide required information when they see it as a standard requirement.

You may wish to advise your client of the following issues:

- the requirement to conduct CDD to comply with the regulations
- whether any electronic verification is to be undertaken during the CDD process
- the requirement to report suspicious transactions

Consider the manner and timing of your communications, for example whether the information will be provided in the standard client care letter or otherwise.

CHAPTER 4 – CUSTOMER DUE DILIGENCE

4.1   General comments

Customer due diligence (CDD) is required by the Money Laundering Regulations 2007 because you can better identify suspicious transactions if you know your customer and understand the reasoning behind the instructions they give you.

4.2   Application

You must conduct CDD on those clients who retain you for services regulated under the regulations (see Chapter 1). Rule 2 of the Solicitors' Code of Conduct is also relevant to all solicitors.

4.3   CDD in general

4.3.1   When is CDD required?

Regulation 7 requires that you conduct CDD when:

- establishing a business relationship
- carrying out an occasional transaction
- you suspect money laundering or terrorist financing
- you doubt the veracity or adequacy of documents, data or information previously obtained for the purpose of CDD

The distinction between occasional transactions and long-lasting business relationships is relevant to the timing of CDD and the storage of records.

Where an occasional transaction is likely to increase in value or develop into a business relationship, consider conducting CDD early in the retainer to avoid delays later. As relationships change, firms must ensure they are compliant with the relevant standard.

There is no obligation to conduct CDD in accordance with the regulations for retainers involving non-regulated activities.

Existing business relationships before 15 December 2007

You must apply CDD measures at appropriate times to existing clients on a risk-sensitive basis. You are not required to apply CDD measures to all existing clients immediately after 15 December 2007. Where you have verified a client's identity to a previously applicable standard then, unless circumstances indicate the contrary, the risk is likely to be low. If you have existing high risk clients that you have previously identified you may consider applying the new CDD standard sooner than for low risk clients.

4.3.2 What is CDD?

Regulation 5 says that CDD comprises:

- identifying the client and verifying their identity on the basis of documents, data or information obtained from a reliable and independent source
- identifying, where there is a beneficial owner who is not the client, the beneficial owner and taking adequate measures, on a risk-sensitive basis, to verify his identity so that you are satisfied that you know who the beneficial owner is. This includes understanding the ownership and control structure of a legal person, trust or similar arrangement.
- obtaining information on the purpose and intended nature of the business relationship

IDENTIFICATION AND VERIFICATION

Identification of a client or a beneficial owner is simply being told or coming to know a client's identifying details, such as their name and address.

Verification is obtaining some evidence which supports this claim of identity.

A RISK-BASED APPROACH

Regulation 7(3) provides that you must:

- determine the required extent of customer due diligence measures on a risk-sensitive basis depending on the type of client, business relationship, product or transaction
- be able to demonstrate to your supervisory authority that you took appropriate measures in view of the risks of money laundering and terrorist financing

You cannot avoid conducting CDD, but you can use a risk-based approach to determine the extent and quality of information required and the steps to be taken to meet the requirements.

You need only obtain information on the purpose and intended nature of your client's use of your services when you are in a business relationship with them. However, it's good practice and required by Rule 2 of the Solicitors' Code of Conduct to obtain such information to ensure you fully understand instructions and closely monitor the development of each retainer, even if it is for an occasional transaction or transactions below the threshold.

4.3.3 Methods of verification

Verification can be completed on the basis of documents, data and information which come from a reliable and independent source. This means that there are a number of ways you can verify a client's identity including:

- obtaining or viewing original documents
- conducting electronic verification
- obtaining information from other regulated persons

INDEPENDENT SOURCE

You need an independent and reliable verification of your client's identity. This can include materials provided by the client, such as a passport.

Consider the cumulative weight of information you have on the client and the risk levels associated with both the client and the retainer.

You are permitted to use a wider range of sources when verifying the identity of the beneficial owner and understanding the ownership and control structure of the client. Often only the client or their representatives can provide you with such information. Apply the requirements in a risk-based manner to a level at which you are satisfied that you know who the beneficial owner is.

DOCUMENTS

You should not ignore obvious forgeries, but you are not required to be an expert in forged documents.

ELECTRONIC VERIFICATION

This will only confirm that someone exists, not that your client is the said person. You should consider the risk implications in respect of the particular retainer and be on the alert for information which may suggest that your client is not the person they say they are. You may mitigate risk by corroborating electronic verification with some other CDD material.

When choosing an electronic verification service provider, you should look for a provider who:

- has proof of registration with the Information Commissioner's Office to store personal data
- can link an applicant to both current and previous circumstances using a range of positive information sources
- accesses negative information sources, such as databases on identity fraud and deceased persons
- accesses a wide range of 'alert' data sources
- has transparent processes enabling you to know what checks are carried out, the results of the checks, and how much certainty they give on the identity of the subject
- allows you to capture and store the information used to verify an identity.

When using electronic verification, you are not required to obtain consent from your client, but they must be informed that this check will take place.

While we believe electronic verification can be a sufficient measure for compliance with money laundering requirements, there may be circumstances where it will not be appropriate. For example, the Council for Mortgage Lenders notes that electronic verification products may not be suitable for fraud prevention purposes, such as verifying that a person's signature is genuine.

4.3.4   Reliance and outsourcing

Reliance has a very specific meaning within the regulations and relates to the process under Regulation 17 where you rely on another regulated person to conduct CDD for you. You remain liable for any failure in the client being appropriately identified. Reliance does not include:

- accepting information from others to verify a client's identity when meeting your own CDD obligations
- electronic verification, which is outsourcing

You need

- the consent of the person on whom you rely for your reliance
- agreement that they will provide you with the CDD material upon request
- the identity of their supervisor for money laundering purposes. Consider checking the register of members for that supervisor, although a personal assurance of their identity may be sufficient where you have reasonable grounds to believe them.

We believe you should ask what CDD enquiries have been undertaken to ensure that they actually comply with the regulations, because you remain liable for non-compliance. This is particularly important when relying on a person outside the UK, and you should be satisfied that the CDD has been conducted to a standard compatible with the third directive, taking into account the ability to use different sources of verification and jurisdictional specific factors. It may not always be appropriate to rely on another person to undertake your CDD checks and you should consider reliance as a risk in itself.

RELIANCE IN THE UK

You can only rely on the following persons in the UK:

- a credit or financial institution which is an authorised person
- a person in the following professions who is supervised by a supervisory authority:

  - auditor
  - insolvency practitioner
  - external accountant
  - tax adviser
  - independent legal professional

RELIANCE IN AN EEA STATE

You can only rely on the following persons in an EEA state:

- a credit or financial institution
- auditor, or EEA equivalent
- insolvency practitioner, or EEA equivalent
- external accountant
- tax adviser
- independent legal professional

if they are both:

- subject to mandatory professional registration recognised by law, and
- supervised for complying with money laundering obligations under Chapter 5, Section 2 of the third directive.

A person will only be supervised in accordance with the third directive if the third directive has been implemented in the EEA state. You can check on the International Bar Association's website on the progress of implementation across Europe.

RELIANCE IN OTHER COUNTRIES

You can only rely on the following persons outside of the EEA:

- credit or financial institution, or equivalent
- auditor, or equivalent
- insolvency practitioner, or equivalent
- external accountant
- tax adviser
- independent legal professional

if they are both:

- subject to mandatory professional registration recognised by law, and
- supervised for complying with money laundering obligations to a standard equivalent to that under Chapter 5, Section 2 of the third directive.

Consult a list of countries where CDD requirements and supervision of credit or financial institutions are considered equivalent to the European Economic Area.

Consult a list of national money laundering legislation around the world, and whether it applies to lawyers.

PASSPORTING CLIENTS BETWEEN JURISDICTIONS

Many firms have branches or affiliated offices ('international offices') in other juris-dictions and will have clients who utilise the services of a number of international offices. It is not considered proportionate for a client to have to provide original identification material to each international office.

Some firms may have a central international database of CDD material on clients to which they can refer. Where this is the case you should review the CDD material to be satisfied that CDD has been completed in accordance with the third directive. If further information is required, you should ensure that it is obtained and added to the central database. Alternatively, you could ensure that the CDD approval controls for the database are sufficient to ensure that all CDD is compliant.

Other firms may wish to rely on their international office to simply provide a letter of confirmation that CDD requirements have been undertaken with respect to the client. This will amount to reliance only if the firm can be relied upon under the terms of Regulation 17 and the CDD is completed in accordance with that regulation.

Finally, firms without a central database may wish to undertake their own CDD measures with respect to the client, but ask their international office to supply copies of the verification material, rather than the client themselves. This will not be reliance, but outsourcing.

It is important to remember that one of your international offices may be acting for a client who is not a PEP in that country, but will be when they are utilising the services of your office. As such, you will need to have in place a process for checking whether a person passported into your office is a PEP and, if so, undertake appropriate enhanced due diligence measures.

UK-based fee earners will have to undertake their own ongoing monitoring of the retainer, even if the international office is also required to do so.

4.3.5 Timing

WHEN MUST CDD BE UNDERTAKEN?

Regulation 9 requires you to verify your client's identity and that of any beneficial owner, before you establish a business relationship or carry out an occasional transaction.

Regulation 11 provides that if you are unable to complete CDD in time, you cannot:

- carry out a transaction with or for the client through a bank account
- establish a business relationship or carry out an occasional transaction

You must also:

- terminate any existing business relationship
- consider making a disclosure to SOCA

Evidence of identity is not required if a one-off transaction involves less than €15,000 or if two or more linked transactions involve less than €15,000 in total. This exception does not apply if there is any suspicion of money laundering or terrorist financing.

EXCEPTIONS TO THE TIMING REQUIREMENT

There are several exceptions to the timing requirement and the prohibition on acting for the client.

However, you should consider why there is a delay in completing CDD, and whether this of itself gives rise to a suspicion which should be disclosed to SOCA.

NORMAL CONDUCT OF BUSINESS

Regulation 9(3) provides that verification may be completed during the establishment of a business relationship (not an occasional transaction), where:

- it is necessary not to interrupt the normal conduct of business, and
- there is little risk of money laundering or terrorist financing occurring

You must complete verification as soon as practicable after the initial contact.

Consider your risk profile when assessing which work can be undertaken on a retainer prior to verification being completed.

Do not permit funds or property to be transferred or final agreements to be signed before completion of full verification.

If you are unable to conduct full verification of the client and beneficial owners, then the prohibition in Regulation 11 will apply.

ASCERTAINING LEGAL POSITION

Regulation 11(2) provides that the prohibition in 11(1) does not apply where:

> A lawyer or other professional adviser is in the course of ascertaining the legal position for their client or performing their task of defending or representing their client in, or concerning legal proceedings, including advice on instituting or avoiding proceedings.

The requirement to cease acting and consider making a report to SOCA when you cannot complete CDD, does not apply when you are providing legal advice or preparing for or engaging in litigation or alternative dispute resolution.

This exception does not apply to transactional work, so take a cautious approach to the distinction between advice and litigation work, and transactional work.

4.4 Ongoing monitoring

Regulation 8 requires that you conduct ongoing monitoring of a business relationship on a risk-sensitive and appropriate basis. Ongoing monitoring is defined as:

- scrutiny of transactions undertaken throughout the course of the relationship (including where necessary, the source of funds), to ensure that the transactions are consistent with your knowledge of the client, their business and the risk profile.
- keeping the documents, data or information obtained for the purpose of applying CDD up-to-date. You must also be aware of obligations to keep clients' personal data updated under the Data Protection Act.

You are not required to:

- conduct the whole CDD process again every few years
- conduct random audits of files
- suspend or terminate a business relationship until you have updated data, information or documents, as long as you are still satisfied you know who your client is, and keep under review any request for further verification material or processes to get that material
- use sophisticated computer analysis packages to review each new retainer for anomalies

Ongoing monitoring will normally be conducted by fee earners handling the retainer, and involves staying alert to suspicious circumstances which may suggest money laundering, terrorist financing, or the provision of false CDD material.

For example, you may have acted for a client in preparing a will and purchasing a modest family home. They may then instruct you in the purchase of a holiday home, the value of which appears to be outside the means of the client's financial situation as you had previously been advised in earlier retainers. While you may be satisfied that you still know the identity of your client, as a part of your ongoing monitoring obligations it would be appropriate in such a case to ask about the source of the funds for this purchase. Depending on your client's willingness to provide you with such information and the answer they provide, you will need to consider whether you are satisfied with that response, want further proof of the source of the funds, or need to discuss making a disclosure to SOCA with your nominated officer.

To ensure that CDD material is kept up-to-date, you should consider reviewing it:

- when taking new instructions from a client, particularly if there has been a gap of over three years between instructions
- when you receive information of a change in identity details
  Relevant issues may include:
- the risk profile of the client and the specific retainer
- whether you hold material on transactional files which would confirm changes in identity
- whether electronic verification may help you find out if your clients' identity details have changed, or to verify any changes

4.5 Records

You are required to keep records of your CDD material.

4.6 CDD on clients

Your firm will need to make its own assessments as to what evidence is appropriate to verify the identity of your clients. We outline a number of sources which may help you make that assessment.

4.6.1 Natural persons

A natural person's identity comprises a number of aspects, including their name, current and past addresses, date of birth, place of birth, physical appearance, employment and financial history, and family circumstances.

Evidence of identity can include:

- identity documents such as passports and photocard driving licences
- other forms of confirmation, including assurances from persons within the regulated sector or those in your firm who have dealt with the person for some time.

In most cases of face to face verification, producing a valid passport or photocard identification should enable most clients to meet the AML/CTF identification requirements.

It is considered good practice to have either:

- one government document which verifies either name and address or name and date of birth
- a government document which verifies the client's full name and another supporting document which verifies their name and either their address or date of birth.

Where it is not possible to obtain such documents, consider the reliability of other sources and the risks associated with the client and the retainer. Electronic verification may be sufficient verification on its own as long as the service provider uses multiple sources of data in the verification process.

Where you are reasonably satisfied that an individual is nationally or internationally known, a record of identification may include a file note of your satisfaction about identity, usually including an address.

UK RESIDENTS

The following sources may be useful for verification of UK-based clients:

- current signed passport
- birth certificate
- current photocard driver's licence
- current EEA member state identity card
- current identity card issued by the Electoral Office for Northern Ireland
- residence permit issued by the Home Office
- firearms certificate or shotgun licence
- photographic registration cards for self-employed individuals and partnerships in the construction industry
- benefit book or original notification letter from the DWP confirming the right to benefits
- council tax bill
- utility bill or statement, or a certificate from a utilities supplier confirming an arrangement to pay services on pre-payment terms
- a cheque or electronic transfer drawn on an account in the name of the client with a credit or financial institution regulated for the purposes of money laundering

- bank, building society or credit union statement or passbook containing current address
- entry in a local or national telephone directory confirming name and address
- confirmation from an electoral register that a person of that name lives at that address
- a recent original mortgage statement from a recognised lender
- solicitor's letter confirming recent house purchase or land registry confirmation of address
- local council or housing association rent card or tenancy agreement
- HMRC self-assessment statement or tax demand
- house or motor insurance certificate
- record of any home visit made
- statement from a member of the firm or other person in the regulated sector who has known the client for a number of years attesting to their identity – bear in mind you may be unable to contact this person to give an assurance supporting that statement at a later date

PERSONS NOT RESIDENT IN THE UK

Where you meet the client you are likely to be able to see the person's passport or national identity card. If you have concerns that the identity document might not be genuine, contact the relevant embassy or consulate.

The client's address may be obtained from:

- an official overseas source
- a reputable directory
- a person regulated for money laundering purposes in the country where the person is resident who confirms that the client is known to them and lives or works at the overseas address given

If documents are in a foreign language you must take appropriate steps to be reasonably satisfied that the documents in fact provide evidence of the client's identity.

Where you do not meet the client, the Regulations state that you must undertake enhanced due diligence measures.

CLIENTS UNABLE TO PRODUCE STANDARD DOCUMENTATION

Sometimes clients are unable to provide standard verification documents. The purpose of the regulations is not to deny people access to legal services for legitimate transactions, but to mitigate the risk of legal services being used for the purposes of money laundering. You should consider whether the inability to provide you with standard verification is consistent with the client's profile and circumstances or whether it might make you suspicious that money laundering or terrorist financing is occurring.

Where you decide that a client has a good reason for not meeting the standard verification requirements, you may accept a letter from an appropriate person who knows the individual and can verify the client's identity.

For example:

- Clients in care homes might be able to provide a letter from the manager.
- Clients without a permanent residence might be able to provide a letter from a householder named on a current council tax bill or a hostel manager, confirming temporary residence.

- A refugee might be able to provide a letter from the Home Office confirming refugee status and granting permission to work, or a Home Office travel document for refugees.
- An asylum seeker might be able to provide their registration card and any other identity documentation they hold, or a letter of assurance as to identity from a community member such as a priest, GP, or local councillor who has knowledge of the client.
- A student or minor might be able to provide a birth certificate and confirmation of their parent's address or confirmation of address from the register of the school or higher education institution.
- A person with mental health problems or mental incapacity might know medical workers, hostel staff, social workers, deputies or guardians appointed by the court who can locate identification documents or confirm the client's identity.

PROFESSIONALS

Where other professionals use your services, you may consult their professional directory to confirm the person's name and business address. It will not be necessary to then confirm the person's home address. You may consult directories for foreign professionals, if you are satisfied it is a valid directory, eg one produced and maintained by their professional body, and you can either translate the information, or understand it already.

4.6.2   Partnerships, limited partnerships and UK LLPs

A partnership is not a separate legal entity, so you must obtain information on the constituent individuals.

Where partnerships or unincorporated businesses are:

- well-known, reputable organisations
- with long histories in their industries, and
- with substantial public information about them, their principals, and controllers
  the following information should be sufficient:
- name
- registered address, if any
- trading address
- nature of business

Other partnerships and unincorporated businesses which are small and have few partners should be treated as private individuals. Where the numbers are larger, they should be treated as private companies.

Where a partnership is made up of regulated professionals, it will be sufficient to confirm the firm's existence and the trading address from a reputable professional directory or search facility with the relevant professional body. Otherwise you should obtain evidence on the identity of at least the partner instructing you and one other partner, and evidence of the firm's trading address.

For a UK LLP, obtain information in accordance with the requirements for companies as outlined below.

4.6.3   Companies

A company is a legal entity in its own right, but conducts its business through representatives. So you must identify and verify the existence of the company. You should consider whether the person instructing you on behalf of the company has the authority to do so

A company's identity comprises its constitution, its business and its legal ownership structure. The key identification particulars are the company's name and its business address, although the registration number and names of directors may also be relevant identification particulars.

Where a company is a well-known household name, you may consider that the level of money laundering and terrorist financing risks are low and apply CDD measures in a manner which is proportionate to that risk.

Where you commence acting for a subsidiary of an existing client, you may have reference to the CDD file for your existing client for verification of details for the subsidiary, provided that the existing client has been identified to the standards of the 2007 regulations.

You will also need to consider the identity of beneficial owners where simplified diligence does not apply.

PUBLIC COMPANIES LISTED IN THE UK

Where a company is either:

- listed and its securities are admitted to trading on a regulated market, or
- a majority-owned and consolidated subsidiary of such a company
- simplified due diligence applies.

For a listed company, this evidence may simply be confirmation of the company's listing on the regulated market. Such evidence may be:

- a copy of the dated page of the website of the relevant stock exchange showing the listing
- a photocopy of the listing in a reputable daily newspaper
- information from a reputable electronic verification service provider or online registry

For a subsidiary of a listed company you will also require evidence of the parent/subsidiary relationship. Such evidence may be:

- the subsidiary's last filed annual return
- a note in the parent's or subsidiary's last audited accounts
- information from a reputable electronic verification service provider or online registry

The regulated market in the UK is the London Stock Exchange. AIM is not considered a regulated market within the UK, but under the risk-based approach you may feel that the due diligence process for listing on AIM gives you equivalent comfort as to the identity of the company under consideration.

Where further CDD is required for a listed company (ie when it is not on a regulated market) obtain relevant particulars of the company's identity.

Verification sources may include:

- a search of the relevant company registry (such as Companies House: www.companies house.gov.uk)
- a copy of the company's certificate of incorporation
- information from a reputable electronic verification service provider

You are still required to conduct ongoing monitoring of the business relationship with a publicly-listed company to enable you to spot suspicious activity.

PRIVATE AND UNLISTED COMPANIES IN THE UK

Private companies are generally subject to a lower level of public disclosure than public companies. In general however, the structure, ownership, purposes and activities of many private companies will be clear and understandable.

The standard identifiers for private companies are:

- full name
- business / registered address
- names of two directors, or equivalent
- nature of business

Other sources for verifying corporate identification may include:

- certificate of incorporation
- details from the relevant company registry, confirming details of the company and of the director, including the director's address
- filed audited accounts
- information from a reputable electronic verification service provider

PUBLIC OVERSEAS COMPANIES

Simplified due diligence applies when:

- a company or its subsidiary is listed on a regulated market subject to specified disclosure obligations

Specified disclosure obligations are disclosure requirements consistent with specified articles of:

- The Prospectus Directive [2003/71/EC]
- The Transparency Obligations directive [2004/109/EC]
- The Market Abuse directive [2003/6/EC]

If a regulated market is located within the EEA, under a risk-based approach you may wish to simply record the steps taken to ascertain the status of the market. Consider a similar approach for non-EEA markets that subject companies to disclosure obligations which are contained in international standards equivalent to specified disclosure obligations in the EU.

Consult a list of countries where CDD requirements and supervision of credit or financial institutions are considered equivalent to the UK.

Consult a list of regulated markets within the EU

Evidence of the company's listed status should be obtained in a manner similar to that for UK public companies. Companies whose listing does not fall within the above requirements should be identified in accordance with the provisions for private companies.

PRIVATE AND UNLISTED OVERSEAS COMPANIES

Obtaining CDD material for these companies can be difficult, particularly regarding beneficial ownership.

You should apply the risk-based approach, looking at the risk of the client generally, the risk of the retainer and the risks presented as a result of the country in which the client is incorporated. Money laundering risks are likely to be lower where the company is incorporated or operating in an EEA state or a country which is a member of FATF.

The company's identity is established in the same way as for UK private and unlisted companies.

Where you are not obtaining original documentation, you may want to consider on a risk-sensitive basis having the documents certified by a person in the regulated sector or another professional whose identity can be checked by reference to a professional directory.

4.6.4   Other arrangements or bodies

TRUSTS

A trust is not a separate legal entity. Your client may be the settlor, the trustee(s) or occasionally the beneficiaries.

UK common law trusts are used extensively in everyday situations and often pose limited risk. They can become more risky if:

- the client requests a trust be used when there seems to be little reason to do so
- the trust is established in a jurisdiction which has limited AML/CTF regulation

In a higher risk situation you should consider either conducting further CDD or enhanced monitoring. This could include:

- conducting CDD on all the trustees, or on the settlor even after the creation of the trust
- asking about the purpose of the trust and the source of the funds used to create it
- obtaining the trust deed or searching an appropriate register maintained in the country of establishment

Your client, whether they are the trustee(s), settlor or beneficiaries, must be identified in accordance with their relevant category (ie natural person, company etc). Where you are acting for more than one trustee it is preferable that you verify the identity of at least two of the trustees. Where the trustee is another regulated person, you may rely on their listing with their supervisory body.

You must consider beneficial ownership issues where you are acting for the trustee(s).

FOUNDATIONS

A foundation is the civil law equivalent to a common law trust and operates in many EEA countries. You should understand why your client is using a solicitor outside of the jurisdiction of establishment, and the statutory requirements for the establishment of the foundation. Then obtain similar information as you would for a trust.

Where the foundation's founder is anonymous, you may consider whether any intermediary or agent is regulated for AML/CTF and whether they can provide assurances on the identity of relevant persons involved with the foundation.

Foundations can also be a loose term for charitable institutions in the UK and the USA – where that is the case they must be verified in accordance with the procedures for verifying charities set out below.

CHARITIES

Charities may take a number of forms. In the UK, you may come across five types of charities:

- small
- registered
- unregistered
- excepted, such as churches
- exempt, such as museums and universities

For registered charities, you should take a record of their full name, registration number and place of business. Details of registered charities can be obtained from:

- the Charity Commission of England and Wales at www.charity-commission.gov.uk
- the Office of the Scottish Charity Regulator at www.oscr.org.uk

Other countries may also have charity regulators which maintain a list of registered charities. You may consider it appropriate to refer to these when verifying the identity of an overseas charity. Currently in Northern Ireland there is no regulator for charities.

For all other types of charities you should consider the business structure of the charity and apply the relevant CDD measures for that business structure. You can also generally get confirmation of their charitable status from HMRC. Further, in applying the risk-based approach to charities it is worth considering whether it is a well-known entity or not. The more obscure the charity, the more likely you are to want to view the constitutional documents of the charity.

Due to the increased interest in some charities and not-for-profit organisations from terrorist organisations you may want to also consult the Bank of England's sanctions list to ensure the charity is not a proscribed organisation.

DECEASED PERSONS' ESTATES

When acting for the executor(s) or administrators of an estate, you should establish their identity using the procedures for natural persons or companies set out above. When acting for more than one executor or administrator, it is preferable to verify the identity of at least two of them. You should consider getting copies of the death certificate, grant of probate or letters of administration.

During the administration of the estate, Regulation 6(8) provides that the beneficial owner is:

- the executor, original or by representation, or
- the administrator for the time being of a deceased person

This definition is wide enough to cover you when you deal with foreign deceased estates that are in the course of administration.

If a will trust is created, and the trustees are different from the executors, the procedures in relation to trusts will need to be followed when the will trust comes into operation.

CHURCHES AND PLACES OF WORSHIP

Places of worship may either register as a charity or can apply for registration as a certified building of worship from the General Register Office (GRO) which will issue a certificate. Further, their charitable tax status will be registered with HMRC. As such, identification details with respect to the church or place of worship may be verified:

- as for a charity
- through the headquarters or regional organisation of the denomination or religion

For UK charities, identification details may be verified:

- with reference to the GRO certificate
- through an enquiry to HMRC

SCHOOLS AND COLLEGES

Schools and colleges may be a registered charity, a private company, an unincorporated association or a government entity and should be verified in accordance with the relevant category.

The Department of Education and Skills maintains lists of approved educational facilities which may assist in verifying the existence of the school or college.

CLUBS AND ASSOCIATIONS

Many of these bear a low money laundering risk, but this depends on the scope of their purposes, activities and geographical spread.

The following information may be relevant to the identity of the club or association:

- full name
- legal status
- purpose
- any registered address
- names of all office holders
  Documents which may verify the existence of the club or association include:
- any articles of association or constitutions
- statement from a bank, building society or credit union
- recent audited accounts
- listing in a local or national telephone directory

PENSION FUNDS

Regulation 13 (7)(c) provides that simplified due diligence is permitted where:

A pension, superannuation or similar scheme which provides retirement benefits to employees, where contributions are made by an employer or by way of deduction from an employee's wages and the scheme rules do not permit the assignment of a member's interest under the scheme (other than an assignment permitted by section 44 of the Welfare Reform and Pensions Act 1999 (disapplication of restrictions on alienation) or section 91(5)(a) of the Pensions Act 1995 (inalienability of occupational pension)).

So you only need evidence that the product is such a scheme and so qualifies for simplified due diligence. Such evidence may include:

- a copy of a page showing the name of the scheme from the most recent definitive deed
- a consolidating deed for the scheme, plus any amending deed subsequent to that date.

Pension funds or superannuation schemes outside the above definition should be subject to CDD according to their specific business structure.

For information on how to conduct CDD on other funds please see the Joint Money Laundering Steering Group's guidance.

4.6.5   Government agencies and councils

The money laundering and terrorist financing risks associated with public authorities varies significantly depending on the nature of the retainer and the home jurisdiction of the public authority. It may be simple to establish that the entity exists, but where there is a heightened risk of corruption or misappropriation of government monies, greater monitoring of retainers should be considered.

The following information may be relevant when establishing a public sector entity's identity:

- full name of the entity
- nature and status of the entity
- address of the entity
- name of the home state authority
- name of the directors or equivalent

Simplified due diligence applies to UK public authorities. Where simplified due diligence does not apply, you may get information verifying the existence of the public sector from:

- official government websites
- a listing in a national or local telephone directory

4.7   CDD on a beneficial owner

4.7.1   General comments

When conducting CDD on a client, you will need to identify any beneficial owners within the meaning of regulation 6 of the Regulations. Note that this definition goes beyond the traditional understanding of the meaning of a beneficial owner.

To identify the beneficial owner, obtain at least their name and record any other identifying details which are readily available. You may decide to use records that are publicly available, ask your client for the relevant information or use other sources.

To assess which identity verification measures are needed, consider the client's risk profile, any business structures involved and the proposed transaction.

The key is to understand the ownership and control structure of the client. A prudent approach is best, monitoring changes in instructions, or transactions which suggest that someone is trying to undertake or manipulate a retainer for criminal ends. Simply ticking boxes is unlikely to satisfy the risk-based approach.

Appropriate verification measures may include:

- a certificate from your client confirming the identity of the beneficial owner
- a copy of the trust deed, partnership agreement or other such document
- shareholder details from an online registry
- the passport of, or electronic verification on, the individual
- other reliable, publicly available information

4.7.2   Assessing the risk

Issues you may consider when assessing the risk of a particular case include:

- why your client is acting on behalf of someone else
- how well you know your client
- whether your client is a regulated person
- the type of business structure involved in the transaction

- where the business structure is based
- the AML/CTF requirements in the jurisdiction where it is based
- why this business structure is being used in this transaction
- how soon property or funds will be provided to the beneficial owner

Only in rare cases will you need to verify a beneficial owner to the same level that you would a client.

When conducting CDD on beneficial owners within a corporate entity or arrangement, you must:

- understand the ownership and control structure of the client as required by Regulation 5(b)
- identify the specific individuals listed in Regulation 6

The level of understanding required depends on the complexity of the structure and the risks associated with the transaction. For example, it may be sufficient to review the trust deed or partnership arrangement and discuss the issue with your client. In the case of a company, you may obtain a company structure chart from your client directly, their website or their annual reports.

It is vital to understand in what capacity your client is instructing you to ensure that you are identifying the correct beneficial owners.

If for example you are acting for Bank A, which is a corporate entity, to purchase new premises for Bank A, then it would be the shareholders and controllers of Bank A who are the beneficial owners. However, if Bank A is a trustee for XYZ Trust and they have instructed you to sell trust property, then Bank A is instructing you on behalf of the arrangement which is XYZ Trust in their capacity as trustee. The beneficial owners in that transaction will be those with specified interests in and/or control of the XYZ Trust.

4.7.3 Agency

Regulation 6(9) says a beneficial owner generally means any individual who ultimately owns or controls the client or on whose behalf a transaction or activity is being conducted.

In these cases, it is presumed the client is himself the beneficial owner, unless the features of the transaction indicate they are acting on someone else's behalf. So you do not have to proactively search for beneficial owners, but to make enquiries when it appears the client is not the beneficial owner.

Situations where a natural person may be acting on behalf of someone else include:

- exercising a power of attorney. The document granting power of attorney may be sufficient to verify the beneficial owner's identity.
- acting as the deputy, administrator or insolvency practitioner. Appointment documents may be sufficient to verify the beneficial owner's identity.
- an appointed broker or other agent to conduct a transaction. A signed letter of appointment may be sufficient to verify the beneficial owner's identity.

You should be alert to the possibility that purported agency relationships are actually being utilised to facilitate a fraud. Understanding the reason for the agency, rather than simply accepting documentary evidence of such at face value, will assist to mitigate this risk. Where a client or retainer is higher risk, you may want to obtain further verification of the beneficial owner's identity in line with the suggested CDD methods to be applied to natural persons.

4.7.4 Companies

Regulation 6(1) defines the beneficial owner of a body corporate as meaning:
  Any individual who:

- as respects any body other than a company whose securities are listed on a regulated market, ultimately owns or controls (whether through direct or indirect ownership or control, including through bearer share holdings) more than 25 per cent of the shares or voting rights in the body, or
- as respects any body corporate, otherwise exercises control over the management of the body

This regulation does not apply to a company listed on a regulated market. It does apply to UK limited liability partnerships.

SHAREHOLDINGS

You should make reasonable and proportionate enquiries to establish whether beneficial owners exist and, where relevant as determined by your risk analysis, verify their identity. These may include:

- getting assurances from the client on the existence and identity of relevant beneficial owners
- getting assurances from other regulated persons more closely involved with the client, particularly in other jurisdictions, on the existence and identity of relevant beneficial owners
- conducting searches on the relevant online registry
- obtaining information from a reputable electronic verification service

Where the holder of the requisite level of shareholding of a company is another company, apply the risk-based approach when deciding whether further enquiries should be undertaken.

A PROPORTIONATE APPROACH

It would be disproportionate to conduct independent searches across multiple entities at multiple layers of a corporate chain to see if, by accumulating very small interests in different entities, a person finally achieves more than a 25 per cent interest in the client corporate entity. You must simply be satisfied that you have an overall understanding of the ownership and control structure of the client company.

Voting rights are only those which are currently exercisable and attributed to the company's issued equity share capital.

COMPANIES WITH CAPITAL IN THE FORM OF BEARER SHARES

These pose a higher laundering risk as it is often difficult to identify beneficial owners and such companies are often incorporated in jurisdictions with lower AML/CTF regulations. You should adopt procedures to establish the identities of the holders and material beneficial owners of such shares and ensure you are notified whenever there is a change of holder and/or beneficial owner. This may be achieved by:

- requiring that the shares be held by a regulated person
- getting an assurance that either such a regulated person or the holder of the shares will notify you of any change of records relating to the shares

CONTROL

A corporate entity can also be subject to control by persons other than shareholders. Such control may rest with those who have power to manage funds or transactions without requiring specific authority to do so, and who would be in a position to override internal procedures and control mechanisms.

You should remain alert to anyone with such powers while you are obtaining a general understanding of the ownership and control structure of the corporate entity. Further enquiries are not likely to be necessary. Monitor situations within the retainer where control structures appear to be bypassed and make further enquiries at that time.

4.7.5 Partnerships

Regulation 6(2) provides that in the case of a partnership (but not a limited liability partnership) the following individuals are beneficial owners:

- any individual ultimately entitled to or who controls (whether directly or indirectly), more than 25 per cent of the capital or profits of the partnership or more than 25 per cent of the voting rights in the partnership, or
- any individual who otherwise exercises control over the management of the partnership

Relevant points to consider when applying this Regulation:

- the property of the entity includes its capital and its profits
- control involves the ability to manage the use of funds or transactions outside of the normal management structure and control mechanisms

You should make reasonable and proportionate enquiries to establish whether beneficial owners exist and, where relevant, verify their identity in a risk-based manner.

Enquiries and verification may be undertaken by:

- receiving assurances from the client on the existence and identity of relevant beneficial owners
- receiving assurance from other regulated persons more closely involved with the client, particularly in other jurisdictions, on the existence and identity of relevant beneficial owners
- reviewing the documentation setting up the partnership such as the partnership agreement or any other profit-sharing agreements

4.7.6 Trusts

Regulation 6(3) sets out three types of beneficial owners of a trust:

- Part A: individual with specified interest – those with at least a 25 per cent specified interest in trust capital
- Part B: class of persons to benefit – those in whose main interest the trust operates
- Part C: individuals who control a trust

You must identify persons within all relevant categories.

NON-INDIVIDUAL BENEFICIARIES

While generally the beneficiaries of a trust will be individuals, they may at times be a company, an entity or an arrangement, such as a charity.

Regulation 6(5) says you will have to apply Regulation 6(1) to a beneficiary company to determine their beneficial owners. This means that:

You should consider for all companies whether anyone exercises control over the beneficiary company outside of the normal management structures. Identify them as a beneficial owner of the client trust. You may ask the client if they are aware of any such person, as this information would not be on a publicly available register and it will generally not be proportionate for you to have direct dealings with the beneficiary company.

- Where the beneficiary company is a private or unlisted company, you should consider whether they have shareholders with more than a 25 per cent interest in the beneficiary company. This can be done by a simple search on Companies House or equivalent online registry.
- If you locate such a shareholder, you should note their identity as a beneficial owner of the client trust. You will have already verified the identity through the company register check. Where there is a tiered structure, eg where, through its shareholding in a such shareholder, another company has more than a 25 per cent interest in the beneficiary company enquire of the client why there is a tiered structure in use and make a risk-based decision, considering the risk of the client generally and the whole retainer, as to whether:

  – further identity enquiries are required
  – you simply identify the second company as the beneficial owner of the client trust and then conduct closer monitoring of any transactions
  – you have a suspicion warranting a disclosure to SOCA, and consider withdrawing from the retainer

The further you look for beneficial owners within beneficial owners the smaller the interest and the harder it is to exercise control. Therefore the risk of laundering or terrorist financing is lower. Consider this when setting proportionate CDD.

If you do not find an individual within either of the above categories, then simply list the beneficiary company as the beneficial owner of the client trust.

Regulation 6(5)(a) does not apply to beneficiaries that are non-corporate entities or another trust. You should still identify them as a beneficial owner of the client trust and consider whether you need to know more about them.

INDIVIDUAL WITH SPECIFIED INTEREST (PART A)

A person has a specified interest if they have a vested interest of the requisite level in possession or remainder or reversion, defeasible or indefeasible.

VESTED INTEREST

This is an interest not subject to any conditions precedent. It is held by the beneficiary completely and inalienably, even if it is still under the control of the trustees at that time.

CONTINGENT INTEREST

This interest is subject to the satisfaction of one or more conditions precedent, such as attaining a specified age or surviving a specified person. Failure to satisfy all conditions precedent results in the failure of the interest.

INTEREST IN POSSESSION

This interest is the right to enjoy the use or possession of the fund and under the regulations relates solely to an interest in the capital of the fund.

INTEREST IN REMAINDER

This is the beneficiary's right to the capital of the fund which is postponed to one or more prior interests in possession in the income of the fund.

INTEREST IN REVERSION

This is the right of the settlor to receive any part of the fund at the end of the trust. It occurs in cases including when the trust fails because all of the beneficiaries die or a life interest terminates and there are no remainder beneficiaries.

DEFEASIBLE INTEREST

An interest is defeasible if it can be terminated in whole or in part, without the consent of the beneficiary, by the happening of an event, such as the failure of a condition subsequent or the exercise by the trustees of a power to terminate or vary the interest.

INDEFEASIBLE INTEREST

An interest is indefeasible if it cannot be terminated in whole or in part without the consent of the beneficiary by the happening of any event.

Defeasible and indefeasible interests are included, so that you consider the beneficiaries who are going to get the property as at the time you are instructed, and conduct CDD on them.

CLASS OF PERSONS TO BENEFIT (PART B)

Part B of the definition in Regulation 6(3) covers any trust that includes persons who do not fit within Part A. Within Part B, you must identify the class of persons in whose main interest the trust operates. All discretionary trusts will fall within Part B.

Note: If a trust has one or more persons who are individuals with a 25 per cent specified interest, as well as other beneficiaries, identify the individuals who fit within the first part of the definition, then consider the rest of the beneficiaries as a class under Part B.

Identification of a class is by description, such as:

- the grandchildren of X
- charity Y
- pension holders and their dependents

When considering in whose main interest a trust is set up or operates, and there are several classes of beneficiary, consider which class is most likely to receive most of the trust property. For example:

- Where a trust is for the issue of X, then the class is the issue of X as there is only one class.

- Where a trust is for the children of X, if they all die, for the grandchildren of X and if they all die, for charity Y, then the class is likely to be the children of X as it is unlikely that they will all die before the funds are disbursed.
- Where a discretionary trust allows for payments to the widow, the children, their spouses and civil partners, the grandchildren, and their spouses and civil partners, then all interests are equal and all classes will need to be identified.

Where in doubt about which class has the main interest, you should identify all classes.

Note: Interests in parts of the trust property can change significantly between retainers, particularly with discretionary trusts. So it is good practice to obtain an update on any changes from the trustees with each set of new retainers your firm receives in relation to a discretionary trust.

CONTROL OF THE TRUST (PART C)

Control is defined as a power, either:

- exercisable alone
- jointly with another person
- with the consent of another person

under the trust instrument or by law to either:

- dispose of, advance, lend, invest, pay or apply trust property
- vary the trusts
- add or remove a person as a beneficiary or to a class of beneficiaries
- appoint or remove trustees
- direct, withhold consent to or veto the exercise of a power such as is mentioned in the options above

The definition of control can include beneficiaries acting collectively where they have the power to take or to direct action.

Regulation 6(5)(b) specifically excludes from the definition of control:

- the power exercisable collectively at common law to vary or extinguish a trust by all of the beneficiaries – see *Saunders* v. *Vautier* [1841] EWHC Ch J82.
- the power of members of a pension fund to influence the investment of the fund's assets
- the power to consent to advancement implied to a person with a life interest under section 32(1)(c) of the Trustee Act 1925
- the powers of beneficiaries to require the appointment or retirement of trustees under Trusts of Land and Appointment of Trustees Act 1996.

IDENTIFYING TRUST BENEFICIAL OWNERS IN PRACTICE

You are only required to make reasonable and proportionate enquiries to establish whether beneficial owners exist and, where relevant, verify their identity. If unsure whether a beneficiary or other person is a beneficial owner, you may consider taking legal advice from a trust practitioner, or identify them and consider whether verification is required.

Enquires and verification may be undertaken by:

- getting assurances from trustees on the existence and identity of beneficial owners
- getting assurances from other regulated persons more closely involved with the client, particularly in other jurisdictions, on existence and identity of beneficial owners
- reviewing the trust deed
- obtaining information from a reputable electronic verification service on details of identified beneficiaries.

4.7.7 Other arrangements and legal entities

Regulation 6(6) provides that where you are dealing with a client who is not a natural person, nor a corporate entity or a trust, then the following individuals are beneficial owners:

- where the individuals who benefit from the entity or arrangement have been determined, any individual who benefits from at least 25 per cent of the property of the entity or arrangement
- where the individuals who benefit from the entity or arrangement have yet to be determined, the class or persons in whose main interest the entity or arrangement is set up or operates
- any individual who exercises control over at least 25 per cent of the property of the entity or arrangement

Unincorporated associations and foundations are examples of entities and arrangements likely to fall within this regulation.

When applying this Regulation relevant points to consider are:

- the property of the entity includes its capital and its profits
- determined benefits are those to which an individual is currently entitled
- contingent benefits or where no determination has been made should be dealt with as a class as benefit has yet to be determined
- a class of persons need only be identified by way of description
- an entity or arrangement is set up for, or operates in, the main interest of the persons who are likely to get most of the property
- control involves the ability to manage the use of funds or transactions outside the normal management structure and control mechanisms
- where you find a body corporate with the requisite interest outlined above, you will need to make further proportionate enquiries as to the beneficial owner of the body corporate

You should make reasonable and proportionate enquiries to establish whether beneficial owners exist and, where relevant, verify their identity in a risk-based manner.

Enquires and verification may be undertaken by:

- asking the client and receiving assurances as to the existence and identity of beneficial owners
- asking other regulated persons more closely involved with the client (particularly in other jurisdictions) and receiving assurances as to the existence and identity of beneficial owners
- reviewing the documentation setting up the entity or arrangement such as its constitution or rules

4.8 Simplified due diligence

Regulation 13 permits simplified due diligence to be undertaken in certain circumstances.

4.8.1 What is simplified due diligence?

You simply have to obtain evidence that the client or products provided are eligible for simplified due diligence. You will not need to obtain information on the nature and purpose of the business relationship or on beneficial owners. You will need to conduct CDD and ongoing monitoring where you suspect money laundering .

4.8.2 Who qualifies for simplified due diligence?

The following clients and products qualify:

- a credit or financial institution which is subject to the requirements of the money laundering directive
- a credit or financial institution in a non-EEA state which is supervised for compliance with requirements similar to the money laundering directive
- companies listed on a regulated EEA state market or a non-EEA market which has similar disclosure requirements to European Community legislation
- beneficial owners of pooled accounts held by a notary or independent legal professional, ie financial services firms are not required to apply CDD to the third party beneficial owners of omnibus accounts held by solicitors, provided the information on the identity of the beneficial owners is available upon request
- UK public authorities
- a non-UK public authority which:

  - is entrusted with public functions pursuant to the treaty on the European Union or the Treaties on the European Communities, or Community secondary legislation
  - has a publicly available, transparent and certain identity
  - has activities and accounting practices which are transparent
  - is accountable to a community institution, the authorities of an EEA state or is otherwise subject to appropriate check and balance procedures

- certain insurance policies, pensions or electronic money products
- products where:

  - they are based on a written contract
  - related transactions are carried out through a regulated credit institution
  - they are not anonymous
  - they are within relevant maximum thresholds
  - realisation for the benefit of a third party is limited
  - investment in assets or claims is only realisable in the long term, cannot be used as collateral and there cannot be accelerated payments, surrender clauses or early termination

For further details on the requirements for qualification for simplified due diligence, see Regulation 13 and Schedule 2 of the regulations.

Consult a list of countries where CDD requirements and supervision of credit or financial institutions are considered equivalent to the UK.

Consult a list of national money laundering legislation around the world, and whether they apply to lawyers.

4.9   Enhanced due diligence

Regulation 14 provides that you will need to apply enhanced due diligence on a risk-sensitive basis where:

- the client is not dealt with face-to-face
- the client is a politically exposed person (PEP)
- there is any other situation which can present a higher risk of money laundering or terrorist financing

The regulations do not set out what will be enhanced due diligence for the last option.

In applying the risk-based approach to the situation you should consider whether it is appropriate to:

- seek further verification of the client or beneficial owner's identity
- obtain more detail on the ownership and control structure of the client
- request further information on the purpose of the retainer or the source of the funds, and/or
- conduct enhanced ongoing monitoring

4.9.1   Non face-to-face clients

A client who is not a natural person can never be physically present for identification purposes and will only ever be represented by an agent. The mere fact that you do not have face-to-face meetings with the agents of an entity or arrangement does not automatically require that enhanced due diligence is undertaken. You should consider the risks associated with the retainer and the client, assess how well standard CDD measures are meeting those risks and decide whether further CDD measures are required.

Where a client is a natural person and they are not physically present for identification purposes, you must undertake enhanced due diligence.

Regulation 14 (2) outlines possible steps which can be taken above standard verification procedures to compensate for the higher risk of non face-to-face transactions. The regulations suggest the following options, although this list is not exhaustive:

- using additional documents, data or information to establish identity. This may involve using electronic verification to confirm documents provided, or using two or three documents from different sources to confirm the information set out in each.
- using supplementary measures to verify or certify the documents supplied or obtain confirmatory certification by a credit or financial institution which is subject to the money laundering directive. You may consider electronic verification to confirm the documents provided. Alternatively consider getting certified copies of documents:

  - When dealing with foreign passports or identity cards, check the requirements for that country with the relevant embassy or consulate.
  - With all other documents, consider whether the certifying person is regulated with respect to the regulations or is otherwise a professional person subject to some sort of regulation or fit and proper person test, who can easily be independently contacted to verify their certification of the documents. Such persons include bank managers, accountants, or local GPs. You may also consider accepting documents certified by the Post Office-provided Identity Checking Service.

- ensuring the first payment in the retainer is through an account opened in the client's name with a credit institution. EU regulation 1781/2006 says credit institutions must provide the payer's name, address and account number with all electronic fund transfers. It entered force on 1 January 2007 and is directly applicable to all member states. Use this to further verify your client's identity.

Further details: Part II – Wire transfers of the JMLSG guidance

If such information is not included on the electronic fund transfer, discuss this with the relevant financial or credit institution. Consider taking up the matter with the FSA, if the institution refuses to give you written confirmation of the details. Take other steps to verify your client's identity.

4.9.2 Politically exposed persons

You must take the following steps to deal with the heightened risk posed by having a client who is a PEP:

- have senior management approval for establishing a business relationship with a PEP
- take adequate measures to establish the source of wealth and source of funds which are involved in the business relationship or occasional transaction
- conduct closer ongoing monitoring of the business relationship

You are not required to actively investigate whether beneficial owners of a client are PEPs. However, where you have a beneficial owner who you know is a PEP, you should consider on a risk-based approach what extra measures, if any, you need to take when dealing with that client.

Further, merely doing work for a non-UK public authority does not mean that you are in a business relationship with a PEP. You should however ensure that you have considered the risks associated with the particular public authority and taken steps to address those risks.

WHO IS A PEP?

A person who has been entrusted within the last year with one of the following prominent public functions by a state other than the UK, a Community institution or an international body:

- heads of state, heads of government, ministers and deputy or assistant ministers
- members of parliament
- members of supreme courts, of constitutional courts, or of other high-level judicial bodies whose decisions are not generally subject to further appeal, except in exceptional circumstances
- members of courts of auditors or of the boards of central banks
- ambassadors, charges d'affairs and high-ranking officers in the armed forces
- members of the administrative, management or supervisory bodies of state-owned enterprises

In addition to the primary PEPs listed above, a PEP also includes:

- family members of a PEP – spouse, partner, children and their spouses or partners, and parents

288

- known close associates of a PEP – persons with whom joint beneficial ownership of a legal entity or legal arrangement is held, with whom there are close business relationships, or who is a sole beneficial owner of a legal entity or arrangement set up by the primary PEP

The regulations only apply to persons appointed by governments and authorities outside the UK, but it may be appropriate, on a risk-based approach to apply some or all of the enhanced due diligence requirements to a person appointed in the UK, who would have been a PEP had they been appointed outside the UK.

HOW TO IDENTIFY PEPS

You are not required to conduct extensive investigations to establish whether a person is a PEP. Just have regard to information that is in your possession or publicly known.

To assess your PEP risk profile, you should consider your existing client base, taking into account the general demographic of your client base, and how many clients you currently know would be a PEP.

If the risk of you acquiring a PEP as a client is low, you may simply wish to ask clients whether they fall within any of the PEP categories. Where they say no, you may reasonably assume the individual is not a PEP unless anything else within the retainer, or that you otherwise become aware of, makes you suspect they may be a PEP.

Where you have a higher risk of having PEPs as clients or you have reason to suspect that a person may actually be a PEP contrary to earlier information, you should consider conducting some form of electronic verification. You may find that a web-based search engine will be sufficient for these purposes, or you may decide that it is more appropriate to conduct electronic checks through a reputable international electronic verification provider.

Note: The range of PEPs is wide and constantly changing, so electronic verification will not give you 100 per cent certainty. You should remain alert to situations suggesting the client is a PEP. Such situations include:

- receiving funds in the retainer from a government account
- correspondence on official letterhead from the client or a related person
- general conversation with the client or person related to the retainer linking the person to a PEP
- news reports which actually come to your attention suggesting your client is a PEP or linked to one

Where you suspect a client is a PEP but cannot establish that for certain, you may consider on a risk-sensitive basis applying aspects of the enhanced due diligence procedures.

SENIOR MANAGEMENT APPROVAL

The regulations do not define senior management, so your firm must decide who that is, on a risk-sensitive basis. Senior management may be:

- the head of a practice group
- another partner who is not involved with the particular file
- the partner supervising the particular file
- the nominated officer
- the managing partner

In any case, it is recommended that you advise those responsible for monitoring risk assessment that a business relationship with a PEP has begun, to help their overall monitoring of the firm's risk profile and compliance.

ESTABLISHING SOURCE OF WEALTH AND FUNDS

Generally this simply involves asking questions of the client about their source of wealth and the source of the funds to be used with each retainer. When you know a person is a PEP, their salary and source of wealth is often publicly available on a register of their interests. This may be relevant for higher risk retainers.

ENHANCED MONITORING

You should ensure that funds paid into your client account come from the account nominated and are for an amount commensurate with the client's known wealth. Ask further questions if they are not.

4.10 Existing clients

Regulation 7(2) states you must apply CDD measures to an existing customer at other appropriate times and on a risk-sensitive basis, repealing the previous exemption for customers with whom you had a business relationship prior to 1 March 2004.

You do not have to ensure all existing clients have been identified and verified by 15 December 2007, nor update all current identification in accordance with the new requirements by that date.

Factors that may trigger a need for CDD include:

- a gap in retainers of three years or more
- a client instructing on a higher risk retainer
- where you develop a suspicion of money laundering or terrorist financing by the client
- an existing high risk client

For all clients, you should ensure ongoing monitoring of the business relationship to identify any suspicious activity.

When conducting CDD on existing clients or a subsidiary of an existing client, you may consider information already on your files which would verify their identity or publicly available information to confirm the information you hold, rather than approaching the client to provide that information initially. It may be appropriate for a fee earner or partner who has known the client for long time to place a certificate on the file providing an assurance as to identity.

4.11 FATF counter measures

Regulation 18 states that the Treasury may direct you not to:

- enter into a business relationship
- carry out an occasional transaction
- proceed further with a business relationship or occasional transaction
- when the client is from a country subject to FATF counter measures.

Your CDD measures will need to ascertain whether your client, and in high risk situations key beneficial owners, are subject to such directions.

The HM Treasury website contains a consolidated list of persons and entities internationally and in the UK to whom financial sanctions apply. You can register for updates of a publication of a financial sanctions release.

4.12 Annex A – Examples of beneficial ownership for a trust

4.12.1 Example 1

DETAILS

A's will provides that after payment of legacies and testamentary expenses his residuary estate passes to his children in equal shares. Three children survive A, one of whom (B) is under 18.

APPLICATION

On A's death each of the children have a vested interest in one third of the residuary estate, notwithstanding that B will not receive his share until he is 18 as he cannot give a valid receipt to the executors, and none of them will be entitled to receive anything until the conclusion of the administration of the estate.

As such all three children should be identified under Part A, after the estate ceases to be in administration.

4.12.2 Example 2

DETAILS

C executed an inter vivos trust in 2000 'for the benefit of my grandchildren who shall be born before 31/12/2020'. At the time he had two grandchildren. C died in 2006, and in 2007 your firm is instructed to act for the trustees. There are now four grandchildren.

APPLICATION

Each of the grandchildren has a vested interest in possession in one quarter of the trust fund, notwithstanding that further grandchildren may be born before 31/12/2020 and their shares may be reduced. Therefore each grandchild has a specified interest in at least 25 per cent of the capital of the trust property and should be identified under Part A.

DEVELOPMENT

In 2015 new trustees are appointed, at which point there are five grandchildren, each of whom has a specified interest in 20 per cent of the fund.

APPLICATION

Your firm will have to apply CDD to the new trustees (either as part of the client CDD or a person who has control) and to the class of beneficiaries under Part B, which will be the grandchildren of C.

4.12.3   Example 3

DETAILS

C's will provides that after payment of legacies and testamentary expenses his residuary estate passes to 'such of my children as shall survive me and attain the age of 21 years'. Three children survive C, one of whom (D) is under 21.

APPLICATION

While the estate is in administration, it is the personal representative who will be the beneficial owner. The two elder children will have been paid out following completion of the administration of the estate, as they have absolute vested interests. D's interest in the one third of the estate is not a specified interest, being subject to a contingency and therefore not vested. As D also does not have control, this leaves you to apply CDD under Part B to the class of one, constituted by D.

4.12.4   Example 4

DETAILS

E executes an inter vivos trust on 31/01/2007, creating a life interest in income for his wife, with remainder to such of their children as shall be living at his wife's death. At the time he has two children.

APPLICATION

The wife has a vested interest in possession, but it is in income, not in the capital of the trust. Therefore she is not a beneficial owner under Part A. As s32(1)(c) of the Trustee Act 1925 is excluded from being defined as control over the trust, she is not a beneficial owner under Part C either.

The children have an interest in the remainder, but it is contingent on them surviving their mother and does not vest until their mother's death. Therefore they should be identified as a class under Part B.

The settlor would be identified under Part A as he also has a vested interest in reversion as he has not provided for the situation which will arise if all of the children pre-decease their mother. Should this happen there will be a total failure of the trust, which will revert to E, or if he has predeceased his wife, to his estate.

The trustees would also be identified under Part C as a result of their control over the trust.

4.12.5   Example 5

DETAILS

F's will provides for a life interest for his wife, with remainder to his children in equal shares. One of the children dies prior to the wife.

APPLICATION

The wife is not a beneficial owner. (see example 4)

The child who has pre-deceased his mother has a vested interest in the remainder as there is no condition precedent that he must survive his mother. Therefore the interest survives him and is capable of being bequeathed by his will or passing under his intestacy.

It will depend on the number of children as to the level of interest each has. If it is under 25 per cent then it would simply be under Part B. If each has at least 25 per cent then they will need to be individually identified under Part A and enquiries will need to be made of the trustee as to who is now entitled to the deceased child's interest.

4.12.6   Example 6

DETAILS

I's will provides for a life interest in favour of his wife, with remainder to his four children in equal shares. The trustee is given express power to vary the shares, in whole or in part.

APPLICATION

This means that the interests of the children are vested but are defeasible. Until the trustee exercises their power to vary the interest, all of the children will be identified under Part A. Once the trustee exercises their power, any children with an interest remaining at 25 per cent or more will continue to be identified under Part A, while the others will be identified under Part B. The trustees will be identified under Part C. The wife is not a beneficial owner (see example 4)

4.12.7   Example 7

DETAILS

J by his will created a life interest in favour of his wife, with the remainder to his three children in equal shares. The trustees are given a power, during the life of the widow, to appoint an interest in all or part of the capital of the fund, without her consent, in favour of such charities as they may select.

APPLICATION

Until the power of appointment is exercised all three children have a vested interest in the remainder and should be identified under Part A.

If for example the power of appointment is exercised and 50 per cent of the fund is to be paid to one specified charity – prior to the distribution it is recommended that the charity be identified under Part A and the children under Part B. After the distribution is made, the children will then return to having a one-third share each and be identified under Part A. As such it is important to obtain updated information when taking on a new retainer for such a trust.

4.12.8   Example 8

DETAILS

N creates an inter vivos trust for his three named grandchildren subject to attaining 21, with substitution for their issue, reserving to himself the power to appoint or remove trustees.

APPLICATION

The three grandchildren have contingent interests and so will be identified under Part B. N has control and should be identified under Part C due to the power to appoint or remove trustees.

4.12.9   Example 9

DETAILS

O creates an inter vivos trust for his three named grandchildren subject to attaining 21, with substitution for their issue, appointing a protector (P) with power to veto any advancement of capital by the trustees under s32 of the Trustee Act 1925 and to appoint or remove trustees.

APPLICATION

The grandchildren have contingent interests and are identified under Part B. Both P and the trustees have control over the trust and should be identified under Part C.

4.12.10   Example 10

DETAILS

Q's will creates discretionary trusts of which his wife and issue are the beneficiaries. He gives his trustees the power, with the consent of his children, to add beneficiaries from amongst the spouses and civil partners of his issue.

APPLICATION

Both the trustees and the children have control of the trust and are subject to identification under Part C, while the wife and all of the issue are discretionary beneficiaries and are to be identified as a class under Part B.

CHAPTER 5 – MONEY LAUNDERING OFFENCES

5.1   General comments

The Proceeds of Crime Act 2002 (POCA) created a single set of money laundering offences applicable throughout the UK to the proceeds of all crimes. It also creates a disclosure regime, which makes it an offence not to disclose knowledge or suspicion of money laundering, but also permits persons to be given consent in certain circumstances to carry out activities which would otherwise constitute money laundering.

5.2   Application

POCA applies to all solicitors, although some offences apply only to persons within the regulated sector, or nominated officers.

5.3 Mental elements

The mental elements which are relevant to offences under Part 7 of POCA are:

- knowledge
- suspicion
- reasonable grounds for suspicion

These are the three mental elements in the actual offences, although the third one only applies to offences relating to the regulated sector. There is also the element of belief on reasonable grounds in the foreign conduct defence to the money laundering offences. A person will have a defence to a principal offence if they know or believe on reasonable grounds that the criminal conduct involved was exempt overseas criminal conduct.

For the principal offences of money laundering the prosecution must prove that the property involved is criminal property. This means that the prosecution must prove that the property was obtained through criminal conduct and that, at the time of the alleged offence, you knew or suspected that it was.

For the failure to disclose offences, where you are acting in the regulated sector, you must disclose if you have knowledge, suspicion or reasonable grounds for suspicion; while if you are not in the regulated sector you will only need to consider making a disclosure if you have actual, subjective knowledge or suspicion.

These terms for the mental elements in the offences are not terms of art; they are not defined within POCA and should be given their everyday meaning. However, case law has provided some guidance on how they should be interpreted.

5.3.1 Knowledge

Knowledge means actual knowledge. There is some suggestion that wilfully shutting one's eyes to the truth may amount to knowledge. However, the current general approach from the criminal courts is that nothing less than actual knowledge will suffice.

5.3.2 Suspicion

The term 'suspects' is one which the court has historically avoided defining; however because of its importance in English criminal law, some general guidance has been given. In the case of *Da Silva* [1996] EWCA Crim 1654, which was prosecuted under the previous money laundering legislation, Longmore LJ stated:

> It seems to us that the essential element in the word 'suspect' and its affiliates, in this context, is that the defendant must think that there is a possibility, which is more than fanciful, that the relevant facts exist. A vague feeling of unease would not suffice.

There is no requirement for the suspicion to be clear or firmly grounded on specific facts, but there must be a degree of satisfaction, not necessarily amounting to belief, but at least extending beyond speculation.

The test for whether you hold a suspicion is a subjective one.

If you think a transaction is suspicious, you are not expected to know the exact nature of the criminal offence or that particular funds were definitely those arising from the crime. You may have noticed something unusual or unexpected and after making enquiries, the facts do not seem normal or make commercial sense. You do not have to have evidence that money laundering is taking place to have suspicion.

Chapter 11 of this practice note contains a number of standard warning signs which may give you a cause for concern; however, whether you have a suspicion is a matter for your own judgement. To help form that judgement, consider talking through the issues with colleagues or with the Law Society. You could take legal advice, possibly from another solicitor on the Law Society's AML directory. Listing causes for concern can also help focus your mind.

If you have not yet formed a suspicion but simply have cause for concern, you may choose to ask the client or others more questions. This choice depends on what you already know, and how easy it is to make enquiries.

If you think your own client is innocent but suspect that another party to a transaction is engaged in money laundering, you may still have to consider referring your client for specialist advice regarding the risk that they may be a party to one of the principal offences.

5.3.3   Reasonable grounds to suspect

The issues here for the solicitor conducting regulated activities are the same as for the mental element of suspicion, except that it is an objective test. Were there factual circumstances from which an honest and reasonable person, engaged in a business in the regulated sector should have inferred knowledge or formed the suspicion that another was engaged in money laundering?

5.4   Principal money laundering offences

5.4.1   General comments

Money laundering offences assume that a criminal offence has occurred in order to generate the criminal property which is now being laundered. This is often known as a predicate offence. No conviction for the predicate offence is necessary for a person to be prosecuted for a money laundering offence.

The principal money laundering offences apply to money laundering activity which occurred on or after 24 February 2003 as a result of the Proceeds of Crime Act 2002 (Commencement No. 4, Transitional Provisions & Savings) Order 2003.

If the money laundering occurred or started before 24 February 2003, the former legislation will apply. If the money laundering occurred or started before 24 February 2003, the former legislation will apply – see the second edition of Money Laundering Legislation: Guidance for Solicitors 2002

However if the money laundering took place after 24 February 2003, the conduct giving rise to the criminal property can occur before that date.

When considering the principal money laundering offences, be aware that it is also an offence to conspire or attempt to launder the proceeds of crime, or to counsel, aid, abet or procure money laundering.

5.4.2   Section 327 – concealing

A person commits an offence if he conceals, disguises, converts, or transfers criminal property, or removes criminal property from England and Wales, Scotland or Northern Ireland.

Concealing or disguising criminal property includes concealing or disguising its nature, source, location, disposition, movement, ownership or any rights connected with it.

5.4.3   Section 328 – arrangements

A person commits an offence if he enters into, or becomes concerned in an arrangement which he knows or suspects facilitates the acquisition, retention, use or control of criminal property by or on behalf of another person.

WHAT IS AN ARRANGEMENT?

Arrangement is not defined in Part 7 of POCA. The arrangement must exist and have practical effects relating to the acquisition, retention, use or control of property.

An agreement to make an arrangement will not always be an arrangement. The test is whether the arrangement does in fact, in the present and not the future, have the effect of facilitating the acquisition, retention, use or control of criminal property by or on behalf of another person.

WHAT IS NOT AN ARRANGEMENT?

Bowman v. *Fels* [2005] EWCA Civ 226 held that s328 does not cover or affect the ordinary conduct of litigation by legal professionals, including any step taken in litigation from the issue of proceedings and the securing of injunctive relief or a freezing order up to its final disposal by judgment.

Our view, supported by Counsel's opinion, is that dividing assets in accordance with the judgment, including the handling of the assets which are criminal property, is not an arrangement. Further, settlements, negotiations, out of court settlements, alternative dispute resolution and tribunal representation are not arrangements. However, the property will generally still remain criminal property and you may need to consider referring your client for specialist advice regarding possible offences they may commit once they come into possession of the property after completion of the settlement.

The recovery of property by a victim of an acquisitive offence will not be committing an offence under either s328 or s329 of the Act.

SHAM LITIGATION

Sham litigation created for the purposes of money laundering remains within the ambit of s328. Our view is that shams arise where an acquisitive criminal offence is committed and settlement negotiations or litigation are intentionally fabricated to launder the proceeds of that separate crime.

A sham can also arise if a whole claim or category of loss is fabricated to launder the criminal property. In this case, money laundering for the purposes of POCA cannot occur until after execution of the judgment or completion of the settlement.

ENTERING INTO OR BECOMING CONCERNED IN AN ARRANGEMENT

To enter into an arrangement is to become a party to it.

To become concerned in an arrangement suggests a wider practical involvement such as taking steps to put the arrangement into effect.

Both entering into and becoming concerned in, describe an act that is the starting point of an involvement in an existing arrangement.

Although the Court did not directly consider the conduct of transactional work, its approach to what constitutes an arrangement under section 328 provides some assistance in interpreting how that section applies in those circumstances.

Our view is that *Bowman* v. *Fels* supports a restricted understanding of the concept of entering into or becoming concerned in an arrangement, with respect to transactional work. In particular:

- entering into or becoming concerned in an arrangement involves an act done at a particular time
- an offence is only committed once the arrangement is actually made, and
- preparatory or intermediate steps in transactional work which does not itself involve the acquisition, retention, use or control of property will not constitute the making of an arrangement under s328
    If you are doing transactional work and become suspicious, you have to consider:
- whether an arrangement exists and, if so, whether you have entered into or become concerned in it or may do so in the future
- if no arrangement exists, whether one may come into existence in the future which you may become concerned in

5.4.4   Section 329 – acquisition, use or possession

A person commits an offence if he acquires, uses or has possession of criminal property.

5.5   Defences to principal money laundering offences

You will have a defence to a principal money laundering offence if:

- you make an authorised disclosure prior to the offence being committed and you gain appropriate consent (the consent defence)
- you intended to make an authorised disclosure but had a reasonable excuse for not doing so (the reasonable excuse defence)

In relation to s.329 you will also have a defence if you received adequate consideration for the criminal property (the adequate consideration defence).

5.5.1   Authorised disclosures

Section 338 authorises you to make a disclosure regarding suspicion of money laundering as a defence to the principal money laundering offences.
    It specifically provides that you can make an authorised disclosure either:

- before money laundering has occurred, and if you have the appropriate consent
- while it is occurring but as soon as you suspect
- after it has occurred, if you had good reason for not disclosing earlier and make the disclosure as soon as practicable.

If a disclosure is authorised, it does not breach any rule which would otherwise restrict it, such as Rule 4 of the Solicitors' Code of Conduct relating to client confidentiality.
    Where your firm has a nominated officer, you should make your disclosure to the nominated officer. The nominated officer will consider your disclosure and decide whether to make an external disclosure to SOCA. If your firm does not have a nominated officer, you should make your disclosure directly to SOCA.

APPROPRIATE CONSENT

If you have a suspicion that a retainer you are acting in will involve dealing with criminal property, you can make an authorised disclosure to SOCA via your nominated officer and seek consent to undertake the further steps in the retainer which would constitute a money laundering offence.

For further information on how to make an authorised disclosure to SOCA and the process by which consent is gained, see chapter 8 of this practice note.

REASONABLE EXCUSE DEFENCE

This defence applies where a person intended to make an authorised disclosure before doing a prohibited act, but had a reasonable excuse for not disclosing. Reasonable excuse has not been defined by the courts, but the scope of the reasonable excuse defence is important for legal professional privilege.

You must make an authorised disclosure where you intend to deal with property in one or more of the ways specified in the money laundering offences, but know or suspect that the property is criminal property.

However, you are prevented from disclosing if your knowledge or suspicion is based on privileged information, and legal professional privilege is not excluded by the crime/fraud exception. You will have a reasonable excuse for not making an authorised disclosure and will not commit a money laundering offence.

There may be other circumstances which would provide a reasonable excuse, however these are likely to be narrow. You should clearly document the reason for not making a disclosure on this ground.

WHERE YOU SUSPECT PART WAY THROUGH

It is not unusual for a transactional matter to seem legitimate early in the retainer, but to develop in such a way as to arouse suspicion later on. It may be that certain steps have already taken place which you now suspect facilitated money laundering; while further steps are yet to be taken which you also suspect will facilitate further money laundering.

Section 338(2A) provides that you may make an authorised disclosure in these circumstances if:

- at the time the initial steps were taken they were not a money laundering offence because you did not have good reason to know or suspect that the property was criminal property; and
- you make a disclosure of your own initiative as soon as practicable after you first know or suspect that criminal property is involved in the retainer.

In such a case you would make a disclosure seeking consent for the rest of the transaction to proceed, while fully documenting the reasons why you came to know or suspect that criminal property was involved and why you did not suspect this to be the case previously.

5.5.2   Adequate consideration defence

This defence applies if there was adequate consideration for acquiring, using and possessing the criminal property, unless you know or suspect that those goods or services may help another to carry out criminal conduct.

The Crown Prosecution Service guidance for prosecutors says the defence applies where professional advisors, such as solicitors or accountants, receive money for or on account of costs, whether from the client or from another person on the client's behalf. Disbursements are also covered. The fees charged must be reasonable, and the defence is not available if the value of the work is significantly less than the money received.

The transfer of funds from client to office account, or vice versa, is covered by the defence.

Returning the balance of an account to a client may be a money laundering offence if you know or suspect the money is criminal property. In that case, you must make an authorised disclosure and obtain consent to deal with the money before you transfer it.

Reaching a matrimonial settlement or an agreement on a retiring partner's interest in a business does not constitute adequate consideration for receipt of criminal property, as in both cases the parties would only be entitled to a share of the legitimately acquired assets of the marriage or the business. This is particularly important where your client would be receiving the property as part of a settlement which would be exempted from s328 due to the case of *Bowman* v. *Fels*.

The defence is more likely to cover situations where:

- a third party seeks to enforce an arms length debt and, unknown to them, is given criminal property in payment for that debt
- a person provides goods or services as part of a legitimate arms length transaction but unknown to them is paid from a bank account which contains the proceeds of crime

5.6 Failure to disclose offences – money laundering

5.6.1 General comments

The failure to disclose provisions in sections 330, 331 and 332 apply where the information on which the knowledge or suspicion is based came to a person on or after 24 February 2003, or where a person in the regulated sector has reasonable grounds for knowledge or suspicion on or after that date.

If the information came to a person before 24 February 2003, the old law applies.

In all three sections, the phrase 'knows or suspects' refers to actual knowledge or suspicion – a subjective test. However, solicitors and nominated officers in the regulated sector will also commit an offence if they fail to report when they have reasonable grounds for knowledge or suspicion – an objective test. On this basis, they may be guilty of the offence under s330 or 331 if they should have known or suspected money laundering.

For all failure to disclose offences you must either:

- know the identity of the money launderer or the whereabouts of the laundered property, or
- believe the information on which your suspicion was based may assist in identifying the money launderer or the whereabouts of the laundered property

5.6.2 Section 330 – failure to disclose: regulated sector

A person commits an offence if

- he knows or suspects, or has reasonable grounds for knowing or suspecting, that another person is engaged in money laundering, and

- the information on which his suspicion is based comes in the course of business in the regulated sector, and
- he fails to disclose that knowledge or suspicion, or reasonable grounds for suspicion, as soon as practicable to a nominated officer or SOCA

Our view is that delays in disclosure arising from taking legal advice or seeking help from the Law Society may be acceptable provided you act promptly to seek advice.

5.6.3   Section 331 – failure to disclose: nominated officer in the regulated sector

A nominated officer in the regulated sector commits a separate offence if, as a result of an internal disclosure under s330, he knows or suspects, or has reasonable grounds for knowing or suspecting, that another person is engaged in money laundering and he fails to disclose as soon as practicable to SOCA.

5.6.4   Section 332 – failure to disclose: nominated officer in the non-regulated sector

An organisation which does not carry out relevant activities and so is not in the regulated sector, may decide on a risk-based approach to set up internal disclosure systems and appoint a person as nominated officer to receive internal disclosures.

A nominated officer in the non-regulated sector commits an offence if, as a result of a disclosure, he knows or suspects that another person is engaged in money laundering and fails to make a disclosure as soon as practicable to SOCA.

For this offence, the test is a subjective one: did you know or suspect in fact?

5.7   Exceptions to failure to disclose offences

There are three situations in which you have not committed an offence for failing to disclose:

- you have a reasonable excuse
- you are a professional legal adviser and the information came to you in privileged circumstances
- you did not receive appropriate training from your employer

The first defence is the only one which applies to all three failure to disclose offences; the other two defences are only specifically provided for persons in the regulated sector who are not nominated officers.

All of the failure to disclose sections also reiterate that the offence will not be committed if the property involved in the suspected money laundering is derived from exempted overseas criminal conduct .

5.7.1   Reasonable excuse

No offence is committed if there is a reasonable excuse for not making a disclosure, but there is no judicial guidance on what might constitute a reasonable excuse.

However, as with reasonable excuse under the principal money laundering offences, where common law legal professional privilege has not been expressly excluded, following the reasoning in *Bowman* v. *Fels*, it is considered that the decision not to make a disclosure because the information came to the person in privileged circumstances would be a reasonable excuse.

You should carefully document any reasons for not making a disclosure under this section.

5.7.2 Privileged circumstances

No offence is committed if the information or other matter giving rise to suspicion comes to a professional legal adviser in privileged circumstances.

You should note that receipt of information in privileged circumstances is not the same as legal professional privilege. It is a creation of POCA designed to comply with the exemptions from reporting set out in the European directives.

Privileged circumstances means information communicated:

- by a client, or a representative of a client, in connection with the giving of legal advice to the client, or
- by a client, or by a representative of a client, seeking legal advice from you
- by a person in connection with legal proceedings or contemplated legal proceedings

The exemption will not apply if information is communicated or given to the solicitor with the intention of furthering a criminal purpose.

The Crown Prosecution Service guidance for prosecutors indicates that if a solicitor forms a genuine, but mistaken, belief that the privileged circumstances exemption applies (for example, the client misleads the solicitor and uses the advice received for a criminal purpose) the solicitor will be able to rely on the reasonable excuse defence.

For a further discussion of privileged circumstances see Chapter 6.

5.7.3 Lack of training

Employees within the regulated sector who have no knowledge or suspicion of money laundering, even though there were reasonable grounds for suspicion, have a defence if they have not received training from their employers. Employers may be prosecuted for a breach of the Money Laundering Regulations 2007 if they fail to train staff.

5.8 Tipping off

The offences of tipping off for money laundering are contained in the Proceeds of Crime Act 2002 as amended by the Proceeds of Crime Act 2002 (Amendment) Regulations 2007 (POCA regulations 2007).

There are also tipping off offences for terrorist property in the Terrorism Act 2000, as amended by the TACT Regulations 2007.

5.8.1 Offences

TIPPING OFF – IN THE REGULATED SECTOR

There are two tipping off offences in S333A of POCA. They apply only to business in the regulated sector.

- **S333A(1)** – disclosing a suspicious activity report (SAR). It is an offence to disclose to a third person that a SAR has been made by any person to the police, HM Revenue and Customs, SOCA or a nominated officer, if that disclosure might prejudice any investigation that might be carried out as a result of the SAR. This offence can only be committed:
  - **after** a disclosure to SOCA or a nominated officer
  - if you know or suspect that by disclosing this information, you are likely to prejudice any investigation related to that SAR

- the information upon which the disclosure is based came to you in the course of business in the regulated sector

- **S333A(3)** – disclosing an investigation. It is an offence to disclose that an investigation into a money laundering offence is being contemplated or carried out if that disclosure is likely to prejudice that investigation. The offence can only be committed if the information on which the disclosure is based came to the person in the course of business in the regulated sector. The key point is that you can commit this offence, even where you are unaware that a SAR was submitted

PREJUDICING AN INVESTIGATION – OUTSIDE THE REGULATED SECTOR

Section 342(1) contains an offence of prejudicing a confiscation, civil recovery or money laundering investigation, if the person making the disclosure knows or suspects that an investigation is being, or is about to be conducted. Section 342(1) was amended by paragraph 8 of the TACT and POCA Regulations 2007. The offence in s342(2)(a) only applies to those outside the regulated sector. The offence in s342(2) (b) applies to everyone.

You only commit the offence in s342(2)(a) if you knew or suspected that the disclosure would, or would be likely to prejudice any investigation.

5.8.2 Defences

TIPPING OFF

The following disclosures are permitted:

- S333B – disclosures within an undertaking or group, including disclosures to a professional legal adviser or relevant professional adviser
- S333C – disclosures between institutions, including disclosures from a professional legal adviser to another professional legal adviser
- S333D – disclosures to your supervisory authority
- S333D(2) – disclosures made by professional legal advisers to their clients for the purpose of dissuading them from engaging in criminal conduct

A person does not commit the main tipping off offence if he does not know or suspect that a disclosure is likely to prejudice an investigation.

S333B – DISCLOSURES WITHIN AN UNDERTAKING OR GROUP ETC

It is not an offence if an employee, officer or partner of a firm discloses that a SAR has been made if it is to an employee, officer or partner of the same undertaking.

A solicitor will not commit a tipping off offence if a disclosure is made to another lawyer either:

- within a different undertaking, if both parties carry on business in an EEA state
- in a country or territory that imposes money laundering requirements equivalent to the EU and both parties share common ownership, management or control

S333C – DISCLOSURES BETWEEN INSTITUTIONS ETC

A solicitor will not commit a tipping off offence if **all** the following criteria are met:

- The disclosure is made to another lawyer in an EEA state, or one with an equivalent AML regime.

- The disclosure relates to a client or former client of both parties, or a transaction involving them both, or the provision of a service involving them both.
- The disclosure is made for the purpose of preventing a money laundering offence.
- Both parties have equivalent professional duties of confidentiality and protection of personal data.

S333D(2) – LIMITED EXCEPTION FOR PROFESSIONAL LEGAL ADVISERS

A solicitor will not commit a tipping off offence if the disclosure is to a client and it is made for the purpose of dissuading the client from engaging in conduct amounting to an offence. This exception and the tipping off offence in s333A apply to those carrying on activities in the regulated sector.

PREJUDICING AN INVESTIGATION

S342(4) – PROFESSIONAL LEGAL ADVISER EXEMPTION

It is a defence to a S342(1) offence that a disclosure is made by a legal adviser to a client, or a client's representative, in connection with the giving of legal advice or to any person in connection with legal proceedings or contemplated legal proceedings.

5.8.3 *Making enquiries of a client*

You should make preliminary enquiries of your client, or a third party, to obtain further information to help you to decide whether you have a suspicion. You may also need to raise questions during a retainer to clarify such issues .

There is nothing in POCA which prevents you making normal enquiries about your client's instructions, and the proposed retainer, in order to remove, if possible, any concerns and enable the firm to decide whether to take on or continue the retainer.

These enquiries will only be tipping off if you disclose that a SAR has been made to SOCA or a nominated officer or that a money laundering investigation is being carried out or contemplated. The offence of tipping off only applies to the regulated sector.

It is not tipping-off to include a paragraph about your obligations under the money laundering legislation in your firm's standard client care letter.

CHAPTER 6 – LEGAL PROFESSIONAL PRIVILEGE

6.1 General comments

Solicitors are under a duty to keep the affairs of their clients confidential, and the circumstances in which they are able to disclose client communications are strictly limited.

However, sections 327–329, 330 and 332 of POCA contain provisions for disclosure of information to be made to SOCA.

Solicitors also have a duty of full disclosure to their clients. However, sections 333A and 342 of POCA prohibit disclosure of information in circumstances where a SAR has been made and/or where it would prejudice an existing or proposed investigation.

This chapter examines the tension between a solicitor's duties and these provisions of POCA. Similar tensions also arise with respect to the Terrorism Act and you should refer to the Law Society's practice note on anti-terrorism in those circumstances.

This chapter should be read in conjunction with Chapter 5 of this practice note and if you are still in doubt as to your position, you should seek independent legal advice. The Law Society's AML directory may be of assistance in locating a solicitor who practises in this area of law.

6.2 Application

This chapter is relevant to any solicitor considering whether to make a disclosure under POCA.

6.3 Duty of confidentiality

A solicitor is professionally and legally obliged to keep the affairs of clients confidential and to ensure that his staff do likewise. The obligations extend to all matters revealed to a solicitor, from whatever source, by a client, or someone acting on the client's behalf. See Solicitors' Code of Conduct – Rule 4.

In exceptional circumstances this general obligation of confidence may be overridden. See Solicitors' Code of Conduct Rule 4 – note 10. However, certain communications can never be disclosed unless statute permits this either expressly or by necessary implication. Such communications are those protected by legal professional privilege (LPP).

6.4 Legal professional privilege

6.4.1 General overview

LPP is a privilege against disclosure, ensuring clients know that certain documents and information provided to lawyers cannot be disclosed at all. It recognises the client's fundamental human right to be candid with his legal adviser, without fear of later disclosure to his prejudice. It is an absolute right and cannot be overridden by any other interest.

LPP does not extend to everything lawyers have a duty to keep confidential. LPP protects only those confidential communications falling under either of the two heads of privilege – advice privilege or litigation privilege.

For the purposes of LPP, a lawyer includes solicitors and their employees, barristers and in-house lawyers. It does not include accountants.

6.4.1 Advice privilege

PRINCIPLE

Communications between a lawyer, acting in his capacity as a lawyer, and a client, are privileged if they are both:

- confidential
- for the purpose of seeking legal advice from a solicitor or providing it to a client

SCOPE

Communications are not privileged merely because a client is speaking or writing to you. The protection applies only to those communications which directly seek or provide advice or which are given in a legal context, that involve the lawyer using his legal skills and which are directly related to the performance of the lawyer's professional duties [Passmore on Privilege 2nd edition 2006].

Case law helps define what advice privilege covers.

Communications subject to advice privilege:

- a solicitor's bill of costs and statement of account [*Chant* v. *Brown* (1852) 9 Hare 790]
- information imparted by prospective clients in advance of a retainer will attract LPP if the communications were made for the purpose of indicating the advice required [*Minster* v. *Priest* [1930] AC 558 per Lord Atkin at 584].

Communications not subject to advice privilege:

- notes of open court proceedings [*Parry* v. *News Group Newspapers* (1990) 140 New Law Journal 1719] are not privileged, as the content of the communication is not confidential.
- conversations, correspondence or meetings with opposing lawyers [*Parry* v. *News Group Newspapers* (1990) 140 New Law Journal 1719] are not privileged, as the content of the communication is not confidential.
- a client account ledger maintained in relation to the client's money [*Nationwide Building Society* v. *Various Solicitors* [1999] P.N.L.R. 53.]
- an appointments diary or time record on an attendance note, time sheet or fee record relating to a client [*R* v. *Manchester Crown Court*, ex *p*. *Rogers* [1999] 1 WLR 832]
- conveyancing documents are not communication so not subject to advice privilege [*R* v. *Inner London Crown Court* ex *p*. *Baines & Baines* [1988] QB 579]

ADVICE WITHIN A TRANSACTION

All communications between a lawyer and his client relating to a transaction in which the lawyer has been instructed for the purpose of obtaining legal advice are covered by advice privilege, notwithstanding that they do not contain advice on matters of law and construction, provided that they are directly related to the performance by the solicitor of his professional duty as legal adviser of his client. [*Three Rivers District Council and others* v. *the Bank of England* [2004] UKHL 48 at 111]

This will mean that where you are providing legal advice in a transactional matter (such as a conveyance) the advice privilege will cover all:

- communications with,
- instructions from, and
- advice given to

the client, including any working papers and drafts prepared, as long as they are directly related to your performance of your professional duties as a legal adviser.

6.4.3 Litigation privilege

PRINCIPLE

This privilege, which is wider than advice privilege, protects confidential communications made after litigation has started, or is reasonably in prospect, between either:

- a lawyer and a client
- a lawyer and an agent, whether or not that agent is a lawyer
- a lawyer and a third party

These communications must be for the sole or dominant purpose of litigation, either:

- for seeking or giving advice in relation to it
- for obtaining evidence to be used in it
- for obtaining information leading to obtaining such evidence

6.4.4 Important points to consider

An original document not brought into existence for these privileged purposes and so not already privileged, does not become privileged merely by being given to a lawyer for advice or other privileged purpose.

Further, where you have a corporate client, communication between you and the employees of a corporate client may not be protected by LPP if the employee cannot be considered to be 'the client' for the purposes of the retainer. As such some employees will be clients, while others will not. [*Three Rivers District Council* v. *the Governor and Company of the Bank of England (no 5)* [2003] QB 1556]

It is not a breach of LPP to discuss a matter with your nominated officer for the purposes of receiving advice on whether to make a disclosure.

6.4.5 Crime/fraud exception

LPP protects advice you give to a client on avoiding committing a crime [*Bullivant* v. *Att-Gen of Victoria* [1901] AC 196] or warning them that proposed actions could attract prosecution [*Butler* v. *Board of Trade* [1971] Ch 680]. LPP does not extend to documents which themselves form part of a criminal or fraudulent act, or communications which take place in order to obtain advice with the intention of carrying out an offence [*R* v. *Cox & Railton* (1884) 14 QBD 153]. It is irrelevant whether or not you are aware that you are being used for that purpose [*Banque Keyser Ullman* v. *Skandia* [1986] 1 Lloyds Rep 336].

INTENTION OF FURTHERING A CRIMINAL PURPOSE

It is not just your client's intention which is relevant for the purpose of ascertaining whether information was communicated for the furtherance of a criminal purpose. It is also sufficient that a third party intends the lawyer/client communication to be made with that purpose (eg where the innocent client is being used by a third party) [*R* v. *Central Criminal Court* ex p. *Francis and Francis* [1989] 1 AC 346].

KNOWING A TRANSACTION CONSTITUTES AN OFFENCE

If you know the transaction you're working on is a principal offence, you risk committing an offence yourself. In these circumstances, communications relating to such a transaction are not privileged and should be disclosed.

SUSPECTING A TRANSACTION CONSTITUTES AN OFFENCE

If you merely suspect a transaction might constitute a money laundering offence, the position is more complex. If the suspicions are correct, communications with the client are not privileged. If the suspicions are unfounded, the communications should remain privileged and are therefore non-disclosable.

PRIMA FACIE EVIDENCE

If you suspect you are unwittingly being involved by your client in a fraud, the courts require prima facie evidence before LPP can be displaced [*O'Rourke* v. *Darbishire* [1920] AC 581]. The sufficiency of that evidence depends on the circumstances: it is easier to infer a prima facie case where there is substantial material available to support an inference of fraud. While you may decide yourself if prima facie evidence exists, you may also ask the court for directions [*Finers* v. *Miro* [1991] 1 WLR 35].

The Crown Prosecution Service guidance for prosecutors indicates that if a solicitor forms a genuine, but mistaken, belief that the privileged circumstances exemption (see 6.5 below) applies (for example, the client misleads the solicitor and uses the advice received for a criminal purpose) the solicitor will be able to rely on the reasonable excuse defence. It is likely that a similar approach would be taken with respect to a genuine, but mistaken, belief that LPP applies.

We believe you should not make a disclosure unless you know of prima facie evidence that you are being used in the furtherance of a crime.

6.5 Privileged circumstances

Quite separately from LPP, POCA recognises another type of communication, one which is given or received in 'privileged circumstances'. This is not the same as LPP, it is merely an exemption from certain provisions of POCA, although in many cases the communication will also be covered by LPP.

The privileged circumstances exemptions are found in the following places:

- POCA – section 330(10) and (11)
- POCA – section333D(2) (repealing and replacing s333(3))
- POCA – section 342(4)
- Terrorism Act – section 19(3) and (5)
- Terrorism Act – section 21A(8)
- Terrorism Act – section 21G(2)

Although the wording is not exactly the same in all these sections, the essential elements of the exemption are:

- you are a professional legal adviser
- the information or material is communicated to you:
- by your client or their representative in connection with you giving legal advice
- by the client or their representative in connection with them seeking legal advice from you
- by any person for the purpose of/in connection with actual or contemplated legal proceedings
- the information or material cannot be communicated or given to you with a view to furthering a criminal purpose

The offence of prejudicing an investigation was amended by section 342(3)(ba) to restrict to work outside the regulated sector. Therefore the privileged circumstances defence only applies to solicitors who are conducting work that falls outside the regulated sector.

The term professional legal adviser includes solicitors, their non-solicitor partners and their employees (see s330(7A) of POCA), barristers and in-house lawyers.

The Society believes that the definition of a representative can be interpreted broadly.

Consider the crime/fraud exception when determining what constitutes the furthering of a criminal purpose.

Finally, section 330(9A) protects the privilege attaching to any disclosure made to a nominated officer for the purposes of obtaining advice about whether or not a disclosure should be made.

6.6 Differences between privileged circumstances and LPP

6.6.1 Protection of advice

When advice is given or received in circumstances where litigation is neither contemplated nor reasonably in prospect, except in very limited circumstances communications between you and third parties will not be protected under the advice arm of LPP.

Privileged circumstances, however, exempt communications regarding advice to be provided to representatives, so this may include communications with:

- a junior employee of a client
- other professionals assisting in a transaction such as surveyors or estate agents

6.6.2 Losing protection by dissemination

Under common law, privileged information can be shared within law firms without losing the protection of LPP and this can include other persons with a common interest, such as co-defendants [*Gotha City* v. *Sotheby's* (no 1) [1998] 1 WLR 114]. As such under common law, privileged material can be put into a data room for the purposes of a transaction and will remain privileged if it is stipulated that privilege is not waived.

For the privileged circumstances exemption to apply, the information must actually be exchanged for the purpose of giving or seeking legal advice. As such the protection is likely to be lost if information is put in a data room and viewed by the other side.

6.6.3 Vulnerability to seizure

It is important to correctly identify whether communications are protected by LPP or if they are merely covered by the privileged circumstances exemption. This is because the privileged circumstances exemption exempts you from certain POCA provisions. It does not provide any of the other LPP protections to those communications. Therefore a communication which is only covered by privileged circumstances, not LPP, will still remain vulnerable to seizure or production under a court order or other such notice from law enforcement.

6.7 When do I disclose?

If the communication is covered by LPP and the crime/fraud exception does not apply, you cannot make a disclosure under POCA.

If the communication was received in privileged circumstances and the crime/fraud exception does not apply, you are exempt from the relevant provisions of POCA, which include making a disclosure to SOCA.

If neither of these situations applies, the communication will still be confidential. However, the material is disclosable under POCA and can be disclosed, whether as an authorised disclosure, or to avoid breaching section 330. Section 337 of POCA permits you to make such a disclosure and provides that you will not be in breach of your professional duty of confidentiality when you do so.

CHAPTER 7 – TERRORIST PROPERTY OFFENCES

7.1 General comments

Terrorist organisations require funds to plan and carry out attacks, train militants, pay their operatives and promote their ideologies. The Terrorism Act 2000 (as amended) criminalises not only the participation in terrorist activities but also the provision of monetary support for terrorist purposes .

7.2 Application

All persons are required to comply with the Terrorism Act. The principal terrorist property offences in ss15–18 apply to all persons and therefore to all solicitors. However, the specific offence of failure to disclose and the two tipping off offences apply only to persons in the regulated sector.

The definition of business in the regulated sector was amended by the Terrorism Act 2000 (Business in the Regulated Sector and Supervisory Authorities) Order 2007 to reflect changes brought about by the third money laundering directive. There are similar changes to the definition of business in the regulated sector in the Proceeds of Crime Act 2002.

7.3 Principal terrorist property offences

7.3.1 Section 15 – fundraising

It is an offence to be involved in fundraising if you have knowledge or reasonable cause to suspect that the money or other property raised may be used for terrorist purposes. You can commit the offence by:

- inviting others to make contributions
- receiving contributions
- making contributions towards terrorist funding, including making gifts and loans.

It is no defence that the money or other property is a payment for goods and services.

7.3.2 Section 16 – use or possession

It is an offence to use or possess money or other property for terrorist purposes, including when you have reasonable cause to suspect they may be used for these purposes.

7.3.3 Section 17 – arrangements

It is an offence to become involved in an arrangement which makes money or other property available to another if you know, or have reasonable cause to suspect it may be used for terrorist purposes.

7.3.4 Section 18 – money laundering

It is an offence to enter into or become concerned in an arrangement facilitating the retention or control of terrorist property by, or on behalf of, another person including, but not limited to the following ways:

- by concealment
- by removal from the jurisdiction
- by transfer to nominees

It is a defence if you did not know, and had no reasonable cause to suspect, that the arrangement related to terrorist property.

- Read about arrangements under POCA in chapter 5

7.4 Defences to principal terrorist property offences

The TACT Regulations 2007 of 26 December 2007 introduced three new defences to the main offences in s15–18. These defences are contained in s21ZA–21ZC.

- **prior consent defence** – you make a disclosure to an authorised person before becoming involved in a transaction or an arrangement, and the person acts with the consent of an authorised officer
- **consent defence** – you are already involved in a transaction or arrangement and make a disclosure, so long as there is a reasonable excuse for failure to make a disclosure in advance
- **reasonable excuse defence** – you intended to make a disclosure but have a reasonable excuse for failing to do so. See 5.7.1 on reasonable excuse

Read chapter 8 for more information on how to make a disclosure and gaining consent.

There are further defences relating to co-operation with the police in s21. You do not commit an offence under s15–18 in the following further circumstances:

- you are acting with the express consent of a constable, including civilian staff at SOCA
- you disclose your suspicion or belief to a constable or SOCA after you become involved in an arrangement or transaction that concerns money or terrorist property, and you provide the information on which your suspicion or belief is based. You must make this disclosure on your own initiative and as soon as reasonably practicable.

The defence of disclosure to a constable or SOCA is also available to an employee who makes a disclosure about terrorist property offences in accordance with the internal reporting procedures laid down by the firm.

7.5 Failure to disclose offences

7.5.1 Non-regulated sector

Section 19 provides that anyone, whether they are a nominated officer or not, must disclose as soon as reasonably practicable to a constable, or SOCA, if they know or suspect that another person has committed a terrorist financing offence based on information which came to them in the course of a trade, profession or employment. The test is subjective.

7.5.2   Regulated sector

Section 21A, inserted by the Anti-Terrorism Crime and Security Act 2001, creates a criminal offence for those in the regulated sector who fail to make a disclosure to either a constable or the firm's nominated officer where there are reasonable grounds for suspecting that another person has committed an offence. This was further expanded by the TACT Regulations 2007 to cover failure to disclose an attempted offence under sections 15–18.

7.6   Defences to failing to disclose

The following are defences to failure to disclose offences under both section 19 and section 21A. Either:

- you had a reasonable excuse for not making the disclosure
- you received the information on which the belief or suspicion is based in privileged circumstances, without an intention of furthering a criminal purpose

The TACT Regulations 2007 introduced an additional defence for those in the regulated sector. A person has a defence where they are employed or are in partnership with a solicitor to provide assistance and support and they receive information concerning terrorist property in privileged circumstances.

Read about privileged circumstances in 5.7.2

It is also a defence under section 19 if you made an internal report in accordance with your employer's reporting procedures.

7.7   Section 21D tipping off offences: regulated sector

- **Section 21D (1) – disclosing a suspicious activity report (SAR).** It is an offence to disclose to a third person that a SAR has been made by any person to the police, HM Revenue and Customs, SOCA or a nominated officer, if that disclosure might prejudice any investigation that might be carried out as a result of the SAR. This offence can only be committed:

  - **after** a disclosure to SOCA or a nominated officer
  - if you know or suspect that by disclosing this information, you are likely to prejudice any investigation related to that SAR
  - the information upon which the disclosure is based came to you in the course of business in the regulated sector

- **Section 21D(3) – disclosing an investigation.** It is an offence to disclose that an investigation into allegations relating to terrorist property offences is being contemplated or carried out if that disclosure is likely to prejudice that investigation. The offence can only be committed if the information on which the disclosure is based came to the person in the course of business in the regulated sector. The key point is that you can commit this offence, even where you are unaware that a SAR was submitted

7.8   Defences to tipping off

7.8.1   Section 21E – disclosures within an undertaking or group etc

It is not an offence if an employee, officer or partner of a firm discloses that a SAR has been made if it is to an employee, officer or partner of the same undertaking.

A solicitor will not commit a tipping off offence if a disclosure is made to another lawyer either:

- within a different undertaking provided that both parties carry on business in an EEA state
- in a country or territory that imposes money laundering requirements equivalent to the EU, and both parties share common ownership, management or control.

7.8.2   Section 21F – other permitted disclosures

A solicitor will not commit a tipping off offence if all the following criteria are met:

- The disclosure is made to another lawyer in an EEA state, or one having an equivalent AML regime.
- The disclosure relates to a client or former client of both parties, or a transaction involving them both, or the provision of a service involving them both.
- The disclosure is made for the purpose of preventing a money laundering offence.
- Both parties have equivalent professional duties of confidentiality and protection of personal data.

7.8.3   Section 21G – limited exception for professional legal advisers

A solicitor will not commit a tipping off offence if the disclosure is to a client and it is made for the purpose of dissuading the client from engaging in conduct amounting to an offence. This exception and the tipping off offence in section 21D apply to the regulated sector.

7.9   Other terrorist property offences in statutory instruments

The Al Qaida and Taliban (United Nations Measures) Order 2006 and the Terrorism (United Nations Measures) Order 2006 create offences of providing funds or economic resources to terrorists. Terrorists can be funded from legitimately obtained income, including charitable donations, so it is difficult to know at what stage legitimate earnings become terrorist assets.

It may be helpful to consult:

- www.hm-treasury.gov.uk – the consolidated sanctions list of the names of suspected terrorists maintained by HM Treasury.
- www.homeoffice.gov.uk – a list of proscribed organisations maintained by the Home Office

7.10   Making enquiries of a client

You will often make preliminary enquiries of your client, or a third party, to obtain further information to help you to decide whether you have a suspicion. You may also need to raise questions during a retainer to clarify such issues.

These enquiries will only amount to tipping off if you disclose that a suspicious activity report has been made, or that an investigation into allegations relating to terrorist property offences is being carried out or contemplated.

CHAPTER 8 – MAKING A DISCLOSURE

8.1   General comments

The disclosure regime for money laundering and terrorist financing is run by the financial intelligence unit within the Serious Organised Crime Agency (SOCA).

SOCA was created on 3 April 2006 by the Serious Organised Crime and Police Act 2005. It is a law enforcement body devoted to dealing with organised crime within the UK and networking with other law enforcement agencies to combat global organised crime.

For full details on SOCA and their activities view their website at: www.soca.gov.uk

8.2 Application

All persons within the regulated sector and nominated officers have obligations under POCA to make disclosures of suspicions of money laundering.

In addition any person may need to make an authorised disclosure about criminal property.

All persons are required to make disclosures to SOCA of suspected terrorist financing.

8.3 Suspicious activity reports

8.3.1 What is a SAR?

A suspicious activity report (SAR) is the name given to the making of a disclosure to SOCA under either POCA or the Terrorism Act.

8.3.2 Who discloses?

Where a firm has a nominated officer, either they or their deputy will make the SAR to SOCA.

8.3.3 When?

You must make a SAR as soon as you are suspicious or know of terrorist financing or money laundering (subject to privilege considerations). Swiftly made SARs avoid delays in fulfilling your client's instructions.

You do not need to wait to ascertain whether or not a person is actually your client before making the disclosure. A SAR can be made about any person whom you suspect is involved in money laundering or terrorist financing.

8.3.4 Types of disclosures

Reports can either take the form of a SAR or a limited intelligence value report (LIVR). SARs will generally be the normal method of reporting, particularly where consent is required; however, LIVRs may be appropriate where you know that a law enforcement agency already has an interest in a matter. SOCA has provided detailed information (PDF) on when LIVRs should be used. If in doubt, complete a SAR form.

8.3.5 How to disclose

FORMS

SOCA has issued a preferred form to be completed when making a SAR, which is likely to become mandatory in the near future. Criminal penalties will apply for its non-use. We encourage you to start using the preferred form now.

SARS ONLINE

You should use SARs online where you have computer access. This securely encrypted system provided by SOCA allows you to:

- register your firm and relevant contact persons
- submit a SAR at any time of day
- receive e-mail confirmations of each SAR submitted

POST OR FAX

SARs can still be submitted in hard copy, although they should be typed and on the preferred form. You will not receive acknowledgement of any SARs sent this way. Where you require consent you should send by fax not by post.

Hard copy SARs should be sent to:

Fax: 020 7238 8256
Post: UK FIU
PO Box 8000
London SE11 5EN

8.3.6 *Information to include*

SOCA has provided information on completing the preferred SARs form.

To speed up consideration of your SAR, it is recommended that you use SOCA's glossary of codes for each reason for suspicion section of the report.

Your regulator number is your firm's ID number. Find this at www.solicitors-online.com or by calling the Solicitors Regulation Authority on 0870 606 2555.

8.3.7 *Getting consent from SOCA to proceed*

You will often be asking SOCA for consent to undertake acts which would be prohibited as a principal money laundering offence. From 26 December 2007, the Terrorism Act 2000 and Proceeds of Crime Act 2002 (Amendment) Regulations 2007 enter force, introducing a consent defence to sections 15–18 of the Terrorism Act 2000. The Regulations introduce s21ZA, which provides a defence if you made a disclosure to an authorised person before becoming involved in a transaction or an arrangement, and the person acts with the consent of an authorised officer.

While SOCA has produced information on obtaining consent, here are a number of key points to remember:

- You only receive consent to the extent to which you asked for it. So it is vital you clearly outline all the remaining steps in the transaction that could be a prohibited act. For example:

  We seek consent to finalise an agreement for sale of property X and to then transfer property X into the name of (purchaser) and following payment of disbursements, pay the proceeds of the sale of the property to (seller).

- The initial notice period is seven working days after the SAR is made, and if consent is refused, the moratorium period is a further 31 calendar days from the date of refusal. If you need consent sooner, you should clearly state the reasons for the urgency in the initial report and perhaps contact SOCA to discuss the situation. SOCA can sometimes give consent in a matter of hours.

- Within the notice and moratorium period you must not do a prohibited act. However this will not prevent you taking other actions on the file, such as writing letters, conducting searches etc.
- SOCA will contact you by telephone to advise that consent has been provided and will then send a follow up letter.

8.3.8 Talking to a SOCA representative

The Financial Intelligence Helpdesk can be contacted on 020 7238 8282. You can contact SOCA on this number for:

- help in submitting a SAR or with the SARs online system
- help on consent issues
- assessing the risk of tipping off so you know whether disclosing information about a particular SAR would prejudice an investigation

8.3.9 Confidentiality of SARs

SOCA is required to treat your SARs confidentially. Where information from a SAR is disclosed for the purposes of law enforcement, care is taken to ensure that the identity of the reporter and their firm is not disclosed to other persons.

If you have specific concerns regarding your safety if you make a SAR, you should raise this with SOCA either in the report or through the helpdesk.

If you fear the confidentiality of a SAR you made has been breached call the SARs confidentiality breach line on 0800 234 6657. In addition, you can e-mail the Law Society at antimoneylaundering@lawsociety.org.uk, so that we can continue to monitor this issue for discussion with SOCA.

8.4 Feedback on SARs

SOCA provides some feedback on the value of SARs they have received, although such feedback will always be anonymised to protect the confidentiality of those who submitted it. Feedback is provided:

- on their website
- in their annual reports
- during SOCA legal sector seminars, details of which are advertised in the Law Society's AML newsletter – Gatekeeper

CHAPTER 9 – ENFORCEMENT

9.1 General comments

The UK AML/CTF regime is one of the most robust in Europe. Breaches of obligations under the regime are backed by disciplinary and criminal penalties.

Law enforcement agencies and regulators are working co-operatively with the regulated sector specifically and solicitors generally to assist compliance and increase understanding of how to effectively mitigate risks. However, be in no doubt of the seriousness of the sanctions for a failure to comply, nor the willingness of supervisory and enforcement bodies to take appropriate action against non-compliance.

9.2 Supervision under the regulations

Regulation 23 provides for several bodies to be supervisory authorities for different parts of the regulated sector.

Where a person in the regulated sector is covered by more than one supervisory authority, either the joint supervisory authorities must negotiate who is to be the sole supervisor of the person, or they must co-operate in the performance of their supervisory duties.

A supervisory authority must:

- monitor effectively the persons it is responsible for
- take necessary measures to ensure their compliance with the requirements of the regulations
- report to SOCA any suspicion that a person it is responsible for has engaged in money laundering or terrorist financing

9.2.1 Solicitors Regulation Authority

The supervisory authority listed in the regulations for solicitors in England and Wales is the Law Society of England and Wales. This responsibility has been delegated in practice to the Solicitors Regulation Authority (SRA).

9.2.2 Other supervisors

Other supervisory authorities which may be of relevance to some solicitors include:

- The Financial Services Authority – www.fsa.org.uk
- The Insolvency Practitioners Association – www.insolvency-practitioners.org.uk
- The Council of Licensed Conveyancers – www.theclc.gov.uk
- The Chartered Institute of Taxation – www.tax.org.uk

Where the SRA reaches agreement with another supervisor about who is to be the supervisory authority for the solicitor, this agreement will be made known to the solicitor in accordance with Regulation 23(3).

In all other cases of supervisory overlap, and where you have questions about AML supervision, contact the SRA.

The SRA will be publishing information for trust and company service providers who are regulated by the SRA and are authorised persons. Details will appear on the SRA's website at www.sra.org.uk, and the Law Society's website at www.lawsociety.org.uk/moneylaundering.

The Joint Money Laundering Steering Group (JMLSG) provides guidance to the financial sector which the FSA considers when assessing compliance with AML/CTF obligations.

9.2.3 Enforcement powers under the regulations

Part 5 of the regulations gives designated authorities a variety of powers for performing their functions under the regulations. They can also impose civil penalties for non-compliance.

The powers are:

- Regulation 37: power to require information from, and attendance of, relevant and connected persons without a warrant
- Regulation 38: power to enter and inspect without a warrant

- Regulation 39: power to obtain a warrant to do things under regulations 37 and 38
- Regulation 40: power to obtain a court order requiring compliance with regulation 37

HM Treasury has stated that designated authorities may use these powers in their role as supervisor, and only on those relevant persons they supervise.

9.3 Disciplinary action

Conduct which fails to comply with AML/CTF obligations may also be a breach of Rule 5 of the Solicitors' Code of Conduct 2007, and result in disciplinary action by the SRA.

For further information on the Solicitors' Code of Conduct go to www.sra.org.uk or contact the professional ethics helpline on 0870 606 2577 (inside the UK), 1100 to 1300 and 1400 to 1600, Monday to Friday.

9.4 Offences and penalties

Not complying with AML/CTF obligations puts you at risk of committing criminal offences. Below is a summary of the offences and the relevant penalties. In addition to the principal offences, you could also be charged with offences of conspiracy, attempt, counselling, aiding, abetting or procuring a principal offence, depending on the circumstances.

9.4.1 POCA

Section	Description	Penalty
327	Conceals, disguises, converts, transfers or removes criminal property	On summary conviction – up to six months' imprisonment or a fine or both
328	Arrangements regarding criminal property	On indictment – up to 14 years' imprisonment or a fine or both
329	Acquires, uses or has possession of criminal property	
330	Failure to disclose knowledge, suspicion or reasonable grounds for suspicion of money laundering – regulated sector	On summary conviction – up to six months' imprisonment or a fine or both
331	Failure to disclose knowledge, suspicion or reasonable grounds for suspicion of money laundering – nominated officer in the regulated sector	On indictment – up to five years' imprisonment or a fine or both
332	Failure to disclose knowledge or suspicion of money laundering – nominated officer in non-regulated sector	

333	Tipping off – before 26 December 2007	On summary conviction – up to six months' imprisonment or a fine or both
333A	Tipping off – regulated sector	On summary conviction – up to three months' imprisonment or a fine not exceeding level 5 or both. On conviction on indictment – up to two years' imprisonment or a fine or both.
342	Prejudicing an investigation	On indictment – up to five years' imprisonment or a fine or both

9.4.2   Terrorism Act

Section	Description	Penalty
15	Fundraising	On summary conviction – up to six months' imprisonment or a fine or both
16	Use and possession	
17	Funding arrangements	On indictment – up to 14 years' imprisonment or a fine or both
18	Money laundering	
19	Failure to disclose	
21A	Failure to disclose – regulated sector	
21	Tipping off – regulated sector	On summary conviction – up to three months' imprisonment or a fine not exceeding level 5 on the standard scale, or both. On conviction on indictment – up to two years' imprisonment, or a fine or both

9.4.3   Regulations

Regulation 45 lists a number of sections, the breach of which is an offence.

Section	Description	Penalty
7 (1)	Applying CDD to new customers	On summary conviction – a fine
7 (2)	Applying CDD to existing customers	On indictment – up to two years' imprisonment or a fine or both
7 (3)	Determining extent of CDD on a risk-sensitive basis and being able to demonstrate this to the SRA	
8 (1)	Conducting ongoing monitoring	

8 (3)	Determining extent of ongoing monitoring on a risk-sensitive basis and being able to demonstrate this to the SRA
9 (2)	Verification prior to the establishment of a business relationship or carrying out of an occasional transaction
11 (1)(a)	Not use a bank account without CDD
11 (1)(b)	Not establish a business relationship or carry out an occasional transaction if no CDD
11 (1)(c)	Terminate existing relationship or occasional transaction if no CDD
14 (1)	Conduct enhanced due diligence
15 (1)	Relates to financial and credit institutions
15 (2)	
16 (1)	
16 (2)	
16 (3)	
16 (4)	
19 (1)	Keep your own records
19 (4)	Keep records others have relied on
19 (5)	Be prepared to provide records others have relied on
19 (6)	Ensure those you rely on are willing to provide records
20 (1)	Establish policies and procedures
21	Train relevant employees
26	Does not relate to solicitors
27 (4)	
33	
Directions under 18	Not to act where Treasury makes a direction

9.5   Joint liability

Regulation 47 provides that offences under the regulations can be committed by a firm as a whole, whether it is a body corporate, partnership or unincorporated association.

However, if it can be shown that the offence was committed with the consent, contrivance or neglect of an officer, partner or member, then both the firm and the individual can be liable.

9.5   Prosecution authorities

The Crown Prosecution Service is a prosecuting authority for offences under POCA, the Terrorism Act and the regulations.

The Revenue and Customs Prosecutions Office is a prosecuting authority for offences under POCA and the regulations.

The FSA is a prosecuting authority under POCA and the regulations as a result of section 402 of the Financial Services and Markets Act 2000.

The Office of Fair Trading, the Local Weights and Measures Authority and the Department of Enterprise, Trade and Investment in Northern Ireland are all prosecuting authorities for breaches of the regulations.

CHAPTER 10 – CIVIL LIABILITY

10.1   General comments

The Proceeds of Crime Act 2002 aims to deprive wrongdoers of the benefits of crime, not compensate the victims. The civil law provides an opportunity for victims to take action against wrongdoers and those who have assisted them, through a claim for constructive trusteeship. Victims often target the professional adviser in civil claims because they are more likely to be able to pay compensation, often by reason of their professional indemnity cover.

If you believe that you may have acted as a constructive trustee, you should seek legal advice.

10.2   Constructive trusteeship

Constructive trusteeship arises as a result of your interference with trust property or involvement in a breach of fiduciary duty. These are traditionally described respectively as knowing receipt and knowing assistance.

Your liability in either case is personal, an equitable liability to account, not proprietary. A constructive trustee has to restore the value of the property they have received or compensate the claimant for the loss resulting from the assistance with a breach of trust or fiduciary duty. See Lord Millett in [2002] 3 WLR 1913,1933.

The state of your knowledge is key to this liability. Records of CDD measures undertaken and disclosures or your notes provide evidence of your knowledge and intentions.

10.3   Knowing receipt

Liability for knowing receipt will exist where a person receives property in circumstances where the property is subject to a trust or fiduciary duty and contrary to that trust applies the property for their use and benefit. Considering each element in turn:

10.3.1   Receipt

- You must have received the property in which the claimant has an equitable proprietary interest.
- The property must be received:

  – in breach of trust
  – in breach of a fiduciary duty, or
  – legitimately, but then misapplied

10.3.2   For your use and benefit

When you receive money, eg as an agent, or, as in the case of a solicitor's client account, as a trustee of a bare trust, then you are not liable for knowing receipt as it is not received for your use or benefit. You may however still be liable for knowing assistance.

Receiving funds that you apply in satisfaction of your fees will however be beneficial receipt and could amount to knowing receipt.

10.3.3   You must be at fault

What constitutes fault here is the subject of some debate. The Court of Appeal in *BCCI* v. *Akinele* [2001] Ch 437 held that the test is whether you acted unconscionably. The test is a subjective one which includes actual knowledge and wilful blindness. The factors the court identified were that:

1.   You need not have acted dishonestly. It is enough to know a fiduciary or trust duty has been breached.
2.   Your knowledge of funds' provenance should be such that it was unconscionable for you to retain any benefit.

It's unclear whether a reckless failure to make enquiries a reasonable person would have made would be sufficient to establish liability. In *Dubai Aluminium Co Ltd* v. *Salaam* [2002] 3 WLR 1913 at 1933 Lord Millett described knowing receipt as dishonest assistance. However, that may well have been specific to the particular facts he was considering.

10.4   Knowing assistance

If you help in a breach of fiduciary or trust duties then you are personally liable for the damage and loss caused. See *Twinsectra* v. *Yardley* [2002] WLR 802.

The requirements to establish liability of this kind are:

10.4.1   Assistance in a breach of trust or fiduciary duty

The breach need not have been fraudulent (see *Royal Brunei Airlines* v. *Tan* [1995] 2 AC 378), and you do not need to know the full details of the trust arrangements you help to breach, nor the obligations incumbent on a trustee/fiduciary.

You assist if you either:

- know that the person you are assisting is not entitled to do the things that they are doing
- have sufficient ground for suspicion of this

10.4.2   You must be at fault

There must be dishonesty, not just knowledge. The test for dishonesty is objective. The Privy Council in *Eurotrust* v. *Barlow Clowes* [2006] 1 All ER 333 stated that the test is whether your conduct is dishonest by the standards of reasonable and honest people, taking into account your specific characteristics and context, ie your intelligence, knowledge at the relevant time, and your experience.

Conscious impropriety is not required; it is enough to have shown wilful blindness by deliberately failing to make the enquiries that a reasonable and honest person would make.

10.5   Making a disclosure to SOCA

10.5.1   Risk of defensive disclosure to SOCA

Where you suspect or know your clients are involving you in circumstances that could amount to one of the principal money laundering offences, you must disclose your suspicions to SOCA, subject to the constraints of LPP, and obtain their permission before allowing the transaction to proceed.

Consent from SOCA only protects you from falling foul of the anti-money laundering regime. It will not defend you from civil liability. In fact, obtaining consent may create the very evidence on which a claimant can rely to found a civil liability.

It is therefore vital that you only disclose to SOCA those situations fulfilling the statutory tests in Part 7 of POCA; knowledge or suspicion of money laundering, or reasonable grounds to suspect money laundering.

10.5.2   While awaiting consent from SOCA

Your position can be difficult. While the client will be expecting you to implement their instructions, you may be unable to do so, or give explanations, as you may risk a tipping off offence.

The client may seek a court order for the return of the funds on the basis that you are breaching their retainer.

Case law provides no direct authority on the point, but a recent ruling on the obligations of banks is helpful in suggesting the courts' likely view of the obligations imposed on solicitors. In *K* v. *Nat West* the Court of Appeal ruled that a bank's contract with the customer was suspended whilst the moratorium period was in place, so the customer had no right to an injunction for return of monies. The court also said that as a matter of discretion, the court would not force the bank to commit a crime.

The Court of Appeal also approved the use of a letter to the court from the bank as evidence of its suspicion. Provision of evidence in these circumstances is permitted under s333(2)(b) of Proceeds of Crime Act as an exception to the tipping off provisions.

10.5.3   Where SOCA consents

In continuing with a transaction you will have to show that either:

- Although you had sufficient suspicion to justify a disclosure to SOCA, your concerns were not such as to render them accountable on a constructive trustee basis. Courts are likely to take into account the fact that you will generally operate in the regulated sector, and assume a degree of sophistication as a result of anti-money laundering training. Solicitors are expected to be able to account for decisions to proceed with transactions.

- Your suspicions were either removed or reduced by subsequent information or investigations.

The Courts have provided limited assistance in this area. *Bank of Scotland* v. *A Limited* [2001] 1 WLR 751 stated that complying with a client's instructions was a commercial risk which a bank had to take. While the court gave some reassurance on the unlikelihood of any finding of dishonesty against an institution that had sought guidance from the court and did not pay funds away, this is of limited assistance because it is for the positive act of paying away funds that protection will be needed.

Such protection is not readily available. In *Amalgamated Metal Trading* v. *City of London Police* [2003] 1 WLR 2711 the court held that while a court could make a declaration on whether particular funds were the proceeds of crime, a full hearing would be required with both the potential victim and the client participating. There would have to be proof on the balance of probabilities that the funds were not the proceeds of crime. In practice this is highly unlikely to be practical.

10.6 Notify your professional indemnity insurers

You must notify your insurers at the earliest opportunity of any circumstances that might give rise to a claim. You should consider notifying your insurers whenever you make a disclosure to SOCA. In particular:

- you may be unable to follow clients' instructions, eg:
  - where consent has not been given by SOCA
  - where you judge you may be exposing yourself to a civil claim, so may face a claim from the client for failure to meet the terms of your retainer

- SOCA has given consent, but where you fear civil liability. Consider whether to not proceed with the transaction.

Any disclosure made to insurers should clearly state any money laundering issues, that a disclosure has been made to SOCA and, if known, SOCA's response.

CHAPTER 11 – MONEY LAUNDERING WARNING SIGNS

11.1 General comments

The Money Laundering Regulations 2007 require you to conduct ongoing monitoring of your business relationships and take steps to be aware of transactions with heightened money laundering or counter-terrorist financing risks.

The Proceeds of Crime Act 2002 requires you to report suspicious transactions.

This chapter highlights a number of warning signs for solicitors generally and for those working in specific sectors, to help you decide whether you have reasons for concern or the basis for a disclosable suspicion.

11.2 General warning signs

Because money launderers are always developing new techniques, no list of examples can be fully comprehensive; however, here are some key factors which may heighten a client's risk profile or give you cause for concern.

11.2.1   Secretive clients

While face-to-face contact with clients is not always necessary, an excessively obstructive or secretive client may be a cause for concern.

11.2.2   Unusual instructions

Instructions that are unusual in themselves, or that are unusual for your firm or your client, may give rise to a cause for concern.

INSTRUCTIONS OUTSIDE YOUR FIRM'S AREA OF EXPERTISE

Taking on work which is outside your firm's normal range of expertise can be risky because money launderers might use such firms to avoid answering too many questions. An inexperienced solicitor might be influenced into taking steps which a more experienced solicitor would not contemplate. Be wary of instructions in niche areas of work in which your firm has no background, but in which the client claims to be an expert.

If your client is based a long way from your offices, consider why you have been instructed. For example, have your services been recommended by another client or is the matter based near your firm? Making these types of enquiries makes good business sense as well as being a sensible anti-money laundering check.

CHANGING INSTRUCTIONS

Instructions or cases that change unexpectedly might be suspicious, especially if there seems to be no logical reason for the changes.

The following situations could give rise to a cause for concern. Consider the Solicitors' Accounts Rules if appropriate.

- a client deposits funds into your client account but then ends the transaction for no apparent reason
- a client tells you that funds are coming from one source and at the last minute the source changes
- a client unexpectedly asks you to send money received into your client account back to its source, to the client or to a third party

UNUSUAL RETAINERS

Be wary of:

- disputes which are settled too easily as this may indicate sham litigation
- loss-making transactions where the loss is avoidable
- dealing with money or property where you suspect that either is being transferred to avoid the attention of a trustee in a bankruptcy case, HMRC, or a law enforcement agency
- settlements paid in cash, or paid directly between parties – for example, if cash is passed directly between sellers and buyers without adequate explanation, it is possible that mortgage fraud or tax evasion is taking place
- complex or unusually large transactions
- unusual patterns of transactions which have no apparent economic purpose

11.2.3   Use of client accounts

Only use client accounts to hold client money for legitimate transactions for clients, or for another proper legal purpose. Putting dirty money through a solicitor's client account can clean it, whether the money is sent back to the client, on to a third party, or invested in some way. Introducing cash into a banking system can become part of the placement stage of money laundering. Therefore, the use of cash may be a warning sign.

Solicitors should not provide a banking service for their clients. However, it can be difficult to draw a distinction between holding client money for a legitimate transaction and acting more like a bank.

For example, when the proceeds of a sale are left with your firm to make payments, these payments may be to mainstream loan companies, but they may also be to more obscure recipients, including private individuals, whose identity is difficult or impossible to check.

ESTABLISH A POLICY ON HANDLING CASH

Large payments made in actual cash may also be a sign of money laundering. It is good practice to establish a policy of not accepting cash payments above a certain limit either at your office or into your bank account.

Clients may attempt to circumvent such a policy by depositing cash directly into your client account at a bank. You may consider advising clients in such circumstances that they might encounter a delay in completion of the final transaction. Avoid disclosing your client account details as far as possible and make it clear that electronic transfer of funds is expected.

If a cash deposit is received, you will need to consider whether you think there is a risk of money laundering taking place and whether it is a circumstance requiring a disclosure to SOCA.

SOURCE OF FUNDS

Accounts staff should monitor whether funds received from clients are from credible sources. For example, it is reasonable for monies to be received from a company if your client is a director of that company and has the authority to use company money for the transaction.

However, if funding is from a source other than your client, you may need to make further enquiries, especially if the client has not told you what they intend to do with the funds before depositing them into your account. If you decide to accept funds from a third party, perhaps because time is short, ask how and why the third party is helping with the funding.

You do not have to make enquiries into every source of funding from other parties. However, you must always be alert to warning signs and in some cases you will need to get more information.

In some circumstances, cleared funds will be essential for transactions and clients may want to provide cash to meet a completion deadline. Assess the risk in these cases and ask questions if necessary.

DISCLOSING CLIENT ACCOUNT DETAILS

Think carefully before you disclose your client account details. They allow money to be deposited into your accounts without your knowledge. If you need to provide your account details, ask the client where the funds will be coming from. Will it be an account in their name, from the UK or abroad? Consider whether you are prepared to accept funds from any source that you are concerned about.

Keep the circulation of client account details to a minimum. Discourage clients from passing the details on to third parties and ask them to use the account details only for previously agreed purposes.

11.2.4   Suspect territory

While there are no longer any countries currently listed on the FATF non co-operative and compliant territories list, this does not mean that all have anti-money laundering standards equivalent to those in the UK. Retainers involving countries which do not have comparative money laundering standards may increase the risk profile of the retainer. The International Bar Association provides a summary of money laundering legislation around the world at: www.anti-moneylaundering.org.

Consider whether extra precautions should be taken when dealing with funds or clients from a particular jurisdiction. This is especially important if the client or funds come from a jurisdiction where the production of drugs, drug trafficking, terrorism or corruption is prevalent.

You can also check whether your client is a proscribed person on the HM Treasury's sanctions lists.

Transparency International provides a corruption perception index which may help when you are considering dealing with clients from other countries.

11.3   Private client work

11.3.1   Administration of estates

The administration of estates is a regulated activity. A deceased person's estate is very unlikely to be actively utilised by criminals as a means for laundering their funds; however, there is still a low risk of money laundering for those working in this area.

SOURCE OF FUNDS

When you are acting either as an executor, or for executors, there is no blanket requirement that you should be satisfied about the history of all of the funds which make up the estate under administration; however you should be aware of the factors which can increase money laundering risks.

Consider the following when administering an estate:

• where estate assets have been earned in a foreign jurisdiction, be aware of the wide definition of criminal conduct in POCA and the provisions relating to overseas criminal conduct
• where estate assets have been earned or are located in a suspect territory, you may need to make further checks about the source of those funds

The wide nature of the offences of 'acquisition, use and possession' in section 329 of POCA may lead to a money laundering offence being committed at an early point in the administration. The section 328 offence may also be relevant.

Be alert from the outset and monitor throughout so that any disclosure can be considered as soon as knowledge or suspicion is formed and problems of delayed consent are avoided. A key benefit of the *Bowman* v. *Fels* judgment is that a solicitor who makes a disclosure is now able to continue work on the matter, so long as they do not transfer funds or take any other irrevocable step.

HOW THE ESTATE MAY INCLUDE CRIMINAL PROPERTY

An extreme example would be where you know or suspect that the deceased person was accused or convicted of acquisitive criminal conduct during their lifetime.

If you know or suspect that the deceased person improperly claimed welfare benefits or had evaded the due payment of tax during their lifetime, criminal property will be included in the estate and so a money laundering disclosure may be required. Information on the financial thresholds for benefits can be obtained from www.dwp. gov.uk or www.hmrc.gov.uk.

While administering an estate, you may discover or suspect that beneficiaries are not intending to pay the correct amount of tax or are avoiding some other financial charge (for example, by failing to disclose gifts received from the deceased less than seven years before death). Although these matters may not actually constitute money laundering (because no criminal conduct has yet occurred so there is no 'criminal property'), you should carefully consider their position in conduct terms with respect to Rule 1.01 of the Solicitors' Code of Conduct.

GRANT OF PROBATE

A UK grant of probate may be required before UK assets can be released, while for overseas assets the relevant local laws will apply. Remain alert to warning signs, for example if the deceased or their business interests are based in a suspect territory.

If the deceased person is from another jurisdiction and a lawyer is dealing with the matter in the home country, it may be helpful to ask that person for information about the deceased to gain some assurances that there are no suspicious circumstances surrounding the estate. The issue of the tax payable on the estate may depend on the jurisdiction concerned.

11.3.2 Trusts

Trust work is a regulated activity.

Trusts can be used as a money laundering vehicle. The key risk period for trusts is when the trust is set up, as if the funds going into the trust are clean, it is only by the trustees using them for criminal purposes that they may form the proceeds of crime.

When setting up a trust, be aware of general money laundering warning signs and consider whether the purpose of the trust could be to launder criminal property. Information about the purpose of the trust, including why any unusual structure or jurisdiction has been used, can help allay concerns. Similarly information about the provider of the funds and those who have control of the funds, as required by the Money Laundering Regulations 2007, will assist.

Whether you act as a trustee yourself, or for trustees, the nature of the work may already require information which will help in assessing money laundering risks, such as the location of assets and the identity of trustees. Again, any involvement of a suspect jurisdiction, especially those with strict bank secrecy and confidentiality rules, or without similar money laundering procedures, may increase the risk profile of the retainer.

If you think a money laundering offence has, or may have, been committed that relates to money or property which already forms part of the trust property, or is intended to do so, consider whether your instructions involve you in a section 328 arrangement offence. If they do, consider the options for making a disclosure.

11.3.3   Charities

In common with trusts, while the majority of charities are used for legitimate reasons, they can be used as money laundering/terrorist financing vehicles.

If you are acting for a charity, consider its purpose and the organisations it is aligned with. If you are receiving money on the charity's behalf from an individual or a company donor, or a bequest from an estate, be alert to unusual circumstances including large sums of money.

There is growing concern about the use of charities for terrorist funding. The Bank of England maintains a list of individuals and organisations for whom you may not provide regulated services.

11.3.4   Powers of attorney/deputyship

Whether acting as, or on behalf of, an attorney or deputy, you should remain alert to money laundering risks.

If you are acting as an attorney you may learn financial information about the donor relating, for example, to non-payment of tax or wrongful receipt of benefits. You will need to consider whether to make a disclosure to SOCA.

Where the public guardian has an interest – because of a deputyship or registered enduring power of attorney – consider whether the Office of the Public Guardian (OPG) needs to be informed. Informing the OPG is unlikely to be tipping off because it is unlikely to prejudice an investigation.

If you discover or suspect that a donee has already completed an improper financial transaction that may amount to a money laundering suspicion, a disclosure to SOCA may be required (depending on whether legal professional privilege applies). However, it may be difficult to decide whether you have a suspicion if the background to the information is a family dispute. You can get legal advice on this through the Law Society's AML directory.

11.4   Property work

11.4.1   Ownership issues

Properties owned by nominee companies or multiple owners may be used as money laundering vehicles to disguise the true owner and/or confuse the audit trail.

Be alert to sudden or unexplained changes in ownership. One form of laundering, known as flipping, involves a property purchase, often using someone else's identity. The property is then quickly sold for a much higher price to the same buyer using another identity. The proceeds of crime are mixed with mortgage funds for the purchase. This process may be repeated several times.

Another potential cause for concern is where a third party is providing the funding for a purchase, but the property is being registered in someone else's name. There may be legitimate reasons for this, such as a family arrangement, but you should be alert to the possibility of being misled about the true ownership of the property. You may wish to undertake further CDD measures on the person providing the funding.

11.4.2   Methods of funding

Many properties are bought with a combination of deposit, mortgage and/or equity from a current property. Usually, as a solicitor, you will have information about how your client intends to fund the transaction, and will expect to be updated if those details change, for example if a mortgage falls through and new funding is obtained.

This is a sensible risk assessment measure which should help you decide whether you need to know more about the transaction.

PRIVATE FUNDING

Usually purchase funds comprise some private funding, with the majority of the purchase price being provided via a mortgage. Transactions that do not involve a mortgage have a higher risk of being fraudulent.

Look out for:

- large payments from private funds, especially if your client has a low income
- payments from a number of individuals or sources

If you are concerned:

- ask your client to explain the source of the funds. Assess whether you think their explanation is valid – for example, the money may have been received from an inheritance or from the sale of another property
- consider whether the beneficial owners were involved in the transaction

Remember that payments made through the mainstream banking system are not guaranteed to be clean.

FUNDS FROM A THIRD PARTY

Third parties often assist with purchases, for example relatives often assist first time home buyers. You may be asked to receive funds directly from those third parties. You will need to decide whether, and to what extent, you need to undertake any CDD measures in relation to the third parties.

Consider whether there are any obvious warning signs and what you know about:

- your client
- the third party
- their relationship
- the proportion of the funding being provided by the third party

Consider your obligations to the lender in these circumstances – you are normally required to advise lenders if the buyers are not funding the balance of the price from their own resources.

DIRECT PAYMENTS BETWEEN BUYERS AND SELLERS

You may discover or suspect that cash has changed hands directly, between a seller and a buyer, for example at a rural auction.

If you are asked to bank the cash in your client account, this presents a problem because the source of the cash is not your client and so checks on the source of the funding can be more difficult. The auction house may be able to assist because of checks they must make under the regulations. However, you may decide to decline the request.

If you suspect that there has been a direct payment between a seller and a buyer, consider whether there are any reasons for concern (attempted avoidance of tax for example) or whether the documentation will include the true purchase price.

A client may tell you that money is changing hands directly when this is not the case. This could be to encourage a mortgage lender to lend more than they would otherwise, because they believe that private funds will contribute to the purchase. In this situation, consider your duties to the lender.

11.4.3   Valuing

An unusual sale price can be an indicator of money laundering. While you are not required to get independent valuations, if you become aware of a significant discrepancy between the sale price and what you would reasonably expect such a property to sell for, consider asking more questions.

Properties may also be sold below the market value to an associate, with a view to obscuring the title to the property while the original owner still maintains beneficial ownership.

11.4.4   Lender issues

You may discover or suspect that a client is attempting to mislead a lender client to improperly inflate a mortgage advance – for example, by misrepresenting the borrower's income or because the seller and buyer are conspiring to overstate the sale price. Transactions which are not at arms length may warrant particularly close consideration.

However, until the improperly obtained mortgage advance is received there is not any criminal property for the purposes of disclosure obligations under POCA.

If you suspect that your client is making a misrepresentation to a mortgagee you must either dissuade them from doing so or consider the ethical implications of continuing with the retainer. Even if you no longer act for the client you may still be under a duty to advise the mortgage company.

If you discover or suspect that a mortgage advance has already been improperly obtained, consider advising the mortgage lender.

If you are acting in a re-mortgage and discover or suspect that a previous mortgage has been improperly obtained, you may need to advise the lender, especially if the re-mortgage is with the same lender. You may also need to consider making a disclosure to SOCA as there is criminal property (the improperly obtained mortgage advance).

LEGAL PROFESSIONAL PRIVILEGE

If your client has made a deliberate misrepresentation on their mortgage application it is likely that the crime/fraud exemption to legal professional privilege will apply, meaning that no waiver to confidentiality will be needed before a disclosure is made.

However, you will need to consider matters on a case-by-case basis and if necessary, seek legal advice, possibly by contacting a solicitor in the AML directory.

TIPPING OFF OFFENCES

You may be concerned that speaking to the lender client conflicts with tipping off offences. A key element of these offences is the likelihood of prejudicing an investigation. This may be a small risk when making disclosures to reputable lenders, and if the lender is your client the legal professional privilege exemption may apply to such a disclosure.

11.4.5   Tax issues

Tax evasion of any type, whether committed by your client or the other party to a transaction, can result in you committing a section 328 arrangements offence.

Abuse of the Stamp Duty Tax procedure may also have money laundering implications, for example if the purchase price is recorded incorrectly.

If a client gives you instructions which offend the Stamp Duty Land Tax procedure, you must consider your position under rule 1.10 of the Solicitors' Code of Conduct. If you discover the evasion after it has occurred, you are obliged to make a disclosure, subject to any legal professional privilege.

11.5 Company and commercial work

The nature of company structures can make them attractive to money launderers because it is possible to obscure true ownership and protect assets for relatively little expense. For this reason solicitors working with companies and in commercial transactions should remain alert throughout their retainers, with existing as well as new clients.

11.5.1 Forming a new company

If you work on the formation of a new company, be alert to any signs that it might be misused for money laundering or terrorist financing.

If the company is being formed in a foreign jurisdiction, it may be helpful to clarify why this is the case. In countries where there are few anti-money laundering requirements, you should make particularly careful checks.

If you are in doubt, it may be better to refuse the retainer.

11.5.2 Holding of funds

If you wish to hold funds as stakeholder or escrow agent in commercial transactions, consider the checks you wish to make about the funds you intend to hold, before the funds are received and whether it would be appropriate to conduct CDD measures on all those on whose behalf you are holding funds.

Consider any proposal that you collect funds from a number of individuals, whether for investment purposes or otherwise. This could lead to wide circulation of your client account details and payments being received from unknown sources.

11.5.3 Private equity

Law firms could be involved in any of the following circumstances:

- the start-up phase of a private equity business where individuals or companies seek to establish a private equity firm (and in certain cases, become authorised to conduct investment business)
- the formation of a private equity fund
- ongoing legal issues relating to a private equity fund
- execution of transactions on behalf of a member of a private equity firm's group of companies, (a private equity sponsor), that will normally involve a vehicle company acting on its behalf, (newco)

WHO IS THE CLIENT?

START-UP PHASE

In this phase, as you will be approached by individuals or a company seeking to become established (and in certain cases authorised) your client would be the individuals or company and you would therefore conduct CDD accordingly.

FORMATION OF PRIVATE EQUITY FUNDS

Your client is likely to be the private equity sponsor or it may be an independent sponsor.

You will rarely, if ever, be advising the fund itself and, unless you are instructed directly by an investor, you will not be considered to be advising the investors in the fund.

You should therefore identify who your client is and apply the CDD measures according to their client type as set out in 4.6.

Where the client is a newco, you will need to obtain documentation evidencing the establishment of the newco and consider the issue of beneficial ownership.

Generally private equity work will be considered at low risk of money laundering or terrorist financing for the following reasons:

- private equity firms in the UK are also covered by the Regulations as a financial institution and they are regulated by the FSA
- investors in private equity funds are generally large institutions, some of which will also be regulated for money laundering purposes. They will have long established relationships with the private equity firm, usually resulting in a well-known investor base
- where the private equity sponsor or fund manager is regulated in the UK, EEA or a comparable jurisdictions, it is likely to have followed CDD processes prior to investors being accepted
- the investment is generally illiquid and the return of capital is unpredictable
- the terms of the fund documentation generally strictly control the transfer of interests and the return of funds to investors

Factors which may alter this risk assessment include:

- where the private equity sponsor or an investor is located in a jurisdiction which is not regulated for money laundering to a standard which is equivalent to the third directive
- where the investor is either an individual or an investment vehicle itself (a private equity fund of funds)
- where the private equity sponsor is seeking to raise funds for the first time

JMLSG has prepared detailed advice on CDD measures for private equity businesses in Part II of its guidance, which you may wish to consider.

The following points should be considered when undertaking CDD measures in relation to private equity work:

- where your client qualifies for simplified due diligence you do not have to identify beneficial owners unless there is a suspicion of money laundering
- where simplified due diligence does not apply you need to consider the business structure of the client and conduct CDD on the client in accordance with that structure
- where there is an appropriately regulated professional closely involved with the client who has detailed knowledge of the beneficial owners of the client, you may consider relying on them in accordance with Regulation 17
- whether an unregulated private entity firm, fund manager or other person involved with the transaction is an appropriate source of information regarding beneficial ownership of the client should be determined on a risk-sensitive basis, issues to consider include:

  - the profile of the private equity sponsor, fund manager, (if different), or such other person

– their track record within the private equity sector
– their willingness to explain identification procedures and provide confirmation that all beneficial owners have been identified

- where you are using another person as an information source for beneficial owners, where there are no beneficial owners within the meaning of Regulation 6, the source may simply confirm their actual knowledge of this, or if beneficial owners do exist, the source should provide you with the identifying details of the beneficial owner or an assurance that the beneficial owners have been identified and that the details will be provided on request.
- where there is a tiered structure, such as a feeder fund or fund of funds structure, you must identify the beneficial owner but you may decide having made enquiries that no such beneficial owners exist even though you have got to the top of the structure.
- where it is envisaged that you will be acting for a newco which is to be utilised at a future point in a flotation or acquisition, it is only once they are established and signed up as a party to the transaction that you need to commence CDD measures on the newco. However once you start acting for a newco, you will need to consider identification for it, and its beneficial owner. You may therefore wish to commence the process of identifying any beneficial owner in advance.

11.5.4 Collective investment schemes

Undertaking work in relation to retainers involving collective investment schemes may pose similar problems when undertaking CDD as for private equity work.

The risk factors with respect to a collective investment scheme will be decreased where:

- the scheme is only open to tax exempt institutional investors
- investment managers are regulated individuals or entities
- a prospectus is issued to invite investment

Factors which will increase the risks include where:

- the scheme is open to non-tax exempt investors
- the scheme or its investors are located in a jurisdiction which is not regulated for money laundering to a standard which is equivalent to the third directive
- neither the scheme nor the investment managers are regulated and do not conduct CDD on the investors

JMLSG have also issued guidance which touches on the area of collective investment schemes, which you may wish to have regard to.

In addition to the points to consider outlined for private equity work, where a collective investment scheme has issued a prospectus it is advisable to review a copy of the prospectus to understand the intended structure of the investment scheme.

CHAPTER 12 – OFFENCES AND REPORTING PRACTICAL EXAMPLES

12.1 General comments

Chapters 5 and 6 of this practice note worked through the theory of the law relating to when a money laundering offence has occurred, the requirements for making a disclosure and when you are unable to make a disclosure because of LPP or are exempted from making a disclosure due to privileged circumstances.

This chapter contains:

- flowcharts to give an overview of how all the obligations link together
- examples to help put the theory into context

This chapter does not replace application of the legislation to your situation; nor should it be viewed without reference to the detailed discussion of the law in the rest of the practice note.

Further examples may be added to future editions of this practice note.

Do I have a suspicion that a principal money laundering offence is occurring?
[Flowchart available to download at **www.lawsociety.org.uk**]

12.2 Principal offences

If you suspect that property involved in a retainer is criminal property, offences under section 327 and section 329 are relatively straightforward to assess. However, an arrangement offence under section 328 may be more complicated, particularly with transactional matters.

12.2.1 Do I have an arrangement?

Under section 328, an arrangement must be created at a particular point in time. If you have formed a suspicion, first consider whether an arrangement already exists. For example, a client may instruct you to act for them in the purchase of a property, including the drafting of the contract and transfer documents. When you are instructed there will already an arrangement between the vendor and the purchaser, but not yet an arrangement for the purposes of section 328.

If an arrangement within section 328 already exists, any steps you take to further that arrangement will probably mean you are concerned in it. In this case, you would immediately need to consider making a disclosure.

12.2.2 No pre-existing arrangement

If there is no pre-existing arrangement, the transactional work you carry out may bring an arrangement under section 328 into existence. You may become concerned in the arrangement by, for example, executing or implementing it, which may lead you to commit an offence under section 328, and possibly under section 327 or 329.

Consider whether you need to make an authorised disclosure to:

- obtain consent to proceed with the transaction
- provide yourself with a defence to the principal money laundering offences

If you are acting within the regulated sector, consider whether you risk committing a failure to disclose offence, if you do not make a disclosure to SOCA.

The following two flowcharts show the issues to consider when deciding whether to make a disclosure to SOCA.

I suspect continuation of a retainer will lead to me being a party to a principal offence. Do I have a defence? [Flowchart available to download at **www.lawsociety.org.uk**]

I suspect someone else of a principal offence, or should reasonably suspect them, and am concerned I may commit a failure to disclose offence. Do I have a defence? [Flowchart available to download at **www.lawsociety.org.uk**]

12.3 Should I make a disclosure?

12.3.1 Property transactions

Considering further the earlier example of a suspect contract for the purchase of a property, the following issues will be relevant when considering the disclosure requirements under POCA.

- If the information on which your suspicion is based is covered by LPP and the crime/fraud exception does not apply, you cannot make a disclosure under POCA.
- If the information was received in privileged circumstances and the crime/fraud exception does not apply, you are exempt from the relevant provisions of POCA, which include making a disclosure to SOCA.
- If neither of these situations applies, the communication will still be confidential. However, the material is disclosable under POCA and an authorised disclosure should be made.

You have the option of withdrawing from the transaction rather than making an authorised disclosure, but you may still need to make a disclosure to avoid committing a failure to disclose offence.

WHAT IF I CANNOT DISCLOSE?

If you decide that either you cannot make a disclosure due to LPP or you are exempt from making a disclosure due to privileged circumstances, you have two options:

- you can approach the client for a waiver of privilege to make a disclosure and obtain consent to carry out the prohibited act, or
- you should consider your ethical obligations and whether you need to withdraw from the transaction

WAIVER OF PRIVILEGE

When approaching your client for a waiver of privilege, you may feel less concerned about tipping off issues if your client is not the suspect party but is engaged in a transaction which involves criminal property. However, if you suspect that your client is implicated in the underlying criminal conduct, consider the tipping off offence and whether it is appropriate to discuss these matters openly with your client.

If you raise the matter with your client and they agree to waive privilege, you can make a disclosure to SOCA on your own or jointly with your client and seek consent if required.

If you are acting for more than one client on a matter, all clients must agree to waive privilege before you can make a disclosure to SOCA.

REFUSAL TO WAIVE PRIVILEGE

Your client, whether sole or one of a number for whom you act, may refuse to waive privilege, either because he does not agree with your suspicions or because he does not wish a disclosure to be made. Unless your client provides further information which removes your suspicions, you must decide whether you are being used in a criminal offence, in which case neither LPP nor privileged circumstances apply.

If your client refuses to waive privilege but accepts that in proceeding with the transaction he may be committing an offence, you might conclude that you are being used in a criminal offence in which case neither exemption applies. In such circumstances it is not appropriate to tell the client that you are making the disclosure, as the risks of tipping off are increased.

If you are unable to make a disclosure, consider the ethical and civil risks of continuing in the retainer and consider withdrawing.

CONSENT AND PROGRESSING THE RETAINER

If you make a disclosure and consent is needed, consider whether you can continue working on the retainer before you receive that consent.

This will depend on whether an arrangement already exists or whether the further work will bring the arrangement into existence. Provided there is no pre-existing arrangement you should be free to continue your preparatory activities. However, the arrangement/prohibited act should not be finalised without appropriate consent.

12.3.2   Company transactions

CRIMINAL PROPERTY IN A COMPANY

The extent of the regulatory and legal obligations affecting companies and businesses means that there is an increased possibility that breaches will have been committed by your client that constitute criminal conduct and give rise to criminal property under POCA.

For example, the Companies Act 1985 contains many offences which will give rise to criminal property as defined by POCA. There does not need to be a criminal conviction, nor even a prosecution underway. If criminal conduct has (or is suspected to have) taken place, and a benefit has been achieved, the result is actual or notional criminal property.

For a number of offences, the only benefit to your client (for the purposes of POCA) is saved costs. For example, it is criminal conduct to fail to notify the Information Commissioner that a company will be processing 'personal data'. The saved notification fee should be treated as criminal property for the purposes of POCA.

It may be difficult to establish whether property or funds which are the subject of the transactions are the 'saved costs' in whole or in part and are therefore tainted. If you are dealing with the whole of a company's business or assets, no distinction is necessary. In other cases, it would be wrong to assume that because some assets are tainted, they all are, or that you are dealing with the tainted ones.

In most cases, unless there is some basis for suspecting that the assets in question result from saved costs, no disclosure/consent may be required in respect of the principal offence. However a disclosure may still be required in respect of the failure to disclose offences.

MERGERS AND ACQUISITIONS

In typical corporate merger/acquisition/sale/take-over transactions, there are a number of issues to consider.

Solicitors acting in company transactions will be acting in the regulated sector and so will have dual disclosure obligations, under the failure to disclose offence and in respect of the principal offences.

Different tests have to be applied to determine whether a disclosure can be made. When you are considering whether you are obliged to make a disclosure to avoid committing a failure to disclose offence, either LPP or privileged circumstances may apply.

When you are considering whether you must make a disclosure as a defence to the principal offences, only LPP is relevant.

For example, when you are acting for a vendor, you may receive information from the client about the target company which is protected under LPP and exempt from disclosure due to privileged circumstances. However, you may receive information from other representatives of the client (such as other professional advisers) which may only be exempt due to privileged circumstances. If information received is initially privileged, you need to consider whether the privilege is lost in the course of the transaction.

The information may be put into a data room and the purchaser, as part of the due diligence inquiries, may raise questions of the vendor's solicitors which, in effect, result in the information being received again by the vendor's solicitor.

That second receipt from the purchaser, or their solicitor, would not be protected by privileged circumstances. It will lose its exemption from disclosure unless the information was also subject to LPP which had not been waived when it was placed in the data room (eg a letter of advice from a solicitor to the vendor).

Consider whether privilege is removed by the crime/fraud exception. You may suspect, or have reasonable grounds to suspect someone of money laundering (which may simply mean they possess the benefits of a criminal offence contrary to section 329). Where the information on which the suspicion is based could be protected by LPP or exempted due to privileged circumstances, consider whether the crime/fraud exception applies.

This may depend on:

- the nature of the transaction
- the amount of the criminal property
- the strength of the evidence

These factors are considered in more detail below with respect to specific types of company sales.

ASSET SALES

In the case of an asset sale, all or some of the assets of the business may be transferred. If any asset transferred to a new owner is criminal property, a money laundering offence may be committed:

- The vendor may commit a section 327 offence by transferring the criminal property.
- Both the vendor and purchaser may be entering into an arrangement contrary to section 328.
- The purchaser may be committing a section 329 offence by possessing the criminal property.

ADEQUATE CONSIDERATION DEFENCE

When looking at the purchaser's position, you will need to consider whether there would be an adequate consideration defence to a section 329 possession offence. This is where the purchase price is reasonable and constitutes adequate consideration for any criminal property obtained. In such a case, should the purchaser effectively be deprived of the benefit of that defence by section 328.

It is a question of interpretation whether sections 328 and 329 should be read together such that, if the defence under section 329 applies, an offence will also not be committed by the vendor under section 328. You should consider this point and take legal advice as appropriate.

DISCLOSURE OBLIGATIONS AFTER COMPLETION

As well as making disclosures relating to the transaction, vendors and purchasers will need to consider disclosure obligations in respect of the position after completion.

The purchaser will, after the transaction, have possession of the assets and may be at risk of committing a section 329 offence (subject to the adequate consideration defence outlined above).

The vendor will have the sale consideration in their possession. If the amount of the criminal property is material, the sale consideration may indirectly represent the underlying criminal property and the vendor may commit an offence under section 329.

Whether the criminal property is material or not will depend on its impact on the sale price. For example, the sale price of a group of assets may be £20m. If the tainted assets represent 10 per cent of the total, and the price for the clean assets alone would be £18m, it is clear that the price being paid is affected by, and represents in part, the criminal property.

If a client commits one of the principal money laundering offences, whether you are acting for the vendor or purchaser, you will be involved in a prohibited act. You will need to make a disclosure along with your clients and obtain appropriate consent.

When considering whether to advise your client about their disclosure obligations, remember the tipping off offences.

AM I PREVENTED FROM REPORTING DUE TO LPP?

Where you are acting for either the purchaser or vendor and conclude that you may have to make a disclosure and seek consent, first consider whether LPP applies. As explained above, this depends on how you received the information on which your suspicion is based.

Generally, when acting for the purchaser, if the information comes from the data room, LPP will not apply. When acting for the vendor, LPP may apply if the information has come from the client for the purpose of obtaining legal advice.

THE CRIME/FRAUD EXCEPTION

Where LPP applies, you will also need to consider whether the crime/fraud exception applies. The test is whether there is prima facie evidence that you are being used for criminal purposes.

Whether the crime/fraud exception applies will also depend on the purpose of the transaction and the amount of criminal property involved. For example, if a company wished to sell assets worth £100m, which included £25 of criminal assets, it would be deemed that the intention was not to use solicitors for criminal purposes but to undertake a legitimate transaction. However, if the amount of criminal property was £75m, the prima facie evidence would be that the company did intend to sell criminal property and the exception would apply to override LPP.

Real cases will not all be so clear-cut. Consider the parties' intentions. If you advise your client of money laundering risks in proceeding with a transaction and the client decides, despite the risks, to continue without making a disclosure, you may have grounds to conclude that there was prima facie evidence of an intention to use your services for criminal purposes and therefore that privilege may be overridden.

Remember that for the purposes of the crime/fraud exception, it is not just the client's intention that is relevant.

Where LPP applies and is not overridden by the crime/fraud exception, it is nonetheless possible for your client to waive the privilege in order for a disclosure to be made.

SHARE SALES

A sale of a company by way of shares gives rise to different considerations to asset sales. Unless shares have been bought using the proceeds of crime they are unlikely to represent criminal property, so their transfer will not usually constitute a section 327 offence (for the vendor), or a section 329 offence (for the purchaser).

However the sale of shares could constitute a section 328 offence, depending on the circumstances, particularly if the criminal property represents a large percentage of the value of the target company. Consent may be needed if:

- the benefit to the target company from the criminal conduct is such that its share price has increased
- as part of the transaction directors will be appointed to the board of the target company and they will use or possess criminal property
- the purpose of the transaction is to launder criminal property. That is, it is not a genuine commercial transaction.

IS THE SHARE VALUE AFFECTED BY CRIMINAL PROPERTY?

If a company has been used to commit criminal offences, some or all of its assets may represent criminal property. The value of the shares may have increased as a result of that criminal activity. When the shares are then sold, by converting a paper profit into cash, the vendor and the purchaser have both been involved in a prohibited arrangement.

For example, if 10 per cent of the profits of a company are earned from criminal activity, it is likely that the share price would be lower if only the legitimate profits were taken into account.

However, if the value of the criminal property is not sufficient to affect the purchase/sale price, the transaction is unlikely to be considered a prohibited arrangement since the vendor does not benefit from the company's criminal conduct. For example, a company is being purchased for £100m and within it is £25 of saved costs. If the costs had been paid by the company, it is unlikely that the price would be £99,999,975. The business is still likely to be valued at £100m.

WHERE CRIMINAL PROPERTY IS IMMATERIAL

Even if the value of criminal property is very small and immaterial to the purchase price, purchasers still need to consider their position after the acquisition. While shareholders do not possess a company's assets, the target company and directors may subsequently transfer, use or possess the assets for the purposes of the principal money laundering offences in sections 327 and 329.

If as part of the transaction, the purchaser proposes appointing new directors to the board of the target company, those directors may need to make a disclosure and seek consent so that they may transfer use or possess and use the criminal property.

In this case, you, and the vendors and the existing and new directors, may still need to make a disclosure (subject to LPP issues), and seek consent, because they will be involved in an arrangement which involves the acquisition, use or control of criminal property by the new directors contrary to section 328.

In summary, the position may be as follows where the amount of the criminal property is immaterial:

- The target company will possess the proceeds of criminal conduct and may need to make a disclosure. If you discover this in privileged circumstances or it is protected by LPP, you cannot make a disclosure unless the fraud/crime exception applies.
- Those individuals or entities which, as a result of the transaction, will be in a position after completion to possess and use criminal property will need to make a disclosure and seek consent before completion.
- The solicitors acting on the transaction and the vendor may also need to make a disclosure if they are involved in an arrangement which facilitates the acquisition or use of criminal property.
- Whenever a disclosure must be made, you must first consider whether privilege applies and, if applicable, whether the fraud/crime exception applies.

SHAREHOLDERS

Generally in a purchase or sale transaction, you will act for the company, not for its shareholders. However it is possible for shareholders to become involved in an arrangement prohibited by section 328. This is most likely to happen when the transaction requires a Class I or Class II circular to shareholders under the listing rules.

Firstly, consider whether the shareholders are, or may become, aware – perhaps through the risk warnings in the circular – of the risk of criminal conduct. Unless they are so aware, they are unlikely to have the necessary suspicion to be at risk of committing a money laundering offence.

Secondly, where shareholders are aware of the criminal conduct, consider whether the amount of criminal property is material to the transaction. That is, it would have an impact on the price or terms. If it is material, by voting in favour of it the shareholders will become concerned in a prohibited arrangement and will be required to make a disclosure and seek consent.

Also consider, in the context of an initial public offering, what risk warnings to include in any prospectus. You may need to give shareholders notice of their disclosure obligations via such a risk warning.

It is good practice to discuss the issue with SOCA to ensure that there are no tipping off concerns if details of the risks are set out in the public circular.

When each shareholder requires consent from SOCA, their express authority to make the disclosure will be required. It may be simplest to ask the shareholders to authorise the board of the vendor to make a disclosure and seek consent on their behalf at the same time as asking them to give conditional approval for the transaction.

OVERSEAS CONDUCT

Where your suspicion of criminal conduct relates in whole or in part to overseas conduct, be aware of the wide definition of criminal conduct.

For example, you might discover or suspect that a company or its foreign subsidiary has improperly manipulated its accounting procedures so that tax is paid in a country with lower tax limits. Or you might form a concern about corrupt payments to overseas commercial agents which might be illegal in the UK .

Even where the conduct is lawful overseas, in serious cases it will still be disclosable if the money laundering is taking place in the UK and the underlying conduct would be criminal if it had occurred in the UK.

341

In some cases the only money laundering activity in the UK may be your involvement in the transaction as a UK solicitor.

AMENDMENTS TO PRACTICE NOTE – FEBRUARY 2008

Introduction

This is a summary of changes made to the AML/CTF practice note in the 22 February 2008 version. It has been updated with advice on recent changes to tipping off offences. The government has substantially changed the tipping off offences in POCA 2002, and introduced new tipping offences and consent defences into the Terrorism Act 2000.

The summary of changes highlights the main changes to assist firms in adapting their policies and procedures. It is not an exhaustive list of amendments nor a detailed explanatory guide to the reasons behind the various amendments.

Chapter 1:

1.4.3

Changes to scope and application sections to reflect changes to POCA due to the POCA Amendment Regulations 2007.

1.4.4

Changes to the scope and application of the Terrorism Act 2000 due to the TACT Amendment Regulations 2007.

1.4.5

Changes to clarify that solicitors should contact the SRA in case of any questions concerning supervision.

Chapter 5:

5.8

There are substantial changes to explain the new tipping off offences that have been introduced through the TACT and POCA Amendment Regulations 2007.

5.8.1

Changes include a full description of the offences and a new section 5.8.1.2 dealing with the offence of prejudicing an investigation (s342(1)). This offence applies to those outside the regulated sector.

5.8.2

Changes to the section on making enquiries. It reflects the position under the two new tipping off offences.

5.8.3.1 – 5.8.3.4

These are new sections to reflect the new defences introduced under the TACT and POCA Amendment Regulations 2007.

Chapter 6

6.5

Changes to include the new exemption of dissuading a client from engaging in criminal activity.

Chapter 7

7.2

Changes to include information about the tipping off offences relating to the TACT and POCA Amendment Regulations 2007.

7.4

Changes to include information on the consent defences.

7.7

A new section explaining the tipping off offences.

7.8

A new section explaining the defences to tipping off.

7.10

A new section about making enquiries of clients.

Chapter 9

9.2.2

Changes to explain that cases of supervisory overlap should be addressed to the SRA.
   Deleted sentence stating that when the standards differ should comply with the higher standard.

9.2.3

Deletion of information on visits to firms by officers of designated authorities.

9.4.1

Changes to the penalties for tipping off resulting from the TACT and POCA Amendment Regulations 2007.

The Law Society's Anti-terrorism Practice Note (19 July 2007)

THE CONFLICTING DUTIES OF MAINTAINING CONFIDENTIALITY AND REPORTING TERRORISM

INTRODUCTION

The Law Society recognises the tension that can exist when the duty of solicitors to advance the interests of their clients may conflict with the interests of the public as a whole. There is a potential for this tension to emerge where solicitors are representing people charged with, or suspected of, serious crime, and in particular, in relation to suspected terrorists.

The right of persons suspected of a criminal offence to communicate in confidence with their legal adviser is a fundamental aspect of their right to have a fair trial. The importance of legal professional privilege has been described thus:

'... there is a clear policy justification for singling out communications between lawyers and their clients from other professional communications. The privilege belongs to the client, but it attaches both to what the client tells his lawyer and to what the lawyer advises his client to do. It is in the interests of the whole community that lawyers give their clients sound advice, accurate as to the law and sensible as to their conduct. The client may not always act upon that advice (which will sometimes place the lawyer in professional difficulty, but that is a separate matter) but there is always a chance that he will. And there is little or no chance of the client taking the right or sensible course if the lawyer's advice is inaccurate or unsound because the lawyer has been given an incomplete or inaccurate picture of the client's position.'[1]

However, The Law Society also recognises that everyone has a public duty, reinforced by the notification offence provisions under consideration in this Practice Note, to co-operate with the authorities in preventing future acts which could result in serious harm to others. Solicitors should never knowingly assist others to commit, or cover up, future crimes.

DISCLAIMER

This Practice Note is not intended to constitute legal advice. Practitioners are strongly recommended to consult specialist lawyers and take full advice on the issues raised in this Practice Note as applicable to themselves and their practices.

---

1 Per Baroness Hale in *Three Rivers District Council* v. *Bank of England (No 6)* [2004] 3 WLR 1274 at paragraph 61, [2005] 1 AC 610

PURPOSE OF THE PRACTICE NOTE

This Practice Note explains the nature of the solicitor's duty of confidentiality to a client, and how the anti-terrorism 'failure to disclose' offence provisions affect this duty.

Put in stark terms, does a solicitor risk imprisonment for failure to disclose information about terrorism that is gained in the course of their professional duties?

FAILURE TO DISCLOSE INFORMATION ABOUT TERRORISM – THE OFFENCES

There are three provisions of the Terrorism Act 2000 ('TA 2000'), which penalise, with the threat of imprisonment, persons who fail to disclose varying degrees of knowledge, belief or suspicion of the commission by others of terrorist offences.

'Disclosure of information: duty' – s 19 TA 2000

Under this section it is an offence for a person not to 'disclose to a constable as soon as reasonably practicable' his or her belief or suspicion, and the information on which it is based, that another person has committed an offence under sections 15 to 18 of the TA 2000,[2] when that belief or suspicion is based on information coming to him or her in the course of a trade, profession, business or employment.

'Failure to disclose: regulated sector' – s 21A TA 2000[3]

If a person knows or suspects, or has reasonable grounds for knowing or suspecting, that another person has committed an offence under sections 15 to 18 of the TA 2000, and the information, or other matter upon which that knowledge, suspicion, reasonable belief is based, came to him or her during the course of business in the regulated sector, the person commits an offence if he or she does not disclose the information or other matter to a constable (or nominated officer) as soon as practicable after it comes to him or her.

'Information about acts of terrorism' – s 38B TA 2000

If a person has information which he or she 'knows or believes might be of material assistance in (a) preventing the commission by another person of an act of terrorism or, (b) in securing the apprehension, prosecution or conviction of another person, in the UK, for an offence involving the commission, preparation or instigation of an act of terrorism,' he or she commits an offence if he does not disclose the information to police as soon as reasonably practicable.

---

2 Offences of fund raising (s 15), use and possession of terrorist property (s 16), funding arrangements (s 17) and money laundering (s 18).

3 For full money laundering guidance on these provisions, reference should be made to the money laundering guidance published by the Money Laundering Task Force of the Law Society at www.lawsociety.org.uk.

THE SOLICITOR'S DUTY OF CLIENT CONFIDENTIALITY

A solicitor is under a professional and legal obligation to keep the affairs of clients confidential and to ensure that all members of his or her staff do likewise.[4] This duty of confidence is fundamental to the fiduciary relationship that exists between solicitor and client. It extends to all matters divulged to a solicitor by a client, or on his or her behalf, from whatever source.

OVERRIDING CONFIDENTIALITY

In certain circumstances confidentiality can be overridden. For solicitors the most relevant instances will arise when:

- A court order, or a statutory obligation, requires them to disclose by compulsion of law, or
- When an exception to the duty of confidentiality arises from the public interest.[5]

Compulsion of law

A court has the power to compel the disclosure of confidential information held by a solicitor. The most common examples of this are the statutory powers exercised by judges to compel production of confidential ('special procedure') material under Schedule 1 of the Police and Criminal Evidence Act 1984 (PACE), and in certain circumstances, the issuing of witness summonses under the Criminal Procedure (Attendance of Witnesses) Act 1965.

A duty to the public to disclose

The circumstances in which a solicitor may make disclosure on grounds related to issues of public interest are very limited. Essentially a solicitor may reveal confidential information only to the extent necessary to prevent the client, or a third party, committing a criminal act that is reasonably believed to be likely to result in serious bodily harm, and in cases of continuing or anticipated child abuse if disclosure is in the public interest.

CONFIDENTIALITY AND LEGAL PROFESSIONAL PRIVILEGE

Certain confidential communications, however, can never be revealed without the consent of the client; they are privileged against disclosure. This protection is called legal professional privilege ('LPP').

In two recent cases, the House of Lords has underlined the policy behind LPP, its necessity and its nature.

---

4 Practice Rule 16E of the Solicitors' Practice (Confidentiality and Disclosure) Amendment Rule 2004, in effect since April 2006. NB: when the new Solicitors' Code of Conduct comes into effect on 1st July 2007 this rule will be incorporated into the Code as Rule 4, and will cease to have effect as a separate Practice Rule.
5 Confidentiality and Disclosure Guidance – Explanatory notes not forming part of Rule 16E, paragraphs 9 – 20.

- 'The policy of legal professional privilege requires that the client should be secure in the knowledge that protected documents and information will not be disclosed at all.'[6]
- '. . . it is necessary in our society, a society in which the restraining and controlling framework is built upon a belief in the rule of law, that communications between clients and lawyers, whereby the clients are hoping for the assistance of the lawyers' legal skills in the management of their (the clients') affairs, should be secure against the possibility of any scrutiny from others, whether the police, the executive, business competitors, inquisitive busy bodies or anyone else. . . .'[7]
- '. . .(LPP is) a fundamental human right long established in the common law. It is a necessary corollary to the right of any person to obtain skilled advice about the law. Such advice cannot be effectively obtained unless the client is able to put all the facts before the adviser without fear that they may afterwards be disclosed and used to his prejudice.'[8]

WHAT COMMUNICATIONS ARE PRIVILEGED?

Not everything that lawyers have a duty to keep confidential is privileged. Only those confidential communications falling under either of the two heads of privilege – 'advice privilege' or 'litigation privilege' – are protected by LPP.

WHO IS A 'LAWYER' FOR SUCH PURPOSES?

This includes solicitors and their employees, barristers, in-house lawyers, but does not include accountants, even if they give legal advice (subject to one very limited exception).

'ADVICE PRIVILEGE'

Communications between a lawyer (acting in his or her capacity as a lawyer) and a client are privileged if they are confidential and for the purpose of seeking legal advice from a lawyer or providing legal advice to a client.

For example:

- conveyancing documents are not communications;[9]
- neither is a client account ledger maintained in relation to the client's moneys;[10]
- nor is an appointments diary or time record on an attendance note, time-sheet or fee record relating to a client;[11]
- a solicitor's bill of costs and statement of account may, in certain circumstances, be privileged;[12]

---

6 Per Lord Hoffmann in *R (Morgan Grenfell & Co Ltd)* v. *Special Commissioner of Income tax and Another* [2002] UKHL 21 at paragraph 30, [2003] 1 AC 563.
7 Per Lord Scott in *Three Rivers District Council* v. *Bank of England* (*ibid*) at paragraph 34.
8 Per Lord Hoffmann in *Morgan Grenfell* (*ibid*) at paragraph 7.
9 *R* v. *Inner London Crown Court ex parte Baines & Baines* [1988] QB 579.
10 *Nationwide Building Society* v. *Various Solicitors* [1999] P.N.L.R. 53. Such entries are not created for the purpose of giving legal advice to a client but are internal records maintained, in part, to discharge a solicitor's professional and disciplinary obligations under the Solicitors' Accounts Rules.
11 *R* v. *Manchester Crown Court, ex parte Rogers* [1999] 1 W.L.R. 832.
12 *Chant* v. *Brown* (1852) 9 Hare 790.

- but notes of open court proceedings,[13] or conversations, correspondence or meetings with opposing lawyers[14] are not privileged, as the content of the communication is not confidential.

Merely because a client is speaking or writing to his or her solicitor does not make that communication privileged – it is only those communications between the solicitor and the client relating to the matter in which the solicitor has been instructed for the purpose of obtaining legal advice that will be privileged. Such communications do not need to 'contain advice on matters of law or construction, provided that they are directly related to the performance by the solicitor of his professional duty as legal adviser of his client.'[15]

'LITIGATION PRIVILEGE'

Under this head the following are privileged:

Confidential communications made, after litigation has started, or is 'reasonably in prospect', between:

- a lawyer and a client
- a lawyer and an agent (whether or not that agent is a lawyer); or
- a lawyer, or his or her client, and a third party;

for the sole or dominant purpose of litigation, whether:

- for seeking or giving advice in relation to it, or
- for obtaining evidence to be used in it, or
- for obtaining information leading to obtaining such evidence.

PRE-EXISTING DOCUMENTS

An original document, which is not brought into existence for either of these privileged purposes and so is not already privileged, does not acquire privileged status merely by being given to a lawyer for advice or otherwise for a privileged purpose.

FRAUD OR ILLEGALITY – THE CRIME/FRAUD EXCEPTION

It is proper for a lawyer to advise a client on how to stay within the law and avoid committing a crime,[16] or to warn a client that proposed actions could attract prosecution,[17] and such advice will be protected by privilege.

LPP does not, however, exist in respect of documents which themselves form part of a criminal or fraudulent act, or communications which take place in order to obtain advice with the intention of carrying out an offence.[18] It is irrelevant whether or not the lawyer is aware that he or she is being used for that purpose.[19] If the lawyer suspects that he or she is unwittingly being involved by their client in a fraud, before they can consider themselves released from the duty of confidentiality, the courts

---

13 *Parry* v. *News Group Newspapers* (1990) 140 New Law Journal 1719.
14 *Parry* (*ibid*).
15 Per Lord Carswell in *Three Rivers DC* v. *Governor of the Bank of England* [2004] (*ibid*) at paragraph 111.
16 *Bullivant* v. *Attorney-General of Victoria* [1901] AC 196.
17 *Butler* v. *Board of Trade* [1971] Ch 680 14; *R* v. *Cox & Railton* (1884) 14 QBD 153.
18 *R* v. *Cox & Railton* (*ibid*).
19 *Banque Keyser Ullman* v. *Skandia* [1986] 1 Lloyds Rep 336.

require there to be strong prima facie evidence before LPP can be displaced.[20] Whilst the lawyer may release himself or herself if such evidence exists, he or she may also raise the issue with the court for an order authorising him or her to make disclosure to the victim.[21]

The general 'crime/fraud exception' principle is restated in the Police and Criminal Evidence Act 1984 ('PACE')[22] at section 10(2), where items held with the intention of furthering a criminal purpose are declared not to be items subject to LPP. It is important to note that the intention to further a criminal purpose need not be that of the client (or the lawyer) – it is sufficient that a third party intends the lawyer/client communication to be made with that purpose (e.g. where the innocent client is being 'used' by a third party).[23]

OVERRIDING PRIVILEGE

By statute

LPP is a fundamental human right; Parliament can of course legislate contrary to fundamental principles of human rights. However, the House of Lords in *Morgan Grenfell* stressed that a parliamentary intention to override rights, such as LPP, must be expressly stated in the statute or appear by necessary implication.[24]

Public duty

Unlike the position in relation to confidential material (see above), there is no public interest exception to LPP. It is therefore prima facie unlawful for a solicitor to disclose a communication if to do so would involve a breach of LPP.

DO SECTIONS 19 AND 21A OF THE TERRORISM ACT 2000 OVERRIDE LPP?

Section 19(5) does not require disclosure by a 'professional legal adviser' of either information which he or she obtains 'in privileged circumstances', or a belief or suspicion based on information which he or she obtains in 'privileged circumstances'.

Section 21A (5) provides that a person does not commit an offence under the section if he or she is a 'professional legal adviser' and the information or other matter came to him or her in 'privileged circumstances'.

Under both provisions, 'privileged circumstances' effectively mirror LPP at common law, and both are subject to the caveat that it will not cover communications in furtherance of a criminal purpose.

A solicitor does not therefore, subject to the caveat, breach these sections of the TA 2000 if he or she fails to disclose information which has come to him or her in privileged circumstances.

---

20 *O'Rourke* v. *Darbishire* [1920] AC 581.
21 *Finers* v. *Miro* [1991] 1 WLR 35.
22 It is also reflected in numerous other criminal statutes – including the Proceeds of Crime Act 2002, s 330 (failure to disclose) and s 333 (tipping off).
23 *R* v. *Central Criminal Court ex parte Francis & Francis* [1989] 1 AC 346.
24 See also *R* v. *Secretary of State for the Home Department, ex parte Simms* [2000] 2 AC 115.

DOES SECTION 38B OF THE TERRORISM ACT 2000 OVERRIDE LPP?

Whilst there is no equivalent provision in this section to that relating to 'professional legal advisers' as in sections 19 and 21A TA 2000, in order to override LPP the statute must do so expressly or by necessary implication.

No express words are used overriding LPP; therefore, only if there is a 'necessary implication' can LPP be overridden.

What is meant by 'a necessary implication'?

Lord Millett expressed the test in *B* v. *Auckland District Law Society*:[25]

> 'A useful test is to write in the words "not being privileged documents" and ask, not "does that produce a reasonable result" or "does it impede the statutory purpose for which production may be required?" but "does that produce an inconsistency?" or "does it stultify the statutory purpose?" The circumstances in which such a question would receive an affirmative answer would be rare.'
>
> This provides helpful assistance in the absence of specific judicial interpretation of s 38B TA 2000. It would seem unlikely that it could be successfully argued that the statutory purpose of s 38B would be stultified if it was to read (adopting the wording in the earlier sections and adapting Lord Millett's formula), "the person commits an offence if he does not disclose the information unless it was obtained in privileged circumstances as soon as reasonably practicable. . .".

In these circumstances, therefore, the Law Society considers that LPP is not overridden by s 38B TA 2000 and that information of the kind referred to in the section, if received in privileged circumstances, cannot be disclosed without the authority of the client.

It is crucial, however, that a solicitor, when in receipt of such information, should be absolutely satisfied that the client's purpose in supplying that information has been for the obtaining of legal advice and is directly related to the performance by the solicitor of his or her professional duty as the legal adviser of the client.

If it is not, then it is not protected by LPP.

It will, however, remain confidential.

The only defence available to an offence under s 38B is that the person charged has a reasonable excuse for not making a disclosure. Is confidentiality a 'reasonable excuse'?

There is a clear duty owed by the solicitor to the public to disclose confidential information to prevent the client, or a third party, committing a criminal act that is reasonably believed to be likely to result in serious bodily harm.

If there is a public duty to disclose in such circumstances, it would seem likely that confidentiality would not amount to a reasonable excuse for non-disclosure under s 38B TA 2000, and that a solicitor prosecuted for failing to disclose such information would have no defence.

It is The Law Society's view that the solicitor must disclose such confidential information as soon as reasonably practicable.

---

25 [2003] 3 WLR 859.

C1

Client identification form

Client Name

Date of Birth

Address

Postcode

[Client No.]

I certify that I have carried out the appropriate client verification procedures as follows:

<u>Individuals (including partnerships and unincorporated businesses)</u> **Tick** ☐

Risk Assessment

I have identified the risk assessment as:

Normal	☐
Enhanced	☐

If enhanced risk, indicate the reason:

Non face-to-face contact	☐	
Politically Exposed Person	☐	
Other higher risk	☐	(Tick as appropriate)

Verification

I have obtained the client(s)'s:

(a) full name
(b) current permanent address
(c) date of birth

by reference to at least one document from each of the following lists:

351

List A *(evidence of name and date of birth)*

(a) current valid full passport
(b) national identity card or resident's permit
(c) current photocard driving licence
(d) firearms certificate
(e) state pension or benefit book
(f) HM Revenue & Customs tax notification.

List B *(evidence of address)*
(a) home visit
(b) electoral roll check
(c) recent utility or local authority council tax bill
(d) recent bank/building society statement
(e) recent mortgage statement
(f) current driving licence (not if used in List A)
(g) local council rent card or tenancy agreement.

Where enhanced risk is indicated the following additional steps have been taken (please specify):

I confirm having seen the original documents and that any photograph of the client bore a good likeness to the client. A copy of each document is attached to this form.

<u>**Corporate**</u>   **Tick** ☐

Risk Assessment

I have identified the risk assessment as:

Simplified	☐
Normal	☐
Enhanced	☐

If enhanced risk, indicate the reason:

Non face-to-face contact	☐	
Other higher risk	☐	(Tick as appropriate)

Verification

Simplified

Where simplified CDD applies I attach evidence of the fact the company is of a description within Regulation 13 of the Money Laundering Regulations 2007.

Normal and Enhanced

I confirm that I have carried out a company search and attach a copy to this form.

Where beneficial owners have been identified I have verified their identity in accordance with the procedures for individuals or companies noted above or I have obtained a verification certificate from the company. I attach a copy of each document/certificate to this form.

Where enhanced risk is indicated the following additional steps have been taken (please specify):

Trusts, nominees and fiduciaries Tick ☐

Risk Assessment

I have identified the risk assessment as:

    Normal ☐
    Enhanced ☐

If enhanced risk, indicate the reason:

    Non face-to-face contact ☐
    Politically Exposed Person ☐
    Other higher risk ☐   (Tick as appropriate)

Verification

I confirm that I have received a certified copy of the trust (and the grant of probate or copy of the will creating the trust in the case of a deceased settlor). The trustees have been identified in accordance with the procedures for individuals or companies noted above.

Where beneficial owners have been identified I have verified their identity in accordance with the procedures for individuals or companies noted above or I have obtained a verification certificate from the trustees. I attach a copy of each document/certificate to this form.

Signed .... Date ....
    (Fee earner)

Where the client has been identified as a PEP the approval of a senior manager must be obtained. The senior manager should sign this form as an indication of approval.

Signed .... Date ....
    (Senior manager)

[*Note: this form provides a basic precedent for a client identification form. It should be developed to suit the needs of individual firms. Reference should be made to **Appendix B1**, the Law Society's Anti-money Laundering Practice Note.*]

353

Precedent for a basic money laundering manual

1. WHAT IS MONEY LAUNDERING?

Money laundering is the process by which the identity of 'dirty money' is changed so that the proceeds of crime appear to originate from a legitimate source. It is important that solicitors and their employees take steps to ensure that their services are not used by those seeking to legitimise the proceeds of crime. Solicitors must be aware that they may be involved in the money laundering process.

It is the policy of *[firm's name]* that we will take no avoidable risks and will cooperate fully with the authorities where necessary. No matter how much we want to help our client, we must not be a party to any form of dishonesty. We must be alert to the possibility that transactions on which we are instructed may involve money laundering.

2. THE FIRM'S POLICY

Recent legislation (in particular the Proceeds of Crime Act 2002, the Serious Organised Crime and Police Act 2005 and the Money Laundering Regulations 2007) has made significant changes to our responsibilities relating to money laundering. These changes are reflected in this manual.

3. THE CRIMINAL OFFENCES

The law relating to money laundering changed in February 2003 as a result of the Proceeds of Crime Act 2002. Amendments were introduced by the Serious Organised Crime and Police Act 2005. These amendments were brought into force at various dates in 2005 and 2006. The Money Laundering Regulations 2007 came into force on 15 December 2007. There are a number of criminal offences relevant to a solicitor's practice. The offences divide into three categories:

A. *Offences where the firm is involved in a client matter or transaction*

It is an offence:

(a) to acquire, use or possess criminal property;
(b) to conceal, disguise, convert, transfer or remove from the UK criminal property; or
(c) to enter into or become concerned in an arrangement which facilitates the acquisition, retention, use or control of another person's criminal property,

in all cases where we know or suspect that this is the case.

Criminal property is defined as constituting or representing a person's benefit from criminal conduct. Criminal conduct for these purposes means any conduct which constitutes a crime in the UK or if undertaken abroad, would have constituted a crime if committed in the UK.

A defence is available where you disclose your knowledge or suspicion to a nominated officer (i.e. a person nominated by the firm to receive internal disclosures).

The firm's nominated officer is *[nominated officer]*. In his/her absence disclosure should be made to *[deputy nominated officer]*.

If you have any knowledge or suspicion which requires reporting, you may initially discuss your concerns with your *[group partner or firm's nominated officer]*. If after such discussion you still have concerns a formal disclosure report should be made to the nominated officer using the Internal Reporting Form.

Note that any disclosure you make must generally be made before the prohibited act (i.e. the act of facilitation or otherwise). If you only become aware of information giving rise to knowledge or suspicion whilst committing the prohibited act (for example, you may have placed money in client account innocently and thereafter discover information which makes you suspicious) you must make your disclosure as soon as possible after you become suspicious. If the disclosure is made after you have committed the prohibited act you will only have a defence **if you can show that there was a good reason for your failure to make the disclosure before the act.**

(A similar offence relating to the laundering of 'terrorist property' appears in the Terrorism Act 2000.)

Formal disclosure report should be made to the nominated officer using the Internal Reporting Form (a copy of which is attached to this document as Appendix 1).

B. Offences following a disclosure report made to the firm's nominated officer

It is an offence to disclose to any person (including our client) that a report has been made to the firm's nominated officer in circumstances where this is likely to prejudice an investigation. (Further, even if no disclosure report has been made, an offence is committed if you know or suspect that a money laundering investigation is or is likely to be conducted and you disclose any information which is likely to prejudice the investigation.)

Once a report has been made to the nominated officer it may be an offence to continue to act for the client without the consent of the nominated officer. The nominated officer can only give consent if (s)he has disclosed details to the Serious Organised Crime Agency (SOCA) and SOCA have, in turn, given consent for the firm to continue to act.

Consequently, once a disclosure has been made to the nominated officer, he must be involved in every decision relating to that client matter and we must not communicate any information concerning the subject matter of the disclosure to the client or to any other person (including your work colleagues) without the express consent of the nominated officer. **Failure to comply with this procedure could lead to a criminal offence being committed.**

C. Offences involving a failure to disclose knowledge or suspicion of money laundering

It is an offence for a person who knows or suspects or who has reasonable grounds for knowing or suspecting that another is engaged in money laundering not to disclose that information where the information came to him in the course of business in the regulated sector.

355

The disclosure should be made to the firm's nominated officer using the same procedures as noted above.

This offence does not require the firm to be acting for a particular client, nor for the firm to be in possession, etc. of criminal property, nor involved in an arrangement which facilitates the acquisition, retention, use or control of criminal property.

Further, the offence is not limited to knowledge or suspicion of our client – it applies to any knowledge or suspicion of money laundering offences committed by any person.

The obligation to report arises simply if the information comes into your possession in the course of our business in the regulated sector. The definition of the regulated sector has been extended significantly. The sector now covers the bulk of our work for clients. Consequently, it is the policy of the firm to assume that all client work falls within the regulated sector and that accordingly all knowledge or suspicion of money laundering must be reported to the nominated officer where the information arises in the course of our business.

The definition of money laundering for these purposes includes the three crimes noted above in category (A). In particular it should be appreciated that the crimes involving 'acquisition, use and possession' and 'concealing, etc'. can be committed by the perpetrator of the crime. A person guilty of theft or tax evasion will also have committed a money laundering offence if he is in possession of criminal property.

Note:

The Court of Appeal's decision in *Bowman* v. *Fels* [2005] EWCA Civ 226 has made changes to the way in which the legislation is to be interpreted. First, generally speaking, the money laundering offences do not apply to most litigation (including consensual resolution of issues in a litigious context). Secondly, the interpretation of the word 'arrangement' (see 3A(c) above) is restricted to the act of facilitation – preparatory acts which do not themselves assist in the acquisition, use, retention or control of criminal property will not give rise to liability. Thirdly, the Court of Appeal's decision has preserved the concept of legal professional privilege. If information is privileged we cannot disclose the information to SOCA unless a waiver of privilege is obtained.

You should continue to report to *[the firm's nominated officer]* any knowledge or suspicion, even if you believe *Bowman* v. *Fels* makes the report unnecessary. *[The firm's nominated officer]* with the assistance of others will decide upon the impact of the judgment in *Bowman* v. *Fels*.

4. THE DANGER SIGNS TO WATCH FOR

Unusual settlement requests: Settlement by cash of any large transaction involving the purchase of property or other investment should give rise to caution. Payment by way of a third party cheque or money transfer where there is a variation between the account holder, the signatory and a prospective investor should give rise to additional enquiries.

Fictitious buyer: Especially if the buyer is introduced to the Firm by a third party (e.g. a broker or an estate agent) who is not well known to you. Beware of clients we never meet – they may be fictitious. Wherever a meeting with the client is not possible, special care is needed.

Unusual instructions: Care should always be taken when dealing with a client who has no discernible reason for using the Firm's services, e.g. clients with distant addresses who could find the same service nearer their home base; or clients whose requirements do not fit into the normal pattern of the Firm's business and could be more easily serviced elsewhere. Similarly care should be taken if you are instructed to remit the net proceeds of sale to the estate agent who was instructed.

Misrepresentation of the purchase price: Make sure that the true cash price for a property which is to be actually paid is the price shown in the contract and the transfer, and is identical to the price shown in the mortgage instructions.

A deposit paid direct: A deposit, perhaps exceeding the normal 10 per cent, paid direct, or said to be direct, to the seller should give rise to concern.

Incomplete contract documentation: Contract documents not fully completed by the seller's representative, e.g. dates missing or the identity of the parties not fully described.

Changes in the purchase price: Adjustments to the purchase price, particularly in high percentage mortgage cases, or allowances off the purchase price for, e.g. works to be carried out.

Unusual transactions: Those which do not follow their normal course or the usual pattern of events.

Large sums of cash: Always be cautious when requested to hold large sums of cash in client account, either pending further instructions from the client or for no other purpose than for onward transmission to a third party. It is the firm's policy not to accept sums of cash in excess of £500 unless prior approval of the firm's nominated officer has been obtained.

The secretive client: A personal client who is reluctant to provide details of his or her identity. Be particularly cautious about the client you do not meet in person.

Suspect territory: Caution should be exercised whenever a client is introduced by an overseas bank, other investor or third party based in countries where production of drugs or drug trafficking may be prevalent.

Mortgage fraud: It is possible that a member of staff may unwittingly assist in a mortgage fraud. This is especially true of staff who deal with any form of conveyancing, whether domestic or commercial. We must therefore be very vigilant to protect our mortgagee clients and ourselves. If you turn a blind eye to any form of dishonesty over mortgages, no matter how small, you could be personally implicated in the fraud. It is important to stress that the penalties are criminal as well as civil.

5. IDENTIFICATION: GENERAL POINTS

5.1. In the light of the requirements contained in the Money Laundering Regulations 2007 it is the firm's policy to verify the identity of all new clients and all existing clients at the start of a new matter unless they have been identified already.

5.2. Documentary evidence must be obtained in accordance with the procedure set out below. It is important that the original of any document is examined and copied. The fee earner should endorse the copy with the words 'original seen' followed by the fee earner's signature.

5.3. Particular care must be taken when acting on corporate and private client matters. The 2007 Regulations require the client's identity and, in specified circumstances, the identity of a "beneficial owner" to be established.

Where we have a corporate client, the beneficial owner is anyone who:

- owns or controls (whether directly or indirectly, including through bearer shares) more than 25% of the shares or voting rights in the body, or
- otherwise exercises control over the management of the body.

Where we are acting on the estate of a deceased person, the beneficial owner is the executor, original or by representation, or administrator for the time being of the deceased person. Where there is an ongoing trust after the estate ceases to be in administration, the beneficial owner of the trust must be identified and verified.

Where we are acting on a trust administration the beneficial owner is:

- An individual with a specified interest in at least 25% of the capital of the trust property (specified interest means a vested interest which is in possession, in remainder or in reversion).
- The class of persons in whose main interest the trust is set up or operates.
- Any individual who controls the trust.

5.4. The identification procedures must be carried out as soon as reasonably practicable after first contact is made between the firm and client. It is not necessary for the firm to wait until the verification process is complete before commencing work for the client. However, if it proves impossible to satisfactorily complete the process **we must cease to act for the client.**

5.5. No client money should be accepted from the client for payment into client account until the verification process has been satisfactorily completed.

5.6. A Client Identification form should be completed and kept on the file.

5.7. The copy of evidence taken to confirm a client's identity must be kept for a period of five years after we have finished acting for the client.

6.   IDENTIFICATION: PROCEDURES

The method for identifying clients will depend upon the type of client. The procedure below and the documentary evidence referred to are not to be taken as an exhaustive list of requirements. A judgement must be made as to whether alternative or additional information should be sought. If in doubt you should seek advice from the nominated officer.

A.   *Companies*

In the case of a corporate client we need to be satisfied that the company exists and that we are dealing with that company. The existence of the company can be determined by making a company search which reveals the following information:

(a)   name and registered address
(b)   registered number
(c)   list of directors
(d)   members or shareholders
(e)   nature of the company's business
(f)   certificate of incorporation
(g)   if a subsidiary, the name of the holding company.

In addition, evidence of the identity of beneficial owners should be obtained in accordance with 5.3 above.

B. Individuals

The following information should be obtained for individuals:

(a) full name
(b) current permanent address (including postcode)
(c) date of birth.

At least one document from each of the following lists should be produced:

List A (evidence of name and date of birth)

(i)   current valid full passport
(ii)   national identity card or resident's permit
(iii) current photocard driving licence
(iv)   firearms certificate
(v)   state pension or benefit book
(vi)   HM Revenue & Customs tax notification

List B (evidence of address)

(i)   home visit
(ii)   electoral roll check
(iii) recent utility or local authority council tax bill
(iv)   recent bank/building society statement
(v)   recent mortgage statement
(vi)   current driving licence (not if used in List A)
(vii) local council rent card or tenancy agreement.

Where joint instructions are received, identification procedures should be applied to each client. If joint clients have the same name and address (e.g. spouses) the verification of the address for one client only is sufficient.

C. Trusts, nominees and fiduciaries

Where the trust is regulated by an independent public body (e.g. the Charities Commission) the evidence of the existence of the trust and the identity of the trustees should be sought from that body.

In other cases a certified copy of the trust (and the grant of probate or copy of the will creating the trust in the case of a deceased settlor) must be obtained. The trustees must also be identified in accordance with the procedures for individuals or companies noted above.

In addition, evidence of the identity of beneficial owners should be obtained in accordance with 5.3 above.

D. Clients where there is no face-to-face contact

Where contact with the client is not face-to face but by post or telephone, it is still necessary to obtain evidence of identity in accordance with the above procedures. Such evidence can be produced by way of an original document or by way of a certi-fied copy provided that the copy is certified by a reputable institution, such as a bank or firm of lawyers, who should verify the name used, the current permanent address and the client's signature. The name and address of the institution providing the certification should be noted and checked by reference to a professional directory.

E. Non-UK Clients

Non-UK individual clients should produce passports or national identity cards together with separate evidence of the client's permanent address obtained from the best source available. PO Box numbers are not sufficient evidence of an address.

Non-UK corporate clients should produce equivalent information to that obtained by making a UK company search. The results of company searches made abroad will depend upon the filing requirements in the local jurisdiction.

If you are unable to obtain satisfactory evidence of identity in accordance with the above procedures you must contact the firm's nominated officer who will advise on any alternative steps which may be taken or consider whether instructions must be terminated.

7. DEPARTMENTAL INSTRUCTIONS

[If appropriate include under this heading typical circumstances where different depart-ments of the firm might find themselves at risk. Details can be found in **Chapter 12** *of this book.]*

8. HELP

Money laundering is real and it will affect us. If you have any concerns regarding the firm's policy and/or your responsibilities contact *[nominated officer]*.

9. CONCLUSION

To minimise the risks of liability:

- **Verify the identity and bona fides of your client:** Meet the client or clients where possible and get to know them.
- **Question unusual instructions:** Make sure that you discuss them fully with your client, and note all such discussions carefully on the file.
- **Discuss any aspects of the transaction which worry you with your client:** For example, if you suspect that your client may have submitted a false mortgage application or references, or if you know or suspect the Lender's valuation exceeds the actual price paid, discuss this with your client and, if you believe they intend to proceed with a fraudulent application, you must refuse to continue to act for the buyer and the mortgagee.
- **Check that the true price is shown in all documentation:** Check that the actual price paid is stated in the contract, transfer and mortgage instructions. Ensure that your client understands that, where you are also acting for the Lender, you will have to report all allowances and incentives to the Mortgagee.
- **Do not witness pre-signed documentation:** No deed should be witnessed by a solicitor or staff unless the person signing does so in the presence of a witness. If a deed is pre-signed, ensure that it is re-signed in the presence of a witness.
- **Verify signatures:** Consider whether signatures on all documents connected with a transaction should be examined and compared with signatures on any other documentation.
- **Make a Company Search:** Where a private company is the seller or the seller has purchased from a private company in the recent past and you suspect that there may be a connection between the company and the seller or the buyer which is being used for improper purposes, then consideration would be given to ascertain the names and addresses of the officers and shareholders which can then be compared with the names of those connected with the transaction and the seller and buyer.

APPENDIX 1

MONEY LAUNDERING INTERNAL REPORTING FORM

*[For a precedent, see **Appendix C3** to this book.]*

APPENDIX 2

CLIENT IDENTIFICATION FORM

*[For a precedent, see **Appendix C1** to this book.]*

C3

Internal reporting form

1. Name of client/s:

   Aliases/Trading names:

2. Address (including postcode,
   telephone, fax, e-mail and contact name):

3. Date of Birth:

4. Summary of instructions:

5. Beneficial Owner(s):

   (a) Name(s) of Beneficial Owner(s):

   (b) Address(es) of Beneficial Owners (including postcode,
   telephone, fax, e-mail and contact name):

6. Evidence of identity (please attach):

7. Value of transaction:

8. Name and address of introducer (if any):

9. Is the client named above the person you know or suspect is involved in money laundering? YES/NO

10. If your answer to 9 is NO:

   (a) Name of person you know or suspect is involved in money laundering:

   (b) Address of person you know or suspect is involved in money laundering:

11. Source and destination of funds:

   (a) source of cash/bank/other securities

   (b) destination

12. The whereabouts of the laundered property:

13. If you are unable to answer 12, do you have information which might assist in identifying the whereabouts of the laundered property? If so, please state this information:

14. Reason for suspicion:

15. Does Professional Privilege apply? YES/NO

16. If Professional Privilege does apply is a waiver of privilege necessary? YES/NO

If NO, give reasons:

Signed .... Date ....

To be completed by nominated officer only:

Report to SOCA? YES/NO

If NO, give reasons:

Date Business completed ....

Record destruction date ....

(If a report has been made to SOCA this record must not be destroyed at the 'date of destruction' without first referring to SOCA)

C4

SOCA reporting forms and guidance notes

The guidance notes explain what information is required in the Standard form template and are to be read in conjunction with the form itself. If you are not completing the form using one of the electronic methods outlined above, the form should be completed on the computer-generated template, which is available to download from the SOCA website, but if this is not possible it should be typed onto a paper copy. A number of fields within the computer-generated template can be completed by selecting options from dropdown menus.

It is important that the relevant information is completed within the appropriate fields and not merely placed within the 'Reasons for Suspicion' field.

There are a number of fields that should be completed in order for a report to be accepted by SOCA. These fields are: Your Ref (even if none), Disclosure Type, New or Update, Source ID, Source Outlet ID, Today's Date, (Main Subject) Surname or Company Name and Reasons for Suspicion. Following this, according to the additional information you have available, a number of fields within each section must be completed if you are filling in that section and are identified below in bold italics.

For a more detailed explanation of the template itself, please contact the SOCA SAR Team at PO Box 8000, London, SE11 5EN.

SUSPICIOUS ACTIVITY REPORT

- Main subject (person or company)
- Address
- ID Information
- Disclosed account details
- Individual transactions with counterparty account details
- Associated subject (person and company)
- (Associated subject) address
- (Associated subject) ID information
- Reason for suspicion

Your ref:

The reference number or alphanumeric identifier that you allocate to the SAR within your own filing system

Sheet no:

The number of pages used to complete the SAR

Disclosure type:

This field should contain the type of offence under which you report (i.e. Crime, Drugs or Terrorism)

Disclosure date:

The date on which the original report is made within your institution New or Update: New is any new suspicious activity or any further activity on a previously reported account/activity or arrangement. An update is any further information that is not a transaction, on a previously reported account/activity or arrangement, e.g. a new address of a subject

Existing disclosure ID:

If you have entered 'Update' in the previous field, please enter here any reference number SOCA may previously have supplied relating to the subject in question

Constructive trust:

Fill this check box if the report relates to an issue of constructive trust Further information: Fill this check box to indicate that you retain further information relating to the report that may be of interest to SOCA or another financial investigator. For example, if your disclosure relates to a mortgage application, it may not always be necessary to provide the full documentation. In this case, indicate its existence here and provide a concise description in the 'Reasons for Suspicion' field. DO NOT SEND THE FURTHER INFORMATION WITH YOUR FORM.

Source ID:

The name of your institution

Source outlet ID:

The name (or sort code) of the branch office from which the report originates

Today's date:

Date report submitted to SOCA (Automatic date field)

MAIN SUBJECT (PERSON OR COMPANY)

This information describes the individual (or company) on whom you wish to report.

Surname:

Subject's family name

Forenames:

Subject's forenames

Title:
Title of subject (Mr, Mrs, Dr etc)

Date of birth:
Date of birth of subject

Gender:
Gender of subject

Occupation:
Occupation of subject

Employer:
Subject's employer

Or:

Company Name:
Company name of subject

Company No:
Company registration number of subject

Type of business:
Type of business of subject

VAT no:
VAT number of subject

Country of Registration:
Country of registration of subject

ADDRESS

Number, street, city/town, county, country.
Full address of subject

Post code:
Post Code of address of subject

Type:

Type of address of subject (i.e. home, accommodation, trading etc)

Current:

Is the address of the subject current, Yes or No

ID INFORMATION

ID Information:

Describes the type of identification offered or taken (e.g. driving licence)

Unique information ID:

Give details of the identification taken (e.g. driving licence number)

Extra information / description:

Give any further information relating to the identification taken, which may be relevant or of use (e.g. if passport, the country of issue)

Other information:

Give any further details that help to identify the subject

DISCLOSED ACCOUNT DETAILS

This information describes an account with which the subject or suspicious activity is connected.

FI ID:

The name of the financial institution that holds the subject's account

Sort Code:

The sort code of the branch office that holds the subject's account

Opened:

Date account opened

Closed:

Date account closed (if applicable)

Turn' Cd:

Turnover credit

Turn' Db:

Turnover debit

Acct. Name:

Account name

Acct No:

Account number

Acct Bal:

Account balance

Bal Date:

Date of the balance

Turn Pd:

Turnover period

INDIVIDUAL TRANSACTIONS WITH COUNTERPARTY ACCOUNT DETAILS

This section contains details of the transaction, or series of transactions that have aroused your suspicion, and details of the counterparties involved.

Date:

The date of the transaction

Amount:

The amount of the transaction

Currency:

The currency concerned in the transaction (e.g. GBP, USD, DEM etc)

Cr/Db:

This field stipulates whether the transaction constitutes a credit or debit in relation to the account identified above

Type:

The type of transaction conducted (e.g. cash, cheque, electronic transfer, mortgage etc)

Notes:

This field is available for further information relating to the transaction identified above

FI ID:

The name of the institution that holds the counterparty account, if applicable

Sort Code:

The sort code of the branch office that holds the counterparty's account

Acct. Name:

The name of the counterparty

Acct. No:

The counterparty's account number

ASSOCIATED SUBJECT (PERSON AND COMPANY)

This information describes the person(s) or companies with which the subject or suspicious activity. It is a person or company that is linked to the main person/company in some direct way and is involved in the suspicious activity. Include the financial institution responsible for that account if it is involved in your suspicions.

Surname:

The associated subject's family name

Forenames:

The associated subject's forenames

Title:

Title of associated subject (Mr, Mrs, Dr etc)

Date of birth:

Date of birth of associated subject

Gender:

Gender of associated subject

Occupation:

Occupation of associated subject

Employer:

Associated subject's employer

Reason for association:

Give details of the connection between the Main Subject and associate subject

Or:

Company name:

The name of the associate company

Company no:

Company number of associated subject

Type of business:

Type of business of associated subject

VAT no:

VAT number of associated subject

Country of registration:

Country of registration of associated subject

Reason for association:

Give details of the connection between the Main Subject and associate subject

Or:

(Associated) subject already exists as main subject of a previous report and is provided for use if you have previously reported on the associated subject.

Existing disclosure ID:

The reference number which SOCA may have provided in relation to previous reports, relating to the associated subject

Your Ref:

The reference number or alphanumeric identifier that you allocated within your own file system to the previous report on the associated subject

Reason for association:

Details of the connection between the Main Subject and associate subject

(ASSOCIATED SUBJECT) ADDRESS

Number, street, city/town, county, country:

Full address of associated subject

Post code:

Post code of address of associated subject

Type:

Type of address of associated subject (i.e. home, accommodation, trading etc)

Current:

Is the address of the associated subject current, Yes or No

(ASSOCIATED SUBJECT) ID INFORMATION

ID information:

Describes the type of Identification offered or taken (e.g. driving licence)

Unique information ID:

Give details of the Identification taken (e.g. driving licence number)

Extra information/description:

Give any further information relating to the Identification taken, which may be relevant or of use (e.g. if passport, country of origin)

General information:

Give any further details that help to identify the subject

REASON FOR SUSPICION

This section requires a clear and thorough explanation of the grounds for your suspicion. (Submissions that do not provide reasons for suspicion cannot be accepted as a SAR by SOCA.)

For further information contact the SOCA UK Financial Intelligence Unit (UKFIU) SAR Team at PO Box 8000, London, SE11 5EN

´ Version 2.1 - Appendix 1

Serious Organised Crime Agency
PO Box 8000
London
SE11 5EN
Tel: 020 7238 8282
Fax: 020 7238 8286

SOURCE REGISTRATION DOCUMENT

IMPORTANT - THE DETAILS IN THIS FORM MUST BE PROVIDED WITH YOUR FIRST DISCLOSURE TO SOCA OR FOLLOWING ANY SUBSEQUENT CHANGE TO THOSE DETAILS.

Institution Name:	
Institution Type:	
Regulator:	
Regulator ID:	
Contact Details (1): Forename:	
Surname:	
Position:	
Address:	
Telephone Details:	
Facsimile Details:	
E-mail Address:	
Contact Details (2): Forename: (where applicable)	
Surname:	
Position:	
Address:	
Telephone Details:	
Facsimile Details:	
E-mail Address:	

Version 2.1 - Appendix 2

Serious Organised Crime Agency
PO Box 8000
London
SE11 5EN
Tel: 020 7238 8282
Fax: 020 7238 8286

DISCLOSURE REPORT DETAILS: STANDARD REPORT:

Reporting Institution:

Your Ref:

Disclosure Reason:

PoCA 2002: ○   Terrorism Act 2000: ○

Branch/Office:

Consent Required: ☐

Disclosure Date: [ ] - [ ] - [ ]   Type: New ○   OR Update ○

D D   M M M   Y Y Y Y

Existing Disclosure ID/s: (where applicable)

Please use whichever sheets you feel are necessary and indicate below how many of each you are submitting.

REPORT SUMMARY:

Number of 'Subject Details' sheet appended relating to a Main Subject: [ ]

Number of 'Additional Details' sheets appended relating to Main Subject: [ ]

Number of 'Subjects Details' sheets appended relating to Associated Subject/s: [ ]

Number of 'Additional Details' sheets' appended relating to Associated Subject/s: [ ]

Number of 'Transaction Detail' sheet/s appended: [ ]

Number of 'Reason For Disclosure Sheets' appended: [ ]

Once completed please collate your sheets in the above mentioned order and then sequentially number your sheets at the bottom of each page. This will ensure that the information is processed in the correct sequence.

Total number of pages submitted including this Header: [ ]

Page 1 of [ ]

■ **SUBJECT DETAILS:**   Version 2.0 - Appendix 3   ■

Subject Type: Main Subject: O   **OR**   Associated Subject: O   (number ☐ of ☐)

Individual's Details:

Subject Status: Suspect : O   **OR**   Victim: O

Surname: [   ]

Forename 1:   [   ]

Forename 2:   [   ]

Occupation: [   ]

DoB: [   ] - [   ] - [   ]   Gender: Male O   Female O
             D D   M M M   Y Y Y Y

Title: Mr O   Mrs O   Miss O   Ms O   Other [   ]

Reason for Association of this subject to the Main Subject (for use only with Associated Subject details)

[   ]

OR

Legal Entity's Details

Subject Status: Suspect : O   **OR**   Victim: O

Legal Entity Name: [   ]

Legal Entity No: [   ]   VAT No: [   ]

Country of Reg: [   ]

Type of Business: [   ]

Reason for Association of this subject to the Main Subject (for use only with Associated Subject details)

[   ]

■   Page ☐ of ☐   ■

375

APPENDIX C4

■   **ADDITIONAL DETAILS:**   Version 2.0 - Appendix 4   ■

Do these details refer to the Main Subject: ○   OR   to an Associated Subject ○

(Please indicate the Associate's number where applicable) ☐

Subject Name: [ ]

Premise No/Name: Current: ☐   Type: [ ]

Street:

City/Town:

County: Post Code:

Country:

Premise No/Name: Current: ☐   Type: [ ]

Street:

City/Town:

County: Post Code:

Country:

Premise No/Name: Current: ☐   Type: [ ]

Street:

City/Town:

County: Post Code:

Country:

Information Type: Unique Information Identifier:

Extra Information / Description

Information Type: Unique Information Identifier:

Extra Information / Description

■   Page [ ] of [ ]   ■

■ **TRANSACTION DETAILS: (Complete if applicable)** ■

MAIN SUBJECT ACCOUNT SUMMARY   Version 2.0 - Appendix 5

Institution Name: [   ]

Account Name: [   ]

Sort Code: [   ]   Account No /Identifier: [   ]

Business Relationship Commenced: (DD-MMM-YYYY) [   ] - [   ] - [   ]   Acct Bal: [   ]

Business Relationship Finished: (DD-MMM-YYYY) [   ] - [   ] - [   ]   Bal Date: (DD-MMM-YYYY) [   ] - [   ] - [   ]

Turnover Period: [   ]   Credit Turnover: [   ]

Debit Turnover: [   ]

TRANSACTION/S

Activity Type: [   ]   Activity Date: (DD-MMM-YYYY) [   ] - [   ] - [   ]

Amount: [   ]   Currency: [   ]   Credit: ○ or Debit: ○

Other party name: [   ]   Account No/ Identifier:

Institution Name or Sort Code: [   ]   [   ]

Activity Type: [   ]   Activity Date: (DD-MMM-YYYY) [   ] - [   ] - [   ]

Amount: [   ]   Currency: [   ]   Credit: ○ or Debit: ○

Other party name: [   ]   Account No/ Identifier:

Institution Name or Sort Code: [   ]   [   ]

Activity Type: [   ]   Activity Date: (DD-MMM-YYYY) [   ] - [   ] - [   ]

Amount: [   ]   Currency: [   ]   Credit: ○ or Debit: ○

Other party name: [   ]   Account No/ Identifier:

Institution Name or Sort Code: [   ]   [   ]

Activity Type: [   ]   Activity Date: (DD-MMM-YYYY) [   ] - [   ] - [   ]

Amount: [   ]   Currency: [   ]   Credit: ○ or Debit: ○

Other party name: [   ]   Account No/ Identifier:

Institution Name or Sort Code: [   ]   [   ]

Page [   ] of [   ]

■ REASON FOR DISCLOSURE: Version 2.0 - Appendix 6   **■**

Main Subject Name: (cross reference purposes)	

Report Activity Assessment
(Please use only where you know or suspect what the offence behind the reported activity may be)

Drugs: ☐   Missing Trader, Inter Community (VAT) ☐   Immigration: ☐   Tobacco/Alcohol Excise Fraud: ☐
         Fraud

Personal Tax Fraud: ☐   Corporate Tax Fraud: ☐   Other Offences: [   ]

Reason for Disclosure:

■   Page [   ] of [   ]   **■**

REASON FOR DISCLOSURE CONTINUATION: Version 2.0 - Appendix 8

Main Subject Name:
(cross reference purposes)

Reason for Disclosure Continuation:

Page ____ of ____

379

GUIDANCE NOTES FOR THE COMPLETION OF THE LIMITED
INTELLIGENCE VALUE REPORT

SCOPE AND PURPOSE

This document provides guidance for the completion of authorised and protected disclosures, under sections 337 and 338 of the Proceeds of Crime Act (2002), in the format categorised as 'Limited Intelligence Value Reports'. This guidance should be read alongside the Limited Intelligence Value Report form (Appendix 7) which has been issued by SOCA. Both the form and guidance have been completed following consultation with organisations representing the Regulated Sector. **Please note that Limited Intelligence Value Reports should only be made under the Proceeds of Crime Act (PoCA). Any reports being made under the Terrorism Act (2000) should be Standard Reports.**

Although none of the fields in the form are mandatory, since the format is not prescribed by law, those submitting disclosures should take account of regulatory and sectoral approved guidance. SOCA's feedback to reporting institutions will assess the quality of reporting against relevant guidance.

HOW TO OBTAIN THE NEW FORMS AND GUIDANCE

'SARs Online' can be used to complete Limited Intelligence Value Reports. The link to this facility is available via the homepage of the SOCA Website at **www.soca.gov.uk** and is freely available to anybody with internet access.

Those organisations which currently use Money.Web or Bulk File submission should continue to submit reports electronically, using the existing input screens or reporting format.

Organisations **not** able to use Money.web, Bulk File Submission or SAR Online, are advised to obtain a copy of the preferred forms. Those reporters who wish to complete reports on their own computer should download the form(s) from the SOCA website (**www.soca.gov.uk**).

If you wish **to complete a report by hand** you should request a special version of the form by telephoning 020 7238 8282. **Please do not complete the version of the form downloaded from the main SOCA website by hand.**

SENDING YOUR REPORT TO SOCA

Those organisations which currently use the Money.Web system or Bulk File Submission method should continue to submit electronic reports in the same way.

SARs Online also allows reports to be submitted electronically and automatically sends a reference number to your email account as proof of submission.

'Limited Intelligence Value Reports' completed on paper forms should be faxed to 020 7238 8286 or posted to PO Box 8000, London SE11 5EN. Disclosures should not be emailed to SOCA.

LIMITED INTELLIGENCE VALUE REPORTS

SOCA recognises that the reporting requirements under Part 7 POCA sometimes result in reports being required in circumstances where there is likely to be limited intelligence value to law enforcement, although wider analysis of such reports may provide useful data. The table below provides guidance on the circumstances that SOCA considers are appropriate for abbreviated information to be provided in the form of a Limited Intelligence Value report. SOCA reserves the right, in all cases, to ask for the Standard Report format to be used and will monitor disclosures submitted to ensure that Limited Intelligence Value reporting is not exploited as a 'short cut' where its use is not justified.

If you are not sure which form to use when making a report you should use the Standard Form.

Type	Detail	Comments
1 Certain classes of crimes committed overseas.	This is intended to apply where the suspicious activity takes place outside the UK and: • Is not a criminal offence in the jurisdiction where committed, and • Relates either to local differences in regulation or social and cultural practices	A Limited Intelligence Value Report is not appropriate to report money laundering relating to serious tax evasion or occasions where the underlying offence is a serious crime such as terrorism, offences relating to drugs, paedophilia etc. In these circumstances, a full report is appropriate. Please note that s102 of SOCPA 2005 removes certain crimes from reporting obligations.
2 Minor irregularities where there is nothing to suggest that these are the result of dishonest behaviour.	Balance discrepancies and minor credit balances not returned because of the administrative costs involved, or other small discrepancies which are judged to have resulted from a mistake rather than dishonest behaviour.	If reporting institutions are satisfied that no criminal property is involved (as defined by s340 (3) of the Proceeds of Crime Act, 2002), they may conclude that a report is not required. However, where reporting institutions feel obliged to make a disclosure, a Limited Intelligence Value report is appropriate.
3 The subject of the report cannot be deduced from the information to hand and the proceeds have disappeared without trace.	This would include bank raids, driving away from a petrol station without paying, shoplifting, retail shrinkage and various cheque and credit card frauds.	Section 330 of POCA (as amended) means that such reports should not be made unless the Suspect, or the means to identify the Subject, is known.

Type	Detail	Comments
4 Accountants, auditors and tax advisers. Multiple instances of suspicion arising during one audit: "Aggregation of incidents to form one report".	Multiple incidents may be aggregated within a single Limited Intelligence Value Report provided that: • Aggregate reports relate to a single audit only. • One or more of the other categories in this table for limited intelligence value reporting is met, for example (3) (above): bank raids, driving away from a petrol station without paying, shoplifting, retail shrinkage and various cheque and credit card frauds; • The reason for the aggregate report is summarised;	The Act refers to reports being made "as soon as practicable". SOCA accepts that this will not always mean "immediately" in the context of an ongoing audit and is content to receive aggregate Limited Intelligence Value Reports within one month of the completion of an audit, provided that during the assignment no time sensitive information is discovered (that may, for example, allow the recovery of proceeds of crime if communicated immediately). Reporters should note that a Standard Report is appropriate should the issue of a Hansard (CoP9) letter by the Inland Revenue, taken with such other information as may be available, cause (or provide reasonable grounds for) knowledge or suspicion of money laundering.
5 Law enforcement prosecutor, regulator or other Government agency already aware of an offence that also happens to be an instance of suspected money laundering.	This category is intended to capture a range of regulatory/procedural offences which are, or may be, already the subject of investigation by another agency. Examples include health and safety offences, environmental offences, and failure to file annual returns with the Companies Registrar.	A Limited Intelligence Value report is appropriate in these cases provided that the reporter has no additional or 'new' information that would be provided as a result of the reporting obligation under PoCA that has not already been made available to another investigating agency. However, any knowledge or suspicion of money laundering relating to serious crime or tax evasion, including cases covered by the Hansard procedure, should be reported in a Standard Report.

Type	Detail	Comments
6 Section 167 (3) Customs and Excise Management Act 1979.	This makes the submission of an incorrect VAT or Customs return, however innocent, a criminal offence.	It is the position of SOCA that a disclosure is not required for innocent error in these circumstances. Where the person knows of the omission and does not rectify the situation there will be a duty to report. Where reporting institutions feel obliged to make a disclosure in these circumstances, a Limited Intelligence Value report may be appropriate
7 Reporting institution served with a Court Order, which prompts suspicion.		A Limited Intelligence Value report may be appropriate except where the suspicion and report relate to matters not covered by the Court Order letter, in which case a report on the Standard Form should be submitted.
8 Where the benefit from criminal conduct is in the form of cost savings, such as breaches of employment law and the illegal copying or distribution of software licences within a company.		However, if there are 'arrangements' in respect of criminal property which require appropriate consent, then a Standard form must always be completed.

COMPLETION INSTRUCTIONS

Source Registration Document (Module 1)

In order to record disclosures and correspond accurately and in a timely manner with the regulated sector, SOCA needs accurate contact details of each reporting organisation. A **Source Registration Document** has been constructed to capture this information as concisely as possible. SOCA already holds such details for organisations which have previously disclosed, therefore **this sheet should only be used by organisations that have never previously reported and then only when making their first report.** It will not be required for each subsequent disclosure. **However, all organisations should use the source registration document to update SOCA about any changes to their contact details in order that SOCA's records can be accurately maintained.**

Institution Name   Please provide details of the Registered and/or Trading name of the company or individual making the report.

Institution Type	Please provide details of the type of company or individual making the report, e.g. Money Transmission Agent, Bank, Estate Agent etc.
Regulator	Please provide details of your regulator, where applicable, (e.g. FSA, Gaming Board of Great Britain etc)
Regulator ID	Please provide details of your regulator's Identity Number, where known to you.
Contact Details (1)	This will be SOCA's primary point of contact with you.
Forename	Please provide full details of your Forename/s.
Surname	Please provide full details of your Surname.
Position	Please provide details as to the position you hold within your employer, where applicable.
Address	Please provide your full postal address details (inc Post Code).
Telephone Details	Please provide details of your principal contact number.
E-mail Address	Please provide details where applicable. The ability to use this medium will enhance the speed of delivery of our correspondence with you.
Contact Details (2)	This will be SOCA's point of contact with you in the absence of (where applicable) the above detailed individual, if applicable.
Name	As above.
Position	As above.
Address	As above.
Telephone Details	As above.
E-mail Address	As above.

Limited Intelligence Value Report *(Module 7)*

Reporting Institution	Please provide details of the company or individual **making** the report. If a Money Laundering Reporting Officer (MLRO) is completing the form it is not essential at any point to mention by name the person making the initial disclosure.
Your Reference	Please provide details of your own reference number relevant to the disclosure in question. **This is an important field as the information supplied will be quoted by SOCA in any correspondence with you relating to this disclosure.**
Branch/Office	This information will enable SOCA to ascertain which of your outlets is reporting the activity, assisting SOCA to decide which law enforcement agency to allocate the disclosure to.
Disclosure Date	The date upon which you submit your report to SOCA. The format DD/MMM/YYYY has been used to prevent any transposition of Day and Month. Please insert two digits in the DD field to state the day, three letters in the MMM field (for example, JAN for January) and four digits to show the year in the YYYY field.

Subject Details

This is the Person/Legal Entity about whom/which the report is being made. Normally, reporters will be in a position to complete one of these fields, although in some circumstances this is not the case. For example, you may be reporting a fraud where the perpetrator is unknown

This section of the sheet can be used to refer to an Individual or a Legal Entity. **However, only one of these sections should be completed**. This sheet should not be used for both an individual and a Legal Entity at the same time.

Subject Status   Please indicate **only one** box from 'Suspect' or 'Victim'.

Suspect should be ticked if you know or suspect or have reasonable grounds for knowing or suspecting that this person is engaged in money laundering.

Victim is the person or entity who/which is harmed by or loses as a result of the criminal activity which you are reporting. To ensure that any intrusion against a victim's privacy is minimised, the victim's details should not, ideally, be included in subject fields. **The personal details of victims should only be included if, in the judgement of the nominated officer, the details are essential to understanding the activity being reported.**

PLEASE COMPLETE EITHER THE INDIVIDUAL'S DETAILS SECTION OF THE SHEET OR THE LEGAL ENTITY SECTION. PLEASE DO NOT COMPLETE BOTH.

Surname   Please provide details, as appropriate.

Forename 1   Please provide details, as appropriate.

Date of Birth   This is an important field. Date of birth information helps law enforcement to positively identify individuals when cross-matching personal data. The format DD/MMM/YYYY has been used to prevent any transposition of Day and Month. Please insert two digits in the DD field to state the day, three letters in the MMM field (for example, JAN for January) and four digits to show the year in the YYYY field.

Gender   Please select from options provided.

Title   Please select from options provided. If the correct title is not shown, please specify the relevant title within the 'Other' field. *Appropriate options are provided with the Field Values List.*

OR

Legal Entity Name   Please provide details as appropriate, e.g. a Company or Charity Name.

Legal Entity Number   Please provide details as appropriate, e.g. a Company or charity Number.

VAT Number   Please provide details as appropriate.

Reason for Disclosure

This area is free text and should include any information not already provided which you feel is relevant to your Report. It should provide details of the reason(s) why you have knowledge or suspicion or reasonable grounds for knowledge or suspicion that another person is engaged in money laundering and why you feel that a Limited Value Report is suitable.

Reason for Disclosure Continuation Sheet (Module/Appendix 8)

Where required, please use this section to continue your reasons for knowledge or suspicion, where the space provided within Appendix 7 is insufficient. Multiples of this module can be utilised as required.

Please ensure that you complete the Main Subject Name at the top of any of these modules completed in order that we may cross reference this module to the rest of your report.

Serious Organised Crime Agency
PO Box 8000
London
SE11 5EN
Tel: 020 7238 8282
Fax: 020 7238 8286

SOCA
SERIOUS ORGANISED CRIME AGENCY

PROCEEDS OF CRIME ACT 2002 - LIMITED INTELLIGENCE VALUE REPORT

Reporting Institution

Your Ref:

Branch/ Office:

Disclosure Date:

D D - M M M - Y Y Y Y

SUBJECT DETAILS:

Individual's Details: Subject Status: Suspect : ◯   **OR**   Victim: ◯

Surname:

Forename:

DoB: D D   M M M   Y Y Y Y   Gender: Male ◯   Female ◯

Title: Mr ◯   Mrs ◯   Miss ◯   Ms ◯   Other

Legal Entity Details: Subject Status: Suspect : ◯   **OR**   Victim: ◯

Legal Entity Name:

Legal entity No: VAT No:

REASON FOR DISCLOSURE:

APPENDIX SEVEN

387

Index